MOGENS HERMAN HANSEN

The Athenian Ecclesia II

OPUSCULA GRAECOLATINA
(Supplementa *Musei Tusculani*)
Edenda curavit Ivan Boserup
Vol. 31

MOGENS HERMAN HANSEN

The Athenian Ecclesia II

A Collection of Articles
1983-1989

MUSEUM TUSCULANUM PRESS
COPENHAGEN 1989

© Mogens Herman Hansen & Museum Tusculanum Press 1989
Printed in Special-Trykkeriet Viborg a-s
ISBN 87-7289-058-4 (paperback)
ISBN 87-7289-060-6 (hardcover)
ISSN 0107-8089

ACKNOWLEDGEMENTS
The author and publishers wish to thank the editors of
Greek, Roman and Byzantine Studies, Classica et Mediaevalia
and *Symbolae Osloenses* for permission
to reproduce the articles from their journals.

Preface

This book completes my studies in the Athenian assembly. In 1983 I published *The Athenian Ecclesia. A Collection of Articles 1976-1983* (herafter *Ath. Eccl.*). In 1987 followed *The Athenian Assembly in the Age of Demosthenes*, a general account intended not only for specialists, but also for students of classics, history and political science, as well as for anyone who takes interest in the history of Ancient Greece and of democracy (herafter *Ath. Ass.*). This third volume includes the articles I have published on the subject in the period 1983-1989. As in the previous collection of articles there are addenda to almost all the articles and a comprehensive index of sources. The most substantial addenda are: (a) a revised inventory of *rhetores kai strategoi*, which now comprises 373 politically active citizens and to which is appended a list of those who are attested as *bouleutai* as well (pages 34-72). (b) A discussion of the political organization of Attica, occasioned by Whitehead's and Osborne's recent books on the demes of Attica and by Traill's new map of 1986 (pages 85-91) (c) A reply to Peter Bicknell on how the Athenians were organized in the Pnyx of the second period (pages 163-56). (d) A reply to Martin Ostwald on the nature of the Heliaia in the archaic and early classical periods (pages 258-61). And finally (e) a redating of Pnyx III. Following Homer Thompson's suggestion in his first report of the excavations (in *Hesperia* I) I am now inclined to believe that the second rebuilding of the Pnyx took place in the Hadrianic period and not in the mid fourth century as Homer Thompson has held since 1943 (page 141).

It remains for me to state my acknowledgements. I would like to thank Niels Bohr Legatet, The Danish Research Council for the Humanities and Copenhagen University for substantial grants which made the publication of this volume possible; and finally I would like to thank Dr. Robin Jackson for reading and commenting on the addenda.

CONTENTS

	Text	Addenda
1. The Athenian »Politicians« 403-322. *GRBS* 24 (1983) 33-55	1-23	(24)
2. *Rhetores* and *Strategoi* in Fourth-Century Athens. *GRBS* 24 (1983) 151-180	25-33	(34-72)
3. Political Activity and the Organization of Attica in the Fourth Century B.C. *GRBS* 24 (1983) 227-38	73-84	(85-91)
4. The Number of *Rhetores* in the Athenian *Ecclesia*, 355-322 B.C. *GRBS* 25 (1984) 123-55	93-125	(126-27)
5. Two Notes on the Pnyx. *GRBS* 26 (1985) 241-50	129-40	(141)
6. The Construction of Pnyx II and the Introduction of Assembly Pay. *ClMed* 37 (1986) 89-98	143-52	(153)
7. The Organization of the Athenian Assembly. A Reply. *GRBS* 29 (1988) 51-58	155-62	(163-65)
8. The Number of *Ecclesiai* in Fourth-Century Athens. [With Fordyce Mitchel] *SymbOslo* 59 (1984) 13-19	167-73	(174-75)
9. How Often Did the Athenian *Ecclesia* Meet? A Reply. *GRBS* 28 (1987) 1-16	177-92	(193-94)
10. What is *Syllogos* at Thuc. 2.22.1? [With Johnny Christensen] *ClMed* 34 (1983) 17-31	195-209	(210-11)
11. *Demos*, *Ekklesia* and *Dikasterion*. A Reply to Martin Ostwald and Josiah Ober. *ClMed* 40 (1989) 101-06	213-18	
12. The Athenian Heliaia from Solon to Aristotle. *ClMed* 33 (1982) 9-47	219-57	(258-61)
13. On the Importance of Institutions in an Analysys of Athenian Democracy. *ClMed* 40 (1989) 108-13	263-69	

14. *Graphe Paranomon* against *Psephismata* not yet
 passed by the *Ekklesia*.
 ClMed 38 (1987) 63-73   271-81

15. Two Notes on Demosthenes' Symbouleutic Speeches.
 ClMed 35 (1984) 57-70   283-96   (297)

Index of Sources   298-324

The articles are reprinted unchanged apart from the asterisks in the margin which refer to the addenda at the end of each article. All cross-references are to the numbers printed at the bottom of the page.

The Athenian 'Politicians', 403-322 B.C.
Mogens Herman Hansen

I

THE TITLE of this paper may seem innocent and straightforward. It presents a historical problem, but does not seem to raise a semantic question. We believe we know what a politician is and we are used to reading about Athenian politicians. Two outstanding examples will suffice. Twenty years ago S. Perlman published an excellent article entitled "The Politicians in the Athenian Democracy of the Fourth Century B.C." (*Athenaeum* 41 [1963] 327-55), and in 1971 W. R. Connor published his seminal study *The New Politicians of Fifth-Century Athens*. It is characteristic of these and similar studies[1] that they are based on two tacit assumptions: (a) that the term politician/*Politiker*/*politicien* covers a sufficiently clear and well-defined concept; and (b) that this concept can be applied in descriptions of ancient societies. I will open my account of the problem by questioning both these assumptions.

It is surprisingly difficult to find out what a politician is and to come up with a definition that can be generally accepted. This word, which is used every day in parliaments, in the newspapers, and in broadcasting, is largely disregarded by students of political science. For example, in the *International Encyclopedia of the Social Sciences* there is no entry "politician," and in the article "Political recruitment and career," the author seems cunningly to avoid it.[2] Similar works of reference in German and French are equally unhelpful. There are scores of books and articles about political parties, and the definition of 'party' is a battle that has been fought among scholars for almost three generations.[3] But it is impossible to find a book or an article defining the concept 'politician' or asking the simple question, Who

---

[1] *Cf.* A. H. M. Jones, *Athenian Democracy* (Oxford 1957) 128-33; R. Sealey, "Callistratos of Aphidna and His Contemporaries," *Historia* 5 (1956) 178-203; M. H. Hansen, *The Sovereignty of the People's Court* (Odense 1974), and *Eisangelia* (Odense 1975); J. Tolbert Roberts, "Athens' So-called Unofficial Politicians," *Hermes* 110 (1982) 354-62.

[2] The article is by Dwaine Marvick. The same observation applies to the entry "Political Participation" by Herbert McClosky.

[3] *Cf.* most recently G. Sartori, *Parties and Party Systems* I (Cambridge 1976).

are 'politicians'? Nevertheless the word is very important in political debates. The 'politicians' are regularly made responsible for a decision or a disaster, and they are often opposed *e.g.* to civil servants, to trade-union leaders, or to the people. So at least students of political terminology in the manner of Weldon[4] ought to pay some attention to the problem and to discuss, if not the meaning, then the uses of the word 'politician'. One exception is the article "Politician" by G. C. Moodie in *A Dictionary of the Social Sciences* (New York 1964): "The term 'politician' is most commonly used to refer to a person actively engaged in the struggle for governmental power and/or office, whose success largely depends upon the favour of others and who, to achieve success, must therefore be skilled in the arts of persuasion, negotiation and compromise. In any given society ... 'politician' will or will not be generally used in a pejorative sense." Developing this definition, Moodie states, *i.a.*, the following modifications: "(a) the term does not normally apply to professional full-time administrators; (b) it does not apply to those who, for all their concern with political power, are neither members of a governing body nor openly aspiring to such office." This is the only definition of 'politician' I have seen,[5] and one swallow does not make a summer. If we turn to the general lexica and dictionaries, we are confronted with much vaguer and broader definitions of the word. A typical definition is "person taking part in politics or much interested in politics; (in a bad sense) person who follows politics as a career, regardless of principle."[6] In 1982 I conducted a poll of the 179 members of the Danish parliament, asking two questions: (a) What is a politician? (b) Who are politicians? I had 62 replies and the definitions ranged from "a person who takes part in politics, *i.e.* all politically active citizens," to "representatives of the people elected by the

---

[4] T. D. Weldon, *A Vocabulary of Politics* (London 1953).

[5] A sociological approach to the problem can be found in Max Weber's paper of 1918 "Politik als Beruf": *Gesammelte politische Schriften* (Tübingen 1958) 493–548. Weber distinguishes between 'Gelegenheitspolitiker' (all politically active citizens) and 'Berufspolitiker' (sometimes living *for* politics but in contemporary societies mostly *by* politics). As Berufspolitiker living 'von der Politik' Weber singles out politische Beamte, Journalisten, Parteibeamte, and Parlamentarier, who however may be Gelegenheitspolitiker or rather 'nebenberufliche' Politiker.

[6] *Oxford Advanced Learner's Dictionary of Current English* (1974); *The Oxford English Dictionary* (1933), "2b One keenly interested in politics; one who engages in party politics, or in political strife, or who makes politics his profession or business; also (esp. in US) in a sinister sense, one who lives by politics as a trade"; *Webster's New International Dictionary* (1937), "(2) one versed or experienced in the science of government; one devoted to politics; a statesman. (3) one addicted to, or actively engaged in, politics as managed by parties ... In modern usage *politician* commonly implies activity in party politics, esp. with a suggestion of artifice or intrigue (versus *statesman*)."

people, comprising ministers, members of the parliament, and (in local government) mayors and councilmen."

The present status of the concept 'politician' seems to be that no one, apart from Moodie, has made a serious attempt to define it, and that there is no agreement about what a politician is and who the politicians are, not even when we strip the word of its pejorative nuance and its metaphorical uses. But this is not in itself a sufficient reason for avoiding it in descriptions of ancient societies. Our word *soul*, for example, as opposed to *body*, is even vaguer and more difficult to grasp; nevertheless it is an obvious and irreproachable word to use in discussions of Greek philosophy and in translations of Plato and Aristotle. With this in mind, we must ask whether the word 'politician' can be used in descriptions of fourth-century Athens, either in the vaguer or in the narrower sense.

In the wider sense, 'politician' denotes all politically active citizens, *i.e.*, in Athens all citizens who attended the *ecclesia*, who took the heliastic oath in order to serve as *nomothetai* or *dicastai*, and who volunteered as candidates in the election or sortition of magistrates. 'Politician' in this sense would be a good translation of *ho politeuomenos* in its wider meaning,[7] and it squares well with the Greek concept of the active citizen. But when scholars speak of the Athenian politicians, it is certainly not this meaning they have in mind. They envisage invariably a much smaller group of 'political leaders' explicitly to be set off against the larger group of active citizens.

So we must turn to the narrower and more technical use according to which politicians are (or aspire to be) members of a governing body elected by the people. But when we transfer this concept to the ancient world we are faced with four problems. (a) A distinguishing mark of the modern politician is that he is elected or at least is a candidate at elections. In Athens election was a condition only for becoming a *strategos*, whereas political leadership was open to any citizen who would address and could persuade the people. (b) In a modern society the (elected) politicians are essentially decision-makers, whereas in Athens the group of citizens called politicians by modern historians never made decisions. On the contrary, they initiated policy by making proposals but left all decisions to the bodies of active citizens.[8] (c) Today the politicians are professionals who make a living by politics, whereas in Athens to be paid for politics was a

---

[7] Lys. 16.18, Isoc. 8.76, Andoc. 2.1, etc.

[8] *Cf.* M. H. Hansen, "Initiative and Decision: the Separation of Powers in Fourth-Century Athens," *GRBS* 22 (1981) 359–65.

* criminal offence. Admittedly, the Athenians often turned a blind eye to perquisites and 'gifts' to a 'political leader', but as soon as he fell from favour with the people, the profit he had made might result in a death-sentence.[9] (d) To be a politician today almost necessarily entails party affiliation. Most historians tend to believe that there were no 'parties' in Athens with which a 'politician' could be affiliated.[10]

These four problems, of course, only reflect the essential difference between direct and representative democracy. But the inference seems to be that the modern concept 'politician' is too closely connected with representative government to be transferred to ancient societies. It is
* worth noting that Finley in his study "Athenian Demagogues" tends to avoid the word 'politician'. Instead he uses the (rare) Greek word 'demagogue' (in a neutral sense) or simply refers to (political) 'leaders',[11] a term often used by students of political theory. Since political leaders do not have to be politicians, Finley's terminology points to a different formulation of the historical problem.

Etymologically, of course, 'politician' is, *via* the Latin *politicus*, derived from the Greek adjective πολιτικός. It is worth noting, however, that the meaning of πολιτικός is 'statesman' and not 'politician'. It is used by philosophers in a complimentary sense about a true political leader. It never occurs as a legal term, and in the orators it is a *hapax*. The neuter τὰ πολιτικά may be used about 'politics', but the masculine πολιτικός occurs only once in some 3000 Teubner pages of Attic rhetoric (Aeschin. 2.184) in a flattering reference to the 'statesman' Euboulos. Another reason for avoiding the word 'politician' for Athenian political leaders: by contrast with 'statesman', which is invariably a complimentary term, 'politician' is at best neutral and regularly pejorative in meaning. In 1968, for example, a Norwegian editor suggested the following definition: "a politician is a man who is so thick-skinned that he can stand up although he is spineless." In accounts of Athenian history, 'politician' is often used as a rendering of the Greek words ῥήτωρ, πολιτευόμενος, or σύμ-

---

[9] *Cf.* Hyp. 3.7–8 (public action against paid political leaders), 1.24–25 (perquisites and gifts to political leaders are tolerated by the Athenians); for political trials *cf.* Hansen, *Eisangelia* (*supra* n.1) 58–65.

[10] O. Reverdin, "Remarques sur la vie politique d'Athènes au Ve siècle," *MusHelv* 2 (1945) 201–12; Jones (*supra* n.1) 130–31; M. I. Finley, "Athenian Demagogues," *Past & Present* 21 (1962) 15; Connor (*supra* p.33) 5–9.

[11] Finley (*supra* n.10), esp. 12–23; only on 14, 18, and 22 is the word 'politician' (cautiously) used. In selecting 'demagogue' as his preferred term for political leader, Finley may have been influenced by Weber, who states (*supra* n.5): "Der 'Demagoge' ist seit dem Verfassungsstaat und vollends seit der Demokratie der Typus des führenden Politikers im Okzident" (513).

βουλος, all of which may be used pejoratively but far more frequently occur in a neutral sense and sometimes even as a compliment. In the United States no member of the Congress would boast, "I am a politician,"[12] but in the speech *On the Crown* Demosthenes states with outspoken pride, ὁ σύμβουλος καὶ ῥήτωρ ἐγώ (18.212), and earlier in the same speech he says μόνος τῶν λεγόντων καὶ πολιτευομένων ἐγώ (173).[13]

Summing up: nowadays most historians agree that the term 'political party' is bound up with representative government and is better avoided in accounts of politics in ancient Greece. I suggest that precisely the same warning applies to the word 'politician', and I shall avoid it hereafter. So both questions posed above must be answered in the negative: (a) 'politician' is a vague concept with no clear meaning and several uses; (b) in its narrower sense, referring to a group of 'political leaders', it cannot be applied to ancient Greek society, unless one explicitly acknowledges 'politician' as an artificial historical term (*i.e.* a convenient translation of *politeuomenos*, *symboulos*, *rhetor*, *strategos*, etc.) which bears little or no relation to the meanings and uses of the word 'politician' in contemporary societies.

II

What language is used by the Athenians themselves when they refer to their political leaders? The most comprehensive expression found in the sources is not a word but a phrase, ῥήτορες καὶ στρατηγοί. This point is best substantiated by quoting some passages from the orators:

Dem. 2.29 = 13.20: πρότερον μὲν γάρ, ὦ ἄνδρες Ἀθηναῖοι, κατὰ συμμορίας εἰσεφέρετε, νυνὶ δὲ πολιτεύεσθε κατὰ συμμορίας. ῥήτωρ ἡγεμὼν ἑκατέρων καὶ στρατηγὸς ὑπὸ τούτῳ καὶ οἱ βοησόμενοι τριακόσιοι· οἱ δὲ ἄλλοι προσνενέμησθε οἱ μὲν ὡς τούτους, οἱ δὲ ὡς ἐκείνους.

Dem. 18.170: πολλάκις δὲ τοῦ κήρυκος ἐρωτῶντος οὐδὲν μᾶλλον ἀνίστατ' οὐδείς, ἁπάντων μὲν τῶν στρατηγῶν παρόντων, ἁπάντων δὲ τῶν ῥητόρων, καλούσης δὲ τῆς πατρίδος τὸν ἐροῦνθ' ὑπὲρ σωτηρίας.

Dem. 18.205: οὐ γὰρ ἐζήτουν οἱ τότ' Ἀθηναῖοι οὔτε ῥήτορ' οὔτε στρατηγὸν δι' ὅτου δουλεύσουσιν εὐτυχῶς ...

---

[12] *Cf.* H. Sperber and T. Trittschuh, *American Political Terms. An Historical Dictionary* (Detroit 1962) 329.

[13] All three terms are used in a positive sense in Dem. 18.94: καὶ μὴν ὅτι μὲν πολλοὺς ἐστεφανώκατ' ἤδη τῶν πολιτευομένων ἅπαντες ἴσασι· δι' ὄντινα δ' ἄλλον ἡ πόλις ἐστεφάνωται, σύμβουλον λέγω καὶ ῥήτορα, πλὴν δι' ἐμέ, οὐδ' ἂν εἷς εἰπεῖν ἔχοι.

Dem. 22.66: πολλῶν μὲν στρατηγῶν ἠδικηκότων τὴν πόλιν, πολλῶν δὲ ῥητόρων ... οὐδενὸς πώποτ' ἐξητάσθης κατήγορος (sc. Androtion; in 24.173 the reference is to both Androtion and Timokrates).
Dem. 23.184: οὐ γὰρ ... χάριν ἐστὶ δίκαιον ὀφείλειν ... ὧν μίκρ' ἀναλίσκων ἰδίᾳ καὶ τοῖς στρατηγοῖς καὶ τοῖς ῥήτορσιν διαπράττεται πρὸς ὑμᾶς ἐπαίνους αὐτοῦ γράφεσθαι.
Dem. Ep. 1.8: φημὶ δὴ χρῆναι μήτε στρατηγῷ μήτε ῥήτορι μήτ' ἰδιώτῃ μηδενὶ τῶν τὰ πρὸ τοῦ γε δοκούντων συνηγωνίσθαι τοῖς καθεστηκόσι μήτε μέμφεσθαι μήτ' ἐπιτιμᾶν μηδένα μηδὲν ὅλως, ἀλλὰ συγχωρῆσαι πᾶσιν τοῖς ἐν τῇ πόλει πεπολιτεῦσθαι τὰ δέοντα ...
Din. 1.90: καὶ πότερα κάλλιόν ἐστι πρὸς δὲ δικαιότερον, ἅπαντ' ἐν τῷ κοινῷ φυλάττεσθαι ἕως ἄν τι δίκαιον ὁ δῆμος βουλεύσηται, ἢ τοὺς ῥήτορας καὶ τῶν στρατηγῶν ἐνίους διηρπακότας ἔχειν;
Din. 1.112: εἰ δὲ ῥήτωρ ἢ στρατηγὸς (ἀναβαίνει συνηγορήσων) ... οὐ προσεκτέον ὑμῖν ἐστι τοῖς τούτων λόγοις.
Din. 2.26: καίτοι, ὦ Ἀθηναῖοι, τί ἂν οἴεσθ' ἐκείνους τοὺς ἄνδρας (our ancestors) ποιῆσαι λαβόντας ἢ στρατηγὸν ἢ ῥήτορα πολίτην ἑαυτῶν δῶρα δεχόμενον ἐπὶ τοῖς τῆς πατρίδος συμφέρουσιν, οἳ τὸν ἀλλότριον (Arthmios of Zeleia) ... οὕτω δικαίως καὶ σωφρόνως ἐξήλασαν;
Din. 3.19: οὐ συνδιέφθαρται τὸ τοῦ δήμου πλῆθος τῶν ῥητόρων καὶ τῶν στρατηγῶν τισιν ...
Hyp. 1.24: [ο]ὐδ[έ] γ' ὁμοίως [ἀδι]κοῦσιν οἱ ἰδιῶται [οἱ λαβ]όντες τὸ χρυσίον [καὶ] οἱ ῥήτορες καὶ οἱ [στρατ]ηγοί. διὰ τί; ὅτι τοῖς [μὲν] ἰδιώταις Ἅρπα[λος ἔ]δωκεν φυλάτ[τειν τ]ὸ χρυσίον, οἱ δὲ [στρατη]γοὶ καὶ οἱ ῥήτο[ρες πρ]άξεων ἕνεκα [εἰλή]φασιν.
Hyp. 3.27: καίτοι σε ἐχρῆν, ἐπείπερ προήρησαι πολιτεύεσθαι, ... μὴ τοὺς ἰδιώτας κρίνειν μηδ' εἰς τούτους νεανιεύεσθαι, ἀλλὰ τῶν ῥητόρων, ἐάν τις ἀδικῇ, τοῦτον κρίνειν, στρατηγὸς ἐάν τις μὴ τὰ δίκαια πράττῃ τοῦτον εἰσαγγέλλειν.

Other passages could be added to this list, both from the orators and from other fourth-century authors,[14] and the inference seems to be that the two words formed a pair denoting one group. Moreover, the frequent juxtaposition of ῥήτορες and στρατηγοί is attested not only in political speeches; the Athenian law code also included at least one *nomos* explicitly referring to ῥήτορες καὶ στρατηγοί and binding on them only. The law is paraphrased by Dinarchus (1.71): καὶ τοὺς μὲν νόμους προλέγειν τῷ ῥήτορι καὶ τῷ στρατηγῷ, <τῷ> τὴν παρὰ τοῦ δήμου πίστιν ἀξιοῦντι λαμβάνειν, παιδοποιεῖσθαι κατὰ τοὺς νόμους, γῆν ἐντὸς ὅρων κεκτῆσθαι, πάσας τὰς δικαίας

[14] Isoc. 5.81, 15.30; Dem. 9.38 (οἱ λέγοντες = ῥήτορες), 24.135 (πολιτευόμενος = ῥήτωρ); Aeschin. 2.184 (πολιτικοί = ῥήτορες), 3.7, 3.146; Din. 1.76 (σύμβουλοι = ῥήτορες); Ar. Eccl. 244–47; Xen. Mem. 2.6.15; Pl. Euthyd. 290C–D (πολιτικοί = ῥήτορες); Arist. Rh. 1388b18, Probl. 916b36.

πίστεις παρακαταθέμενον, οὕτως ἀξιοῦν προεστάναι τοῦ δήμου.[15] We do not know whether this *nomos* was strictly enforced. I tend to doubt it. But it shows that the combined group of ῥήτορες and στρατηγοί was not only acknowledged as a political fact but also endorsed in the laws so as to form a part of the democratic constitution.

Thus, in fourth-century Athens the phrase ῥήτορες καὶ στρατηγοί is the nearest equivalent of what we with a much vaguer and less formal term call 'politicians' or 'political leaders'. The Athenians of course had other less comprehensive and less technical words for political leaders; these will be discussed after a closer examination of the two terms ῥήτωρ and στρατηγός.

The board of ten annually elected *strategoi* has been studied frequently and needs no further presentation; but what does ῥήτωρ mean in a political context? An examination of all preserved speeches shows that *rhetor* denotes a citizen who moves a *psephisma* in the *ecclesia*[16] or in the *boule*[17] or a *nomos* before the *nomothetai*[18] or brings a public action before the *dicasteria*.[19] In a wider sense a *rhetor* is a speaker addressing the *ecclesia*[20] or the *boule*[21] (either supporting

---

[15] In the sections leading up to the paraphrase Deinarchos is attacking Demosthenes, who was a *rhetor* but never a *strategos*. So *strategos* was probably juxtaposed with *rhetor* in the paraphrase because the two words appeared together in the law. If the requirement for *rhetores* had been mentioned in one part of the law code and the requirement for *strategoi* in another, Deinarchos' paraphrase is inexplicable. Admittedly, he refers to τοὺς νόμους and not τὸν νόμον, but it is well known that the orators made no distinction here between singular and plural, often using them indiscriminately in references to one law, sometimes running for a few lines only: cf. e.g. Dem. 24.20 and 24, 41–43, 105 and 114; 43.50–51. The requirement to own land and to have legitimate children is also mentioned in the spurious Draconian constitution as binding on *strategoi* and *hipparchoi* (Arist. *Ath.Pol.* 4.2) and in the much-disputed decree of Themistocles as binding on trierarchs (Meiggs/Lewis 23.20–22). So the paraphrase by Deinarchos is the only reliable source we have for the requirement.

[16] Aeschin. 3.55 ὁ αὐτὸς οὗτος ῥήτωρ ἔγραψε τὸν πόλεμον. *Cf.* Lys. 13.72; Dem. 3.22; 18.219; 22.70; 23.201; 59.43, 105; Aeschin. 1.188; 3.16, 31, 203–04.

[17] Lys. 22.2 ἐπειδὴ γὰρ οἱ πρυτάνεις ἀπέδοσαν εἰς τὴν βουλὴν περὶ αὐτῶν, οὕτως ὠργίσθησαν αὐτοῖς, ὥστε ἔλεγόν τινες τῶν ῥητόρων ὡς ἀκρίτους αὐτοὺς χρὴ τοῖς ἕνδεκα παραδοῦναι θανάτῳ ζημιῶσαι.

[18] Dem. 24.142 οἱ δὲ παρ' ἡμῖν ῥήτορες ... πρῶτον μὲν ὅσοι μῆνες μικροῦ δέουσι νομοθετεῖν τὰ αὑτοῖς συμφέροντα ..., *cf.* 123–24.

[19] Din. 1.100 τί γάρ ἐστι ῥήτορος δημοτικοῦ καὶ μισοῦντος τοὺς κατὰ τῆς πόλεως λέγοντας καὶ γράφοντας; ... οὐ κρίνειν ἀλλήλους; οὐκ εἰσαγγέλλειν; οὐ γράφεσθαι παρανόμων; Dem. 58.62, 59.43; Aeschin. 1.34; Lycurg. 1.31; Isoc. 8.129.

[20] Aeschin. 2.74 ἀνιστάμενοι δὲ οἱ συντεταγμένοι ῥήτορες, περὶ μὲν τῆς σωτηρίας τῆς πόλεως οὐδ' ἐνεχείρουν λέγειν ... ; Lys. 12.72; Dem. 12.14; 18.170; 19.23; *Prooem.* 53.1; *Ep.* 2.10; Aeschin. 1.28, 30, 186; 2.161; 3.2, 4; Hyp. 3.1, 4, 8, 9, 29; Isoc. 14.4; 15.138.

[21] Lys. 30.22 ἡ βουλὴ ἡ <ἀεὶ> βουλεύουσα ... ἀναγκάζεται ... τῶν ῥητόρων τοῖς <τὰ> πονηρότατα λέγουσι πείθεσθαι; Dem. 22.37, 24.147, 51.2.

or opposing a *psephisma* moved by another *rhetor*) or a *synegoros* addressing the court (either for the prosecution or for the defence).[22] Moreover, in opposition to the modern terms 'politician' or 'political leader', *rhetor* was a legal technical term occurring not only in the law on ῥήτορες καὶ στρατηγοί quoted above but also in several others explicitly aimed at *rhetores*:

(a) Most important is the law regulating the *dokimasia* of *rhetores*, quoted by Aischines (1.28-32): δοκιμασία, φησί, [ὁ νομοθέτης] ῥητόρων· ἐάν τις λέγῃ ἐν τῷ δήμῳ τὸν πατέρα τύπτων ἢ τὴν μητέρα, ἢ μὴ τρέφων, ἢ μὴ παρέχων οἴκησιν ... ἢ τὰς στρατείας ... μὴ ἐστρατευμένος, ὅσαι ἂν αὐτῷ προσταχθῶσιν, ἢ τὴν ἀσπίδα ἀποβεβληκώς ... ἢ πεπορνευμένος ... ἢ ἡταιρηκώς ... ἢ τὰ πατρῷα ... κατεδηδοκώς, ἢ ὧν ἂν κληρονόμος γένηται, ... δοκιμασίαν ... μὲν ἐπαγγειλάτω Ἀθηναίων ὁ βουλόμενος οἷς ἔξεστιν.[23]

(b) Next comes ὁ εἰσαγγελτικὸς νόμος, quoted by Hypereides (3.7-8): an εἰσαγγελία has to take place ἐάν τις ... ῥήτωρ ὢν μὴ λέγῃ τὰ ἄριστα τῷ δήμῳ τῷ Ἀθηναίων χρήματα λαμβάνων.

(c) Third, we have two important lexicographical notes referring to a ῥητορικὴ γραφή. The first is in Harpokration: ῥητορικὴ γραφή· Ἰσαῖος ἐν τῷ πρὸς Εὐκλείδην. ἔοικε ῥητορικὴ γραφὴ καλεῖσθαι ἡ κατὰ ῥήτορος γράψαντός τι ἢ εἰπόντος ἢ πράξαντος παράνομον, ὥσπερ λέγεται καὶ πρυτανικὴ ἡ κατὰ πρυτάνεως καὶ ἐπιστατικὴ ἡ κατ' ἐπιστάτου. The second note comes from the *Lexicon Rhetoricum Cantabrigiense*: ῥητορική· Ἰσαῖος ἐν τῷ πρὸς Εὐκλείδην περὶ χωρίου. τὰς γνώμας ἃς εἰσῆγον εἰς τὸ δικαστήριον μετὰ ψηφίσματος. καὶ Ὑπερείδης ἐν τῷ κατὰ Αὐτοκλέους προδοσίας, 'ῥητορικῆς ἐκ δήμου'. ἔστι γὰρ καὶ ἐκ βουλῆς, οἷον εἰ τὰ αὐτὰ ἔδοξε τῷ δήμῳ καὶ τῇ βουλῇ. Harpokration, quoting Isaeus, obviously refers to the law regulating the *graphe paranomon*, and so does the *Lex. Cant.*, in which I follow Sauppe in emending γνώμας to γραφάς. And I take the obscure phrase μετὰ ψηφίσματος to be a reflection of the fact that, in a *graphe paranomon*, the *psephisma* was quoted *verbatim* in the indictment (*cf.* Aeschin. 3.199-200).

(d) Finally, Aischines (1.34-35) quotes τοὺς νόμους τοὺς περὶ τῆς εὐκοσμίας κειμένους τῶν ῥητόρων. The document inserted in the speech may be spurious,[24] but Aischines' reference to the law indicates that the word *rhetor* was used.

In (a) and (b) *rhetor* denotes any citizen who addresses the *ecclesia* and so, *a fortiori*, any citizen who moves a decree (*cf. infra*). In (c)

[22] Lycurg. 1.43 τίς ἂν ἢ δικαστὴς φιλόπολις καὶ εὐσεβεῖν βουλόμενος ψήφῳ ἀπολύσειεν, ἢ ῥήτωρ κληθεὶς τῷ προδότῃ τῆς πόλεως βοηθήσειε; Isae. 1.7; Dem. 20.74, 21.190, 48.36; Din. 1.112; Lycurg. 1.43. (In notes 16-22 I have confined myself to references to the orators. References to other sources and more references to the orators can be found in Hansen [*supra* n.8] 369.)

[23] *Cf.* further Aeschin. 1.186, Lys. fr.86-88, Lycurg. fr.18 Conomis.

[24] *Cf.* E. Drerup, "Über die bei den attischen Rednern eingelegten Urkunden," *NJbb* Suppl. 24 (1898) 307-08.

the defendant in a *graphe paranomon* is *per definitionem* a *rhetor* moving a *psephisma*,[25] and that is undoubtedly the reason why the *graphe paranomon* was also called a ῥητορικὴ γραφή. It is worth noting that the reference in the preserved laws is primarily to the *rhetores* in the *ecclesia*, and not to *rhetores* addressing the *boule*, the *nomothetai*, or the *dicasteria*. In the third law, however, the implication is that *rhetores* comprise speakers in the *boule*, since a *graphe paranomon* could be brought not only against decrees of the people, but also against decrees of the *boule*.[26] So I have little doubt that, if more laws were preserved, we would also have evidence of *rhetor* as a legal term denoting a speaker addressing one of the other bodies of government.

If we turn from laws to decrees, a first impression is that we have disappointingly little evidence of ῥήτωρ as the official designation of the citizen who addresses the *ecclesia* or the *boule*. The one example I can cite is an entrenchment clause in the Brea decree of *ca* 445: ἐ]ὰν δέ τις ἐπιφσεφίζει παρὰ τέ[ν στέλεν ἒ ῥρέ]τορ ἀγορεύει ... [ἄτιμον] ἔναι ... (*IG* I³ 46.24ff). But it is idiomatic in Attic decrees to use verbs rather than nouns. ἐγραμμάτευε, ἐπρυτάνευε, ἐπεστάτει are obvious examples. Now the verb corresponding to ῥήτωρ is λέγειν/εἰπεῖν/ῥηθῆναι. The obligatory reference, in the preamble, to the proposer of a decree is ὁ δεῖνα εἶπε, where, in my opinion, the aorist εἶπε is the verbal equivalent of the noun ῥήτωρ. The present tense λέγειν is also used about a ῥήτωρ, for example in *IG* II² 223A.4 κρίσιν ποιῆσαι τῶν λεγόντων ἐν τεῖ βουλῆι.

So the *rhetores* formed an integral and constitutionally recognized part of the Athenian democracy. Admittedly, a *rhetor* was neither elected nor selected by lot, but was volunteering: but he was officially invited to do so. All decisions were made by the large political bodies—the *ecclesia* (assisted by the *boule*), the *nomothetai*, and the *dicasteria*. But all initiatives were left to ὁ βουλόμενος Ἀθηναίων οἷς ἔξεστιν.[27] A *rhetor* was a citizen who took it upon himself to address the *ecclesia*, the *boule*, the *nomothetai*, or the *dicasteria*, and consequently to perform the rôle of ὁ βουλόμενος. Like being an ἐκκλησιαστής or a νομοθέτης or a δικαστής, to be a ῥήτωρ was essentially a one-day business. A citizen was *rhetor* insofar as he mounted the *bema* and addressed his fellow citizens and insofar as he was responsible for the speech he made. Beyond that he was, constitutionally

---

[25] Arist. *Pol.* 1255a8 ῥήτορα γράφονται παρανόμων.
[26] Dem. 47.34 γενομένου τοίνυν τοῦ ψηφίσματος τούτου ἐν τῇ βουλῇ, καὶ οὐδενὸς γραφομένου παρανόμων, ἀλλὰ κυρίου ὄντος ...
[27] The rôle of ὁ βουλόμενος is discussed and the sources are collected in Hansen (*supra* n.8) 359-60.

speaking, no longer a *rhetor* when he had descended from the *bema*. In recognition of his official position he, like the *archai*, had to wear a crown while addressing the assembly.[28] Admittedly, he was subjected neither to an initial *dokimasia* nor to *euthynai* in consequence of his speech. But he was certainly not irresponsible, as maintained by some historians.[29] On the contrary, the Athenians had forged much more dangerous weapons against the *rhetores* than against *archai* or *presbeis*. Apart from the δοκιμασία ῥητόρων, which was rarely used, the Athenians had created a whole series of public actions directly and often exclusively applying to *rhetores*. As a proposer of a *psephisma* (of the *demos* or of the *boule*), a *rhetor* was liable to be prosecuted by a γραφὴ παρανόμων. As the proposer of a *nomos* he might be put on trial by a γραφὴ νόμον μὴ ἐπιτήδειον θεῖναι. As a prosecutor in a public action he risked a fine of 1000 drachmas plus partial *atimia* if he withdrew his action before the hearing or if he obtained less than 1/5 of the votes of the jurors.[30] It was less dangerous to support or oppose a proposal made by another citizen, but a *rhetor* who made a profit from addressing his fellow citizens could be indicted by an εἰσαγγελία εἰς τὸν δῆμον or a προβολή or a γραφή to the *thesmothetai*.[31] We know of more than one hundred applications of these public actions against the relatively small group of *rhetores*, whereas the sources provide us with only some ten examples of the *euthynai* resulting in a public action, although every year some 1200 Athenian *archai*, in addition to an unknown number of *presbeis*, had to submit to *euthynai*.[32]

---

[28] Ar. *Eccl.* 131, *Eq.* 1227, *Av.* 463.
[29] E.g. C. Hignett, *A History of the Athenian Constitution* (Oxford 1952) 263. For further references see Roberts (*supra* n.1) 355-56.
[30] For the *graphe paranomon* and the *graphe nomon me epitedeion theinai cf.* Hansen (*supra* n.1: 1974); for the fine of 1000 drachmas and partial *atimia*, Hansen (1975) 29-30.
[31] *Eisangelia*, Hyp. 3.7-8; *probole*, Arist. *Ath.Pol.* 43.5; *graphe* to the *thesmothetai*, Dem. 46.26.
[32] Known applications of *euthynai* are: Kallias in 449 (Dem. 19.273); Phormion in 428 (schol. Ar. *Pax* 347); Paches in 427 (Plut. *Nic.* 6); Polystratos in 410 (Lys. 20); Eratosthenes in 403 (Lys. 12); Epikrates in 394-392 (Lys. 27.1); Pamphilos in 388 (Xen. *Hell.* 5.1.2; schol. Ar. *Plut.* 174; Dem. 40.20, 22); Melanopos before 361 (Arist. *Rh.* 1374b 25f); Melanopos before 353 (Dem. 24.127); Timarchos in 348 (Aeschin. 1.113); Theodoros in 347 (Din. fr.xxx Conomis); Aischines in 343 (Dem. 19, Aeschin. 2); Lykourgos in 336-324 (Din. fr.viii); Demosthenes ca 330 (Plut. *Mor.* 845F); Hermias ca 325 (Din. fr.xlii). In several cases we have no precise information about the type of action applied, and some of the trials listed above may not be *euthynai*, but e.g. an application of a *graphe klopes*. Roberts (*supra* n.1) argues that the politicians were responsible *qua* being *archai* and accordingly subjected to *euthynai*. She is right in stressing the responsibility of the political leaders, but she overrates the *euthynai* and does not discuss the far more important types of public action aimed directly at *rhetores* and *strategoi*.

III

Thus far I have concentrated on the constitutional aspect of the term *rhetor*. By law, any citizen is a *rhetor* in so far as he acts as *ho boulomenos* and addresses the *ecclesia*, the *boule*, the *nomothetai*, or the *dicasteria*. Since democracy in principle involved the participation of all citizens, the inference is that, in an ideal democracy, all *rhetores* combined would constitute the entire *demos*. But in Athens citizenship did not entail an obligation to act as *ho boulomenos* and to become a *rhetor*.[33] There was a considerable gap between the ideal and the real democracy, and according to their political participation, Athenian citizens may be divided into four groups:

(a) Citizens who never attended the *ecclesia* and never joined the panel of 6000 jurors (from which *nomothetai* and *dicastai* were appointed) and never presented themselves as candidates at the annual sortition of *bouleutai* and other *archai*. They are the passive citizens censured by Perikles in the funeral speech (Thuc. 2.40.2), but praised by Plato, if they are philosophers: λέγωμεν δή ... περὶ τῶν κορυφαίων (τί γὰρ ἄν τις τούς γε φαύλως διατρίβοντας ἐν φιλοσοφίᾳ λέγοι;) οὗτοι δέ που ἐκ νέων πρῶτον μὲν εἰς ἀγορὰν οὐκ ἴσασι τὴν ὁδόν, οὐδὲ ὅπου δικαστήριον ἢ βουλευτήριον ἤ τι κοινὸν ἄλλο τῆς πόλεως συνέδριον. νόμους δὲ καὶ ψηφίσματα λεγόμενα ἢ γεγραμμένα οὔτε ὁρῶσιν οὔτε ἀκούουσι· σπουδαὶ δὲ ἑταιριῶν ἐπ' ἀρχὰς καὶ σύνοδοι καὶ δεῖπνα καὶ σὺν αὐλητρίσι κῶμοι, οὐδὲ ὄναρ πράττειν προσίσταται αὐτοῖς.[34] It is surprising, however, even in the forensic speeches to find prosecutors and defendants who almost take a pride in telling the jurors that they have never (before) visited the *agora* and never been to the *bouleuterion* or the *dicasteria*:

Pl. *Ap.* 17D: νῦν ἐγὼ πρῶτον ἐπὶ δικαστήριον ἀναβέβηκα, ἔτη γεγονὼς ἑβδομήκοντα· ἀτεχνῶς οὖν ξένως ἔχω τῆς ἐνθάδε λέξεως.

Lys. 19.55: περὶ δ' ἐμαυτοῦ βραχέα βούλομαι ὑμῖν εἰπεῖν. ἐγὼ γὰρ ἔτη γεγονὼς ἤδη τριάκοντα οὔτε τῷ πατρὶ οὐδὲν πώποτε ἀντεῖπον, οὔτε τῶν πολιτῶν οὐδείς μοι ἐνεκάλεσεν, ἐγγύς τε οἰκῶν τῆς ἀγορᾶς οὔτε πρὸς δικαστηρίῳ οὔτε πρὸς βουλευτηρίῳ ὤφθην οὐδεπώποτε, πρὶν ταύτην τὴν συμφορὰν γενέσθαι.

Is. 1.1: καὶ τότε μὲν οὕτως ὑπ' αὐτοῦ σωφρόνως ἐπαιδευόμεθα, ὥστ' οὐδὲ ἀκροασόμενοι οὐδέποτε ἤλθομεν ἐπὶ δικαστήριον, νῦν δὲ ἀγωνιούμενοι περὶ πάντων ἥκομεν τῶν ὑπαρχόντων.

---

[33] Dem. 19.99 οὐδένα γὰρ τὰ κοινὰ πράττειν ὑμεῖς κελεύετε οὐδ' ἀναγκάζετε· ἀλλ' ἐπειδάν τις ἑαυτὸν πείσας δύνασθαι προσέλθῃ, ... εὐνοϊκῶς δέχεσθε καὶ οὐ φθονερῶς, ἀλλὰ καὶ χειροτονεῖτε καὶ τὰ ὑμέτερ' αὐτῶν ἐγχειρίζετε.

[34] *Tht.* 176C–D; *cf. Ap.* 17D, 32A.

Isoc. 15.38: ἐμὲ δ' οὐδεὶς πώποθ' ἑώρακεν οὔτ' ἐν τοῖς συνεδρίοις οὔτε περὶ τὰς ἀνακρίσεις οὔτ' ἐπὶ τοῖς δικαστηρίοις οὔτε πρὸς τοῖς διαιτηταῖς, ἀλλ' οὕτως ἀπέχομαι τούτων ἁπάντων ὡς οὐδεὶς ἄλλος τῶν πολιτῶν.

In a court, to admit frankly to political inactivity would, in my opinion, amount to an insult of the jurors who were performing their civic duties. On the contrary, the topos is found in passages where the intended effect is *captatio benevolentiae*.[35] It is of no consequence whether or not the speaker is telling the truth. The citizen who professes his passivity to the active citizens is a topos which shows that to be an *apragmon* was certainly a respectable attitude even among active Athenian citizens.[36] It is only natural that we have no similar evidence for the citizens who never or hardly ever visited the *ecclesia*. A passive citizen could be forced to go to court either as a defendant or as a plaintiff, and then the topos is appropriate. But no citizen could be forced to go to the *ecclesia*, and logographers hardly ever wrote symbouleutic speeches. Therefore we do not have and probably shall never find an orator stating, "Regularly I never attend the *ecclesia*, but in this case ... " So we must look for other types of evidence. Plato's description of the passive citizen (quoted *supra*) includes the *ecclesia* (*psephismata*), but Plato is not a good source for the ideology of the Athenian democratic citizens. A much better source is Euripides, who in *Orestes* 917ff describes the honest farmer whose trustworthiness is only increased by the fact that he hardly ever comes to the city and attends the assembly. The setting is Argos, but the audience was Athenian and the play probably reflects a view accepted by many Athenian democrats. The ideology must of course be connected with the fact that the assembly-place on the Pnyx could accommodate only a fraction of the adult male population.

(b) Citizens who attended the *ecclesia*, who served as *bouleutai*, and who manned the panel of 6000 jurors, but who restricted themselves to listening and voting without ever addressing the assemblies. There is ample evidence that this was a very common type of citizen. Commenting on the 'Solonian' *dokimasia* of male prostitutes, Demosthenes imputes to Solon the following reason for restricting the

---

[35] In all four cases the speaker's purpose is of course to persuade the jurors that he is not a sycophant. For this purpose, however, it would have been sufficient to deny any prior appearance in court as a prosecutor or defendant. All four speakers take the further step of denying any involvement in the administration of justice. The clients of Lysias and Isaeus are probably too young to have served as jurors; so they emphasize that they have never *listened* to a trial in a *dicasterion*. The two old men, Socrates and Isocrates, emphasize that they have never even been jurors. So in all four cases the alleged total ignorance of the lawcourts is intended as an argument in favour of the speaker.

[36] *Cf.* A. W. Gomme, *A Historical Commentary on Thucydides* II (Oxford 1956) 121–22.

law to those who make proposals or address the *ecclesia* (22.30): πολλαχόθεν μὲν οὖν ἄν τις ἴδοι τοῦτο, οὐχ ἥκιστα δ' ἐκ τούτου τοῦ νόμου, μήτε λέγειν μήτε γράφειν ἐξεῖναι τοῖς ἡταιρηκόσιν. ἑώρα γὰρ ἐκεῖνο, ὅτι τοῖς πολλοῖς ὑμῶν ἐξὸν λέγειν οὐ λέγετε. A few sections later (36) he makes a similar statement about the councillors: τῷ γὰρ [sc. τῶν βουλευτῶν] ἐστιν ὄνειδος, εἰ σιωπῶντος αὐτοῦ καὶ μηδὲν γράφοντος, ἴσως δ' οὐδὲ τὰ πόλλ' εἰς τὸ βουλευτήριον εἰσιόντος, μὴ λάβοι ἡ βουλὴ τὸν στέφανον; And Aischines has the following statement to make about the ordinary juror (3.233): ἔπειτ' ἔξεισιν ἐκ τοῦ δικαστηρίου ὁ τοιοῦτος κριτὴς ἑαυτὸν μὲν ἀσθενῆ πεποιηκώς, ἰσχυρὸν δὲ τὸν ῥήτορα. ἀνὴρ γὰρ ἰδιώτης ἐν πόλει δημοκρατουμένῃ νόμῳ καὶ ψήφῳ βασιλεύει· ὅταν δ' ἑτέρῳ ταῦτα παραδῷ, καταλέλυκε τὴν αὐτὸς αὑτοῦ δυναστείαν. Aischines' portrait of the ordinary juror is confirmed by the preserved dicastic *pinakia*. In *Athenian Bronze Allotment Plates* (1972) John Kroll collected 82 dicastic *pinakia* of the fourth century with 161 attested uses. The names of 65 citizens are either preserved or can be restored. But not a single one of these 65 citizens is known as a *rhetor*, a *strategos*, or an ambassador.

(c) Citizens who conform to the democratic ideal. They took it upon themselves occasionally to act as *ho boulomenos*, but they avoided any regular or 'professional' involvement in politics. They were emphatic in stating that they were *idiotai*, and they did not like to be grouped with those *rhetores* who took the platform incessantly. This type of citizen is regularly praised by the orators, as can be seen from the following four quotations, one referring to each of the four major assemblies—the *ecclesia*, the *boule*, the *nomothetai*, and the *dicasteria*:

Aeschin. 3.220: ἐν μὲν γὰρ ταῖς ὀλιγαρχίαις οὐχ ὁ βουλόμενος, ἀλλ' ὁ δυναστεύων δημηγορεῖ, ἐν δὲ ταῖς δημοκρατίαις ὁ βουλόμενος καὶ ὅταν αὐτῷ δοκῇ. καὶ τὸ μὲν διὰ χρόνου λέγειν σημεῖόν ἐστιν ἐπὶ τῶν καιρῶν καὶ τοῦ συμφέροντος ἀνδρὸς πολιτευομένου, τὸ δὲ μηδεμίαν παραλείπειν ἡμέραν ἐργαζομένου καὶ μισθαρνοῦντος.

Dem. 22.37: εἰ μὲν ἀπογνώσεσθε, ἐπὶ τοῖς λέγουσι τὸ βουλευτήριον ἔσται, ἐὰν δὲ καταγνῶτε, ἐπὶ τοῖς ἰδιώταις· ἑορακότες γὰρ οἱ πολλοὶ διὰ τὴν τῶν λεγόντων πονηρίαν τήνδ' ἀφῃρημένην τὴν βουλὴν τὸν στέφανον, οὐχὶ προήσονται τούτοις τὰς πράξεις, ἀλλὰ τὰ βέλτιστ' ἐροῦσιν αὐτοί. εἰ δὲ γενήσεται τοῦτο καὶ τῶν ἠθάδων καὶ συνεστηκότων ῥητόρων ἀπαλλαγήσεσθε, ὄψεσθ', ὦ ἄνδρες Ἀθηναῖοι, πάνθ' ἃ προσήκει γιγνόμενα.

Dem. 24.66: οὔτε γὰρ ὡς οὐκ ἐναντίος ἔσθ' ὁ νόμος τοῖς ἄλλοις δεικνύειν ἕξει, οὔθ' ὡς δι' ἀπειρίαν ἰδιώτην αὐτὸν ὄντα τοῦτ' ἔλαθεν δύναιτ' ἂν πεῖσαι· πάλαι γὰρ μισθοῦ καὶ γράφων καὶ νόμους εἰσφέρων ὦπται.

Dem. 23.4: ἐπειδὴ γάρ, οὐχὶ τῶν ἐνοχλούντων ὑμᾶς οὐδὲ τῶν πολιτευομένων καὶ πιστευομένων παρ' ὑμῖν ὤν, πρᾶγμα τηλικοῦτόν φημι δείξειν πεπραγμένον, ἐὰν, ὅσον ἐστὶν ἐν ὑμῖν, συναγωνίσησθέ μοι καὶ προθύμως ἀκούσητε, τοῦτό τε σώσετε καὶ ποιήσετε μὴ κατοκνεῖν, ἐάν τίς τι καὶ ἡμῶν οἴεται δύνασθαι ποιῆσαι τὴν πόλιν ἀγαθόν. οἰήσεται δέ, ἂν μὴ χαλεπὸν εἶναι νομίζῃ τὸ παρ᾿ ὑμῖν λόγου τυχεῖν. νῦν δὲ πολλοῖς τοῦτο φοβουμένοις, λέγειν μὲν ἴσως οὐ δεινοῖς, βελτίοσι δ᾿ ἀνθρωποῖς τῶν δεινῶν, οὐδὲ σκοπεῖν ἐπέρχεται τῶν κοινῶν οὐδέν.

It is worth noting that *idiotes*, in these and similar passages, does not denote the passive citizen, but the active ordinary citizen in a true democracy. This almost technical use of the word is to be found not only in the speeches but also in inscriptions.[37]

(d) Finally, the orators refer with the greatest frequency to a small group of citizens who regularly addressed the *ecclesia*, proposed laws and decrees, and frequented the courts as prosecutors or *synegoroi*. *Rhetor* is by far the most common designation attested for this group of citizens, but we also find them called πολιτευόμενοι,[38] sometimes σύμβουλοι,[39] occasionally δημαγωγοί (in a neutral sense),[40] and only

---

[37] Apart from the passages just quoted, *idiotes* is applied to a proposer of a decree (Aeschin. 3.214) and of a *nomos* (Dem. 23.62, Andoc. 1.83), to a speaker in the *ecclesia* (Dem. *Prooem.* 13, Hyp. 3.13), and to a prosecutor in a public action (Dem. 53.2, Lys. 5.3). Furthermore, *idiotai* are sometimes appointed *presbeis* (IG II² 16.19, 204.82) or *archai* (Dem. 24.112, Hyp. 1.25). So, in a political context, *idiotes* has a whole range of denotations: (a) a citizen who avoids all involvement with the affairs of the city (Aeschin. 3.252), (b) a citizen who, as a listener, attends a public meeting (Ant. 6.24, Dem. 19.17, Aeschin. 3.125), (c) a citizen who is a voting member of one of the political assemblies (Aeschin. 3.233), (d) a citizen who occasionally acts as *ho boulomenos*, *cf.* the references *supra* 45f.

[38] *Politeuomenos* is a common term but vaguer than *rhetor*. In its broader sense it means 'one who acts as a citizen' and may refer to any politically active citizen or to the entire body of citizens (*supra* n.7). Most occurrences, however, indicate the meaning 'political leader', regularly without reference to any specific form of political initiative (Lys. 25.27; Dem. 3.29–31; 8.68; 10.46, 70; 13.35; 15.33; 17.23; 19.12, 285; 22.52; 23.209; 24.155, 164, 192–93; 26.1–6, 18; 39.3; 52.28; 58.23; *Prooem.* 12.2; *Ep.* 2.9; 3.15, 27, 33, 45; Aeschin. 3.8, 235–36; Din. 1.96; 2.15; Isoc. 7.55; 15.132). If *politeuomenos* is connected with a body of government, it denotes in most cases a proposer or speaker in the *ecclesia* (Dem. 8.32–33; 18.173, 301; 20.132; Aeschin. 1.195; 2.64; Isoc. 15.231) and only rarely a citizen addressing the *boule* (Dem. 22.36), the *nomothetai* (Dem. 20.91), or the *dicasteria* (Dem. 23.4, 24.157). *Politeuomenos* is sometimes juxtaposed with *rhetor* (Dem. 13.20; 18.94, 278; Isoc. 15.231) and once with *strategos* (Dem. 24.135) These references are fairly exhaustive but not complete. I have concentrated on the participle, although other forms of the verb have the same uses.

[39] As one would expect from the rhetorical term συμβουλευτικὸς λόγος, *symboulos* is used exclusively about proposers and speakers in the *ecclesia*: Dem. 18.66 τί τὸν σύμβουλον ἔδει λέγειν ἢ γράφειν τὸν Ἀθήνησιν ... ὃς συνῄδειν μὲν ἐκ παντὸς τοῦ χρόνου μέχρι τῆς ἡμέρας ἀφ᾿ ἧς αὐτὸς ἐπὶ τὸ βῆμ᾿ ἀνέβην; Aeschin. 1.120 ὁ τοῦ δήμου σύμβουλος (*cf.* Dem. 1.16; 7.1; 18.66, 94, 189; 22.77; 58.62; Aeschin. 1.26; Hyp. 1.28; Din. 1.38–40; etc.). *Symboulos* and *rhetor* are juxtaposed in Dem. 18.94, 212; 58.62; Din. 1.38–40. *Symbouloi* and *strategoi* are juxtaposed in Din. 1.76. The verb συμβουλεύειν has the same meaning (*e.g.* Dem. 9.3–4) but may occasionally be applied to somebody who advises a *dicasterion* (Dem. 20.167).

[40] *Demagogos* means 'leader of the people' sometimes in a positive sense (Lys. 27.10; Aeschin. 3.78, 226; Hyp. 1.16; Din. 1.31, 53), sometimes in a neutral sense (Dem.

one time πολιτικοί.⁴¹ By contrast with *rhetor*, neither *politeuomenos* nor *symboulos* nor *demagogos* is used in documents as a technical term. Furthermore, an examination of all occurrences of the word *rhetor* in the orators shows that, in most cases, it denotes specifically the citizen who *habitually* took political initiatives.⁴² And when ῥή-τορες καὶ στρατηγοί are juxtaposed, the reference is invariably to this smaller group of 'political leaders', to the exclusion of active citizens who only at intervals acted as *hoi boulomenoi*. Apart from all the general references, the term *rhetor* is applied to the following fourth-century 'political leaders':⁴³

Aischines (Dem. 18.130, 308, 318; 19.23)
Androtion (Dem. 22.37, 70)
Aristogeiton (Dem. 25.62)
Aristophon (Dem. 18.219, Hyp. 3.28)
Autokles (Hyp. fr.97 Jensen)
Demades (Din. 1.100-01)
Demosthenes (Dem. 18.94, 212, 246, 319; 21.189; 25.38; 32.31; *Ep.* 2.10; Aeschin. 3.55, 73, 148; Din. 1.86, 100-02; Hyp. 1.12, 21)
Diopeithes of Sphettos (Hyp. 3.29)

26.4, Aeschin. 3.134, Hyp. 1.22, Din. 1.99), and only twice in a pejorative sense (Lys. 25.9, Din. 1.10, *cf.* δημαγωγεῖν in Dem. 8.34). In most cases there is no reference to a specific body of government; if any, then to the *ecclesia* (Din. 1.31). *Demagogoi* and *strategoi* are juxtaposed in Hyp. 1.22. *Demagogos* occurs in Andoc. 4.27, which is however a late composition. *Cf.* furthermore Pytheas fr.4 (Baiter/Sauppe 311).

⁴¹ The only occurrence of *politikos* is Aeschin. 2.184 (*cf. supra* 36), and the orators never use the word *demegoros*, which may occur in other texts (*e.g.* Xen. *Mem.* 2.6.15; *Hell.* 6.2.39, 6.3.3).

⁴² *Cf. supra* 39f with nn.16-22. In the orators the word *rhetor* is used in its legal sense in references to *nomoi* (Aeschin. 1.28, 34, 186; 3.2; Din. 1.71; Lycurg. fr.18 Conomis; Hyp. 3.1, 4, 8). In some cases it applies to a proposer of a specific decree (Lys. 13.72; Dem. 22.70; 59.105; Aeschin. 3.31, 203), and once it is used about a citizen who at intervals addresses the *ecclesia* (Dem. 18.308). In all other cases the reference is to the *rhetores* in the political sense.

⁴³ Some historians suggest a different grouping of the politically active citizens, distinguishing between (a) citizens who attend the meetings, (b) minor politicians, and (c) the true political leaders, *cf.* Jones (*supra* n.1) 128-33 and Perlman (*supra* n.1) 328-30. Jones gives the following description of (b): "There was throughout Athenian history a class of semi-professional politicians, at first consisting of the gentry, later partly of the gentry and partly of poor men of rhetorical talent. These were the people who held the elective offices, were chosen as envoys to foreign states, proposed motions in the council and in the assembly, and prosecuted (and defended) in political trials" (130). There was indeed some kind of 'hierarchy' within the group of *rhetores* (*cf. e.g.* Dem. 2.29, Hyp. 1.12), but Jones' description of the minor politician fits Demosthenes, Demades, and Lykourgos better than Aristogeiton or Theokrines, and the distinction between major and minor politicians tends to obliterate the distinction between groups (c) and (d) above, which is, however, well attested in the sources. Consequently I will in this paper treat the group of *rhetores* as a whole and reserve a discussion of the hierarchy within the group for a future study.

Kallistratos (Dem. 18.219, Hyp. 3.1)
Kephalos (Dem. 18.219, Din. 1.38)
Ktesiphon (Aeschin. 3.31, 203-04)
Lykourgos (Lyc. 1.31)
Philokrates (Hyp. 3.29)
Philostratos (Dem. 42.21)
Polyeuktos of Sphettos (Din. 1.100)
Stephanos (Dem. 59.43)
Theokrines (Dem. 58.62ff)
Thrasyboulos (of Kollytos?) (Dem. 18.219)
Timarchos (Aeschin. 1.112, 188)
Timokrates (Dem. 24.124)

Summing up: in the Athenian democracy of the fourth century, we are faced with two different uses of the important political term *rhetor*. As a legal term it occurs in *nomoi* and signifies any citizen who addresses his fellow citizens in the assemblies—groups (c) and (d) above. But in the speeches *rhetor* is almost invariably used as a political term in the much narrower sense of a citizen who addresses his fellow-citizens habitually, sometimes even professionally—group (d) above to the exclusion of (c)—and the citizen who only once or at intervals performs the part of *ho boulomenos* is described as an *idiotes*, to be distinguished from the *rhetores* proper.

The clash between these two uses of the term *rhetor* is best illustrated by Hypereides in the speech *For Euxenippos*, who had been elected by the people to sleep in the Amphiaraion and then to tell in the following *ecclesia* what the god had revealed to him. He performed his task; but when he had reported his dream to the people in the *ecclesia*, Polyeuktos (of Kydantidai?) suspected foul play and indicted Euxenippos by an εἰσαγγελία εἰς τὸν δῆμον, based on the third section of the eisangeltic law: ἐάν τις ῥήτωρ ὢν μὴ λέγῃ τὰ ἄριστα τῷ δήμῳ τῷ Ἀθηναίων χρήματα λαμβάνων.[44] Euxenippos was defended by Hypereides, and one of the basic arguments put forward by the defence is that Euxenippos is not a *rhetor* but a private citizen (*idiotes*), and so he is not liable to be prosecuted by an *eisangelia* which is reserved for *rhetores*, i.e. citizens who regularly take a political initiative (Hyp. 3.3, 9, 11, 27-30). In his *graphe paranomon* against Ktesiphon, Aischines anticipates that his opponent will rely on precisely the same line of defence: Ktesiphon has admittedly proposed and carried the *psephisma*, but he is an *idiotes* and not a *rhetor* (Aeschin. 3.214). Now apart from the *eisangelia*, Euxenippos cannot be connected with

---

[44] *Cf.* Hansen (*supra* n.1: 1975) Catalogue no. 124.

any other political activity, but since he has addressed the *ecclesia*, he must have been a *rhetor* in the legal sense. The two different uses of *rhetor* in Athens illustrate a common phenomenon in societies of all periods: a gap between the constitution and how it works.

IV

I have argued that *rhetores* and *strategoi* are regularly grouped together when the reference is to 'political leaders' in general. Having discussed the *rhetores*, I turn to the distinction between *rhetores* and *strategoi*. It is well known that in the fifth century the two different tasks of being a *rhetor* and a *strategos* were regularly performed by the same men, whereas in the fourth the two functions tended to become more and more separated.[45] In the *Ath. Pol.* 28.2–3 Aristotle enumerates thirteen Athenian προστάται after Kleisthenes down to the end of the Peloponnesian War. Eleven were *strategoi*, the twelfth may have been a *strategos*; only the thirteenth, Kallikrates of Paiania, was certainly a *prostates* without being a *strategos*.[46] After the restoration of the democracy, however, a sharp division developed, so that policy-making was left to a group of *rhetores* who were no longer elected *strategoi*, whereas the wars were conducted by a group of professional *strategoi* who tended to keep away from the *bema* on the Pnyx. Of the 77 known *strategoi* of the period 403–322, only 11 or 12 are recorded as proposers of decrees or speakers in the *ecclesia*. In the first half of the fourth century at least some political leaders were still elected *strategoi*, but after the Social War, Phokion was the only man of any importance to combine the *strategia* with addressing the *ecclesia*.[47]

---

[45] *Cf.* Jones (*supra* n.1) 128, Perlman (*supra* n.1) 347; C. Mossé, *La fin de la démocratie athénienne* (Paris 1962) 269–73; J. K. Davies, *Wealth and the Power of Wealth in Classical Athens* (New York 1981) 124–31.

[46] Xanthippos (480/479), Miltiades (490/489), Themistokles (481/0), Aristeides (479/8), Ephialtes (?), Kimon (478/7), Perikles (454/3), Thoukydides (444/3), Nikias (427/6), Kleon (424/3), Theramenes (411/0), Kleophon (?), Kallikrates. The year is that of the first attested *strategia*; *cf.* C. W. Fornara, *The Athenian Board of Generals from 501 to 404* (*Historia* Einzelschr. 16 [1971]). Concerning Ephialtes see Fornara 46 n.24, concerning Kleophon 70 with n.126. Connor (*supra* p.33) has argued convincingly that a new type of 'politician' appeared after the death of Perikles. The 'new politicians', however, were regularly *strategoi*, and in this respect there is no difference between the new and the old politicians. The first source mentioning a separation of civilian and military political leaders is Lys. 13.7: τοὺς τοῦ δήμου προεστηκότας καὶ τοὺς στρατηγοῦντας καὶ ταξιαρχοῦντας. But the splitting up of *rhetores* and *strategoi* is basically a fourth-century phenomenon, and most marked after 355.

[47] For the period 403–355: Rhinon of Paiania, Thrasyboulos of Steiria, Archinos of Koile, Anytos, Aristophon of Azenia, Kallistratos of Aphidna, Timotheos of Ana-

And the prosopographical statistics support the general comments on the change in leadership which can be found in the orators and in later sources:

Isoc. 8.54–55: τοσοῦτον δὲ διαφέρομεν τῶν προγόνων, ὅσον ἐκεῖνοι μὲν τοὺς αὐτοὺς προστάτας τε τῆς πόλεως ἐποιοῦντο καὶ στρατηγοὺς ᾑροῦντο νομίζοντες τὸν ἐπὶ τοῦ βήματος τὰ βέλτιστα συμβουλεῦσαι δυνάμενον, τὸν αὐτὸν τοῦτον ἄριστ' ἂν βουλεύσασθαι καὶ καθ' αὐτὸν γενόμενον, ἡμεῖς δὲ τοὐναντίον τούτων ποιοῦμεν· οἷς μὲν γὰρ περὶ τῶν μεγίστων συμβούλοις χρώμεθα, τούτους μὲν οὐκ ἀξιοῦμεν στρατηγοὺς χειροτονεῖν ὡς νοῦν οὐκ ἔχοντας, οἷς δ' οὐδεὶς ἂν οὔτε περὶ τῶν ἰδίων οὔτε περὶ τῶν κοινῶν συμβουλεύσαιτο, τούτους δ' αὐτοκράτορας ἐκπέμπομεν ὡς ἐκεῖ σοφωτέρους ἐσομένους καὶ ῥᾷον βουλευσομένους περὶ τῶν Ἑλληνικῶν πραγμάτων ἢ περὶ τῶν ἐνθάδε προτιθεμένων.

Aeschin. 3.146: εἰ δέ τις αὐτῷ (Demosthenes) τῶν στρατηγῶν ἀντείποι, καταδουλούμενος τοὺς ἄρχοντας καὶ συνεθίζων μηδὲν αὐτῷ ἀντιλέγειν διαδικασίαν ἔφη γράψειν τῷ βήματι πρὸς τὸ στρατήγιον· πλείω γὰρ ὑμᾶς ἀγαθὰ ὑφ' ἑαυτοῦ ἔφη ἀπὸ τοῦ βήματος πεπονθέναι, ἢ ὑπὸ τῶν στρατηγῶν ἐκ τοῦ στρατηγίου.

Plut. Phoc. 7.5: ὁρῶν δὲ (Phokion) τοὺς τὰ κοινὰ πράσσοντας τότε διῃρημένους ὥσπερ ἀπὸ κλήρου τὸ στρατήγιον καὶ τὸ βῆμα, καὶ τοὺς μὲν λέγοντας ἐν τῷ δήμῳ καὶ γράφοντας μόνον, ὧν Εὔβουλος ἦν καὶ Ἀριστοφῶν καὶ Δημοσθένης καὶ Λυκοῦργος καὶ Ὑπερείδης, Διοπείθη δὲ καὶ Μενεσθέα καὶ Λεωσθένη καὶ Χάρητα τῷ στρατηγεῖν καὶ πολεμεῖν αὔξοντας ἑαυτούς, ἐβούλετο τὴν Περικλέους καὶ Ἀριστείδου καὶ Σόλωνος πολιτείαν ὥσπερ ὁλόκληρον καὶ διηρμοσμένην ἐν ἀμφοῖν ἀναλαβεῖν καὶ ἀποδοῦναι.[48]

The reason for the separation of the *strategoi* from the *rhetores* is lucidly stated by Aristotle at *Politics* 1305a7–15: ἐπὶ δὲ τῶν ἀρχαίων, ὅτε γένοιτο ὁ αὐτὸς δημαγωγὸς καὶ στρατηγός, εἰς τυραννίδα μετέβαλλον· σχεδὸν γὰρ οἱ πλεῖστοι τῶν ἀρχαίων τυράννων ἐκ δημαγωγῶν γεγόνασιν. αἴτιον δὲ τοῦ τότε μὲν γίγνεσθαι νῦν δὲ μή, ὅτι τότε μὲν οἱ δημαγωγοὶ ἦσαν ἐκ τῶν στρατηγούντων (οὐ γάρ πω δεινοὶ ἦσαν λέγειν), νῦν δὲ τῆς ῥητορικῆς ηὐξημένης οἱ δυνάμενοι λέγειν δημαγωγοῦσι μέν, δι' ἀπειρίαν δὲ τῶν πολεμικῶν οὐκ ἐπιτίθενται,

---

phlystos, Exekestides of Thorikos. For the period 355–322: Phokion of Potamos, Melanopos of Aixone, Nausikles of Oe, Philokles of Eroiadai. For Anytos as a fourth-century *strategos* cf. Pl. *Meno* 90B, αἱροῦνται γοῦν αὐτὸν ἐπὶ τὰς μεγίστας ἀρχάς. The dramatic date of the dialogue is after the restoration of the democracy in 403, perhaps 402: J. E. Thomas, *Musings on the* Meno (The Hague 1980) 22. A twelfth *strategos* who was probably also a *rhetor* is Polyeuktos (Hyp. fr.xlv [182–84 Sauppe]), identified by Kirchner *PA* 11947 with Polyeuktos of Kydantidai.

[48] The rhetorical juxtaposition of βῆμα and στρατήγιον both in Aischines and in Plutarch indicates that Plutarch had the Aischines passage in mind here. The separation of *rhetores* and *strategoi* is also emphasized in Isoc. 15.136; Dem. 12.19; 18.212, 246; Din. 1.76; Plut. *Mor.* 486D, 812F.

πλὴν εἴ που βραχύ τι γέγονε τοιοῦτον. So a growing professionalism (both in rhetoric and in warfare) produced its regular effect: a division of labour. To the account given by Aristotle we must add that in the fourth century citizen armies tended to be replaced by mercenary forces commanded by condottieri, some of whom were not even native Athenians but only naturalized in order to be elected *strategoi*. The outstanding example is Charidemos of Oreos.[49] A naturalized condottiere or an Athenian mercenary leader, who for years might be in the service of a tyrant or a barbarian prince, is not the obvious type of person to persuade the Athenians in the *ecclesia*, and the result was that the leading *rhetores* had to fight the battles in the ranks,[50] whereas the *strategoi* attended the *ecclesiai* and voted without ever addressing the people.

On the basis of the undeniable and important distinction between *rhetores* and *strategoi*, modern historians sometimes identify the *rhetores* with the politicians, as opposed to the *strategoi* who are no longer to be regarded as proper 'political leaders'.[51] There may be some truth in this, but I emphasize a caution stated by Raphael Sealey: "it is well known that in fourth-century Athens the profession of general and politician tended to diverge. The tendency should not be overestimated."[52] As argued above, when the sources refer to 'political leaders' in general they regularly mention both *rhetores* and *strategoi*. One can think of several good reasons for this common practice.

Like other Greek *poleis*, Athens was regularly at war. After a period of peace (403-395) the Athenians joined the Corinthian War (395-386), and then the war against Sparta in alliance with Thebes (379-371). In the 360's the Athenians fought regularly in the Aegean, *i.a.* to recover Amphipolis, and sometimes in Hellas as well, now in alliance with Sparta against Thebes. The Social War was fought and lost in 357-355, and the first war against Philip dragged on for eleven years (357-346). The more formidable second war against Philip was over in two years (340-338), and after the defeat at Chaironeia Athens experienced her only long period of peace and prosperity until Antipater put an end to the democracy after the Lamian War (323-

---

[49] For a short biography see J. K. Davies, *Athenian Propertied Families* (Oxford 1971) 570-71. Other examples are Philiskos (*PA* 14430), Polystratos (12070), and Strabax (12911).

[50] Both Demades (Diod. 16.87.1) and Demosthenes (Plut. *Dem.* 20.2, *Mor.* 845F) fought in the battle of Chaironeia as ordinary hoplites.

[51] Jones (*supra* n.1) 128, Perlman (*supra* n.1) 347; Davies (*supra* n.45) 124ff.

[52] Sealey (*supra* n.1) 178-79.

322). Admittedly, warfare was not continuous and battles were fought only occasionally, but Athens nearly always had a squadron operating somewhere in the Aegean or Ionian Sea and sometimes an army operating somewhere in Hellas. When peace is the exception and war the rule, political leaders tend to include generals, and the Athenians can certainly testify to the principle stated by Clausewitz: war is politics carried on by other means.

Second, the splitting up of the 'political leaders' into a group of *rhetores* and a group of *strategoi* resulted in close collaboration between members of the two groups. This is perhaps best illustrated by Demosthenes in his description of Athenian political behaviour in the *Second Olynthiac* (2.29, quoted *supra* 37), but many other sources can be adduced: Aischines describes Chares' collaboration with citizens who dominated the *ecclesia* (2.71), and collaboration between *rhetores* and *strategoi* is also discussed in Isocrates' defence of Timotheos (15.136ff), in Philip's letter to the Athenians (Dem. 12.19), and in Plato's *Euthydemus* (290C–D).

Third, tradition is always an important factor, especially for the Athenians who cherished the idea of an ancestral constitution and tended to believe that reaction was the only true form of progress. For almost a century the Athenians had been used to political leaders who both commanded the armed forces and addressed the *ecclesia* and the *dicasteria*. In the fourth century, when the *strategoi* tended to become professional generals and left the political initiatives to citizens acting as *hoi boulomenoi*, the Athenians' first reaction, in my opinion, would be to believe that the group of leaders now comprised *both* generals *and* orators. And so they coined the phrase ῥήτορες καὶ στρατηγοί. The juxtaposition of *rhetores* and *strategoi* does not occur in the sources before the 350's. It may of course be accidental, but it may also reflect the Athenians' adaptation to a change in political leadership during the first half of the fourth century.

Fourth, one of the important political activities in Athens was to serve on an embassy. The *presbeis* were elected by the *ecclesia*, and of the 94 envoys known in our period 32 are attested also as *rhetores* in the *ecclesia* and 11 also as *strategoi*.[53] The *rhetores* outweigh the *strategoi*, but, on the other hand, to be an envoy was an activity that tended to bind together the *rhetores* and the *strategoi*, especially since the *strategoi* who served as envoys would have to make a report on

[53] Konon of Anaphlystos (*PA* 8707), Eunomos (*PA* 5861), Thrasyboulos of Kollytos, Kallistratos of Aphidna, Kallias of Alopeke, Autokles of Euonymon, Aristophon of Azenia, Melanopos of Aixone, Nausikles of Oe, Phokion (of Potamos?), Ephialtes (*PA* 6156).

their mission to the *boule* and the *ecclesia* and would become *rhetores*, at least in the technical legal sense of the word.

Finally, the distinction between *rhetores* and *strategoi* is most marked if we focus on the *rhetores* in the *ecclesia*. But some *strategoi* are also known as *rhetores* addressing the *boule* or the *nomothetai*, and more appeared before the *dicasteria* as prosecutors or *synegoroi*. Many political battles were fought not in the *ecclesia* but in the people's court. Political trials were still brought by *strategoi*, and it was quite common, for both prosecutor and defendant, to call on a *strategos* to be his *synegoros*.[54] If we take into account that *rhetor* denotes not only policy-makers in the *ecclesia* but also the citizens appearing before the *boule*, the *nomothetai*,[55] and the *dicasteria*, the number of *strategoi* who were also *rhetores* rises from 11 or 12 to 17 or 18 with several more activities attested. Including ambassadors, the figure rises to 22–23. In conclusion, *rhetores* and *strategoi* were diverging groups throughout the fourth century, which is probably the reason why the Athenians had to use two words instead of one when referring to their 'political leaders'; but there was still a considerable overlap which must not be underrated.[56]

V

In conclusion, the comprehensive term for political leaders in fourth-century Athens was ῥήτορες καὶ στρατηγοί, not *rhetores* to the exclusion of *strategoi*, and the juxtaposition of *rhetores* and *strategoi* was not only a political fact but also acknowledged in the law code. There was indeed an increasing separation of *rhetores* and *strategoi* due to a growing professionalism both in rhetoric and in warfare.

---

[54] Aeschin. 3.7 μήτε τὰς τῶν στρατηγῶν συνηγορίας, οἳ ἐπὶ πολὺν ἤδη χρόνον συνεργοῦντές τισι τῶν ῥητόρων λυμαίνονται τὴν πολιτείαν; 196 οἱ γὰρ ἀγαθοὶ στρατηγοὶ ὑμῖν καὶ τῶν τὰς σιτήσεις τινὲς εὑρημένων ἐξαιτοῦνται τὰς γραφὰς τῶν παρανόμων ... The following *strategoi* are known also as *synegoroi*: Iphikrates of Rhamnous, Aristophon of Azenia, Phokion (of Potamos?), Nausikles of Oe, Philochares of Kothokidai. The following *strategoi* are known as public prosecutors: Archinos of Koile, Konon of Anaphlystos (*PA* 8707), Kallistratos of Aphidna, Iphikrates of Rhamnous, Melanopos of Aixone, Aristophon of Azenia, Chares of Angele.

[55] Three, perhaps four, *strategoi* are also known as proposers of *nomoi*: Agyrrhios of Kollytos, Archinos of Koile, Aristophon of Azenia, and perhaps Kephisophon of Aphidna, whose name however is only restored in *IG* II² 244.2.

[56] Several *strategoi*, for whom no activity as *rhetor* is *attested*, are nevertheless described in our sources as outstanding *rhetores*: Autokles of Euonymon (Xen. *Hell.* 6.3.7), Eunomos (*PA* 5861: Isoc. 15.93), Leosthenes of Kephale (*PA* 9141: Aeschin. 2.124), and Thrasyboulos of Kollytos (?) (Dem. 18.219).

Political leadership tended to be split up between the *rhetores* who dominated the *ecclesia* and the *strategoi* who commanded the armies in the constant wars. But there were some *strategoi* who were still active in the *ecclesia*; both *rhetores* and *strategoi* influenced foreign policy by being elected ambassadors, and in the *dicasteria* it was still common to see a *strategos* as a prosecutor or as a *synegoros* in a political action. *Rhetor* was a technical legal term denoting the citizen who performed the task of *ho boulomenos* in the decision-making assemblies. A *rhetor* was the proposer of decrees of the *demos* or the *boule*, of laws passed by the *nomothetai*, or he was a prosecutor in a political public action. Furthermore, a *rhetor* addressed the *ecclesia*, the *boule*, or the *nomothetai* supporting or opposing a proposal made by another *rhetor* or he was a *synegoros* for the prosecutor or the defendant in a political action. By contrast with the modern 'politician' a *rhetor* was not elected—he volunteered; he was never entrusted with making decisions but only expected to take initiatives; he might collaborate with other *rhetores* or with a *strategos*, but he was not affiliated with any party or any broader group among the voters in the decision-making bodies. To be a *rhetor* was essentially a one-day business, and ideally the political initiatives should have been distributed among all citizens so that a citizen only occasionally would assume the responsibility of being a *rhetor*. In fact a small group of active citizens dominated the decision-making assemblies by taking initiatives habitually, sometimes almost professionally. And as a result the word *rhetor* developed a new meaning different from the legal use of the term. As a legal term *rhetor* denoted any citizen who addressed the decision-making bodies, no matter whether he did it occasionally or frequently. As a political term *rhetor* tended to denote only those who habitually addressed the assemblies to the exclusion of the occasional *rhetor*, who was called *idiotes* and often contrasted with the *rhetores* in the political sense. Consequently, the Athenian citizens can be divided into four groups according to their political participation: (a) passive citizens, (b) active citizens who attended the assemblies and voted but never addressed the people or the jurors, (c) the *idiotai* who occasionally acted as *hoi boulomenoi*, being *rhetores* in the legal sense, and (d) the *rhetores* in the political sense who regularly addressed the assemblies and assumed the responsibility for most of the initiatives. Modern scholarship tends to overlook the difference between (c) and (d), emphasizing instead a subdivision of (d) into major and minor *rhetores*. A kind of hierarchy within (d) can indeed be traced in the sources, but must not obliterate the existence of (c). There was of course no sharp distinction between (c) and (d), and the group of *rhetores* in the political meaning seems also to have been much larger than often assumed. But this problem will be reserved for a future study. Finally, the accountability of the *rhetores* and the *strategoi* was more far-reaching than the accountability of all the *archai* selected by lot. Especially the *graphe paranomon* (against *rhetores*) and the *eisangelia* (frequently used against *strategoi*) were dangerous weapons against the 'political leaders', whereas the obligatory *euthynai* against *archai*, as far as the sources go, only infrequently resulted in a public action.[57]

THE INSTITUTE FOR ADVANCED STUDY
March, 1983

---

[57] I would like to thank the Institute for Advanced Study in Princeton for appointing me a visiting member for spring 1983, the Commission for Educational Exchange between Denmark and the United States for appointing me a Fulbright Scholar for the same period, and the Danish Research Council for the Humanities for supporting me with a grant-in-aid.

ADDENDA

4: Perquisites and »gifts« to political leaders have been studied by: H. Wankel, 'Die Korruption in der rednerischen Topik und in der Realität des klassischen Athen,' *Korruption im Altertum* ed. W. Schuller (München 1982) 29-53; B.S. Strauss, 'The Cultural Significance of Bribery and Embezzlement in Athenian Politics: The Evidence of the Period 403-386 B.C.,' *AW* 11 (1985) 67-74; F. D. Harvey, 'Dona Ferentes: Some Aspects of Bribery in Greek Politics,' *Crux ... Essays ... G.E.M. de Ste Croix* (Exeter 1985) 76-117.

4: Finley's article is now reprinted as chapter 2 of *Democracy Ancient and Modern* (2nd ed. New Brunswick 1985) 38-75.

5: Recent studies of political participation and political leadership in classical Athens are: M.I. Finley, *Politics in the Ancient World* (Cambridge 1983) chapter 4: Popular participation (70-84); C. Mossé, 'Politeuomenoi and idiôtai. L'affirmation d'une classe politique à Athènes au IVe s.,' *REA* 86 (1984) 193-200; D. Lotze, 'Die Teilhabe des Bürgers an Regierung und Rechtsprechung in den Organen der direkten Demokratie des klassischen Athen,' *Kultur und Fortschritt in der Blütezeit der griechischen Polis* ed. E. Kluwe (Berlin 1985) 52-76; R.A. Knox, 'So Mischievous a Beaste? The Athenian *Demos* and its treatment of its Politicians,' *G&R* 32 (1985) 132-61; J. Bleicken, *Die athenische Demokratie* (Paderborn 1985) 231-53; B. S. Strauss, *Athens After the Peloponnesian War* (New York 1986) 11-41; P.J. Rhodes, 'Political Activity in Classical Athens,' *JHS* 106 (1986) 132-44; R.K. Sinclair, *Democracy and Participation in Athens* (Cambridge 1988) 106-90. J. Ober, *Mass and Elite in Democratic Athens. Rhetoric, Ideology and the Power of the People* (Princeton 1989).

11: On the ideological aspects of the »passive« citizen cf. L.B. Carter, *The Quiet Athenian* (Oxford 1986).

17: Cf. J.T. Roberts, 'Paradigm Lost: Tritle, Plutarch and Athenian Politics in the fourth century,' *AHB* 1 (1987) 34-35; Sinclair (*supra ad* page 5) 136-62; Ober (*supra ad* page 5) 119-121.

Rhetores and Strategoi in Fourth-Century Athens

Mogens Herman Hansen

CONCERNING POLITICAL LEADERSHIP in classical Athens historians have posed a number of interesting questions: Were the Athenian 'politicians' recruited from the propertied families? Did they become rich in consequence of their political careers? Did they belong to the city demes or to the inland and coastal demes? Did they often serve as *archai* selected by lot? How often were they put on trial? But as a basis for their arguments historians tend either to draw up a random list of so-called politicians or to adduce five, ten, or fifteen examples of named political leaders, from which to draw conclusions.[1] In the absence of a list of political leaders, this is of course the only possible method, and doubtless the answers offered are often along the right lines. Nevertheless, given the very good sources available on fourth-century Athens, it is worth while to delimit the concept 'political leader' and accordingly draw up a list of persons meeting the criteria, so as to have a more rigorous basis for addressing questions of the sort mentioned above. In an earlier article[2] I argued that in fourth-century Athens the phrase ῥήτορες καὶ στρατηγοί is the nearest equivalent of what we, with a much vaguer and less formal term, call 'politicians' or 'political leaders'. Accordingly, I present here the application of that principle, an inventory which is basically a list of *rhetores* and *strategoi*. First however it is necessary to discuss whom to include and why.

---

[1] Several lists of *strategoi* have been published (see *infra* n.23). Lists of 'politicians' can be found in *e.g.* P. Cloché, "Les hommes politiques et la justice populaire dans l'Athènes du ive siècle," *Historia* 9 (1960) 80–95; J. Talbert Roberts, "Athens' So-called Unofficial Politicians," *Hermes* 110 (1982) 354–62. A good but incomplete list of ambassadors and proposers of decrees and speakers addressing the *ecclesia* in the period 359–322 can be found in J. Sundwall, *Epigraphische Beiträge zur sozial-politischen Geschichte Athens* (*Klio* Beih. 4 [1906]) 59–74. For conclusions based on a selection of examples see A. W. Gomme, *The Population of Athens in the Fifth and Fourth Centuries* (Oxford 1933) 37–39 (distribution over demes); S. Perlman, "The Politicians in the Athenian Democracy of the Fourth Century B.C.," *Athenaeum* 41 (1963) 327–55 (participation in trials, social composition, etc.).

[2] M. H. Hansen, "The Athenian 'Politicians', 403–322 B.C.," *GRBS* 24 (1983) 33–55.

In recording the *strategoi* I include only members of the Athenian board of ten and omit the generals who commanded the forces on Samos, Skyros, Lemnos, and Imbros.³ But of the elected military officials, the *strategoi* were only first in rank: why not include the hipparchs, taxiarchs, and phylarchs? There is some slight evidence that taxiarchs or hipparchs might be reckoned among the political leaders. Describing the oligarchic revolution of 404, Lysias mentions τοὺς τοῦ δήμου προεστηκότας καὶ στρατηγοῦντας καὶ τοὺς ταξιαρχοῦντας (13.7, *cf.* also 26.20), and Xenophon advises a hipparch to collaborate with the *rhetores* in the council (*Hipp.* 1.8). There is however a substantial gulf between these scattered remarks and the constant juxtaposition of *rhetores* and *strategoi*, and our prosopographical knowledge does not support the inclusion of the other elected officers.⁴ Of 39 known fourth-century hipparchs, taxiarchs, and phylarchs, three, completing the '*cursus honorum*', came to be *strategoi* and are accordingly recorded in this capacity. But only two are known also as *rhetores* and only one as an ambassador. Hence I prefer to record only the ten *strategoi*, and exclude all other elected military officials.⁵

In recording the *rhetores* I follow the definition argued in my former article, and so I include: proposers of *psephismata* in the *ecclesia* or in the *boule*; proposers of *nomoi* before the *nomothetai*; prosecutors and defendants in political public actions; speakers addressing the *ecclesia* or the *boule*; *synegoroi* addressing the *dicasteria* (either for the prosecution or for the defence). Two problems, however, need a more detailed investigation. As to prosecutors, defendants, and *synegoroi*, we must define the concept 'political public action'; and as to speakers addressing the *ecclesia* and the *boule*, we must decide whether or not to include the ambassadors.

'Public prosecutors' in Athens comprised all citizens who brought any public action (δημόσιος ἀγών). But the Athenians had more than fifty different types of public action, ranging from *e.g.* the public action

---

³ Arist. *Ath.Pol.* 62.2, *cf.* P. J. Rhodes, *A Commentary on the Aristotelian* Athenaion Politeia (Oxford 1981) 695.

⁴ A complete list of taxiarchs, phylarchs, and hipparchs can be found in J. K. Davies, *Wealth and the Power of Wealth in Classical Athens* (New York 1981) 151-55. Apart from broken names, Davies records, for the fourth century, 8 taxiarchs (Philokles II should be deleted, as he is an ephebic officer and not a genuine taxiarch), 20 phylarchs, and 12 hipparchs. Lykophron served both as phylarch and as hipparch. So the sum is 39.

⁵ The three *strategoi* are Demainetos of Paiania, Euetion of Kephisia, and Philokles of Eroiadai. The two *rhetores* are Meidias of Anagyrous (*PA* 9719) and, presumably, Menites of Kydathenaion. The ambassador is Orthoboulos of Kerameis. For the '*cursus honorum*' *cf.* Davies (*supra* n.4) 122 with n.56.

for locking up a man on the pretense that he is an adulterer (γραφὴ ἀδίκως εἰρχθῆναι ὡς μοιχόν) to the public action against unconstitutional proposals (γραφὴ παρανόμων).[6] The former action had no direct connection with politics, and in this and many similar public actions the prosecutor would often be one of the relatives or friends of the injured person (who was in this case the detained man).[7] So within the group of public actions we must look for specifically political types of public action, i.e. public actions brought against *rhetores* or *strategoi* in their capacity of being *rhetores* or *strategoi*. The two most obvious types of public action meeting this requirement are the γραφὴ παρανόμων (invariably brought against *rhetores*) and the εἰσαγγελία (frequently brought against *strategoi* and sometimes against *rhetores*). To the γραφὴ παρανόμων (involving *psephismata* passed by the *ecclesia* or the *boule*) must be added the corresponding γραφὴ νόμον μὴ ἐπιτήδειον θεῖναι (involving *nomoi* passed by the *nomothetai*), and in addition to the εἰσαγγελία we must record applications of the ἀπόφασις, introduced ca 350 and brought against the same types of offender as the εἰσαγγελία, the main difference being that the council of the Areopagos was entrusted with the preliminary investigation. Next, prosecutors and *synegoroi* in the δοκιμασία ῥητόρων must be recorded, and so must attested cases of the προβολή, when brought against sycophants or against a man who did not fulfill what he had promised the Athenian *demos*; both types of action seem to have been used only infrequently.[8]

---

[6] J. H. Lipsius, *Das attische Recht und Rechtsverfahren* I–III (Leipzig 1905–15), discusses forty different types of *graphe* (spurious *graphai* are not included in the count). Apart from the *graphai* we have the following types of public action: ἀπαγωγή/ἔνδειξις/ἐφήγησις, ἀπογραφή, ἀπόφασις, δοκιμασία τῶν ῥητόρων, εἰσαγγελία, εὔθυναι, προβολή, and φάσις.

[7] Cf. E. Ruschenbusch, *Untersuchungen zur Geschichte des athenischen Strafrechts* (Köln 1968) 58–60.

[8] For the period 403–322 we know of 36 applications of the γραφὴ παρανόμων, 62 of the εἰσαγγελία εἰς τὸν δῆμον, 5–6 of the γραφὴ νόμον μὴ ἐπιτήδειον θεῖναι, 15–16 of the ἀπόφασις. The inventory includes, of course, only those cases in which we know the name(s) of the prosecutor(s) and/or defendant(s). Apart from Aischines' ἐπαγγελία against Timarchos, the only other known application of the δοκιμασία τῶν ῥητόρων is Lysitheos' ἐπαγγελία against Theomnestos (Lys. 10.1, where I follow Gernet/Bizos in emending εἰσήγγελλε to ἐπήγγελλε). In Aeschin. 1.64 we hear that Aristophon threatened to bring a *dokimasia rhetoron* against Hegesandros. When used against offences committed during a festival, the προβολή (Dem. 21.8–10) was not a political public action (although it could sometimes be used by political leaders against their opponents, cf. Dem. 21). The only known case of a *probole* against sycophants falls outside our period, viz. the *probole* against the prosecutors of the generals in 406 (Xen. *Hell.* 1.7.35). Of the *probole* for not fulfilling one's promises to the *demos* (Arist. *Ath.Pol.* 43.5) we have only one attested case, Euboulos' *probole* against Aristophon (Dem. 21.218 with scholia).

What brings together these public actions is not only the fact that they were explicitly aimed at *rhetores* and/or *strategoi*, but also some significant procedural regulations. The *graphe paranomon*, the *eisangelia*, and the *apophasis* were probably the only types of public action for which the *thesmothetai* could appoint a *dicasterion* manned with more than 500 jurors.[9] Furthermore, by contrast with other types of public action, these procedures involved the *ecclesia* in the initial phase before the hearing by a *dicasterion*; in the *graphe paranomon* the indictment against the proposer of a decree was often lodged under oath (ὑπωμοσία) during the *ecclesia*, either before or after the people had voted on the *psephisma*.[10] In a *graphe nomon me epitedeion theinai*, the σύνδικοι, speaking in defence of the *nomos*, might be appointed by the *ecclesia* (Dem. 20.146). The *dokimasia ton rhetoron* was opened by an ἐπαγγελία brought in the *ecclesia* (Aeschin. 1.81). The *eisangelia* was brought in the *ecclesia* (Arist. *Ath.Pol.* 43.3) and so was the *probole* (43.5). Finally, the *apophasis* was initiated by a decree of the people ordering the council of the Areopagos to conduct the preliminary investigation and report to the *ecclesia*, which then referred the case to a *dicasterion* (Din. 1.51).

More problematical is whether or not to register known cases of εὔθυναι. The *euthynai* apply primarily to *archai* and, apart from speakers in the *boule*, *rhetores* were not *archai*. On the other hand, my inventory includes not only councillors addressing the *boule*, but also *strategoi* and some elected treasurers, who were *archai*, and ambassadors, who by contrast with other *rhetores* (cf. infra) had to submit to *euthynai*. It would be misleading to omit *euthynai* of *strategoi*, councillors, and ambassadors, and so these cases of *euthynai* are included, but not instances of *euthynai* against other *archai*. The problem is of surprisingly little practical importance. Although more than 1200 Athenian officials had to submit to *euthynai* every year,[11] the sources, covering a period of more than one hundred years, provide us only some ten examples of the *euthynai* resulting in a public action.[12] In the fourth century, there is not a single attested case of *euthynai* against a councillor, and *euthynai* against other officials included in my list amount to one against a general (Pamphilos, 389/8), one against an elected trea-

---

[9] *Cf.* M. H. Hansen, *Eisangelia* (Odense 1975) 10 n.14. The same procedural rule may apply to the *graphe nomon me epitedeion theinai*, but we have no information.
[10] *Lex.Cant. s.v.* ὑπωμοσία; *cf.* also Lipsius (*supra* n.6) 393–94.
[11] 500 *bouleutai* + *ca* 700 other *archai* (Arist. *Ath.Pol.* 24.3, defended by M. H. Hansen, "Seven Hundred *Archai* in Classical Athens," *GRBS* 21 [1980] 151–73) + and unknown number of *presbeis* and other officials.
[12] *Cf.* Hansen (*supra* n.2) 42 n.32.

surer (?) (Lykourgos, 336-324), and two against ambassadors (Epikrates, 394-392; Aischines, 343/2). I have included these examples, and I stress how few they are only to emphasize that the *euthynai* (against *archai* and other officials) were of very little importance by comparison with the *graphe paranomon* and the *eisangelia* against *rhetores* and *strategoi*.

Another problem is raised by the *endeixis* when brought against an *atimos* who exercised his citizen rights. Insofar as the citizen put on trial had only attended a festival or served as a juror or the like, there is no reason to include the *endeixis* in an inventory of *rhetores* and *strategoi*. But if the defendant was an *atimos* who had addressed the *ecclesia* or served on an embassy, the case must be regarded as a 'political public action', and the known applications of this form of *endeixis* are accordingly included in the inventory.[13]

This list, I believe, exhausts the 'political public actions'. There may of course have been others unknown to us, and we must admit further that any public action, and sometimes even private actions, might be misused for political purposes. Antiphon 6, for example, was delivered in a *dike phonou* by a defendant who claims that he has been put on trial for political reasons. But we have no speech for the prosecution, and so we must suspend judgement in this and many similar cases (*e.g.* the speech *Against Theokrines*, Dem. 58).

Finally, since the types of public action discussed above were brought against *rhetores* and *strategoi* in their capacity of being *rhetores* and *strategoi*, I naturally record not only the prosecutors and their *synegoroi* but also the defendants and the *synegoroi* speaking for the defence.

The next major issue is whether or not to include ambassadors among the *rhetores*. They were elected by the *ecclesia* (occasionally by the *boule*), and so, once appointed, they can no longer be regarded as volunteers. Moreover, by contrast with proposers, public prosecutors, and speakers addressing the political assemblies, the *presbeis* had to submit to *euthynai* after their mission.[14] In these two respects they differ from *rhetores*. On the other hand, they had to make a report on their mission both to the *boule* and to the *ecclesia*. So they were *rhe-*

---

[13] *Endeixis* against a citizen who served as a juror: Dem. 21.182. Applications of *endeixis* against *rhetores* are the trials of Philon of Koile in 402 (Isoc. 18.22: ambassador), Andokides in 400 (occasioned by the Mysteries, but *cf.* Lys. 6.33 for Andokides as a *rhetor*), Polyeuktos (of Kydantidai?) in 326/5 (Din. fr.ii Conomis), and Aristogeiton in 325/4 (Dem. 25.4 etc., Din. 2.13 etc.).

[14] *Cf.* D. J. Mosley, *Envoys and Diplomacy in Ancient Greece* (*Historia* Einzelschr. 22 [1973]) 39.

tores in the legal sense, and subject to be put on trial by an *eisangelia* warranted by the third section of the νόμος εἰσαγγελτικός, prescribing an *eisangelia ἐάν τις ... ῥήτωρ ὢν μὴ λέγῃ τὰ ἄριστα τῷ δήμῳ τῷ Ἀθηναίων χρήματα λαμβάνων* (Hyp. 3.7-8). This is precisely what happened to the four ambassadors sent to Sparta in 392/1. In consequence of their report, Kallistratos brought an *eisangelia* against them, and all were sentenced to death. In 368/7 Timagoras suffered the same fate after his embassy to the king of Persia.[15] But were ambassadors also regarded as *rhetores* in the political sense? Several sources strongly indicate that they were. In the speech *On the Crown* Demosthenes takes pride in telling the jurors that he both moved the decree by which ambassadors were sent to Thebes in 339 and served as an ambassador, thereby surpassing all previous *rhetores* (18.219): καίτοι πολλοὶ παρ' ὑμῖν, ἄνδρες Ἀθηναῖοι, γεγόνασι ῥήτορες ἔνδοξοι καὶ μεγάλοι πρὸ ἐμοῦ, Καλλίστρατος ἐκεῖνος, Ἀριστοφῶν, Κέφαλος, Θρασύβουλος, ἕτεροι μυρίοι· ἀλλ' ὅμως οὐδεὶς πώποτε τούτων διὰ παντὸς ἔδωκεν ἑαυτὸν εἰς οὐδὲν τῇ πόλει, ἀλλ' ὁ μὲν γράφων οὐκ ἂν ἐπρέσβευσεν, ὁ δὲ πρεσβεύων οὐκ ἂν ἔγραψεν. All four *rhetores* mentioned by Demosthenes did in fact serve on various embassies, and three of them are also known as proposers of decrees. Demosthenes has no intention of emphasizing any subdivision of *rhetores* into two mutually exclusive groups of proposers and ambassadors; his point is that a *rhetor* who had proposed and carried a decree concerning an embassy did not normally serve on the embassy warranted by his decree. On the other hand, he states explicitly that the group of famous *rhetores*, the political leaders, included both proposers of decrees and ambassadors. Aischines takes the same view in his description of Timarchos (1.120, αἰσχύνομαι γὰρ ὑπὲρ τῆς πόλεως, εἰ Τίμαρχος, ὁ τοῦ δήμου σύμβουλος καὶ τὰς εἰς τὴν Ἑλλάδα τολμῶν πρεσβείας πρεσβεύειν κτλ.) and in his description of Demosthenes (3.73, ὁ γὰρ μισαλέξανδρος καὶ μισοφίλιππος ὑμῖν οὑτοσὶ ῥήτωρ δὶς ἐπρέσβευσεν εἰς Μακεδονίαν, ἐξὸν μηδὲ ἅπαξ κτλ.). What connects the speaker addressing the people or the jurors with the ambassador is the art of rhetoric, and eloquence is often mentioned as essential for being a good ambassador.[16] So ambassa-

---

[15] Kallistratos' *eisangelia* against Andokides, Epikrates, Euboulides, and Kratinos: Philoch. *FGrHist* 328 F 149; Leon's against Timagoras: Dem. 19.191.

[16] *Cf.* Xen. *Hell.* 6.3.7, μετὰ τοῦτον Αὐτοκλῆς, μάλα δοκῶν ἐπιστρεφὴς εἶναι ῥήτωρ, ὧδε ἠγόρευεν (ambassador to Sparta in 372/1); Aeschin. 3.139, Λεωδάμας ὁ Ἀχαρνεύς, οὐχ ἧττον Δημοσθένους λέγειν δυνάμενος (ambassador to Thebes, 370's); Aeschin. 3.242, οὐ γὰρ δή που τοῦτό γε σκήψῃ, ὡς οὐ δυνατὸς εἶ λέγειν (Ktesiphon), καὶ γὰρ ἂν ἄτοπόν σοι συμβαίνοι εἰ πρώην μὲν ποθ' ὑπέμεινας πρεσβευτὴς ὡς Κλεοπάτραν τὴν Φιλίππου θυγατέρα χειροτονεῖσθαι ... νυνὶ δὲ οὐ φήσεις δύνασθαι λέγειν

dors deserve inclusion in an inventory of ῥήτορες καὶ στρατηγοί, since they seem to have been regarded as *rhetores*, not only in the legal sense but also in the political sense of the term.

The phrase ῥήτορες καὶ στραγηγοί seems to cover almost all the important aspects of political leadership in both domestic policy, foreign policy, and military command. There is however one important exception: fiscal policy. In the course of the fourth century the Athenians created some very important financial offices which, like the *strategia*, were filled by election. Most important are ὁ ταμίας στρατιωτικῶν, οἱ ἐπὶ τὸ θεωρικόν, and ὁ ἐπὶ τῇ διοικήσει (attested only for the last years of our period).[17] Euboulos, Demosthenes, Lykourgos, and Demades were all elected to fill one of these offices, but none was ever a *strategos*. The fifth-century merging of *rhetores* and *strategoi* seems to have been replaced, in the period 355-322, by a merging of *rhetores* and elected treasurers. Again, the trend must not be overrated, but in the so-called Lycurgan period, political leadership was often connected with serving as an elected treasurer. Yet the financial officials were neither *rhetores* nor *strategoi*. We do not know how the Athenians reacted to this new change in political leadership. It is not uncommon that a change in political opinion and terminology requires some adaptation and comes later than the change in political institutions. In the *Ath. Pol.* Aristotle devotes only a few lines to the Theoric Board and the treasurer of the military fund (43.1, 47.2, 49.3), and ὁ ἐπὶ τῇ διοικήσει is passed over in silence. The orators have a few references to the Theoric Board but none to ὁ ἐπὶ τῇ διοικήσει. The democracy was abolished in 322 and at the same time the literary sources stop. The elected financial treasurers were not covered by the terms ῥήτορες καὶ στρατηγοί or οἱ πολιτευόμενοι or οἱ σύμβουλοι. But they were certainly 'political leaders', and I have recorded the eleven known instances in the inventory.

Athenian citizens who fulfill one or more of these requirements consitute an inventory of 368 persons who were politically active in the sense that they were either *rhetores* or *strategoi* or (in a few cases) elected treasurers. This list, I believe, can provide a more exact basis for addressing questions of the sort mentioned at the beginning of this article.

(argument adduced by Aischines to prove that Ktesiphon is a *rhetor* [*cf.* 3.31] and not an *idiotes* [*cf.* 3.214]); Dem. 18.179, οὐκ εἶπον μὲν ταῦτα, οὐκ ἔγραψα δέ, οὐδ' ἔγραψα μέν, οὐκ ἐπρέσβευσα δέ, οὐδ' ἐπρέσβευσα μέν, οὐκ ἔπεισα δὲ τοὺς Θηβαίους ... (Demosthenes' policy towards Thebes in 339).

[17] *Cf.* Rhodes (*supra* n.3) 513-16 with further references.

Inventory: ῥήτορες καὶ στρατηγοί, 403–322 B.C.

The following catalogue of Athenian 'political leaders' includes first the name (with patronymic and demotic if known), then the number given in Kirchner's *Prosopographia Attica* and, if the man is of the liturgical class, reference to Davies' *Athenian Properties Families*. Broken names are not included. Some of the citizens registered were active before 403 and others after 322, but I record only political activities within the period 403–322.[18] The inventory lists political activities in the following order:

(1) Proposal of a decree in the *ecclesia*. To move a probouleumatic decree is regarded as one political activity, and so proposers of probouleumatic decrees are recorded only as proposers of decrees in the *ecclesia*, but not in the *boule*.

(2) Proposal of a decree in the *boule*.

(3) Proposal of a *nomos* before the *nomothetai*. I believe that all *nomoi* in the fourth century were passed by the *nomothetai*.[19] Accordingly, all proposers of *nomoi* are recorded separately from proposers of *psephismata* in the *ecclesia*, although the *nomothetai* are explicitly mentioned in ten *nomoi* only, seven preserved on stone (of which one is unpublished) and three referred to in literary sources.

(4) Prosecution in a political public action. These actions comprise the γραφὴ παρανόμων, the γραφὴ νόμον μὴ ἐπιτήδειον θεῖναι, the εἰσαγγελία,[20] the ἀπόφασις, the δοκιμασία ῥητόρων, the προβολή if brought against sycophants or citizens deceiving the people, the εὔθυναι if brought against *strategoi*, elected treasurers, or ambassadors, and the ἔνδειξις if brought against an *atimos* acting as a *rhetor*.[21]

(5) Speech delivered in the *ecclesia*. Information about a speech by the proposer of a decree is not recorded separately under this heading, but only under the proposal. For a few major *rhetores*, e.g. Demosthenes and Demades, I have not thought it necessary to record all the possible occasions for speeches delivered in the assembly.[22]

(6) Speech delivered in the *boule*.

(7) *Synegoria* for the prosecutor or for the defendant.

(8) Defence in a political public action.

(9) Mission as an ambassador. To be an ambassador is regarded as one political activity only, and the obligatory reports on the mission to the *boule* and the *ecclesia* are recorded here and not earlier under speeches delivered in the *ecclesia* or the *boule*.

---

[18] So I omit e.g. Anytos' *strategia* in 409/8 (Diod. 13.64.6) and Derkylos of Hagnous' *strategia* dated 319/8 by F. Mitchel, *Hesperia* 33 (1964) 341–42.

[19] *Cf.* M. H. Hansen, "Did the Athenian *Ecclesia* Legislate after 403/2?" *GRBS* 20 (1979) 27–53.

[20] For the sake of completeness I include the (few) manifest examples of misuse of the εἰσαγγελία εἰς τὸν δῆμον, e.g. against Agasikles, and the few examples of εἰσαγγελία εἰς τὴν βουλήν, i.e. against Nikomachos, Timarchos, and Theophemos.

[21] The numbers stated after references to the *graphe paranomon*, *eisangelia*, and *endeixis* are to the catalogues of trials in M. H. Hansen, *The Sovereignty* (Odense 1974), *Eisangelia* (Odense 1975), and *Apagoge, Endeixis and Ephegesis* (Odense 1976). In many cases we have only circumstantial evidence for the classification of the type of action, and the problems are discussed in these catalogues.

[22] The problem whether or not Demosthenes' symbouleutic speeches were delivered in support of proposals will be discussed in my forthcoming article "A Note on Demosthenes' Symbouleutic Speeches," *ClMed* 35 (1984).

(10) *Strategia*.²³
(11) Administration of public money as an elected treasurer. These comprise ὁ ταμίας στρατιωτικῶν, οἱ ἐπὶ τὸ θεωρικόν, and ὁ ἐπὶ τῇ διοικήσει. I do not record the ἐπιμελητὴς τῶν κρηνῶν because this important office was probably technical rather than political, and I omit as well the extraordinary officials, *e.g.* the σιτώνης and the τειχοποιοί.

The references to the sources are fairly complete but not exhaustive. Especially for some decrees and public actions frequently referred to in literary sources, it would be pointless in this context to print all references. For most of the political public actions full documentation is given in my monographs cited under (4) *supra*. For the decrees I must ask the reader to await the completion of my Inventory of decrees of 403–322 B.C. mentioned in literary sources.

---

²³ By contrast with the *rhetores*, the *strategoi* have been carefully studied; earlier lists can be found in K. J. Beloch, *Die attische Politik seit Perikles* (Leipzig 1884); Sundwall (*supra* n.1); A. Krause, *Attische Strategenlisten bis 146 v. Chr.* (Weimar 1914); Davies (*supra* n.4). The problem whether an Athenian military commander is a member of the board of *strategoi* deserves a proper investigation. In most cases there is a *communis opinio* (not always well founded) which I have followed, apart from some difficult cases (*e.g.* Iphikrates before 390, Antiochos [Aeschin. 7.73], etc.).

UPDATED INVENTORY OF *RHETORES* AND *STRATEGOI* (1988)

Ἀγάθων (*PA* 81). Defendant in an *eisangelia* (no. 127), 325/4 (Dem. 25.47).

Ἀγασίας Χαιριγένους Ἰκαριεύς (*PA* 95 + 97). Proposes in the *boule* an honorary decree for Phyleus, 336/5 (*IG* II^2 330.25, 32).

Ἀγασικλῆς Ἁλιμούσιος (*PA* 100). Defendant in an *eisangelia* (no. 115), 336-324 (Hyp. 3.3, Din. fr.xvi Con.).

Ἁγνίας (not in *PA*). Ambassador to the king of Persia in 397/6 (*Hell. Oxy.* 7.1, Androt. *FGrHist* 324F18 = Philoch. 328F147).

Ἁγνίας Πολέμωνος ἐξ Οἴου (*PA* 133, *APF*). Ambassador to ? in the 370s (Is. 11.8). Cf. Develin 294.

Ἁγνωνίδης Νικοξένου Περγασῆθεν (*PA* 176). Proposes a decree of the people concerning naval equipment, 325/4 (*IG* II^2 1629.13-15 etc.). Defendant in an *apophasis* in 324/3 (Hyp. 1.40, Din. fr. xxvi Con.).

Ἀγύρριος Κολλυτεύς (*PA* 179, *APF*). Proposes four *nomoi* (?): (1) introduction of the ἐκκλησιαστικόν of one obol; (2) increase of the ἐκκλησιαστικόν to three obols, before 392 (Arist. *Ath. Pol.* 41.3); (3) introduction (?) of the *theorikon*, date unknown (Harp. *s. v.*); (4) introduction of an 8 1/3 % grain tax, 374/3 (unpublished: *ASCSA Newsletter* Spring 1987,8). *Synegoros* for Kephisios in an *endeixis* (no. 10) in 400/399 (Andoc. 1.133). *Strategos* in 389/8 (Xen. *Hell.* 4.8.31).

Ἀδείμαντος Λευκολοφίδου Σκαμβωνίδης (*PA* 202). Defendant in an *eisangelia* (no. 68), 393/2 (Dem. 19.191).

Ἀθηνίων Ἀραφήνιος (*PA* 240). Ambassador to Olynthus in 376/5 (?) (*IG* II^2 36.8).

Ἀθηνόδωρος (*PA* 259). Proposes a decree of the people concerning honours for Iphitos, 394-387 (*IG* II^2 26.6-7).

Ἀθηνόδωρος (*PA* 260). Proposes a decree of the people concerning the Asklepieion, 355/4 (?). (*IG* II^2 47.23), cf. Develin 284.

Αἴσιμος (*PA* 311). Addresses the *ecclesia*, 397/6 (*Hell. Oxy.* 6.2). Ambassador to (1) Chios in 384/3 (*IG* II^2 34.36-37, (2) Methymna in 378/7 (*IG* II^2 42.19-20).

Αἰσχίνης (*PA* 333). Ambassador to Thessaly, 361/0 (?) (*IG* II^2 175.3).

Αἰσχίνης Ἀτρομήτου Κοθωκίδης (*PA* 354, *APF*). Brings an *epangelia* against Timarchos, 346/5 (Aeschin. 1.81); attempts to bring an *eisangelia* (no. 110) against Demosthenes, 343 (?) 3.223-24); brings a *graphe paranomon* (no. 30) against Ktesiphon, 330/329 (3.8). Elected *syndikos* in the Delian affair, 343 (?) Dem. 18.134). Addresses the *ecclesia* frequently (Dem. 18.136, 140, 285; 19.10, 35, 113, 209, 304, 310, as well as his reports to the *boule* and *ecclesia* in his capacity as ambassador). Defendant in an *euthynai* charged with *parapresbeia*, 343/2 (Dem. 19.2, 103, 211). Ambassador (1) to Arcadia in 348/7 (?) (Aeschin. 2.79), (2) three times to Philip in 347/6 (1: Dem. 19.13; Aeschin. 2.18; 2: Dem.

UPDATED INVENTORY OF *RHETORES* AND *STRATEGOI* (1988)

19.17, Aeschin. 2.82; 3: Dem. 19.121, 126, Aeschin. 2.94-95), (3) as *pylagoros* in 340/339 (Aeschin. 3.115), (4) to Philip in 338/7 (Dem. 18.282, Aeschin. 3.227).

Ἀλεξίμαχος Χαρίνου(?) Πήληξ (*PA* 545). Proposes a decree of the people concerning Kersebleptes, 347/6 (Aeschin. 2.83, 85). For the patronymic cf. *Hesperia* 47 (1978) 90 line 54.

Ἀλκίμαχος Κηφισίου Ἀγγελῆθεν (*PA* 615). Ambassador to Byzantion, 378/7 (*IG* II² 41.21). For the patronymic cf. *IG* II² 5228.

Ἀλκίμαχος Ἀναγυράσιος (*PA* 616). *Strategos*, 364/3 (schol. Aeschin. 2.31), 357/6 (*IG* II² 124.22), 355 4 (?) (Dem. 47.50, 78; Harp *s. v.*).

Ἀλκίμαχος ...ε...ἐγ Μυρρινούττης (*PA* 622). Proposes in the *ecclesia* a decree of unknown content, 335/4 (EM 13067, of which only the first lines have been published, cf. *SEG* XXI 272). Proposes in the *boule* a decree concerning a quadrireme, 325/4 (*IG* II² 1629.273). Patronymic according to squeeze.

Ἀμεινιάδης (*PA* 664). Addresses the *ecclesia* and advises the people to consult the Delphic oracle, 339/8 (Aeschin. 3.130).

Ἀνδοκίδης Λεωγόρου Κυδαθηναιεύς (*PA* 828, *APF*). Proposes in the *ecclesia* to conclude peace with Sparta, 392/1 (Andoc. 3.41). Defendant in an *endeixis* (no. 10) in 400/399 (1.8, 10). Defendant in an *eisangelia* (no. 70) in 392/1 (Philoch. F149a). Addresses the *ecclesia* and the *boule* from 403 and thereafter (Lys. 6.33). Ambassador to Sparta in 392/1 (Philoch.).

Ἀνδρομένης (*PA* 882). Proposes in the *ecclesia* a rider to an honorary decree for Pythodoros, 363/2 (*I. Délos* I 88.30).

Ἀνδροτίων Ἄνδρωνος Γαργήττιος (*PA* 913 + 915, *APF*). Proposes five decrees of the people: (1) concerning temple treasures, before 365/4(?) (*IG* II² 216a.13, b.6; 217.13); (2) melting down the *pompeia*, before 356/5 (Dem. 22.70, 24.178); (3) recovering arrears of *eisphora*, 356/5 (?) (Dem. 22.48, 24.160); (4) honours for the *boule* of 356/5 (Dem. 22.5, 8-10); (5) honours for the Bosporan princes, 347/6 (*IG* II² 212.8). Brings a *graphe paranomon* (no. 13) against Euktemon in 355/4 (Dem. 24.13-14). Addresses the *ecclesia*: (1) concerning the *graphe paranomon* (no. 12), 355/4 (Dem. 22.59); (2) concerning the recovery of 9 1/2 talents, 354/3 (Dem. 24.13); (3) concerning Karia, 351 (?) (Arist. *Rh.* 1406b27); (4) in reply to Artaxerxes' envoys, 344/3 (Didymos *In Dem.* 18.14). *Synegoros* for Timokrates in a *graphe nomon me epitedion theinai*, 354/3 (Dem. 24.158-59). Defendant in a *graphe paranomon* (no. 12), 355/4 (Dem. 22). Ambassador to Mausolos in 355/4 (Dem. 24.12).

Ἄνδρων ἐκ Κεραμέων (*PA* 924). Ambassador to Keos, *ca* 350 (*IG* II² 1128.39).

Ἀντιγένης (*PA* 985). Addresses the *boule* frequently in 356/5 (Dem. 22.38). Probably *synegoros* for Androtion in the *graphe paranomon* (no. 12) of 355/4 (Dem. 22.38).

Ἀντίδοτος Ἀπολλοδώρου Συπαλήττιος (*PA* 1019). Proposes in the *boule* an open *probouleuma* concerning the Kitian merchants' application for erecting a temple, 333/2 (*IG* II² 337.7-8).

Ἀντίμαχος (*PA* 1108). Ambassador to Thrace in 356/5 (*IG* II² 127.36).

Ἀντίμαχος (*PA* 1110). Defendant in an *eisangelia* (no. 81), 373/2 (Dem. 49.9-10, 47).

Ἀντιμέδων (*PA* 1134). Proposes a decree of the people concerning the Tenedians, before 342 (Dem. 58.35). Defendant in a *graphe paranomon* (no. 24), before 342 (Dem. 58.35).

Ἀντισθένης Ἀντιφάτους Κυθήρριος (*PA* 1184 + 1194 + 1196 + 1197, *APF*). Strategos after 380 (?) (Xen. *Mem.* 3.4.1).

Ἀντίφιλος (*PA* 1264). Strategos in 323/2 (Diod. 18.13.6); 322/1 (Diod. 18.17.6).

Ἀντιφῶν (*PA* 1280). Ambassador to Philip in 359/8 (Theopomp. *FGrHist* 115F30).

Ἀντιφῶν (*PA* 1281). Defendant in an *apophasis*, 343 (?) (Dem. 18.133, Din. 1.63).

Ἄνυτος Ἀνθεμίωνος Εὐωνυμεύς (*PA* 1324 + 1322 [?], *APF*). *Synegoros* for Andokides in an *endeixis* (no. 10), 400/399 (Andoc. 1.150). Addresses the *ecclesia* in 397/6 (*Hell. Oxy.* 6.2). Strategos in 403/2 (?) (Pl. *Meno* 90B).

Ἀπολλόδωρος Πασίωνος Ἀχαρνεύς (*PA* 1411, *APF*). Proposes a decree of the people concerning τὰ περιόντα, 349/8 (Dem. 59.4). Brings an *eisangelia* in 361/0 against (1) Autokles of Euonymon (no. 90), (2) Timomachos of Acharnai (no. 91), (3) Kallippos of Aixone (no. 92), (4) Timotheos of Anaphlystos (no. 93), (5) Menon of Potamos (no. 95): Dem. 36.53. Defendant in a *graphe paranomon* (no. 18), 349/8 (Dem. 59.3-8).

Ἀπολλόδωρος ὁ Κυζικηνός (*PA* 1458). Strategos 403/2-400/399, (Pl. *Ion* 541 C).

Ἀριστίων (*PA* 1734). Proposes in the *ecclesia* an honorary decree, before 378/7 (*IG* II² 72.3).

Ἀριστογείτων (*PA* 1774). Ambassador to Dareios III, 333/2 (Curt. 3.13.15).

Ἀριστογείτων Κυδιμάχου (*PA* 1775). Proposes a decree of the people ordering execution without trial of Hierokles, 335-330 (Dem. 25.87, hypoth. 1; Din. 2.12). Brings a *graphe paranomon* (no. 27) against Hypereides, 338/7 (Hyp. fr.32-36, 38-41; Aristog. fr.iii; Dem. 26.11). Brings *eisangeliai* (1) against Hegemon (no. 120), *ca* 331 (Dem. 25.47); (2) against Demokles (no. 128), 325/4 (Dem. 25.47). Brings *graphai* and *eisangeliai* against Demosthenes (Dem. 25.37), Demades (Dem. 25.47), and others (Dem. 25.94, 26.17; Din. 2.12). Addresses the *ecclesia* in connection with the *eisangelia* (no. 127) againt Agathon, 325/4 (Dem. 25.47). Is frequently addressing the *ecclesia* (Dem. 25.41-42, 64; *Ep.* 3.16; Din. 2.12) and proposing decrees (Dem. 25.94, 26.17; Din. 2.12). Defendant in a *graphe paranomon* (no. 29), 335-330 (Dem. 25 hypoth. 1-3). Defendant in an *endeixis* (no. 32), 325/4 (Dem. 25.6, 26.1; Din. 2.13).

UPDATED INVENTORY OF *RHETORES* AND *STRATEGOI* (1988)

Defendant in an *apophasis* in consequence of the Harpalos affair, 324/3 (Din. 2).

Ἀριστόδημος (not in *PA*). Ambassador (1) to Philip in 348/7 (Aeschin. 2.15), (2) three times (?) to Philip in 347/6 (1: Aeschin. 2.52; 2 [?]: Dem. 19.163-65; 3 [?]: 19.121), (3) to Thessaly and Magnesia in 343/2 (Aeschin. 3.83). Aristodemos was a citizen of Metapontion, but I follow A. Schaefer, *Demosthenes und seine Zeit*² I (Leipzig 1885) 246, in believing that he must have been naturalized, cf. Osborne *PT* 134.

Ἀριστοκλῆς (*PA* 1851). Ambassador to Sparta, 372/1 (Xen. *Hell.* 6.3.2).

Ἀριστοκράτης (*PA* 1897). Proposes in the *ecclesia* an honorary decree for Charidemos, 353/2 (Dem. 23.1, 14). Defendant in a *graphe paranomon* (no. 14) in 352/1 (Dem. 23.18).

Ἀριστόμαχος Κριτοδήμου Ἀλωπεκῆθεν (*PA* 1969, *APF*). Addresses the *ecclesia* as the representative of Charidemos and Kersebleptes, 353/2 (Dem. 23.13, 110).

Ἀριστόνικος Ἀριστοτέλους Μαραθώνιος (*PA* 2023 + 2028). Proposes a decree of the people against pirates, 335/4 (*IG* II² 1623.280-82). Proposes a *nomos* about the Panathenaia, 336-34 (*Hesperia* 28 [1959] 239-47). Proposes numerous other *nomoi*, before 322 (Ath. 226A-C [Alexis frr.125-26 K.]). Defendant in an *apophasis* in consequence of the Harpalos affair, 324/3 (Din. fr.xxvii, *aparasema* 4 Con.).

Ἀριστόνικος Νικοφάνους Ἀναγυράσιος (*PA* 2025). Proposes in the *ecclesia* an honorary decree for Demosthenes, 341/0 (Dem. 18.83, Plut. *Mor.* 848D).

Ἀριστόξενος Κηφισοδότου (*PA* 2044). Proposes in the *ecclesia* an honorary decree for Amphis, 332/1 (*IG* II² 347.9-11).

Ἀριστοπείθης Φυλάσιος (?) (*PA* 2046). Ambassador to Lesbos, 368/7 (*IG* II² 107.33).

Ἀριστοτέλης Μαραθώνιος (*PA* 2065). Proposes a decree of the people concerning membership of the Second Naval Confederacy, 378/7 (*IG* II² 43.7, 91). Ambassador to Thebes, 378/7 (*IG* II² 43.76).

Ἀριστοφάνης Νικοφήμου (*PA* 2082, *APF*). Ambassador (1) to Sicily, 394/3 (Lys. 19.19; allegedly sent by Konon but probably officially elected, *cf. infra s. v.* Εὐριππίδης); (2) to Cyprus, 390/389 (Lys. 19.23).

Ἀριστοφῶν (not in *PA*). Proposes a decree of the people relating to Samos, 324-322 (*AthMitt* 72 [1957] 156-64 no. 1).

Ἀριστοφῶν Ἀριστοφάνους Ἀζηνιεύς (*PA* 2108, *APF*). Proposes twelve decrees of the people: (1) payment of *xenikon* in the Agora, 403/2 (Dem. 57.31-34); (2) repayment to Gelarchos of five talents, 403/2 (Dem. 20.149); (3) relating to Keos, 363/2 (Hyp. fr.44); (4) Athenian relations with Ioulis, 363/2 (*IG* II² 111.4); (5) mobilization of triremes, 362/1 (Dem. 50.4-6); (6) concerning Poteidaia, 361/0 (?) (*IG* II² 118.4): (7) unknown content, 357/6 (*IG* II² 121.9);

(8) proxeny for Lachares, 355/4 (*IG* II² 130.8; (9) appointment of *zetetai*, 355/4 (Dem. 24.11); (10-11) two decrees against Philip, 346-340 (Dem. 18.70, 75); (12) honours for the Kephallenians, 343/2 (*IG* II² 224.6-7). Proposes a *nomos* concerning citizenship, 403/2 (Ath. 577B). Brings five (?) *eisangeliai*: (1) against Leosthenes (?) (*cf.* no. 88 n.1), 362/1 (Hyp. 3.1); (2) against Leosthenes' trierarchs (no. 142), 362/1 (Dem. 51.8-9); (3) against Timotheos (no. 101), 356/5 (Din. 3.17); (4) against Iphikrates (no. 100), 356/5 (Polyaen. 3.9.- 29); (5) against Menestheus (?) (no. 102), 356/5 (Isoc. 15.129). Opposes (in the *ecclesia*?) making peace with Philip, 347/6 (Theopomp. F166). *Syndikos* elected to defend Leptines' law, 355/4 (Dem. 20.146). Defendant in a *graphe paranomon* (no. 10), 363/2 (schol. Aeschin. 1.64). Defendant in an *eisangelia* (no. 97), 361-343 (Hyp. 3.28). Defendant in a *probole*, 370-350 (?) (Dem. 21.218 with schol.). Acquitted in 75 *graphai paranomon* (Aeschin. 3.194). Ambassador to Thebes, unknown date (Aeschin. 3.139). *Strategos* in 363/2 (schol. Aeschin. 1.64).

Ἀρίστων (*PA* 2140). Brings an *eisangelia* (no. 119) against Lykophron, ca 333 (Hyp. 2.1, 2, 8).

Ἀριστώνυμος Ἀριστονίκου (not in *PA*). Proposes in the *ecclesia* an honorary decree for the Pellaneans, 345/4 (*IG* II² 220.7-8, 28-29).

Ἁρμόδιος Προξένου Ἀφιδναῖος (*PA* 2234, *APF*). Brings a *graphe paranomon* (no. 9) against the honorary decree for Iphikrates, 371/0 (Lys. frr.36, 43).

Ἀρχέδημος Ἀρχίου Παιονίδης (*PA* 2325). Proposes a decree of the people concerning envoys from Echinos, 349/8 (*IG* II² 208.5-6).

Ἀρχέδημος Πήληξ (*PA* 2326). Ambassador to Thebes, 370s (Aeschin. 3.139).

Ἀρχίας Ἀχεστορίδου Χολαργεύς (*PA* 2481, *APF*). Probably *synegoros* for Androtion in the *graphe paranomon* (no. 12) of 355/4 (Dem. 22.40).

Ἀρχῖνος (not in *PA*). Defendant in an *apophasis*, 325/4 (Din. 1.63). (*PA* at 15437 accepts the emendation Χαρῖνον).

Ἀρχῖνος ἐκ Κοίλης (*PA* 2526). Proposes two decrees of the people (1): an honorary decree for the democrats from Phyle, 403/2 (Aeschin. 3.187, *Hesperia* 10 [1941] 287 no. 78); (2) decree about adopting the Ionic Alphabet, 403/2 (Σ ad Dion. Thr., ed. A. Hilgard, I.3 183.18). Supports in the *boule* a decree ordering execution without trial of a citizen who did not respect the amnesty, 403/2 (Arist. *Ath.Pol.* 40.2). Proposes two *nomoi*: (1) on *paragraphe* 403/2 (Isoc. 18.2); (2) on *prytaneia* and *epobelia*, ca. 403-399 (Σ ad Aeschin. 1.163). Brings a *graphe paranomon* (no. 4) against Thrasyboulos, 403-401 (Aeschin. 3.195, Arist. *Ath.Pol.* 40.2; Plut. *Mor.* 835F-836A). *Strategos*, frequently serving on the board (Dem. 24.135). In *IG* II² 10.1-2 the proposer is Archinos according to Wilhelm's restoration (Tod II 100), but Osborne restores Thrasyboulos (*Naturalization in Athens*: D 6).

UPDATED INVENTORY OF *RHETORES* AND *STRATEGOI* (1988)

Ἀστύφιλος Φιλάγρου Ἁλαιεύς (*PA* 2662 + 2663 + 2664). Proposes two decrees of the people: (1) alliance with Methymna, 378/7 (*IG* II² 42.3); (2) unknown content, 373/2 (*Hesperia* 3 [1934] 2-3 no. 3). For the identifications see *Agora* XV 7.7 with p. 370.

Αὐτοκλῆς Στρομβιχίδου Εὐωνυμεύς (*PA* 2727, *APF*). Defendant in an *eisangelia* (no. 90), 361/0 (Dem. 36.53). Ambassador to Sparta, 372/1 (Xen. *Hell.* 6.3.2). *Strategos* in 368/7 (Diod. 15.71.3) and 362/1 (Dem. 23.104, 50.4).

Αὐτόλυκος Π--- (*PA* 2746). Proposes the amendment to a decree of the people concerning Mytilene, 368/7 (*IG* II² 107.30). Addresses the *ecclesia* on behalf of the council of the Areopagos, 346/5 (Aeschin. 1.81ff.). Defendant in an *eisangelia* (no. 113), 338/7 (Lycurg. 1.53). Ambassador to Lesbos, 368/7 (*IG* II² 107.32). For the demotic cf. *Hesperia* 52 (1983) 106 *d* 10.

Ἀφαρεύς Ἰσοκράτους Ἐρχιεύς (*PA* 2769, *APF*). Addresses the *ecclesia* (Plut. *Mor.* 839C, ὁ δ᾽ Ἀφαρεὺς συνέγραψε μὲν λόγους οὐ πολλοὺς δὲ, δικανικούς τε καὶ συμβουλευτικούς; Aphareus may have been a logographer, but logographers hardly ever wrote symbouleutic speeches).

Ἀφόβητος Ἀτρομήτου Κοθωκίδης (*PA* 2775, *APF*). *Synegoros* for Aischines in his *euthynai*, 343/2 (Aeschin. 2.179, Dem. 19.237). Ambassador (1) to Philip in 347/6 (Aeschin. 2.94, Dem. 19.124); (2) to the king of Persia, before 343 (Aeschin. 2.149). Elected treasurer, before 343 (Aeschin. 2.149, ὅτε αὐτὸν ἐπὶ τὴν διοίκησιν εἵλεσθε).

Ἀχιλλεύς (*PA* 2796). Ambassador to Alexander, 332/1 (Arr. *Anab.* 3.6.2).

Ἀφηφίων Βαθίππου (*PA* 2808). Brings a *graphe nomon me epitedeion theinai* against Leptines' law on *ateleia*, 355/4 (Dem. 20.144).

Βάθιππος (*PA* 2814). Brings a *graphe nomon me epitedeion theinai* against Leptines' law on *ateleia*, 356/5 (Dem. 20.144).

Βλέπυρος Πειθάνδρου Παιονίδης (*PA* 2881). Proposes an amendment to a decree of the people of unknown content, in or after 354/3 (*IG* II² 189.7).

Βράχυλλος Βαθύλλου Ἐρχιεύς (*PA* 2928). Proposes in the *ecclesia* an honorary decree, *ca* 330 (*IG* II² 408.5). Proposes in the *boule* an honorary decree for Eudoxos, 343/2 (*IG* II² 223C.10).

Γλαυκέτης (*PA* 2946). Brings a *graphe paranomon* (no. 13) against Euktemon, 355/4 (Dem. 24.13-14). Addresses the *ecclesia*, 355/4 (Dem. 24.13). Ambassador to Mausolos, 355/4 (Dem. 24.12-13).

Γλαύκων (*PA* 3011). Proposes a decree of the people concerning envoys, 358/7 (Dem. 23.172, 177).

Γνάθιος Προβαλίσιος (?) (*PA* 3043, *APF*?). Proposes in the *boule* an alliance with Eretria, 394/3 (*IG* II² 16.6); for the date cf. *AJP* 100 (1979) 398-400; 101 (1980) 462-69.

Γνάθων Λαχιάδης (not in *PA*). Proposes a decree of the people of unknown content, *init. s.* iv. (*Hesperia* 26 [1957] 207 no. 53); for the demotic see *Hesperia* 52 (1983) 106 no. 1.ii.e.8.

Δεινίας Ἐρχιεύς (*PA* 3163, *APF*). *Syndikos* elected to defend Leptines' law, 355/4 (Dem. 20.146).

Δεινοκράτης Κλεομβρότου Ἀχαρνεύς (*PA* 3181 + 3185, *APF*). *Strategos*, 336/5 (*IG* II² 1628.351, 370; 1629.871, 890).

Δεινόστρατος Δεινιάδου Ἀγχυλῆθεν (*PA* 3191 + 3192). Proposes in the *boule* an honorary decree for Phanodemos, 343/2 (*IG* II² 223A.4).

Δέρχυλος Αὐτοχλέους Ἁγνούσιος (*PA* 3248 + 3249, *APF*). Ambassador to Philip three times in 347/6 (Aeschin. 2.47; Dem. 19.175; Aeschin. 2.140).

Δημάδης Δημέου Παιανιεύς (*PA* 3263, *APF*). Proposes 22 decrees of the people: (1) conclusion of peace with Philip, 338/7 (Dem. 18.285, Diod. 16.87.3, Demades 1.9); (2) *koine eirene* and membership in the Corinthian League, 338/7 (Plut. *Phoc.* 16.5); (3) honours for Euthykrates, 338-336 (Hyp. fr.80); (4) concerning Lemnos, 337/6 (*Hesperia* 9 [1940] 325-27 no. 35); (5) citizenship for Alkimachos, 337/6 (*IG* II² 239 [*SEG* XXI 267], Harp. *s. v.* Ἀλκίμαχος); (6) proxeny for ?, 337/6 (*IG* II² 240.7); (7) unknown content, 337/6 (*IG* II² 241.5-6); (8) honours for Philip, 336/5 (Demades 1.9, Diod. 16.92.1-2); (9) conclusion of peace with Alexander, 336/5 (?) (Demades 1.14); (10) election of ten envoys to be sent to Alexander, 335/4 (Arr. *Anab.* 1.10.3); (11) reply to Alexander's request for extradition of ten leading Athenians, 335/4 (Diod. 17.15.3); (12) unknown content, 334/3 (*IG* II² 335 [*SEG* XXI 274.10-11]); (13) citizenship for Amyntor, 334/3 (*IG* II² 405.4-5 [*SEG* XXI 275]); (14) honours for ?, 332/1 (*IG* II² 346.12-13); (15) honours for Eurylochos, 332/1 (?) (*IG* II² 399; cf. *BSA* 79 [1984] 229-35); (16) condemnation of triremes, two or more decrees, 330/329 (*IG* II² 1627.247-48); (17) honours for ?, 329/8 (*IG* II² 353.9-10); (18) collection of naval debts, 326/5 (*IG* II² 1629.520); (19) concerning *epidoseis*, 326/5 (*IG* II² 1629.869); (20) concerning the deification of Alexander, 324/3 (Ael. *VH* 5.12); (21) election of envoys to be sent to Antipater, 322/1 (Plut. *Phoc.* 26.3); (22) sentence of death passed on the anti-Macedonian Athenian leaders (Arr. *FGrHist* 156F9.13). Brings numerous *eisangeliai* (Polyeuktos fr.1 Baiter/Sauppe). Convicted in three *graphai paranomon* (Diod. 18.18.2), the first (no. 28) in 338-336 (Hyp. fr.80-91), the second (no. 38) in 324/3 (Ath. 251 B, Ael. *VH* 5.12). Defendant in an *apophasis* in consequence of the Harpalos affair, 324/3 (Din. 1.89). Ambassador (1) to Philip, 338/7 (*Suda* 415 *s. v.* Δημάδης); (2) to Alexander, 335/4 (Plut. *Dem.* 23.6, Diod. 17.15.4-5); (3) to Antipater, 322/1 (Diod. 18.18.2). *Tamias stratiotikon*, 334/3 (*IG* II² 1493-95 [*SEG* XXI 552]).

Δημαίνετος Δημέου (?) Παιανιεύς (?) (*PA* 3265 + 3276, *APF*). *Strategos*, before 388 (Aeschin. 2.79); in 388/7 (Xen. *Hell.* 5.1.10, 26).

UPDATED INVENTORY OF *RHETORES* AND *STRATEGOI* (1988)

Δημέας Δημάδου Παιανιεύς (*PA* 3322, *APF*). Proposes in the *ecclesia* a citizenship decree for ?, before 321 (*Hesperia* 13 [1944] 231-33 no. 5). Addresses the *ecclesia*, before 322 (Ath. 591 F).

Δημέας Σφήττιος (*PA* 3325). Proposes in the *boule* an honorary decree for Lykourgos, before 324 (*IG* II² 3207: I follow Wilhelm in taking this to be the lower part of *IG* II² 457 and to record the honours bestowed on Lykourgos; see *Attische Urkunden* III [1925] 3-6 [*Akademieschr.* I 463ff]).

Δημήτριος Εὐχτήμονος 'Αφιδναῖος (*PA* 3392). Proposes a decree of the people concerning the cult of Amphiaraos, 332/1 (*Syll.*³ 287.9).

Δημήτριος Φανοστράτου Φαληρεύς (*PA* 3455, *APF*). Ambassador to Antipater, 322 (Demetr. *Eloc.* 289).

Δημοκλείδης (*PA* 3476). Ambassador to Chios, 384/3 (*IG* II² 34.37).

Δημοκλῆς (*PA* 3487). Defendant in an *eisangelia* (no. 128), 325/4 (Dem. 25.47).

Δημοκράτης Δημοκλέους 'Αφιδναῖος (*PA* 3521, *APF*). Exhorts the *boule* to pass a decree summoning Aristodemos, 347/6 (Aeschin. 2.17). Addresses the *ecclesia*, 338/7 (Plut. *Mor.* 803D). *Synegoros* for Philippides in a *graphe paranomon* (no. 32), 336/5 (Hyp. 4.2-3).

Δημομέλης Δήμωνος Παιανιεύς (*PA* 3554, *APF*). Proposes in the *ecclesia* an honorary decree for Demosthenes, 339/8 (Dem. 19.222-23). Defendant in a *graphe paranomon* (no. 26), 339/8 (Dem. 18.222, 249).

Δημοσθένης Δημοκλέους Λαμπτρεύς (*PA* 3593). Proposes two decrees of the people: (1) honours for the *epimeletai* of the Amphiaraion, 329/8 (*Syll.*³ 298.9-10); (2) honours for Herakleides of Salamis, 325/4 (*IG* II² 360.5).

Δημοσθένης Δημοσθένους Παιανιεύς (*PA* 3597, *APF*). Proposes 39 decrees of the people: (1) proposal for an expeditionary force and a smaller permanent force, 352/1 (Dem. 4.13-29, 30, 33); (2) honours for Aristodemos, 347/6 (Aeschin. 2.17); (3) safe conduct for the envoys from Philip, 347/6 (Aeschin. 2.53-54); (4) honours for the first embassy to Philip, 347/6 (Dem. 19.234, Aeschin. 2.46); (5) instructing the *prytaneis* to summon the *ecclesia* on 18-19 Elaphebolion 346 (Aeschin. 2.61); (6) providing for an embassy to the Peloponnese, 345/4 (Dem. 18.79); (7) concerning Ainos, before 342 (Dem. 58.36-37, 43); (8) providing for an embassy to Euboia, 343/2 (Dem. 18.79); (9) ordering *apophasis* against Proxenos, 346-343 (Din. 1.63); (10) death sentence passed on Anaxinos, 343 (?) (Aeschin. 3.224); (11) alliance with Chalkis, 342/1 (Aeschin. 3.92-93); (12) providing for a campaign against Oreos, 341/0 (Dem. 18.79); (13) providing for embassies to Eretria and Oreos, 341/0 (Aeschin. 3.95-101); (14) providing for a campaign against Eretria, 341/0 (Dem. 18.79); (15) appointment of *nomothetai*, 340/339 (Dem. 18.102-07, *cf. Ath. Eccl.* 175); (16) squadrons sent to the Chersonese, to Byzantion, etc., 340/339 (Dem. 18.80); (17) declaration of war against Philip, 340/339 (Philoch. F55); (18) honours for Phokinos,

Nikandros, and Dexippos, 340/339 (*IG* II^2 231.6); (19) providing for envoys to Thebes, 339/8 (Dem. 18.177-79); (20) alliance with Thebes, 339/8 (Aeschin. 3.142-45); (21) transferring revenue from the theoric to the stratiotic fund, 339/8 (Philoch. F56A); (22) providing for garrisons, 338/7 (Dem. 18.248); (23) providing for the repair of the walls, 338/7 (Dem. 18.248); (24) providing for the mending of the moats, 338/7 (Dem. 18.248); (25) judicial powers to the Areopagos, 338/7 (?) (Din. 1.62, 82-83); (26) providing for a partial demobilization and the despatch of embassies, 338/7 (Din. 1.78-80); (27) prescribing meetings of the *phylai* for the repair of the walls, 338/7 (Aeschin. 3.27); (28) providing for armed assistance to Thebes, 335/4 (Diod. 17.8.6); (29) honours for the Bosporan princes, *ca* 330 (Din. 1.43); (30) citizenship for Kallias of Chalkis, *ca* 330 (Aeschin. 3.85, Hyp. 1.20); (31) citizenship for Taurosthenes, *ca* 330 (Aeschin. 3.85, Hyp. 1.20); (32) citizenship for Chairephilos and his sons, before 324 (Din. 1.43); (33) citizenship for Epigenes, before 324 (Din. 1.43); (34) citizenship for Konon, before 324 (Din. 1.43); (35) unknown content, before 324 (Din. fr.xlvii Con.); (36) ordering the arrest of Harpalos and confiscation of his money, 324 (Hyp. 1.8-9, Din. 1.89); (37) instructing the Areopagos to investigate the Harpalos affair, 324/3 (Din. 1.82-83); (38) honours for Diphilos, 324/3 (Din. 1.43; fr.xli Con.); (39) proposal to worship only the acknowledged deities, 324/3 (Din. 1.94). Proposes four decrees of the *boule*: (1) despatching ambassadors to the cities to be visited by Aristodemos, 347/6 (Aeschin. 2.19); (2) instructing the *prytaneis* to summon an *ecclesia* on 8 Elaphebolion 346 (Aeschin. 3.66-67); (3) *proedria* for the envoys from Philip, 347/6 (Dem. 18.28, Aeschin. 2.55); (4) instructing the second embassy to leave Athens forthwith, 347/6 (Dem. 18.25-29, 19.154). Proposes a *nomos* on trierarchs, 340/339 (Dem. 18.102-07, Din. 1.42). Brings (1) an *eisangelia* (no. 111) against Anaxinos, 343 (?) (Aeschin. 3.223-24); (2) an *apophasis* against Archinos, 345/4 (Din. 1.63); (3) an *eisangelia* (no. 129) against Kallimedon, 324/3 (Din. 1.94); (4) an *euthynai* against Aischines, 343/2 (Dem. 19.17). *Synegoros* for (1) Euthykles in an *eisangelia* (no. 96), 360/359 (Aeschin. 3.52); (2) Ktesippos in a *graphe nomon me epitedeion theinai*, 355/4 (Dem. 20 hypoth. 3); (3) Philokrates in a *graphe paranomon* (no. 17), 348/7 (Aeschin. 2.14); (4) Timarchos in a *dokimasia rhetoron*, 346/5 (Aeschin. 1.166ff); (5) Phanostratos in a *graphe paranomon* (no. 29), 335-330 (Dem. 25 hypoth. 2); (6) Ktesiphon in a *graphe paranomon* (no. 30), 330/329 (Dem. 18.5 etc.); (7) Lykourgos in an *endeixis* (no. 32), 325/4 (Aristogeiton fr.1). Defendant (1) in a *graphe paranomon* (no. 22), before 342 (Dem. 58.23, 36-37, 42-44); (2) in a *graphe paranomon* (no. 25), 340/339 (Dem. 18.102-07); (3) in a *graphe paranomon* (no. 37), before 324 (Din. fr.xlvii Con.); (4) in an *apophasis* in consequence of the Harpalos affair, 324/3 (Hyp. 1, Din. 1); in numerous *graphai (paranomon), eisangeliai*, and *euthynai*, 338/7 (Dem. 18.249). Ambassador (1) to Philip three times, 347/6 (Aeschin. 2.18; Dem. 19.17; Dem. 19.121 [elected], 122 [*exomosia*]); (2) to the Peloponnese, 345/4 (Dem. 6.19-

27); (3) *pylagoros*, 344/3 (Aeschin. 3.113); (4) to the Peloponnese, 343/2 (Dem. 9.72); (5) to Byzantion and Thrace, 342/1 (?) (Dem. 18.244, Aeschin. 3.256); (6) to Thessaly, 341/0 (?) (Dem. 18.244); (7) to the Peloponnese and Arkadia, 341/0 (Aeschin. 3.97, 256); (8) to Thebes, 339/8 (Dem. 18.179); (9) to the allies overseas, 338/7 (Din. 1.80); to Alexander, 336/5 (Aeschin. 3.161); (11) to the Peloponnese, 335/4 (Plut. *Mor.* 851B); (12) to Arkadia, 323/2 (Plut. *Dem.* 27.4-5). Member of the Theoric Board, 337/6 (Aeschin. 3.24).

Δημόστρατος 'Αριστοφῶντος 'Αζηνιεύς (*PA* 3617, *APF*). Ambassador to Sparta, 372/1 (Xen. *Hell.* 6.3.2).

Δημοτίων (*PA* 3646). Addresses the *ecclesia* 366/5 (Xen. *Hell.* 7.4.4).

Δημόφιλος (*PA* 3664). Proposes a decree of the people ordering a *diapsephisis ton aston*, 346/5 (Aeschin. 1.86, schol. Aeschin. 1.77).

Δημόφιλος Δημοφίλου 'Αχαρνεύς (*PA* 3675, *APF*). Proposes two decrees of the people: (1) concerning naval equipment, 324/3 or earlier (*IG* II² 1631.655-58); (2) honours for ?, before 318/7 (*IG* II² 421.3-4).

Δημοφῶν (*PA* 3693). *Strategos*, 379/8 (Diod. 15.26.2).

Δημοχάρης Λάχητος Λευκονοεύς (*PA* 3716, *APF*). Addresses the *ecclesia*, 322/1 (Plut. *Mor.* 847D).

Δήμων Δημομέλους Παιανιεύς (*PA* 3736, *APF*). Proposes the dcecree of the people by which Demosthenes is recalled, 323/2 (Plut. *Dem.* 27.6, *Mor.* 846D).

Δικαιογένης Μενεξένου Κυδαθηναιεύς (*PA* 3776, *APF*). *Strategos* in 324/3 (*IG* II² 1631.380f, Reinmuth no. 15b.4-6) and 323/2 (*IG* II² 1631.215).

Διογείτων (*PA* 3790). Proposes in the *ecclesia* an honorary decree for Timaphenides, ca. 370 (*IG* II² 152.7-8; cf. *SEG* XIV 44).

Διογνίδης (not in *PA*). Defendant in an *eisangelia* (no. 122), 331-324 (Hyp. 3.3).

Διόδωρος (*PA* 3919). Brings a *graphe nomon me epitedeion theinai* against Timokrates, 354/3 (Dem. 24.64, hypoth. 1). *Synegoros* for Euktemon in a *graphe paranomon* (no. 12), 355/4 (Dem. 22.1, hypoth. 1.1).

Διοκλῆς (*PA* 3987). Brings a *graphe nomon me epitedeion theinai* against (?), 400-380 (Lys. frr.86-87). It is in fact only an assumption that Lysias' speech πρὸς Διοκλέα ὑπὲρ τοῦ κατὰ τῶν ῥητόρων νόμου was written for a client who defended a law about *rhetores* against a *graphe nomon me epitedeion theinai* brought by Diokles.

Διοκλῆς (*PA* 3989). Proposes a *nomos* concerning the coming into force of *nomoi*, ca 400 (Dem. 24.42).

Διοκλῆς 'Αλωπεκῆθεν (*PA* 3990 + 4015, *APF*). *Strategos*, 357/6 (*IG* II² 124.23, Polyaen. 5.29, Dem. 21.174).

Διονύσιος (*PA* 4092). Defendant in an *eisangelia* (no. 74), 388/7 (Dem. 19.180). *Strategos*, 388/7 (Xen. *Hell.* 5.1.26, Dem. 19.180).

Διονύσιος (PA 4095). ὁ ἐπὶ τῆς διοικήσεως, ca 330 (Din. fr.xiii Con.).

Διοπείθης Διφίλου Σουνιεύς (PA 4327, APF). Strategos, 343/2 (Philoch. F158); 342/1 (Dem. 8.28); 341/0 (Arist. Rh. 1386a14, Aristogeiton fr.3.2).

Διοπείθης Διοπείθους Σφήττιος (PA 4328, APF). Proposes two decrees of the people: (1) amendment to honours for Dioskourides, 346/5 (IG II² 218.22-23); (2) concerning Philip, 346-340 (Dem. 18.70). Defendant in an eisangelia (no. 98), 361-343 (Hyp. 3.29).

Διότιμος 'Ολυμπιοδώρου (?) Εὐωνυμεύς (?) (PA 4370, APF). Strategos, 390/389 (schol. Aristid. Panath. 172.4); 388/7 (Xen. Hell. 5.1.7,25).

Διότιμος Διοπείθους Εὐωνυμεύς (PA 4384, APF). Strategos, 338/7 (IG II² 1628.396f, 1623.200f [?]); 337/6 (IG II² 1623.200ff); 335/4 (IG II² 1623.277-78); 334/3 (IG II² 114; SEG XXI 276); ca 330 (IG II² 408.7-8).

Διοφάνης Κηφισιεύς (PA 4409). Proposes in the boule an honorary decree for Lykourgos, before 324 (IG II² 3207, cf. supra Δημέας Σφήττιος).

Διόφαντος (PA 4421; = 4435?). Ambassador to Alexander, 332/1 (Arr. Anab. 3.6.2).

Διόφαντος Φρασικλείδου Μυρρινούσιος (PA 4435, APF). Proposes two decrees of the people: (1) unknown content, 337/6 (IG II² 242.6-7); (2) honours for Kalliteles, 337/6 (IG II² 243.6-7). Proposes in the boule a decree relating to a trireme, 337/6 (?) (IG II² 1623.210-12).

Διόφαντος Θρασυμήδους Σφήττιος (PA 4438). Proposes three decrees of the people: (1) honours for Koroibos, 368/7 (IG II² 106.6); (2) honours for the envoys from Mytilene, 368/7 (IG II² 107.8); (3) celebrating the defence of Thermopylai, 352/1 (Dem. 19.86). Member of the Theoric Board, 360-350 (?) (schol. Aeschin. 3.24 Schultz). For the patronymic see Hesperia 26 (1957) 3 no. S2.13.

Δίφιλος Διοπείθους Σουνιεύς (PA 4467 + 4487, APF). Proposes a nomos relating to the navy, 323/2 or earlier (IG II² 1631.511, 1632.19). Addresses the ecclesia with a speech written by Deinarchos or Demosthenes, 324/3 (Din. fr.xli Con.).

Δίων (PA 4491). Ambassador (1) to?, 394/3 (IG II² 1424a.350); (2) to Tiribazos 392/1 (Xen. Hell. 4.8.13).

Διώνδας (PA 4524). Brings a graphe paranomon (no. 26) against Hypereides, 339/8 (Dem. 18.222, 249). Plut. Mor. 848D records also a graphe paranomon against Aristonikos, probably confusing the honorary decree for Demosthenes proposed by Aristonikos with that proposed by Hypereides.

Δρωπίδης 'Ερμίππου 'Αφιδναῖος (PA 4575 + 4576). Ambassador to Dareios III, 333/2 (Curt. 3.13.15). For the patronymic and demotic see Hesperia 19 (1950) 261 no. 19.22.

'Εμμενίδης (PA 4687). Proposes a decree of the people relating to the Eleusinion, 332/1 or earlier (IG II² 1544.30).

UPDATED INVENTORY OF *RHETORES* AND *STRATEGOI* (1988)

Ἔμπεδος Ὀῆθεν (*PA* 4696a). Ambassador to Thessaly, 361/0 (?) (*IG* II^2 175.2-3).

Ἐξηκεστίδης (*PA* 4710). Proposes in the *ecclesia* an alliance with Thessaly, 361/0 (*IG* II^2 116.8).

Ἐξηκεστίδης Χαρίου Θορίκιος (*PA* 4718, *APF*). *Strategos*, 357/6 (*IG* II^2 124.22).

Ἐξηκεστίδης Παλληνεύς (*PA* 4721). Ambassador to Byzantion, 378/7 (*IG* II^2 41.18).

Ἐπικράτης Κηφισιεύς (*PA* 4859, *APF*). Addresses the *ecclesia*, 397/6 (*Hell.Oxy.* 7.2, schol. Ar. *Eccl.* 71). Defendant (1) in an *euthynai* (?) as *presbeus*, 394-392 (?) (Lys. 27.1); (2) in an *eisangelia* (no. 69), 392/1 (Philoch. F149a). Ambassador (1) to the king of Persia, 394-392 (Plato Com. frr.119, 122 K.); (2) to Sparta, 392/1 (Dem. 19.277-80, Philoch.).

Ἐπικράτης ..οτήτου Παλληνεύς (*PA* 4863, *APF*). Proposes a decree of the people concerning appointment of *nomothetai*, 354/3 (Dem. 24.27). Proposes two *nomoi*: (1) concerning the fincancing of a festival, 354/3 (unpublished); (2) concerning the *epheboi*, 336/5 (?) (Harp. s. v. Ἐπικράτης = Lycurg. fr.v.3 Con.).

Ἐπικράτης Μενεστράτου Παλληνεύς (*PA* 4909, *APF*). Proposes in the *ecclesia* an amendment to an honorary decree for Pythodoros, 369/8 (*I.Délos* I 88.15).

Ἐπιτέλης Σωιναύτου Περγασῆθεν (*PA* 4963). Proposes in the *ecclesia* an honorary decree for Lapyris, 323/2 (*IG* II^2 365.6-7). Patronymic suppl. M.J. Osborne.

Ἐπιχάρης (*PA* 4976). Proposes en the *ecclesia* an amendment to a proxeny decree, before 353/2 (*IG* II^2 188.13).

Ἐπιχάρης Λαμπτρεύς (*PA* 4991). *Synegoros* for Kephisios in an *endeixis* (no. 10), 400/399 (Andoc. 1.95).

Ἐπιχάρης Χολλείδης (*APF* 58-59). Proposes in the *ecclesia* an honorary decree for Charidemos, before 342 (Dem. 58.30-34). Defendant in a *graphe paranomon* (no. 23), before 342 (Dem. 58.30).

Ἐργοκλῆς (*PA* 5052, *APF*). Defendant in an *eisangelia* (no. 73), 390/389 (lys. 28, 29; Dem. 19.180). *Strategos*, 390/389 (Lys. 28.2, 12).

Ἐργόφιλος (*PA* 5062). Defendant in an *eisangelia* (no. 86), 363/2 (Dem. 19.180, Arist. *Rh.* 1380b10). *Strategos*, 363/2 (Dem. 23.104).

Ἕρμιππος Πόριος (*PA* 5116). Ambassador to Olynthos, 376/5 (?) (*IG* II^2 36.7).

Ἑρμογένης Ἱππονίκου (?) Ἀλωπεκῆθεν (*PA* 5119, *APF*). Ambassador to Tiribazos 392/1 (Xen. *Hell.* 4.8.13).

Εὐβουλίδης Ἀντιφίλου Ἁλιμούσιος (*PA* 5323). Proposes in the *ecclesia* an honorary decree for Dioskourides, 346/5 (*IG* II^2 218.6-7).

Εὐβουλίδης Ἐπικλείδου Ἐλευσίνιος (*PA* 5325). Defendant in an *eisangelia* (no. 72), 392/1 (Philoch. F149a). Ambassador to Sparta, 392/1 (Philoch.). For the patronymic *cf. IG* II^2 2811.

Εὔβουλος Σπινθάρου Προβαλίσιος (*PA* 5369). Proposes three decrees of the people: (1) recalling Xenophon (?), 370-360 (?) (Diog. Laert. 2.59); (2) inviting envoys from all Greek *poleis* to Athens, 348/7 (?) (Dem. 19.304); (3) concerning Philip, 346-340 (Dem. 18.70, 75). Proposes a *nomos* concerning the theoric fund, 349/8 (schol. Dem. 1.1 p. 9.1). Brings a *probole* against Aristophon, *ca* 370-350 (Dem. 21.218 with schol.). *Synegoros* for Aischines in an *euthynai*, 343/2 (Dem. 19.290, Aeschin. 2.184). Member of the Theoric Board, *ca* 350 (Aeschin. 3.25).

Εὔδημος Κυδαθηναιεύς (*PA* 5401). Proposes a *nomos*, 382/1 (Dem. 24.138). Defendant in a *graphe nomon me epitedeion theinai*, 382/1 (Dem. 24.138).

Εὐδίδακτος Λαμπτρεύς (*PA* 5414). Ambassador to Delphoi, 352/1 (*IG* II^2 204.83).

Εὔδοξος Θεαγγέλου Συπαλήττιος (*PA* 5439). Addresses the *boule* frequently, 343/2 (*IG* II^2 223C.10-12).

Εὐετίων Πυθαγγέλου Κηφισιεύς (*PA* 5461+5462, *APF*). *Strategos*, 323/2 (*IG* II^2 505.18, Diod. 18.15.9).

Εὐετίων Αὐτοκλείδου Σφήττιος (*PA* 5463, *APF*). Proposes in the *boule* a decree concerning the priest of Asklepios, 328/7 (*IG* II^2 354.32).

Εὐήγορος Φιλοίνου Παιανιεύς (*PA* 5466, *APF*). Proposes a *nomos* concerning *probolai* in the *ecclesia*, before 350 (Dem. 21.10).

Εὐθυκλῆς Θριάσιος (*PA* 5581, *APF*). Brings an *eisangelia* (no. 96) against Kephisodotos, 360/359 (Dem. 23.5, 165-68). Brings a *graphe paranomon* (no. 14) against Aristokrates, 352/1 (Dem. 23.5; hypoth. 1.2, 2.4).

Εὐθύμαχος (*PA* 5624). Proposes in the *ecclesia* an honorary decree for Xennias, 353/2 (*IG* II^2 138.4), cf. *Hesperia* 54 (1985) 309-12 no. 1.

Εὐκλείδης (*PA* 5678). Ambassador to Philip, 345/4 (?) (Dem. 19.162 with schol. p. 392.8).

Εὐκράτης Ἀριστοτίμου Πειραιεύς (*PA* 5762). Proposes a *nomos* against tyranny, 337/6 (*Hesperia* 21 [1952] 355-59 no. 5).

Εὐκτήμων (*PA* 5784). Proposes a decree of the people ordering the collection of 9 1/2 talents, 355/4 (Dem. 24.11-14, *cf* 9). Brings a *graphe paranomon* (no. 12) against Androtion, 355/4 (Dem. 22.1, 3). *Synegoros* for Diodoros in a *graphe nomon me epitedeion theinai*, 354/3 (Dem. 24.10, hypoth. 2.5). Defendant in a *graphe paranomon* (no. 13), 355/4 (Dem. 24.9, 11-15).

Εὔνομος (*PA* 5861). Ambassador to Sicily, 394/3 (Lys. 19.19): perhaps sent privately by Konon and not officially elected, but *cf. infra* Εὐριππίδης. *Strategos*, 388/7 (Xen. *Hell.* 5.1.5, 7-9).

Εὔνομος Κυδιμάχου (*PA* 5863). *Synegoros* for Aristogeiton in an *endeixis* (no. 32), 325/4 (Dem. 25.55).

Εὐξένιππος Ἐθελοκράτους Λαμπτρεύς (*PA* 5886+5888, *APF*). Addresses the *ecclesia*

UPDATED INVENTORY OF *RHETORES* AND *STRATEGOI* (1988)

and reports on his dream in the Amphiaraion, *ca* 330-324 (Hyp. 3.14). Defendant in an *eisangelia* (no. 124), *ca* 330-324 (Hyp. 3).

Εὐξίθεος (*PA* 5901). Proposes in the *ecclesia* an honorary decree for Xanthippos, before 378/7 (*IG* II² 60.4).

Εὐριππίδης 'Αδειμάντου Μυρρινούσιος (*PA* 5949 + 5955 + 5956, *APF*). Proposes two decrees of the people: (1) honours for Eukles, *ca* 403/2 (*IG* II² 145.3-4, *cf.* Rhodes, *Athenian Boule* 85); (2) concerning *eisphora*, before 393 (Ar. *Eccl.* 825 with schol.). Ambassador to Sicily, 394/3 (Arist. *Rh.* 1384b15 with schol. 106-07 Rabe).

Εὐφίλητος Εὐφιλήτου Κηφισιεύς (*PA* 6054, *APF*). Proposes in the *ecclesia* an honorary decree for Euphron, 323/2 (*IG* II² 448.6).

Εὐφρόσυνος Παιανιεύς (*PA* 6123). Ambassador to Keos, *ca* 350 (*IG* II² 1128.39-40).

'Εφιάλτης (*PA* 6156). Ambassador to the king of Persia, 341/0 (?) (Plut. *Mor.* 847F). *Strategos*, 350/349 (Philoch. F155).

'Ηγέμαχος Χαιρήμονος Περιθοίδης (*PA* 6282). Proposes in the *boule* an honorary decree for the *epheboi* of Kekropis, 334/3 (*IG* II² 1156.36).

'Ηγήμων (*PA* 6290). Proposes two *nomoi*: (1) concerning the *theorika*, before 330 (Aeschin. 3.25); (2) concerning naval equipment, before 326 (*IG* II² 1628.300). Defendant in an *eisangelia* (no. 120), *ca* 331 (Dem. 25.47).

'Ηγήσανδρος 'Ηγησίου Σουνιεύς (*PA* 6307, *APF*). Proposes a decree of the people concerning Andros, 357/6 (*IG* II² 123.7). Opposes Aristophon in the *ecclesia*, before 346/5 (Aeschin. 1.64). *Synegoros* for Timarchos in the *dokimasia rhetoron*, 346/5 (Aeschin. 1.71).

'Ηγησίλεως Προβαλίσιος (?) (*PA* 6339). *Strategos*, 363/2 (Ephoros *FGrHist* 70F85, Diod. 15.84.2); 349/8 (Dem. 19.290 with schol. (513, Dilts).

'Ηγήσιππος 'Ηγησίου Σουνιεύς (*PA* 6351, *APF*). Proposes six decrees of the people: (1) concerning Eretria, 357/6 (*IG* II² 125.1); (2) honours for some Akarnanians, 338/7 (*IG* II² 237.5-6); (3) alliance with Phokis, 356/5 (Aeschin. 3.118); (4) reply to Python, 344/3 (Dem. 7.23-26); (5) reply to Philip's letter, 343/2 (Dem. 7.46); (6) relating to Philip, 346-340 (Dem. 18.75). Brings (1) a *graphe paranomon* (no. 11) against Kallippos, *ca* 357 (Dem. 7.43); (2) an *eisangelia* (no. 99) against some traitors, 357/6 (*IG* II² 125.7-9). *Synegoros* for Timarchos in the *dokimasia rhetoron*, 346/5 (Aeschin. 1.71). Ambassador (1) to Philip, 344/3 (Dem. 19.331); (2) to the Peloponnese, 343/2 (Dem. 9.72).

'Ηρακλείδης ὁ Κλαζομένιος (*PA* 6489). Proposes a *nomos* (?) by which the ἐκκλησιαστικόν is raised from one to two obols, before 393 (Arist. *Ath.Pol.* 41.3). *Strategos*, 403/2-400/399 (Pl. *Ion* 541 D).

Θεαίτητος 'Ερχιεύς (*PA* 6631). Addresses the *ecclesia* concerning the alliance with the Thessalians, 361/0 (*IG* II² 116.45, cf. Tod II 147).

Θεόδωρος 'Αντιφάνου 'Αλωπεκῆθεν (PA 6854). Proposes in the *ecclesia* an honorary decree for Phyleus, 335/4 (*IG* II² 330.5).

Θεοζοτίδης 'Αθμονεύς (PA 6913 + 6914, *APF*). Proposes two decrees of the people: (1) concerning the orphans of the democrats, 403/2 (?) (*Hesperia* 40 [1971] 280-301 no. 7); (2) honours for ?, ca 400 (*IG* II² 5.11 [*SEG* XIV 36]). Defendant in a *graphe paranomon* (no. 5), 403/2 (?) (*P.Hib.* 1.14 = Lys. fr.vi Gernet/Bizos). For the demotic cf. *SEG* XXVIII 190.

Θεοκρίνης Ὑβάδης (PA 6946). Brings four *graphai paranomon* (nos. 21-24), before 342: (1) against Thoukydides (Dem. 58.23, 36-38); (2) against Demosthenes (Dem. 58.23, 36, 42-44); (3) against Epichares (Dem. 58.1, 30-34, 70); (4) against Antimedon (Dem. 58.35).

Θεομένης Ὀῆθεν (PA 6957). Proposes in the *ecclesia* an honorary decree for Lykourgos, before 324 (*IG* II² 3207). Proposes in the *boule* an honorary decree for Lykourgos, before 324 (*IG* II² 3207), cf. *supra* Δημέας Σφήττιος.

Θεόμνηστος (PA 6962). Addresses the *ecclesia*, 394-384 (Lys. 10.1). Defendant in a *dokimasia rhetoron*, 394-384 (Lys. 10.1 Gernet/Bizos).

Θεόπομπος (PA 7016). Ambassador to Mytilene, 378/7 (*IG* II² 40.7).

Θεότιμος (PA 7055). Defendant in an *eisangelia* (no. 94), 361/0 (?) (Hyp. 3.1). Strategos, 361/0 (?) (Hyp.).

Θεόφημος Εὐωνυμεύς (PA 7094, *APF*). Defendant in an *eisangelia* (no. 144), 357/6 (Dem. 47.41-44).

Θεόφιλος Μελίτωνος 'Αλωπεκῆθεν (PA 7126). Synegoros for Lykophron in an *eisangelia* (no. 119), 332/2 (?) (Hyp. 2.20, *P. Oxy.* 1607).

Θηβαγένης 'Ελευσίνιος (PA 7231). Ambassador to Dionysios of Heraklea, 330-328 (*IG* II² 360.45).

Θουκλείδης Αἰαντίδος φυλῆς (not in *PA*). Strategos, 394/3 (*IG* II² 5221.2-4).

Θουκυδίδης (PA 7265). Proposes a decree of the people concerning *syntaxis* paid by the Ainians, before 342 (Dem. 58.36-38). Defendant in a *graphe paranomon* (no. 21), before 342 (Dem. 58.23, 36-38).

Θρασύβουλος Θράσωνος 'Ερχιεύς (PA 7304, *APF*). Strategos (?), 353/2 (*IG* II² 1613.270); strategos, 326/5 (*IG* II² 1628.40-41; 2969).

Θρασύβουλος Θράσωνος Κολλυτεύς (PA 7305, *APF*). Defendant in two *eisangeliai* (nos. 75, 76): (1) 388/7 (Lys. 26.21-24, Dem. 24.134); (2) 383/2 (Lys. 26.21-23, Dem. 24.134). Ambassador to Thebes, 378/7 (Aeschin. 3.138, *IG* II² 43.76). Strategos, 388/7 (Xen. *Hell.* 5.1.26); 373/2 (*Hesperia* 8 [1939] 3-5 no. 2).

Θρασύβουλος Λύκου Στειριεύς (PA 7310, *APF*). Proposes three decrees of the people: (1) citizenship to democrats, 403/2 (Arist. *Ath.Pol.* 40.2, Aeschin. 3.195); (2) second grant of citizenship to democrats, 401/0 (*IG* II² 10.1, Osborne D 6); (3) alliance with Boiotia, 395/4 (Xen. *Hell.* 3.5.16). Addresses the *ecclesia*, 397/6

UPDATED INVENTORY OF RHETORES AND STRATEGOI (1988)

(Hell. Oxy. 6.2). Defendant in a graphe paranomon (no. 4), 403/2 (?) (Arist. Ath. Pol. 40.2, Aeschin. 3.195). Strategos, 395/4 (Paus. 3.5.4, Lys. 16.15); 390/389 (Xen. Hell. 4.8.25-31).

Θρασυκλῆς ἐξ Οἴου (PA 7327). Pylagoros, 340/339 (Aeschin. 3.115).

Θρασυκλῆς Παλληνεύς (PA 7328). Ambassador to Olynthos, 376/5 (?) (IG II² 36.6).

Θράσυλλος Πανδιονίδος φυλῆς (PA 7338). Synegoros for Andokides in an endeixis (no. 10), 400/399 (Andoc. 1.150).

Θράσων Ἐρχιεύς (PA 7384, APF). Ambassador (1) to Thebes, 379-371 (Aeschin. 3.138, Din. 1.38); (2) to Thrace, 356/5 (IG II² 127.37).

Ἰατροκλῆς Πασιφῶντος (PA 7442). Addresses the boule, 347/6 (Aeschin. 2.16). Ambassador three times to Philip, 347/6 (1: Aeschin. 2.20; 2: Dem. 19.197-98, Aeschin. 2.126; 3 [?]: Dem. 19.121).

Ἱεροκλείδης Τιμοστράτου Ἀλωπεκῆθεν (PA 7463). Proposes two decrees of the people: (1) honours for Theogenes, 349/8 (IG II² 206.5-7, 26-27); (2) unknown content, 349/8 (IG II² 209.5).

Ἱερώνυμος (PA 7552). Strategos, 395/4 (Lys. fr.123, Diod. 14.81.4).

Ἱερώνυμος Οἰκωφέλους Ῥαμνούσιος (PA 7570). Proposes in the ecclesia an honorary decree for Kallikratides, ca 330 (IG II² 415.11).

Ἱμεραῖος Φανοστράτου Φαληρεύς (PA 7578, APF). Elected prosecutor in the apophasis in consequence of the Harpalos affair, 324/3 (Plut. Mor. 846C). Defendant in an eisangelia (no. 130), 336-322 (Din. fr.xiv Con.).

Ἱππόστρατος Ἐτεαρχίδου Παλληνεύς (PA 7669). Proposes a decree of the people concerning Elaious, 341/0 (IG II² 228.7-8).

Ἱπποχάρης Ἀλωπεκῆθεν (PA 7670). Proposes in the ecclesia an honorary decree for Phyleus, 336/5 (IG II² 330.26, 50).

Ἰφικράτης Ἰφικράτους Ῥαμνούσιος (PA 7736, APF). Ambassador to Dareios III, 333/2 (Arr. Anab. 2.15.2-14, Curt. 3.13.15).

Ἰφικράτης Τιμοθέου Ῥαμνούσιος (PA 7737, APF). Brings eisangeliai against (1) Timotheos (no. 80), 373/2 (Dem. 49.9, Lys. fr.228); (2) Antimachos (no 81), 373/2 (Dem. 49.9-10). Synegoros for ? in a graphe paranomon (no. 9), 371/0 (Lys. fr.xviii). Defendant in an eisangelia (no. 100), 356/5 (Lys. fr.lxv, Dion. Hal. Lys. 480). Strategos, 390/389 (Diod. 14.92.2); 389/8 (Xen. Hell. 4.8.34); 388/7 (Hell. 5.1.7, 25); 373/2 (Dem. 49.22, Hell. 6.2.13-39); 372/1 (Hell. 6.3.3); 370/369 (Hell. 6.5.49); 368/7 (Aeschin. 2.27); 367/6, 366/5, 365/4 (Dem. 23.149); 364/3 (Dem. 23.149, schol. Aeschin. 2.31), deposed; 357/6 (IG II² 124.20); 356/5 (Dion. Hal. Lys. 480, Lys. fr.lxv). Mercenary leader before 390, cf. Xen. Hell. 4.5.13 ἄρχων versus στρατηγῶν. Perhaps strategos in 369/8 (Polyaen. 3.9.20).

Καλλίας (not in PA). Strategos, 341/0 (Dem. 12.5). According to Schäfer (II 492.3) the reference is to Kallias of Chalkis, but I follow H. Weil, *Les harangues de Démosthène*³ (Paris 1912) 407, in believing that ὁ παρ' ὑμῶν στρατηγός probably denotes a regular elected Athenian general.

Καλλίας Ἱππονίκου Ἀλωπεκῆθεν (*PA* 7826, *APF*). Ambassador to Sparta three times (Xen. *Hell.* 6.3.4), the third time in 372/1 (*Hell.* 6.3.2). Strategos in 391/0 (*Hell.* 4.5.13).

Καλλίας Ἄβρωνος Βατῆθεν (*PA* 7856, *APF*). Tamias stratiotikon, 338/7 (Plut. *Mor.* 842F).

Καλλικράτης (not in *PA*). Brings a *graphe paranomon* (no. 37) against Demosthenes, date unknown (Din. fr.xlii Sauppe).

Καλλικράτης Χαροπίδου Λαμπτρεύς (*PA* 7946 + 7973 + 8213). Proposes two decrees of the people: (1) honours for Kephisodoros, 346/5 (*IG* II² 215.5-6); (2) concerning the Tenedians, 340/339 (*IG* II² 233.5).

Καλλιμέδων (*PA* 8030, *APF*). Ambassador to Tiribazos, 392/1 (Xen. *Hell.* 4.8.13).

Καλλιμέδων Καλλικράτους Κολλυτεύς (*PA* 8032, *APF*). Defendant in an *eisangelia* (no. 129), 324/3 (Din. 1.94).

Κάλλιππος Φίλωνος Αἰξωνεύς (*PA* 8065, *APF*). Defendant in an *eisangelia* (no. 92), 361/0 (Dem. 36.53).

Κάλλιππος Παιανιεύς (*PA* 8078). Proposes a decree of the people concerning klerouchs near Kardia, ca 357 (Dem. 7.42-43). Defendant in a *graphe paranomon* (no. 11), ca 357 (Dem. 7.42-43).

Καλλισθένης (*PA* 8088). Ambassador to Tiribazos, 392/1 (Xen. *Hell.* 4.8.13).

Καλλισθένης (*PA* 8089). Defendant in an *eisangelia* (no. 85), 363/2 (Aeschin. 2.30, Arist. *Rh.* 1380b10ff). Strategos in 363/2 (Aeschin. 2.30).

Καλλισθένης (*PA* 8090). Proposes two decrees of the people: (1) alliance with Ketriporis, Lyppeios, and Grabos, 356/5 (*IG* II² 127.7); (2) concerning the evacuation of Attika, 347/6 (Dem. 18.37, 19.86 + schol.). Defendant in an *eisangelia* (no. 118), after 336 (Din. fr.xix Con.).

Καλλισθένης Χαροπίδου Τρινεμεύς (*PA* 8106). Proposes in the *boule* an honorary decree for three councillors, 328/7 (*Agora* XV 49.41).

Καλλίστρατος Καλλικράτους Ἀφιδναῖος (*PA* 8157 + 8129 + 8130, *APF*). Proposes four decrees of the people: (1) impeachment of four ambassadors to Sparta, 392/1 (Philoch. F149a); (2) rider to an honorary decree for Polychartides and Alkibiades, 378-376 (?) (*IG* II² 84.9-10); (3) armed assistance to the Lakedaimonians, 370/369 (Dem. 59.27); (4) answer to the Mytilenian ambassadors, 369/8 (*IG* II² 107.36). Brings six *eisangeliai*: (1-4) against the four ambassadors to Sparta (nos. 69-72), 392/1 (Philoch. F149a); (5) against Timotheos (no. 80), 373/2 (Dem. 49.9-10); (6) against Antimachos (no. 81), 373/2 (Dem. 49.9-10). Brings an *euthynai* (?) against Melanopos, before 361

UPDATED INVENTORY OF RHETORES AND STRATEGOI (1988)

(Arist. *Rh.* 1374b25-26). Defendant in (1) an *eisangelia* (no. 83), 366/5 (Arist. *Rh.* 1364a19-23); (2) an *eisangelia* (no. 87), 362/1 (Hyp. 3.1-2). Ambassador (1) to Sparta, 372/1 (Xen. *Hell.* 6.3.3); (2) to Arkadia and Messene, 363/2 (Nep. *Epam.* 6, Arist. *Rh.* 1418b10). *Strategos*, 378/7 (Diod. 15.29.7); 373/2 (Xen. *Hell.* 6.2.39); 372/1 (*Hell.* 6.3.3).

Καλλίστρατος Θορίκιος (*PA* 8168). Proposes in the *boule* a decree concerning naval equipment, 330/329 or earlier (*IG* II² 1627.374-95 etc.).

Κέφαλος Κολλυτεύς (*PA* 8277). Proposes two decrees of the people: (1) rider to honours for Phanokritos, 387/6 (*IG* II² 29.6); (2) armed assistance to Thebes against Sparta, 379/8 (Din. 1.39). Proposes innumerable decrees (Aeschin. 3.194). *Synegoros* for Andokides in an *endeixis* (no. 10), 400/399 (Andoc. 1.150). Ambassador to Chios, 384/3 (*IG* II² 34.35-36).

Κήδων (*PA* 8281). *Strategos*, 376/5 (Diod. 15.34.5).

Κηφίσιος (*PA* 8288). Brings an *endeixis* (no. 10) against Andokides, 400/399 (Andoc. 1.33, 121-22).

Κηφισόδοτος (not in *PA*). Proposes in the *ecclesia* an honorary decree for Demades, 336/5 (*Lex.Patm.* 159f s. v. ἑκατόμπεδον). Defendant in a *graphe paranomon* (no. 31), 336/5 (*Lex.Patm.*).

Κηφισόδοτος 'Αρχίππου (?) 'Αχαρνεύς (?) (*PA* 8313 + 8326). Addresses the *boule* as *synegoros* for Apollodoros, 360/359 (Dem. 51.1). Defendant in an *eisangelia* (no. 96), 360/359 (Dem. 23.167, Aeschin. 3.51-52). *Strategos*, 360/359 (Dem. 23.163). For the demotic *cf.* Anaxandrides fr.41.18. For the patronymic *cf. IG* II² 5787a.

Κηφισόδοτος Εὐαρχίδου 'Αχαρνεύς (*PA* 8327). Proposes in the *boule* an honorary decree for Herakleides of Salamis, 330-328 (*IG* II² 360.51).

Κηφισόδοτος ἐκ Κεραμέων (*PA* 8331). Proposes four decrees of the people: (1) concerning the command of the allied forces, 369/8 (Xen. *Hell.* 7.1.12-14); (2) concerning the Aitolian League, '367/6 (*Hesperia* 8 [1939] 5-12 no. 3); (3) honours for Straton of Sidon, ca 364 (?) (*IG* II² 141.30); (4) providing for armed assistance sent to Euboia, 358/7 (Arist. *Rh.* 1411a6-11). Addresses the *ecclesia* opposing Chares, 348/7 (Arist. *Rh.* 1411a6). *Syndikos* elected to defend Leptines' law, 355/4 (Dem. 20.146, 150). Ambassador to Sparta, 372/1 (Xen. *Hell.* 6.3.2).

Κηφισόδωρος (*PA* 8351). Addresses the *ecclesia*, before 329 (?) (Timokles fr.16 K.).

Κηφισοφῶν Κεφαλίωνος 'Αφιδναῖος (*PA* 8410, *APF*). *Strategos*, 345/4 (?) (*IG* II 701 = II² 1443.112-13, *cf. APF*); 342/1 (Philoch. F159); 341/0 (?) (*IG* II² 1623.35-37, *cf. APF*); 340/339 (*IG* II² 1628.438, 1629.959). Member of the Theoric Board, 343/2 (*IG* II² 223C.6). In *IG* II² 244.2 his name is restored as the proposer of the *nomos* for repair of the walls.

Κηφισοφῶν Παιανιεύς (*PA* 8400 + 8401 + 8415 + 8416, *APF*). Proposes in the *ecclesia* an honorary decree for the Samians, 403/2 (*IG* II² 1.42, 51).

Κηφισοφῶν Καλλιβίου Παιανιεύς (*PA* 8417, *APF*). Proposes four decrees of the people: (1) concerning a message sent to Chares, 347/6 (*Ath. Eccl.* 45, 64) (Aeschin. 2.73); (2) honours for the *boule*, 343/2 (*IG* II² 223B.7-9); (3) concerning Philip, 346-340 (Dem. 18.75); (4) rider to honours for Asklepiodoros, 337/6 (*IG* II² 276.23-24). Addresses the *ecclesia* in support of Philokrates, 347/6 (Dem. 18.21).

Κηφισοφῶν Λυσιφῶντος Χολαργεύς (*PA* 8419). Proposes a decree of the people regulating the despatch of a squadron to the Adriatic, 325/4 (*IG* II² 1629.170). Defendant in an *apophasis* in consequence of the Harpalos affair, 324/3 (Din. 1.45; for the identification *cf. APF* 149).

Κίμων Λακιάδης (?) (*PA* 8424, *APF*). Ambassador to Philip three (?) times in 347/6 (1: Aeschin. 2.21; 2 [?]: Dem. 19.163-65; 3 [?]: Dem. 19.121).

Κινησίας Μέλητος (*PA* 8438). Proposes in the *boule* (?) an honorary dcecree for Dionysios I, 394/3 (*IG* II² 18.5). Brings a *graphe paranomon* (no. 6) against Phanias, 400-380 (Lys. fr.143).

Κλειτόμαχος (not in *PA*). Ambassador to the Peloponnese, 343/2 (Dem. 9.72 *vulg.*, *om.* **SFYO**). The names of Kleitomachos and Lykourgos are omitted by the best MSS.: but Plut. *Mor.* 841E shows that Lykourgos did serve on the embassy, and so I am prepared to accept Kleitomachos as well.

Κλεόβουλος Γλαύκου Ἀχαρνεύς (*PA* 8558, *APF*). *Strategos*, 389/8 (Aeschin. 2.78).

Κόνων Τιμοθέου Ἀναφλύστιος (*PA* 8707, *APF*). Brings an *eisangelia* (no. 68) against Adeimantos, 393/2 (?) (Dem. 19.191). Ambassador to Tiribazos, 392/1 (Xen. *Hell.* 4.8.13). *Strategos* (?), 394/3, 393/2 (?) (Harp. *s. v.* ξενικὸν ἐν Κορίνθῳ).

Κόνων Τιμοθέου Ἀναφλύστιος (*PA* 8708, *APF*). *Strategos*, 334/3 (*IG* II² 2970.5 [*SEG* XXII 148]); 333/2 (*IG* II² 2976.9, *Hesperia* 9 [1940] 62-63 no. 8.ii9-10).

Κρατῖνος (*PA* 8752). Proposes three decrees of the people: (1) honours for Astykrates, 363/2 (*IG* II² 109a.7, b.8); (2) honours for ?, 354/3 (*IG* II² 134.6); (3) honours for Democharis, before 353/2 (*IG* II² 172.3-4). Addresses the *ecclesia*, 363/2 (*SEG* XXI 241.4).

Κρατῖνος Σφήττιος (*PA* 8757a). Defendant in an *eisangelia* (no. 71), 392/1 (Philoch. F149a). Ambassador to Sparta, 392/1 (Philoch.).

Κρίτιος (*PA* 8798). Proposes in the *ecclesia* an alliance with the Korkyraeans, the Akarnanians, and the Kephallenians, 375/4 (*IG* II² 96.4-5).

Κτησικλῆς (*PA* 8861). *Strategos*, 393/2 (?) (Lys. 9.6); 374/3 (Diod. 15.46.3); 373/2 (Xen. *Hell.* 6.2.10 [νησικλεα or στησικλεα], Diod. 15.47.4).

Κτησικλῆς Βατῆθεν (*PA* 8868). Proposes in the *boule* an honorary decree for Lykourgos, before 324 (*IG* II² 3207, *cf. supra* Δημέας Σφήττιος).

Κτησιφῶν (*PA* 8893). Addresses the *ecclesia* in support of a conclusion of peace with Philip, 347/6 (Dem. 19.12). Ambassador (1) to Philip, 348/7 (Aeschin.

2.12); (2) to Philip three (?) times, 347/6 (1: Aeschin. 2.42; 2 [?]: Dem. 19.163-65; 3 [?]: Dem. 19.121).

Κτησιφῶν (*PA* 8894). Proposes in the *ecclesia* an honorary decree for Demosthenes, 337/6 (Aeschin. 3.12, 34, 49, 53, 101, 155, 236-37, etc.). Defendant in a *graphe paranomon* (no. 30), 330/329 (Aeschin. 3.9, Dem. 18.13, etc.). Ambassador to Kleopatra, 330/329 (Aeschin. 3.242).

Κυδίας (*PA* 8924). Addresses the *ecclesia* concerning klerouchs to Samos, 365-362 (Arist. *Rh.* 1384b32).

Λάχης Λάχητος (?) Αἰξωνεύς (?) (*PA* 9018). *Strategos*, 364/3 (Diod. 15.79.1).

Λεόντιχος (*PA* 9036). *Strategos*, 388/7 (Xen. *Hell.* 5.1.26).

Λεπτίνης ἐκ Κοίλης (*PA* 9046, *APF*). Proposes a *nomos* on *ateleia*, 356/5 (Dem. 20.95, 128, etc.). Addresses the *ecclesia* concerning an alliance with Sparta, 370/369 (Arist. *Rh.* 1411a4-5). Elected *syndikos* defending his own law, 355/4 (Dem. 20.144, 146): Leptines is not defendant (20.144), but probably the fifth *syndikos* (20.146, *cf.* Dem. 24.23 referring to the similar *nomothesia*).

Λεωδάμας Ἐρασιστράτου (?) Ἀχαρνεύς (*PA* 9077, *APF*). Brings a *graphe paranomon* (no. 7) against ?, 376/5 (Dem. 20.146). Brings two *eisangeliai*: (1) against Kallistratos (no. 83), 366/5 (Arist. *Rh.* 1364a19-21); (2) against Chabrias (no. 84), 366/5 (*Rh.* 1364a21-23). Elected *syndikos* defending Leptines' law, 355/4 (Dem. 20.146). Ambassador to Thebes, 370's (Aeschin. 3.139).

Λεωκράτης (*PA* 9083). Defendant in an *eisangelia* (no. 121), 331/0 (Lycurg. 1.1, Aeschin. 3.252).

Λέων (*PA* 9101). Brings an *eisangelia* (no. 82) against Timagoras, 368/7 (Dem. 19.191, Xen. *Hell.* 7.1.38). Ambassador to the king of Persia, 368/7 (*Hell.* 7.1.33).

Λεωσθένης Κεφαλῆθεν (*PA* 9141, *APF*). Defendant in an *eisangelia* (no. 88), 362/1 (Hyp. 3.1-2). *Strategos*, 362/1 (Diod. 15.95.2).

Λεωσθένης Λεωσθένους Κεφαλῆθεν (*PA* 9142 + 9144, *APF*). Addresses the *boule*, 323/2 (Diod. 17.111.3). *Strategos*, 324/3 (Reinmuth no. 15.b4-6); 323/2 (Plut. *Phoc.* 23, Paus. 1.25.5).

Λύκαιθος (*PA* 9189). Ambassador to Sparta, 372/1 (Xen. *Hell.* 6.3.2).

Λυκῖνος (*PA* 9198). Brings a *graphe paranomon* (no. 17) against Philokrates, 348/7 (Aeschin. 2.14, 3.62).

Λυκολέων (*PA* 9226). *Synegoros* for Chabrias in an *eisangelia* (no. 84), 366/5 (Arist. *Rh.* 1411b6-7).

Λυκοῦργος Λυκόφρονος Βουτάδης (*PA* 9251 + 9247, *APF*). Proposes eleven decrees of the people: (1) honours for ?, 336/5 (*IG* II^2 328.8-9); (2) the despatch of a squadron against pirates, 335/4 (*IG* II^2 1623.281-82); (3) honours for Diotimos, 334/3 (*IG* II^2 414a [*SEG* XXI 276], Plut. *Mor.* 844A). (4) payment concerning the Eleusinion, 333/2 or earlier (*IG* II² 1673.65); (5) permitting the Kitians to erect a temple, 333/2 (*IG* II² 337.31-32); (6) honours for a Plataean, 332/1 (*IG* II² 345.9-10); (7) honours for Neoptolemos, 338-330 (Dem. 18.114, Plut. *Mor.* 843F); (8) honours for Eudemos, 330/329 (*IG* II² 351.10-11); (9) payment to *hieropoioi*, 329/8 (?) (*IG* II² 1672.303); (10) honours for an *epimeletes*, 328/7 (*IG* II² 452.11 [*SEG* XXI 284]); (11) honours for Sopatros, before 324 (*Hesperia* 43 [1974] 322-24 no. 3). Proposes in the *boule* a decree concerning a sacrifice, 329/8 (?) (*IG* II² 1672.302). Proposes six *nomoi*: (1) concerning various offerings, 335/4 (*IG* II² 333.14); (2) concerning comic actors; (3) concerning statues and authorized texts of Aischylos, Sophokles, and Euripides; (4) prohibition against buying freeborn captives for slaves; (5) concerning a festival of Poseidon; (6) concerning women's transport to Eleusis by carriage, all before 324 (Plut. *Mor.* 841F-842A). Brings four *eisangeliai*: (1) against Lysikles (no. 112), 338/7 (Lycurg. fr.xii Con); (2) against Autolykos (no. 113),338/7 (fr.iii); (3) against Leokrates (no. 121), 331/0 (Lycurg. 1.1, 5, etc.); (4) against Menesaichmos (no. 126), before 325/4 (fr.xiv). Brings an *endeixis* (no. 32) against Aristogeiton, 325/4 (Dem. 25.1, 14; Din. 2.13). Addresses the *ecclesia* (1) opposing the extradition of ten leading Athenians, 335/4 (Plut. *Phoc.* 9.10); (2) opposing the deification of Alexander, 324/3 (Plut. *Mor.* 842D). *Synegoros* (1) for Ariston in an *eisangelia* (no. 119), ca 333 (Lycurg. frr.x-xi Con); (2) for Polyeuktos of Kydantidai in an *eisangelia* (no. 124), 330-324 (Hyp. 3.12); (3) for Polyeuktos of Sphettos in a *graphe paranomon* (nos. 31, 36 [?], 336/5 (Lycurg. fr.ix Con.). Defendant in an *euthynai*, before 324 (Din. fr.viii Con-.). Ambassador to the Peloponnese, 343/2 (Dem. 9.72 [om. **SFYO**]; Plut. *Mor.* 841E). ὁ ἐπὶ τῇ διοικήσει, 330's and 320's (Hyp. fr.139).

Λυκόφρων (*PA* 9255). Defendant in an *eisangelia* (no. 119), ca 333 (Hyp. 2.3, 20).

Λυσίθεος (*PA* 9399). Brings a *dokimasia rhetoron* against Theomnestos, 394-384 (Lys. 10.1): I follow Gernet/Bizos in emending εἰσήγγελλε to ἐπήγγελλε, cf. *JHS* 100 (1980) 89.

Λυσικλῆς (*PA* 9422). Defendant in an *eisangelia* (no. 112), 338/7 (Lycurg. fr.xii Con.). *Strategos*, 338/7 (Diod. 16.88.1).

Λυσικράτης Οἰναῖος (*PA* 9465). Ambassador to Thrace, 356/5 (*IG* II² 127.36).

Λυσίστρατος (*PA* 9598). *Strategos*, 366/5 (?) (Xen. *Vect.* 3.7).

Μαντίας Μαντιθέου Θορίκιος (*PA* 9667, *APF*). *Strategos*, 360/359 (Diod. 16.2.6).

Μαντίθεος (*PA* 9674, cf. *APF* 364). Addresses the *ecclesia*, ca 400 (Lys. 16.20).

Μειδίας Κηφισοδώρου Ἀναγυράσιος (*PA* 9719, *APF*). Proposes some *nomoi* concerning the cavalry, 349/8 (Dem. 21.173; Goodwin *ad loc.* suggests that Meidias as a hipparch, procured the enactment of laws he did not personally propose). Addresses the *ecclesia* (1) accusing the retiring *boule*, 356/5 (Dem. 22.10); (2) accusing the *hippeis*, 349/8 (Dem. 21.197); (3) on numerous other occasions

UPDATED INVENTORY OF *RHETORES* AND *STRATEGOI* (1988)

(Dem. 21.153, 202). Addresses the *boule* suggesting the arrest of Aristarchos, 348/7 (Dem. 21.116). *Pylagoros*, 340/339 (Aeschin. 3.115).

Μειδίας Μειδίου 'Αναγυράσιος (*PA* 9720, *APF*). Proposes in the *ecclesia* an honorary decree for Phokion, before 322 (Hyp. fr.150). Defendant in a *graphe paranomon* (no. 39), before 322 (Hyp. fr.150).

Μελάντης Ποτάμιος (*PA* 9779 + 9780). Brings a public action against Demosthenes, 338/7 (Dem. 18.249). Melantes is mentioned as one of Demosthenes' prosecutors in the period after Chaironeia. The type of public action employed was either a *graphe (paranomon)* or an *eisangelia* or an *euthynai, cf.* Hansen, *Eisangelia* 10-11.

Μελάνωπος Λάχητος Αἰξωνεύς (*PA* 9788). Proposes a decree of the people appointing a *keryx*, 366/5 (*IG* II^2 145.13). Brings a *graphe paranomon* (no. 13) against Euktemon, 355/4 (Dem. 24.13-14). Addresses the *ecclesia* frequently (Plut. *Dem.* 13.3). Defendant in an *euthynai* (1) before 361 (Arist. *Rh.* 1374b25); (2) before 353 (Dem. 24.127). Ambassador (1) to Sparta, 372/1 (Xen. *Hell.* 6.3.2); (2) to Egypt, before 354 (Dem. 24.127); (3) to Mausolos, 355/4 (Dem. 24.12). *Strategos*, 355/4 (*IG* II^2 150, restored).

Μέλητος (*PA* 9825). *Synegoros* for Kephisios in an *endeixis* (no. 10), 400/399 (Andoc. 1.94).

Μενέλαος Μενελόχου Μυρρινούσιος (*PA* 9963, *APF*). Ambassador to the king of Persia, 341/0 (?) (Lycurg. 1.24).

Μενέξενος (*PA* 9972). Proposes two decrees of the people: (1) amendment to honours for Straton of Sidon, 364/3 (?) (*IG* II^2 141.29); (2) repayment to Athens of a debt of 3 talents, before 363/2 (*IG* II^2 111.8-9).

Μενέσαιχμος (*PA* 9983). Elected prosecutor in the *apophasis* in consequence of the Harpalos affair, 324/3 (Plut. *Mor.* 846C). Defendant in an *eisangelia* (no. 126), 325/4 (Lycurg. fr.xiv Con.). ὁ ἐπὶ τῇ διοικήσει, before 324 (Dion. Hal. *Din.* 660, *cf.* Sauppe 343).

Μενεσθεύς 'Ιφικράτους 'Ραμνούσιος (*PA* 9988, *APF*). Defendant in an *eisangelia* (no. 102), 356/5 (Isoc. 15.129, Dion. Hal. *Din.* 668). *Strategos*, 356/5 (Dion. Hal. *Din.* 668, Nep. *Timoth.* 3.2); 333/2 (?) (Dem. 17.20).

Μένων Ποτάμιος (*PA* 10085). Defendant in an *eisangelia* (no. 95), 361/0 (Dem. 36.53). *Strategos*, 362/1 (Dem. 50.12); 357/6 (*IG* II^2 124.21).

Μοιροκλῆς 'Ελευσίνιος (?) (*PA* 10400 + 10401). Proposes a decree of the people concerning offences against *emporoi*, before 342 (Dem. 58.53, 56). Addresses the assembly although formally imprisoned, before 324 (Dem. *Ep.* 3.16; *cf.* *Hesperia* 8 [1939] 180).

Μολοττός (*PA* 10403). *Strategos*, 349/8 (Plut. *Phoc.* 14.2, Paus. 1.36.4).

Μονιππίδης (*PA* 10414). Proposes in the *ecclesia* an honorary decree for Kleonymides, 403/2 (*IG* II² 7.3-4). Proposes in the *boule* an honorary decree for the sons of Apemantos, 403/2 (*IG* II² 6.7).

Ναυσικλῆς Κλεάρχου 'Οῆθεν (*PA* 10552, *APF*). Proposes a decree of the people concerning naval equipment, 334/3 (*IG* II² 1623.313); responsible proposer of several of Demosthenes' decrees, 338/7 (Aeschin. 3.159). Proposes in the *ecclesia* the election of Aischines as envoy to Philip, 347/6 (Aeschin. 2.18). *Synegoros* for Aischines in an *euthynai*, 343/2 (Aeschin. 2.184). Ambassador to Philip three (?) times, 347/6 (1; Dem. 19 hypoth. 2.4; 2 [?]: Dem. 19.163-65; 3 [?]: Dem. 19.121). *Strategos*, 352/1 (Diod. 16.37.3); before 334/3 (*IG* II² 1623.329-30).

Νεοπτόλεμος Σκύριος (*PA* 10647). Addresses the *ecclesia* in support of peace with Philip, 347/6 (Dem. 19.12, 315).

Νικήρατος Νικίου Κυδαντίδης (*PA* 10742, *APF*). *Tamias stratiotikon*, 345/4 or 344/3 (*IG* II² 1443.13).

Νικόμαχος (*PA* 10934). Defendant in an *eisangelia* (no. 140), 399/8 (Lys. 30).

Νικομένης (*PA* 10968). Proposes in the *ecclesia* (?) a decree (*nomos?*) about citizenship, 403/2 (?) (schol. Aeschin. 1.39; *cf. Ath. Eccl.* 166, 177).

Νικόστρατος Θοραιεύς (*PA* 11029). Ambassador to Olynthos, 376/5 (?) (*IG* II² 36.4).

Νικοφῶν (not in *PA*). Proposes a *nomos* on silver coinage, 375/4 (*Hesperia* 43 [1974] 157-88).

Νόθιππος Λυσίου Διομειεύς (*PA* 11131). Proposes in the *ecclesia* an honorary decree for Rheboulas, 331/0 (*IG* II² 349.9-10).

Ξενόδοκος 'Αχαρνεύς (*PA* 11192). Ambassador to Byzantion, 378/7 (*IG* II² 41.19).

Ξενοκλείδης (*PA* 11197). Addresses the *ecclesia* opposing Kallistratos, 370/369 (Dem. 59.26-27).

Ξενοκλῆς Ξεινίδος Σφήττιος (*PA* 11234, *APF*). ὁ ἐπὶ τῇ διοικήσει, *ca* 330 (?) (*Hesperia* 29 [1960] 2-4 no. 3).

Ξενότιμος (not in *PA*). Proposes in the *boule* an honorary decree for Kommaios, *ca*. 400 (*IG* II² 77 + *Add*.; *cf. IG* I³ p.196).

'Ορθόβουλος ἐκ Κεραμέων (*PA* 11489). Ambassador to Byzantion, 378/7 (*IG* II² 41.17).

Πάμφιλος Εὐφιλήτου Κηφισιεύς (*PA* 11531, *APF*). Proposes in the *ecclesia* an amendment to an honorary decree for Euphron, 323/2 (*IG* II² 448.31).

Πάμφιλος 'Αχερδούσιος (*PA* 11540). Brings an *eisangelia* (no. 143) against Timarchos, 361/0 (Aeschin. 1.109-12).

Πάμφιλος Κειριάδης (*PA* 11545, *APF*). Defendant in an *euthynai* (?), 389/8 (?)

UPDATED INVENTORY OF *RHETORES* AND *STRATEGOI* (1988)

(Ar. *Plut.* 174-75 with schol.; Plat. *Com.* fr.14 K.; Dem. 40.20, 22). *Strategos*, 390/389, 389/8 (Xen. *Hell.* 5.1.2).

Πάνδιος (*PA* 11575). Proposes two decrees of the people: (1) honours for Dionysios, 369/8 (*IG* II² 103.6); (2) alliance with Dionysios, 368/7 (*IG* II² 105.6). Proposes in the *boule* a decree concerning repairs to the Amphiaraion at Oropos, 369/8 (*AE* [1923] 36ff).

Πάταιχος 'Ελευσίνιος (*PA* 11676-79, *APF*). Addresses the *ecclesia* although formally imprisoned, before 324 (Dem. *Ep.* 3.16).

Πεισιάναξ Σουνιεύς (*PA* 11776, *APF*). Ambassador to Thrace, 357/6 (*IG* II² 127.15, 31).

Περίανδρος Πολυαράτου Χολαργεύς (*PA* 11800, *APF*). Proposes in the *ecclesia* an alliance with the Peloponnesian *poleis*, 362/1 (*IG* II² 112.5-6). Proposes a *nomos* on naval symmories, 358/7 (Dem. 47.21).

Πιστίας (*PA* 11823). Prosecutor in an *apophasis* against the speaker of Deinarchos 1 (?), 336-324 (Din. 1.48-53). Defendant in an *eisangelia* (no. 117), 336-324 (Din. 1.48-53, fr.xv Con.).

Πολίαγρος (*PA* 11893). Proposes a decree of the people concerning Klazomenai, 387/6 (*IG* II² 28.3).

Πολύευκτος Καλλικράτους 'Εστιαιόθεν (*PA* 11943). Proposes in the *boule* a decree concerning a naval debt, 324/3 (*IG* II² 1631.350-51).

Πολύευκτος Τιμοκράτους Κριωεύς (*PA* 11946, *APF*). Proposes in the *ecclesia* an amendment to the honorary decree for the Bosporan princes, 347/6 (*IG* II² 212.65-66).

Πολύευκτος Κυδαντίδης (*PA* 11947 + 11928 + 11927 [?]). Proposes two decrees of the people: (1) concerning some triremes, 326/5 (*IG* II² 1628.38-39); (2) concerning Oropos, 330-324 (Hyp. 3.15-17). Brings an *eisangelia* (no. 124) against Euxenippos, 330-324 (Hyp. 3.41, *cf.* 12). Defendant in (1) a *graphe paranomon* (no. 35), 330-324 (Hyp. 3.15-18); (2) an *endeixis* (no. 31), 326/5 (Din. fr.ii Con.); (3) an *apophasis*, 324/3 (Din. 1.58-59). *Synedros* in the Korinthian *synedrion*, before 324 (Hyp. 3.20, *cf.* G. T. Griffith, *History of Macedonia* II [Oxford 1979] 638 n. 1).

Πολύευκτος (*PA* 11947 [?]). *Strategos*, 360-322 (Hyp. fr.xlv.182-84). According to *PA* the reference is to Polyeuktos of Kydantidai.

Πολύευκτος Σωστράτου Σφήττιος (*PA* 11925 + 11934 + 11950). Proposes four decrees of the people: (1) concerning Neapolis, 356/5 (*IG* II² 128.8); (2) honours for ?, 332/1 (*IG* II² 344.11-12); (3) honours for Theophantos, 332/1 (*IG* II² 368.8, *cf.* Walbank in *ZPE* 48 [1982] 266-but 9 [?] spaces for the demotic); (4) honours for Dionysios, 326/5 (*IG* II² 363.7-8 [*SEG* XII 89]). Brings a *graphe paranomon* (no. 31) against Kephisodotos, 336/5 (Polyeuktos frr.1-2 Sauppe). Defendant in an *apophasis* in consequence of the Harpalos affair, 324/3 (Din. 1.100). Ambassador (1) to the Peloponnese, 343/2 (Dem. 9.72, Plut. Mor. 841E); (2) to Arkadia, 323/2 (Plut. Mor. 846C-D).

Πολυκράτης Πολυκράτους (not in PA). Proposes in the ecclesia an honorary decree for Orontes, 340/39 (?) (IG II² 207a.2).

Πολύξενος (not in PA). Syndikos in the Delian affair (?), 343 (?) (Sauppe 344 no. lxxi).

Πολύχαρμος (PA 12105). Addresses the ecclesia regularly, 4th c. (?) (Plut. Mor. 726B).

Προκλείδης Πανταλέοντος ἐκ Κεραμέων (PA 12200). Proposes in the ecclesia an honorary decree for Androkles, 328/7 (IG II² 354.8-9).

Προκλῆς (PA 12208). Elected prosecutor in the apophasis in consequence of the Harpalos affair, 324/3 (Plut. Mor. 846C).

Πρόξενος ‘Αρμοδίου ’Αφιδναῖος (PA 12270, APF). Defendant in an apophasis, 346-343 (Dem. 19.280 and schol., Din. 1.63). Strategos, 347/6 (Aeschin. 2.133); 340/339 (?) (IG II² 207d.23); 339/8 (Polyaen. 4.2.8).

Πρωτόμαχος (not in PA). Strategos, 339/8 (?) (FGrHist 390Fl.31).

Πυθέας (PA 12342). Elected prosecutor in the apophasis in consequence of the Harpalos affair, 324/3 (Plut. Mor. 846C, Dem. Ep. 3.29, Pytheas fr.iii). Addresses the ecclesia opposing the deification of Alexander, 324/3 (Plut. Mor. 804B). Defendant in an eisangelia (no. 116), 336-324 (Din. fr.vi Con.).

Πυθοκλῆς Πυθοδώρου ἐκ Κήδων (PA 12444, APF). Addresses the ecclesia opposing Demosthenes, 338/7 (Dem. 18.285).

Πυθόνικος (PA 12458 [?]). Proposes in the boule a proxeny decree for Komaios, ca. 400 (IG II² 77 + Add.; cf. IG I³ p.196).

Πύρρανδρος ’Αναφλύστιος (PA 12496). Proposes in the ecclesia an alliance with the Chalkidians, 378/7 (IG II² 44.7). Addresses the ecclesia commenting on a report made by the Areopagos, 347/6 (Aeschin. 1.84). Ambassador (1) to Byzantion, 378/7 (IG II² 41.20); (2) to Thebes, 378/7 (IG II² 43.76, Aeschin. 3.139).

‘Ρίνων Χαρικλέους Παιανιεύς (PA 12532, APF). Strategos, 403/2 (Arist. Ath.Pol. 38.4).

Σάτυρος (PA 12575). Proposes in the ecclesia an honorary decree for Menelaos, 363/2 (IG II² 110.6, 20).

Σκίτων (not in PA). Proposes a decree of the people, before 347 (Dem. 21.182). Defendant in a graphe paranomon (no. 19), before 347 (Dem. 21.182).

Σμίκρος (not in PA). Proposes a decree of the people, before 347 (Dem. 21.182). Defendant in a graphe paranomon (no. 20), before 347 (Dem. 21.182).

Σπουδίας (PA 12861). Strategos, 368/7 (IG II² 104.3).

UPDATED INVENTORY OF *RHETORES* AND *STRATEGOI* (1988)

Στέφανος (*PA* 12879). Proposes a decree of the people concerning a water-pipe, after 336 (Din. fr.xviii Con.). Defendant in a *graphe paranomon* (no. 33), after 336 (Din.).

Στέφανος (not in *PA*). Proposes in the *ecclesia* an alliance with Thebes, 378/7 (*IG* II² 40.4 [*Staatsvertr.* II 255]).

Στέφανος 'Αντιδωρίδου 'Εροιάδης (*PA* 12887). Proposes in the *ecclesia* an alliance with Mytilene, 347/6 (*IG* II² 213.5). Regularly moves decrees on behalf of others (Dem. 59.43). Brings a *graphe paranomon* (no. 18) against Apollodoros, 349/8 (Dem. 59.5). Ambassador to Philip, 347/6 (third embassy) (Aeschin. 2.140).

Στρατοκλῆς Λακιάδης (?) (*PA* 12931 + 12941). *Strategos*, 339/8 (Aeschin. 3.143); 338/7 (Polyaen. 4.2.2). For the demotic cf. *Hesperia* 33 [1964] 55-58 no. 16.

Στρατοκλῆς Εὐθυδήμου Διομειεύς (*PA* 12938, *APF*). Elected prosecutor in the *apophasis* in consequence of the Harpalos affair, 324/3 (Din. 1.1).

Σωσικλῆς (*PA* 13232). Brings a public action against Demosthenes, 338/7 (Dem. 18.249, cf. *supra* Μελάντης).

Σώφιλος (*PA* 13414). Proposes two decrees of the people: (1) honours for Phil---, 394/3 (*IG* II² 19.4-5); (2) honours for Euagoras, 394/3 (*IG* II² 20 [*Hesperia* 48 (1979) 180-93]).

Σώφιλος 'Αριστοτέλους Φυλάσιος (*PA* 13422). *Strategos*, 334/3 (*IG* II² 2970.6 = Reinmuth no. 4); 333/2 (*Hesperia* 9 [1940] no. 8.ii.11).

Ταυρέας (*PA* 13430). Addresses the *ecclesia* although formally imprisoned, before 324 (Dem. *Ep.* 3.16). = Ταυρέας Πυθοκλέους Πιθεύς ? (*Agora* XV 62.220).

Τεισαμενὸς Μηχανιῶνος (*PA* 13443). Proposes a decree of the people regulating the codification of the laws, 403/2 (Andoc. 1.83-84).

Τελεσήγορος Κολλυτεύς (?) (*PA* 13512). Ambassador to the king of Persia, 397/6 (*Hell. Oxy.* 7.1).

Τηλέμαχος Θεαγγέλου 'Αχαρνεύς (*PA* 13562). Proposes three decrees of the people: (1) unknown content, 339/8 (*Hesperia* 7 [1938] 291-92 no. 18); (2-3) honours for Herakleides, 330-328 (*IG* II² 360.28, 46).

Τιμαγόρας (*PA* 13595). Defendant in an *eisangelia* (no. 82), 368/7 (Xen. *Hell.* 7.1.38, Dem. 19.191). Ambassador to the king of Persia, 368/7 (Xen. *Hell.* 7.1.33).

Τίμαρχος 'Αριζήλου Σφήττιος (*PA* 13636). Proposes two decrees of the people: (1) concerning export of weapons to Philip, 347/6 (Dem. 19.286-87); (2) concering public works on the Pnyx, 346/5 (Aeschin. 1.81). Proposes more than one hundred decrees (Aeschin. 1 hypoth., *Suda s. v.*). Brings a *graphe nomon me epitedeion theinai*, 346/5 (Aeschin. 1.34). Addresses the *boule* frequently, 347/6 (Aeschin. 1.80). Defendant in (1) an *eisangelia* (no. 143), 361/0 (Aeschin.

1.109-12); (2) a *dokimasia rhetoron*, 346/5 (Aeschin. 1.2, 81). Ambassador on several occasions to unknown destinations, before 346/5 (Aeschin. 1.120).

Τιμόθεος Κόνωνος 'Αναφλύστιος (*PA* 13700, *APF*). Addresses the *ecclesia* in support of a campaign to Euboia, 358/7 (Dem. 8.74-75). Defendant in three *eisangeliai*: (1) 373/2 (no. 80: Dem. 49.9-10); (2) *ca* 360 (no. 93: Dem. 36.53); (3) 356/5 (no. 101: Isoc. 15.129, Din. 1.14-16). *Strategos*, 378/7 (Diod. 15.29.7); 376/5 (Xen. *Hell.* 5.4.63); 375/4 (*Hell.* 5.4.66); 374/3 (*Hell.* 6.2.11, Dem. 49.-6); 373/2 (Dem. 49.9, 22), deposed; 367/6 (Dem. 15.9); 366/5 (*IG* II^2 108.10); 365/4 (Isoc. 15.112-13); 364/3 (Dem. 23.149, schol. Aeschin. 2.31); 363/2 (*IG* II^2 110.6); 360/359 (schol. Aeschin. 2.31); 356/5 (Diod. 16.21.1, Dion. Hal. *Lys.* 480).

Τιμοκράτης 'Αντιφῶντος Κριωεύς (*PA* 13772, *APF*). Proposes two *nomoi*: (1) amendment to the eisangeltic law, before 353 (Dem. 24.63); (2) concerning debtors to the state, 354/3 (Dem. 24.39-40, 71). Defendant in a *graphe nomon me epitedeion theinai*, 354/3 (Dem. 24.17, 33).

Τιμόμαχος 'Αχαρνεύς (*PA* 13797, *APF*). Defendant in an *eisangelia* (no. 91), 361/0 (Hyp. 3.1-2). *Strategos*, 367/6 (Xen. *Hell.* 7.1.41); 361/0 (Dem. 50.14).

Τιμόνοθος (*PA* 13799). Ambassador to Lesbos, 368/7 (*IG* II^2 107.32).

Τιμωνίδης (*PA* 13855). Proposes in the *ecclesia* a decree of unknown content, 353/2 (*IG* II^2 139.6).

Ὑπερείδης Γλαυκίππου Κολλυτεύς (*PA* 13912, *APF*). Proposes two decrees of the people: (1) honours for Demosthenes, 339/8 (Dem. 18.223); (2) enfranchising *atimoi*, metics and slaves, 338/7 (Dem. 26.11; Lycurg. 1.36-37, 41; Hyp. fr.32-33). Brings four *graphai paranomon* against (1) Aristophon (no. 10), 363/2 (schol. Aeschin. 1.64); (2) Demades of Paiania (no. 28), 338-336 (Hyp. fr.xiii, *P. Oxy.* 3360); (3) ? (no. 34), after *ca* 335 (Hyp. fr.xxii); (4) Meidias (no. 39), before 322 (Hyp. fr.xxxiii). Brings three *eisangeliai* against: (1) Aristophon (no. 97), 361-343 (Hyp. 3.28); (2) Diopeithes of Sphettos (no. 98), 361-343 (Hyp. 3.29); (3) Philokrates (no. 109), 344/3 (Hyp. 3.29, Dem. 19.116). Addresses the *ecclesia* (Plut. *Mor.* 848E; Hyp. frr.172, 190, 194, 195-96; *P. Oxy.* 3360). *Synegoros* for: (1) Apollodoros in an *eisangelia* (no. 90), 361/0 (Hyp. fr.x); (2) ? in a *graphe paranomon* (no. 32), 336/5 (Hyp. 4); (3) Chairephilos in an *apophasis*, after *ca* 345 (Hyp. fr.lix, *P. Oxy.* 2686); (4) Euxenippos in an *eisangelia* (no. 124), 330-324 (Hyp. 3.41). *Syndikos* in the Delian affair, 343 (?) (Hyp. fr.xii, Dem. 18.134). Elected prosecutor in the *apophasis* in consequence of the Harpalos affair, 324/3 (Hyp. 1). Defendant in two *graphai paranomon*, (1) 339/8 (no. 26: Hyp. fr.xviii); (2) 338/7 (no. 27: Hyp. fr.vi, Aristogeiton fr.iii). Ambassador to (1) Thasos, 361/0 (?) (Hyp. fr.xxiii); (2) Rhodes, 342/1 (Hyp. fr.xlviii); (3) Kythnos (?), 338/7 (Hyp. fr.xxviii); (4) Elis, 332/1 (Hyp. fr.xxv, *P. Oxy.* 3360); (5) the Peloponnese, 323/2 (Just. 13.5.10).

UPDATED INVENTORY OF *RHETORES* AND *STRATEGOI* (1988)

Φαιδρός Καλλίου Σφήττιος (*PA* 13964, *APF*). *Strategos*, 347/6 (*IG* II² 213.8); 334/3 or earlier (*IG* II² 1623.240); 323/2 (Strab. 10.1.6).

Φαίνιππος 'Αζηνιεύς (*PA* 13980). Ambassador to Olynthos, 376/5 (?) (*IG* II² 36.5).

Φανίας (*PA* 14009). *Strategos*, 388/7 (Xen. *Hell.* 5.1.26).

Φανίας (*PA* 14010). Proposes in the *ecclesia* a decree of unknown content, 400-380 (Lys. fr.143). Defendant in a *graphe paranomon* (no. 6), 400-380 (Lys. fr.143).

Φανόδημος Διύλλου Θυμαιτάδης (*PA* 14033). Proposes a decree of the people honouring Amphiaraos, 332/1 (*IG* VII 4252.9-10). Proposes in the *boule* an honorary decree for the retiring *boule*, 343/2 (*IG* II² 223B.1). Proposes a *nomos* on the Amphiaraion, before 332/1 (*Syll.*³ 287.10). Honoured as the best *rhetor* in the *boule*, 343/2 (*IG* II² 223A.6).

Φανόστρατος (*PA* 14097). Brings a *graphe paranomon* (no. 29) against Aristogeiton, 335-330 (Dem. 25 hypoth. 2).

Φειδιάδης (*PA* 14145). Defendant in an *eisangelia* (no. 114), 336-324 (Din. fr.xxiv Con.).

Φερεκλείδης Φερεκλέους Περιθοίδης (*PA* 14187). *Strategos*, ca. 333/2 (*IG* II² 2968.5); 324/3 (Reinmuth no. 15b.4-6, *IG* II² 2968).

Φίλαγρος (*PA* 14203). Proposes in the *ecclesia* an honorary decree for ?, 382/1 (?) (*IG* II² 2.8-9).

Φιλέας 'Αντιγένου Παιονίδης (*PA* 14232+14242). Proposes in the *ecclesia* an honorary decree for an actor, 331/0 (*IG* II² 348.6).

Φιλέφιος Λαμπτρεύς (*PA* 14256). Addresses the *ecclesia* regularly, 390-380 (?) (Baiter/Sauppe 244, *cf.* Dem. 24.134).

Φιλημονίδης (not in *PA*). *Strategos*, ca 330 (*Hesperia* Suppl. 8 [1949] 274).

Φιλΐνος (*PA* 14304). Addresses the *nomothetai* or the *dicastai*, opposing or supporting Lykourgos' *nomos* on bronze statues of the tragic poets, before 324 (Philinos fr.3).

Φιλιππίδης (*PA* 14351). Proposes three decrees of the people: (1-2) unknown content, before 336 (Hyp. 4.11); (3) honours for the board of *proedroi*, 336/5 (Hyp. 4.4-6). Defendant in three *graphai paranomon*: (1-2) before 336 (Hyp. 4.11; (3) 336/5 (no. 32: Hyp. 4).

Φίλιππος (*PA* 14374). Addresses the *boule* frequently, 356/5 (Dem. 22.38). *Synegoros* for Androtion in a *graphe paranomon* (no. 12), 355/4 (Dem. 22.38).

Φίλιππος Φιλίππου (not in *PA*). Proposes a *nomos* of unknown content, before 353 (Dem. 24.138). Defendant in a *graphe nomon me epitedeion theinai*, before 353 (Dem. 24.138).

Φιλόδημος Αυτοκλέους 'Εροιάδης (*PA* 14488, *APF*). Proposes in the *ecclesia* an amendment to an honorary decree for Aratos, 340/339 (*IG* II² 232.18-19).

Φιλοκλῆς Φορμίωνος 'Εροιάδης (*PA* 14521 + 14541, *APF*). Proposes a decree of the people concerning Harpalos, 324/3 (Din. 3.2, 5). Defendant in an *apophasis* in consequence of the Harpalos affair, 324/3 (Din. 3, Dem. *Ep.* 3.31). *Strategos* more than ten times before 324 (Din. 3.12); 325/4 (Din. 3.1).

Φιλοκράτης 'Εφιάλτου (*PA* 14586). *Strategos*, 390/389 (Xen. *Hell.* 4.8.24).

Φιλοκράτης Πυθοδώρου 'Αγνούσιος (*PA* 14599 + 14576). Proposes nine decrees of the people: (1) honours for ?, before 353/2 (*IG* II² 182.5); (2) amendment to honours for Apollodoros and ?, before 353/2 (*IG* II² 182.6); (3) concerning the *hiera orgas*, 352/1 (Androt. F30, Philoch. F155, *IG* II² 204.54-55); (4) concerning envoys from Philip, 348/7 (Aeschin. 2.13); (5) election of ten ambassadors to Philip, 347/6 (Aeschin. 2.18); (6) peace and alliance with Philip, 347/6 (Dem. 18.21, Aeschin. 3.54); (7) concerning the oath on the peace, 347/6 (Aeschin. 3.74); (8) honours for Philip and appointment of ambassadors, 347/6 (Dem. 19.47-48); (9) concerning Philip, 346-343 (Dem. 18.75). Defendant in (1) a *graphe paranomon* (no. 17), 348/7 (Aeschin. 2.13-14); (2) an *eisangelia* (no. 109) 344/3 (Hyp. 3.29-30). Ambassador to Philip three times, 347/6 (1: Aeschin. 2.18, 47; 2: Dem. 19.189; 3: Dem. 19.121). For the patronymic *cf.* *Hesperia* 5 (1936) 393-413 no. 10.46, 111.

Φιλοκράτης 'Επικράτου 'Ελευσίνιος (*PA* 14609). Brings a public action against Demosthenes, 338/7 (Dem. 18.249, *cf. supra* Μελάντης). *Synegoros* for Aristogeiton in an *endeixis* (no. 32), 325/4 (Dem. 25.44).

Φιλόστρατος Διονυσίου Κολωνῆθεν (*PA* 14734, *APF*). *Synegoros* for Leodamas in an *eisangelia* (no. 84), 366/5 (Dem. 21.64).

Φιλοχάρης 'Ατρομήτου Κοθωκίδης (*PA* 14775, *APF*). *Synegoros* for Aischines in an *euthynai*, 343/2 (Aeschin. 2.179, Dem. 19.237). *Strategos*, 345/4, 344/3, 343/2 (Aeschin. 2.149).

Φιλοχάρης 'Ραμνούσιος (*PA* 14779). *Strategos* 357/6 (*IG* II² 124.21).

Φίλων (*PA* 14805). *Strategos*, 329/8 (*IG* II² 1672.271-72; *cf. Syll.*² 587 n.180).

Φίλων Καλλίππου (?) Αἰξωνεύς (?) (*PA* 14825, *APF*). Defendant in an *eisangelia* (no. 89), *ca* 360 (?) (Hyp. 3.1-2). *Strategos* (?), *ca* 360 (?) (Hyp. 3.1-2; *cf.* Hansen, *Eisangelia* no. 87 n.4).

Φίλων ἐκ Κοίλης (*PA* 14847). Defendant in an *endeixis* (no. 8), 403/2 (Isoc. 18.22). Elected ambassador, 403/2 (Isoc.).

Φιλωτάδης Φιλοστράτου Παλληνεύς (*PA* 14927). Proposes in the *ecclesia* an honorary decree for Apollonides, 354/3 (*IG* II² 136.10-11).

Φοξίας (*PA* 14942). Proposes in the *ecclesia* an honorary decree for Pythodoros, 369/8 (*I.Délos* I 88.5).

Φορμίσιος (*PA* 14945). Proposes a decree of the people restricting citizen rights to

UPDATED INVENTORY OF *RHETORES* AND *STRATEGOI* (1988)

owners of landed property, 403/2 (Dion. Hal. *Lys.* 526). Ambassador to the king of Persia, 394-392 (?) (Plato Com. fr.119 K.).

Φορμίων (*PA* 14950). *Strategos*, 368/7 (*IG* II² 104.2).

Φορμίων (*PA* 14952). *Synegoros* for Apsephion in a *graphe nomon me epitedeion theinai*, 355/4 (Dem. 20.51, 100, 159, hypoth. 2.3).

Φρύνων Διογνήτου 'Ραμνούσιος (*PA* 15032). Proposes a decree of the people concerning envoys to Philip, 348/7 (Aeschin. 2.12). Ambassador to Philip, (1) 348/7 (Aeschin. 2.12); (2) three (?) times in 347/6 (1: Dem. 19 hypoth. 2.4; 2: Dem. 19.189, 197; 3 [?]: Dem. 19.121). For the patronymic *cf. PA* 3868.

Φυλεύς Παυσανίου Οἰναῖος (*PA* 15045). Proposes in the *boule* an honorary decree for Herakleides, 325/4 (*IG* II² 360.66).

Φυρχῖνος (*PA* 15051). Addresses the *ecclesia* in support of Lykourgos, 331/0 (Lycurg. 1.19).

Φωκίων Φώκου Ποτάμιος (?) (*PA* 15076, *APF*). Addresses the *ecclesia* regularly (Plut. *Phoc.* 7.5-6). *Synegoros* for Aischines in an *euthynai*, 343/2 (Aeschin. 2.184). Ambassador (1) to Philip, 338/7 (Nep. *Phoc.* 1.3, Plut. *Phoc.* 17.6); (2) to Alexander, 335/4 (Plut. 17.6); (3) to Antipater, 322/1 (Diod. 18.18.2). *Strategos* forty-five times (Plut. 8.2); 349/8 (Dem. 21.164); 344/3 (Plut. 15.1); 343/2 (Aeschin. 2.184); 342/1 (?) (Polyaen. 5.21); 341/0 (Philoch. F160, Diod. 16.74.1); 340/339 (*IG* II² 1628.437, 1629.958, *IG* II² 207C.12, 14); 339/8 (Plut. *Phoc.* 16.1); 338/7 (Plut. 16.4); 335/4 (Plut. 17.1); 323/2 (Plut. 25.1). For the demotic *cf. Agora* XV 42.206.

Φῶκος (*PA* 15082). Proposes in the *boule* a decree concerning the Apatouria, 366/5 or 323/2 (Ath. 171E).

Χαβρίας Κτησίππου Αἰξωνεύς (*PA* 15086, *APF*). Defendant in an *eisangelia* (no. 84), 366/5 (Dem. 21.64). *Strategos*, 390/389 (*IG* II² 21.2, Diod. 14.92.2); 389/8 (schol. Aristid. *Panath.* 172.3-4); 388/7 (Xen. *Hell.* 5.1.10); 387/6 (Nep. *Chabr.* 2.2); 379/8 (*Hell.* 5.4.14); 378/7 (Diod. 15.29.7); 377/6 (Diod. 15.30.5); 376/5 (*Hell.* 5.4.61); 373/2 (*Hell.* 6.2.39); 369/8 (*Hell.* 7.1.25); 366/5 (?) (schol. Dem. 21.64); 363/2 (*IG* II² 111.18); 359/8 (Dem. 23.171); 357/6 (*IG* II² 124.20).

Χαιρέδημος (*PA* 15112 + 15113). Proposes a decree of the people concerning the collection of naval equipment, 357/6 (Dem. 47.20).

Χαιρέφιλος Φειδωνος (?) Παιανιεύς (*PA* 15187, *APF*). Defendant in an *apophasis*, ca 330-322 (Hyp. fr.lix, *P.Oxy.* 2686).

Χαιρημονίδης (not in *PA*). Proposes a *nomos* on *aparchai*, before 353 (*IG* II² 140.9, 33).

Χαιριωνίδης Λυσανίου Φλυεύς (*PA* 15269). Proposes in the *ecclesia* an honorary decree for Pytheas, 333/2 (*IG* II² 338.6-7).

Χάρης Θεοχάρους 'Αγγελῆθεν (*PA* 15292, *APF*). Brings an *eisangelia* (no. 114) against Pheidiades, 336-324 (Din. fr.xxiv Con.). *Strategos*, 367/6 (Xen. *Hell.* 7.2.18, Diod. 15.75.3); 366/5 (*Hell.* 7.4.5); 362/1 (Diod. 15.95.3); 358/7 (Dem. 23.173); 357/6 (*IG* II² 124.20); 356/5 (*IG* II² 127.17, Diod. 16.22.1-22.2); 355/4 (*FGrHist.* 105.4); 354/3 (Polyaen. 4.2.22); 353/2 (Theopomp. F249); 349/8 (Philoch. F49); 348/7 (schol. Aristid. *Panath.* 179; Philoch. F51, 156); 347/6 (Aeschin. 2.90-92); 346/5 (Aeschin. 1.132ff); 343/2 (schol. Dem. 7.15; 58.38);341/0 (*IG* II² 228.11); 340/339 (Plut. *Phoc.* 14.3-4, *IG* II² 207c.12, d.1); 339/8 (Polyaen. 4.2.8); 338/7 (Diod. 16.85.2, 7); before 324/3 (Plut. *Mor.* 848E).

Χαρίδημος (*PA* 15370). Ambassador to Philip, 359/8 (Theopomp. F30).

Χαρίδημος Φιλοξένου 'Αχαρνεύς (*PA* 15380, *APF*). *Strategos*, 351/0 (Dem. 3.5); 349/8 (Philoch. F50); 340/339 *IG* II² 207c.12, d.1); 338/7 (Plut. *Phoc.* 16.4).

Χαρικλείδης (*PA* 15396). Proposes a decree of the people, 333/2 (?) (*IG* II² 1673.9 cf. *SEG* XXXIV 122).

Χαρικλῆς (*PA* 15403). Defendant in an *apophasis* in consequence of the Harpalos affair, 324/3 (Plut. *Phoc.* 22.4).

Χαρῖνος (*PA* 15437). Brings a *graphe paranomon* (no. 21) against Thoukydides, before 342 (Dem. 58.37-38).

This inventory of 368 politically active Athenian citizens raises a methodological question: does the catalogue, as it purports, include all *known* Athenian citizens who volunteered as *rhetores* or were elected *strategoi* or treasurers? Not quite, and I append a list of citizens who, in the literary sources, are called *politeuomenoi* or *symbouloi* or are described in another way as *rhetores*, but are never once attested as having performed one of the listed political activities:

'Αριστομήδης Κολλυτεύς (?) (*PA* 2014, 2013 Add., cf. *APF* 65): Dem. 10.70-74.
Γλαύκιππος 'Υπερείδου Κολλυτεύς (*PA* 2987, *APF*): Plut. *Mor.* 848D.
Εὐθύδικος (*PA* 5552): Dem. *Ep.* 3.31, Din. 1.33.
Εὐκτήμων Λουσιεύς (*PA* 5800): Dem. 21.103, 139.
Ἠλεῖος (*PA* 6400): Din. 1.38.
Θρασύβουλος Θρασυβούλου Στειριεύς (*PA* 7309, *APF*): Dem. 19.280, 290.
Κάλλιππος Λαμπτρεύς (*PA* 8074): Dem. 52.28.
Λύκων Θορίκιος (*PA* 9271): Pl. *Ap.* 23E, Diog. Laert. 2.38.
Νεοπτόλεμος 'Αντικλέους Μελιτεύς (*PA* 10652, *APF*): Dem. 18.114, 21.215.
Ξενότιμος (*PA* 11266): Isoc. 18.11.
Φιλόνεικος (*PA* 14675): Dem. 19.291.

This list shows that an inventory based on attested political activities cannot be complete, owing to the scattered nature of our attestations. Complete sources would probably lead to the inclusion of all eleven citizens listed above, and of many others as well, but this problem will be reserved for a future study of the number of Athenian ῥήτορες καὶ στρατηγοί.[24]

THE INSTITUTE FOR ADVANCED STUDY
March, 1983

UPDATED INVENTORY OF *RHETORES* AND *STRATEGOI* (1988)

ADDENDA

This revised version of my inventory includes the *Addenda et Corrigenda* printed in *GRBS* 28 (1987) 209-11. It results from my further study of fourth-century Athens, but some corrigenda I owe to Robert Develin, who kindly allowed me to see the typescript of his monumental *Athenian Officials 684-321 B.C.* (Cambridge 1989). Some other corrigenda and addenda stem from my visit to Melbourne in September - October 1988, where Michael Osborne was kind enough to let me use his prosopographical file of Athenians which, when completed, will appear as the second volume of the *Oxford Lexicon of Greek Personal Names*. My work with the file has only confirmed my expectation that this volume will revolutionize the study of Athenian history.

Four persons have been deleted from the inventory: (1) Κτησίας (*PA* 8838) cf. *IG* I^3 1454 and Develin 113. (2) Μενίτης Μένωνος Κυδαθηναιεύς (*PA* 10055) cf. *IG* I^3 48 *bis*. (3) Φίλιππος (*PA* 14373): in *IG* II^2 114.4 Kirchner, following Koehler, restored Φιλ[ιππο]ς, but there are so many alternatives (αγρο, αιθο, ανθη, αργο, ησιο, ιαδη, ισχο, ιστο, οθεο, οχλη etc., all attested in fourth-century sources as names of Athenian citizens) that the restoration should be taken *exempli gratia*. Thus Φίλιππος must be deleted from the inventory since we have evidence of a broken name only. (4) Φράσμων (*PA* 14988) cf. *IG* I^3 228.

In three cases activities first ascribed to one person are now believed to have been performed by two homonymous persons: (1) Ἁγνίας Πολέμωνος ἐξ Οἴου (*PA* 133) cf. S. Humphreys in *CP* 78 (1983) 224f and Develin 206 & 294. (2) Ἀθηνόδωρος (*PA* 259 + 260) cf. Develin 282 & 284: the downdating of *IG* II^2 47 entails that *PA* 260 should (again) be dissociated from *PA* 259, who, in the period 394-87, proposed and carried *IG* II^2 26. (3) Ἐξηκεστίδης Χαρίου Θορίκιος (*PA* 4710 + 4718): The identification of *PA* 4710 with *PA* 4718, judiciously discussed by Davies in *APF* 175-76, is so uncertain that it cannot be upheld.

The following six persons have been added to the inventory: (1) Ἀπολλόδωρος ὁ Κυζικηνός (*PA* 1458). (2) Ἀρχέδημος Πήληξ (*PA* 2326): all other references to *PA* 2326 concern the last years of the Peloponnesian War. In Aeschin. 3.139, however, the context strongly indicates a date in the 370's rather than before 403; cf. Develin 226. (3) Ξενότιμος (not in *PA*). (4) Πεισιάναξ Σουνιεύς (*PA* 11776). (5) Πρωτόμαχος (non in *PA*). (6) Πυθόνικος (*PA* 12458?).

Though precise dating of political activities is not of primary importance for my inventory I have devoted much time and energy to chronological problems. Dating, especially of *strategiai*, is often difficult, and in a number of cases my inventory of 1983 gives a different year from that which Develin now prints in his *Athenian Officials*. In the revised version of my inventory printed here, I have sometimes changed my mind; in other cases I have left a discrepancy and have nothing to add since, in my opinion, the sources do not allow us to make a clear choice between two years. But occasionally I have felt that it might be helpful for the user of the inventory to know my reasons for either keeping or changing the date I first offered. The five comments printed below are illustrations of chronological problems. More could be added but would, I fear, result in an undue emphasis on the chronological aspects of the inventory.

(1) The military operations in the Hellespont in the summer of 387 cannot be dated exactly, but the sources give some indications. After a naval victory and the arrival of reinforcements (Xen. *Hell.* 5.1.27) Antalkidas "prevented the ships from the Pontos from sailing to Athens" (28). Thus, the victory should be dated to the (early?) summer of 387 as assumed by Hamilton, *Sparta's Bitter Victories* (Ithaca 1979) 309-11 and not to the autumn of 387 (after the sailing season?) as suggested by Merkelbach in *ZPE* 5 (1970) 33 followed by Harding no. 26. A further inference is that the Athenian commanders Demainetos, Dionysios, Leontichos and Phanias (Xen. *Hell.* 5.1.26) must have served on the board of generals of 388/7, and not on the board of 387/6 as suggested by Develin 217-18. Whether they were re-elected and served both years is, as usual, a moot point. I follow my regular practice of recording a *strategos* in one year only, unless he is explicitly attested as being in command both before and after the turn of the year.

(2) *IG* II² 36 records the names of five envoys sent to Olynthos: Ἀθηνίων Ἀραφήνιος, Ἕρμιππος Πόριος, Θρασυκλῆς Παλληνεύς, Νικόστρατος Θοραιεύς and Φαίνιππος Ἀζηνιεύς. In *Hesperia* 40 (1971) 149-50 no. 3 R. S. Stroud restored *EM* 12917 to be a second copy of the treaty between Athens and the Chalkidians. But very few letters are left and Stroud emphasizes that he offers a *possible* restoration. Thus, I cannot follow Develin (220) in dating *IG* II² 36 to 384/3 instead of 376/5 as suggested by S. Accame, *La lega ateniese* 87ff followed by Lewis in *BSA* 49 (1954) 33 n. 14.

(3) According to Dion. *ad Amm.* 4 the trial of Timokrates (Dem. 24) took place in the archonship of Thoudemos (353/2). In *BSA* 49 (1954) 32, however, Lewis, following Kahle, suggested 354/3 because all the documents inserted in Dem. 24 state that Pandionis is the first prytany (Dem. 24.27, 39, 71). This piece of information rules out 353/2 but is perfectly compatible with 354/3. Let me add another argument which supports the earlier date of Dem. 24. The decree inserted in Dem. 24.27 records the name of the proposer, Epikrates, without patronymic and demotic. But the reform whereby the proposer's patronymic and demotic were in-

variably added to the name took place in the course of 354/3, cf. *infra* page 93 with note 6. Consequently, the decree inserted in Dem. 24.27 must have been proposed and carried in the first prytany of 354/3, not of 353/2.

(4) On the chronology of the Athenian embassy to Dareios III I follow Bosworth, *Commentary on Arrian* 2.15.2 (pages 233-34). On this particular question I believe that Curtius must be preferred to Arrian, and the date of the embassy of Aristogeiton, Dropides and Iphikrates is 333/2, not 330/29 as suggested by Develin 385 & 392.

(5) According to Pittakis' transcription of *IG* II^2 207a (to be preferred to Rangabé's printed in *IG*), the name of the proposer (Πολυκράτης) is followed by his patronymic (Πολυκράτους) and demotic (now lost). A proposer's name with patronymic and demotic added shows that the *terminus post quem* is 354/3, cf. *infra* page 93 with note 6. Next, in line 12 there is a reference to the *thesmothetai* in the archonship of Nikomachos (341/0). The only formula that points to an earlier date is ἐπεστάτει in line 2. But the change from ἐπεστάτει to τῶν προέδρων ἐπεψήφιζεν was gradual; the older formula is attested in 346/5 (*IG* II^2 217-18) and plausibly restored in *IG* II^2 227 of 342/1. Thus, *IG* II^2 207a was probably passed in the archonship of Theophrastos (340/39) or, possibly, in the following year; the war referred to is the war between Athens and Philip 340-38, and the Orontes honoured is Orontes II, not the Orontes who led the Satraps' revolt in the late 360s. This date fits the four *strategoi* mentioned in *IG* II^2 207b-d, i.e. Πρόξενος (Ἁρμοδίου Ἀφιδναῖος), Φωκίων (Φώκου Ποτάμιος), Χάρης (Θεοχάρους Ἀγγελῆθεν) and Χαρίδημος (Φιλοξένου Ἀχαρνεύς). For recent treatments of the chronology of *IG* II^2 207 cf. Osborne, *Naturalization* I 52-54 (D 12); II 61-80; Moysey in *ZPE* 69 (1987) 93-100 and Develin in *ZPE* 73 (1988) 75-81.

Other changes which require some discussion but relate to single persons are listed below in alphabetical order:

Ἀριστόξενος Κηφισοδότου. In *IG* II^2 347.9-10 -ενος is almost certainly -ξενος, cf. Dornseiff/Hansen p. 269, and [...ṣ...]ξενος is either (1) Ἀριστόξενος or (2) Ἐμπεδόξενος or (3) Τιμησίξενος (*Ibidem*). (2) and (3) are not attested in Attica, whereas we now have seven attestations of (1). Thus, Koehler's restoration [Ἀριστόξ]ενος is probably correct. The demotic Πειραιεύς (?), however, should be deleted. [...ṣ...]ευς could be Πειραιεύς (cf. *IG* II^2 1028 Col. III 109), but it could also be Κηφισιεύς (cf. *IG* II^2 1965.9). Thus, on the demotic, I now prefer to suspend judgement.

Ἀριστοπείθης Φυλάσιος (?). For the demotic cf. Ἀριστοπείθης [-]νύμου Φυλάσιος (321/0; *IG* II^2 2840.5; 2841.5), the only other attestation in Attica of the name 'Αριστοπείθης and thus presumably a relative of the envoy of 368/7.

'Αριστοφῶν 'Αριστοφάνους 'Αζηνιεύς. *IG* II² 289.6 (decree no. 13) was probably moved by an unknown *rhetor*, cf. *infra* page 106 no. 13.

Αὐτόλυκος Π—. For the demotic cf. *Hesperia* 52 (1983) 106 d 10. Since Αὐτόλυκος (*PA* 2746) was convicted in 338/7 (Lycurg. 1.53) he cannot plausibly be identified with the Αὐτόλυκος Θορίκιος (not in *PA*) who was *kosmetes* in the 330's *SEG* XXIII 78.15, (cf. F. Mitchel in *ZPE* 19 [1975] 242-43).

'Εμμενίδης. In the *Addenda et Corrigenda* (*GRBS* 28 [1987] 210) I suggested 'Εμμενίδης ἐκ Κοίλης cf. *IG* II² 208.4f (349/8). But equally possible is 'Εμμενίδης 'Εκαλεύς cf. *Agora* XV 42.263 (336/5). Thus I retract my suggestion and suspend judgement on the demotic of the 'Εμμενίδης who proposed and carried *IG* II² 1544.30 (333/2).

'Ηρακλείδης ὁ Κλαζομένιος. On his *strategia* cf. J.D. Moore in *GRBS* 15 (1974) 433 and *IG* II² 8 + 65 cf. M.B. Walbank in *ZPE* 51 (1983) 183f.

Θουκλείδης. In *IG* II² 5221.3 [-]υκλε[-] are the letters to be seen on the stone. But the only alternative to [Θο]υκλ[είδης] is [Βο]υκλ[είδης] which is attested only once in Attic inscriptions: *IG* II² 1009 Col. II 76 + 2457.7 (cf. *AE* [50/51] 41 n. 19).

Μοιροκλῆς. As usual Demosthenes reports the name without patronymic and demotic. But Μοιροκλῆς is a rare name, and a case can be made for identifying the *rhetor* mentioned in the literary sources (*PA* 10400) with either Μοιροκλῆς Καλλίππου 'Ελευσίνιος (*IG* II² 6043) or Μοιροκλῆς Εὐθυδήμου 'Ελευσίνιος (*IG* II² 1191.5-6; 2845.1; *Hesperia* 8 [1939] 176-80; *SEG* XXVIII 103.14-15) and/or Μοιροκλῆς ('Ελευσίνιος) (*IG* II 1672.210). Thus, the demotic can be established with some confidence, but not the patronymic.

Μολοττός. In the light of Μολοττός 'Ιφιστιάδης, *bouleutes* in 336/5 (*Agora* XV 42.303) I am inclined to retract the identification of Μολοττός, the *strategos* of 349/8, with Μολοττός Εὐνόμου 'Αφιδναῖος, recorded as *Diaitetes* in *IG* II² 1927.129). Cf. furthermore, Ruschenbusch's discussion of the date of *IG* II² 1927 in *ZPE* 49 (1982) 267-81.

Πάνδιος Σωχλέους ἐξ Οἴου. Kirchner joined Πάνδιος, the proposer of *IG* II² 103 (369/8) and 105 (368/7) with the *grammateus* of 355/4: Πάνδιος Σωχλέους ἐξ Οἴου (*IG* II² 130-33). But later discoveries have left us with at least two alternatives: Πάνδιος 'Αχαρνεύς s. IV a (*IG* II² 5830) and Πάνδιος Τειθράσιος med. s. IV a (*SEG* XXIV 151.6). Thus, I am inclined to question Kirchner's identification and to leave the proposer of *IG* II² 103 and

UPDATED INVENTORY OF *RHETORES* AND *STRATEGOI* (1988)

105 without patronymic and demotic. — In *Chiron* 16 (1986) 85ff D. Knoepfler, followed by Develin 253, suggests that the Πάνδιος who moved the probouleumatic decree *IG* II² 103 also moved the decree of the *boule* published by Leonardos in *AE* (1923) 36ff. I am inclined to accept the identification.

Πολυκράτης Πολυκράτους. According to Pittakis' transcription of *IG* II² 207 the name of the proposer was Πολυκράτης Πολυκράτους (demotic), cf. *supra* page 67.

Φίλαγρος. Cf. M.B. Walbank, *ClViews* 1 (1982) 259-74, but cf. also D. M. Lewis in *SEG* XXXII 32 and Develin 227.

Χάρης Θεοχάρους 'Αγγελῆθεν. On the *strategia* in 346/5 cf. M.M. Markle in *CQ* 24 (1974) 260 n. 1.

Χαρίδημος Φιλοξένου 'Αχαρνεύς. Referring to *IG* II² 118.7 Develin 268 has Χαρίδημος as *strategos* in 361/0. But Charidemos can have been a member of the board of generals of 361/0 only if he had been naturalized in the late 360's (as assumed by Osborne T 51) and not in the early 350's (as indicated by Dem. 23.141 and assumed by most others, e.g. by Davies in *APF* 571). Osborne's updating of the naturalization of Charidemos, however, is based on his updating of *IG* II² 207. But if we can trust Pittakis' transcription, the honorary decree for Orontes must be dated 340/39 or slightly later, cf. *supra* page 67. Accordingly, there is no reason to question the traditional dating of the naturalization of Charidemos and, in *IG* II² 118, he must be referred to as a mercenary leader, not as a member of the board of generals.

RHETORES AND *STRATEGOI* ATTESTED AS *BOULEUTAI*.

Of the 373 ῥήτορες καὶ στρατηγοί 80 are attested as members of the council of five hundred as well. Of these, 27 moved decrees of the council and 34 moved probouleumatic decrees (there is a slight overlap between the two groups); furthermore, 6 are attested as *rhetores* in the *boule*, whereas 17 are known as *bouleutai* only because they are recorded in the bouleutic lists or prytany inscriptions. In the following list B signifies member of the *boule*; BD proposer of a decree of the *boule*; BD (prop) proposer of a *probouleuma*; PD proposer of a probouleumatic decree; and RB *rhetor* in the *boule*.

Ἀγασίας Χαιριγένους Ἰκαριεύς 336/5 (*IG* II² 330.32); BD.
Ἀγγύρριος Κολλυτεύς 403/2 (*IG* II² 1.41-42); B.
Ἀλεξίμαχος Χαρίνου Πήληξ 371/0 (*Hesperia* 47 [1978] 90-91 line 54); B.
Ἀλκίμαχος ......ου ἐγ Μυρρινούττης 325/4 (*IG* II² 1629.273); BD.
Ἀντιγένης 356/5 (Dem. 22.38); RB.
Ἀνδροτίων ῎Ανδρωνος Γαργήττιος 373/2? (*IG* II² 61.6-7); B; 356/5 (Dem. 22); PD.
Ἀντίδοτος Ἀπολλοδώρου Συπαλήττιος 333/2 (*IG* II² 337.7-8); BD (prob).
Ἀπολλόδωρος Πασίωνος Ἀχαρνεύς 349/8 (Dem. 59.4); PD.
Ἀριστογείτων Κυδιμάχου 325/4 (Din. 2.13); B.
Ἀριστοκράτης 353/2 (Dem. 23.14); BD (prob).
Ἀριστοφῶν Ἀριστοφάνους Ἀζηνιεύς 357/6 (*IG* II² 121.9); PD; 355/4 (*IG* II² 130.8); PD.
Ἀρχέδημος Ἀρχίου Παιονίδης 349/8 (*IG* II² 208.5-6); PD.
Ἀρχίας Ἀχεστορίδου Χολαργεύς 356/5 (Dem. 22.40); B.
Ἀστύφιλος Φιλάγρου Ἁλαιεύς 378/7 (*IG* II² 42.3; *Agora* XV 7.7); PD.
Βράχυλλος Βαθύλλου Ἐρχιεύς 343/2 (*IG* II² 223C 10); BD.
Γνάθιος Προβαλίσιος 394/3 (*IG* II² 16.6); BD or PD.
Γνάθων Λακιάδης *init. s.* IV (*Hesperia* 26 [1957] 207 no. 53); PD.
Δεινόστρατος Δεινιάδου Ἀγχυλῆθεν 343/2 (*IG* II² 223A 4; *Agora* XV 36.21); BD.
Δημάδης Δημέου Παιανιεύς 336/5 (*Agora* XV 42.145); B; 320/19 (*SEG* XXI 305); PD.
Δημέας Σφήττιος *ante* 324 (*IG* II² 3207); BD.
Δημήτριος Εὐκτήμονος Ἀφιδναῖος 328/7 (*Agora* XV 49.24); B.
Δημοσθένης Δημοσθένους Παιανιεύς 347/6 (Aeschin. 3.62 etc); BD, PD, RD.
Διογείτων ca. 370 (*IG* II² 152.7-8); PD.
Διοφάνης Κηφισιεύς *ante* 324 (*IG* II² 3207); BD.
Διάφαντος Φρασικλείδου Μυρρινούσιος 337/6 (*IG* II² 242.6-7; 243.6-7; 1623.210-12); BD, PD.
Διάφαντος Θρασυμήδους Σφήττιος 368/7 (*IG* II² 106.6); PD.
῎Εμπεδος Οῆθεν 328/7 (*Agora* XV 49.13); B.
Ἐπικράτης ..οτήτου Παλληνεύς 335/4 (*Agora* XV 43.214-15); B.
Ἐπιτέλης Σωιναύτου Περγασῆθεν 336/5 (*Agora* XV 42.42); B.
Εὐβουλίδης Ἀντιφίλου Ἁλιμούσιος 346/5 (Dem. 57.8; *IG* II² 218.6-7); PD.

UPDATED INVENTORY OF *RHETORES* AND *STRATEGOI* (1988)

Εὔδοξος Θεαγγέλου Συπαλήττιος 343/2 (*IG* II² 223C 10-12); RB.

Εὐετίων Αὐτοκλείδου Σφήττιος 328/7 (*Agora* XV 49.12); B.

Εὐξίθεος *ante* 378/7 (*IG* II² 60.4); PD.

Ἡγέμαχος Χαιρήμονος Περιθοίδης 334/3 (*IG* II² 1156.36); BD.

Ἡγήσανδρος Ἡγησίου Σουνιεύς 357/6 (*IG* II² 123.7); PD.

Θεόδωρος Ἀντιφάνου Ἀλωπεκῆθεν 334/3 (*Agora* XV 44.56); B.

Θεοζοτίδης Ἀθμονεύς 403/2 (*Hesperia* 40 [1971] 280-301 no. 7); PD.

Θεοκρίνης Ὑβάδης 328/7 (*Agora* XV 49.14); B.

Θεομένης Ὀῆθεν *ante* 324 (*IG* II² 3207); BD.

Ἱεροκλείδης Τιμοστράτου Ἀλωπεκῆθεν 349/8 (*IG* II² 206.5-7); PD.

Ἱερώνυμος Οἰκωφέλους Ῥαμνούσιος ca. 330 (*IG* II² 415.11); PD.

Ἱπποχάρης Ἀλωπεκῆθεν 336/5 (*IG* II² 330.26, 50); PD.

Καλλικράτης Χαροπίδου Λαμπτρεύς 346/5 (*IG* II² 215.5-6); PD.

Καλλισθένης 356/5 (*IG* II² 127.7); PD.

Καλλισθένης Χαροπίδου Τρινεμεύς (*Agora* XV 49.41); PD.

Καλλίστρατος Καλλικράτους Ἀφιδναῖος 369/8 (*IG* II² 107.36); PD.

Καλλίστρατος Θορίκιος ca. 330 (*IG* II² 1627.374-95); BD.

Κηφισόδοτος Εὐαρχίδου Ἀχαρνεύς 330-28 (*IG* II² 360.51); BD.

Κηφισόδοτος ἐκ Κεραμέων 367/6 (*Hesperia* 8 [1939] 5-12 no. 3); PD.

Κηφισοφῶν Παιανιεύς 403/2 (*IG* II² 1.42, 51); PD.

Κινησίας Μέλητος 394/3 (*IG* II² 18.5); BD.

Κρατῖνος 363/2 (*IG* II² 109a7, b8); PD.

Κρίτιος 375/4 (*IG* II² 96.4-5); PD.

Κτησικλῆς Βατῆθεν *ante* 324 (*IG* II² 3207); BD.

Κτησιφῶν 337/6 (Dem. 18.9, 53, 118-9); BD (prob.).

Λυκοῦργος Λυκόφρονος Βουτάδης 336/5 (*IG* II² 328.8-9); PD; 329/8 (*IG* II² 1672.302); BD.

Μειδίας Κηφισοδώρου Ἀναγυράσιος 348/7 (Dem. 21.111, 116, 161); RB.

Μειδίας Μειδίου Ἀναγυράσιος 304/3 (*Agora* XV 61.177); B.

Μελάνωπος Λάχητος Αἰξωνεύς 366/5 (*IG* II² 145.13); PD.

Μονιππίδης 403/2 (*IG* II² 6.7); BD.

Νόθιππος Λυσίου Διομειεύς 331/0 (*IG* II² 349.9-10); PD.

Πάνδιος 369/8 (*AE* [1923] 26ff); BD.

Περίανδρος Πολυαράτου Χολαργεύς 362/1 (*IG* II² 112.5-6); BD (prob)? cf. Rhodes 69.

Πολύευκτος Καλλικράτους Ἑστιαιόθεν 324/3 (*IG* II² 1631.350-1); BD.

Πολύευκτος Κυδαντίδης ca. 330-22 (Din. fr. 2.2, Conomis); B.

Πολύευκτος Σωστράτου Σφήττιος 356/5 (*IG* II² 128.8); PD.

Πυθόνικος ca. 400 (*IG* II² 77 + Add); BD.

Πύρρανδρος Ἀναφλύστιος 378/7 (*IG* II² 44.7); PD.

Ταυρέας Πυθοκλέους Πιθεύς 303/2 (?) (*Agora* XV 62.220); B.

Τηλέμαχος Θεαγγέλου Ἀχαρνεύς 339/8 (*Hesperia* 7 [1938] 291-2 no. 18); PD.

Τίμαρχος Ἀριζήλου Σφήττιος 361/0 (Aeschin. 1.109); B; 347/6 (Aeschin. 1.80; Dem. 19.286-87); RB; PD.

Φανόδημος Διύλλου Θυμαιτάδης 343/2 (*IG* II² 223B 1); BD.

Φιλέας Ἀντιγένου Παιονίδης 336/5 (*Agora* XV 42.244); B.

Φίλιππος 356/5 (Dem: 22.38); RB.

Φιλόδημος Αὐτοκλέους Ἐροιάδης ca. 350 (*Agora* XV 22.11); B.

Φιλωτάδης Φιλοστράτου Παλληνεύς 354/3 (*IG* II² 136.10-11); PD.

Φοξίας 369/8 (*I. Délos* I 88.5). PD.

Φυλεύς Παυσανίου Οἰναῖος 325/4 (*IG* II² 360.66); BD (prop).

Φωκίων Φώκου Ποτάμιος 336/5 (*Agora* XV 42.206); B.

Φῶκος 366/5 or 323/2 (Ath. 171 E); BD.

Political Activity and the Organization of Attica in the Fourth Century B.C.

Mogens Herman Hansen

IT IS GENERALLY BELIEVED that the political organization of Attica introduced by Kleisthenes in the years after 508/7 was maintained unchanged for two hundred years. Most historians hold, with Traill's fundamental study,[1] that the creation and distribution of 139 (?) constitutional demes over thirty *trittyes* and ten *phylai* was upheld from *ca* 500 to 307/6 B.C. and that the number of seats in the *boule* assigned to each deme goes back to Kleisthenes, although the attested quotas are all later than the restoration of the democracy in 403/2.[2]

An essential aspect of Kleisthenes' reforms was to combine membership in a deme with residence in the deme (Arist. *Ath.Pol.* 21.4); but as deme membership was made hereditary, all scholars acknowledge that the original territorial organization of the citizen body must have become increasingly artificial in the course of the classical period. So the student of fourth-century Athenian institutions is faced with two basic questions: (1) to what degree was the original settlement pattern preserved, *i.e.* how many fourth-century citizens happened to reside in the deme to which they belonged? (2) to what degree was the political organization preserved, *i.e.* was the distribution of politically active citizens over the three Attic districts (Asty, Paralia, Mesogaios) the same in the fourth century as when Kleisthenes created the districts and fixed the bouleutic quotas for all the demes? I shall begin with the second question.

For the relation between deme membership and political activity we have three types of evidence: (a) inscriptions recording *bouleutai* and so the bouleutic quotas, *i.e.* the number of seats in the *boule* assigned to each deme (and accordingly to each of the thirty *trittyes* and

---

[1] J. S. TRAILL, *The Political Organization of Attica* (*Hesperia* Suppl. 14 [1975], hereafter 'Traill'). In this article I accept Traill's conclusions as to the location of demes and their distribution over *trittyes* and tribes.

[2] Bouleutic quotas go back to Kleisthenes, *cf.* Traill 103. No attested bouleutic quotas earlier than the fourth century, *cf. Athenian Agora* XV 2–56. We have only one prytany dedication from the fifth century, which Traill believes to be incomplete (*Agora* XV 1). On this inscription and *IG* I³ 1040 see *infra* n.10.

three districts); (b) prosopographical information in all sources about citizens acting as *rhetores* and *strategoi*; (c) dicastic *pinakia* recording the names and demotics of citizens who served as jurors. As the bouleutic quotas have been discussed frequently, I focus here on the other two types of evidence and their relation to the bouleutic quotas.

I have previously published an inventory of 368 citizens attested as proposers, speakers, prosecutors, ambassadors, and generals in the period 403-322.³ The demotic is known (or conjectured) for 211 of these; to this figure we can add 29 proposers and ambassadors for whom fragmentary inscriptions record the demotic but not the name.⁴ A total of 240 citizens is too small a sample for a study of single demes,⁵ but quite sufficient to investigate the distribution of *rhetores* and *strategoi*⁶ over the three districts:

District	Total	Percentage
Asty	63	26%
Paralia	86	36%
Mesogaios	91	38%

We have from fourth-century Athens 190 bronze allotment plates.⁷ The *pinakia* were used for two different purposes: the daily sortition

---

³ "*Rhetores* and *Strategoi* in Fourth-Century Athens," *GRBS* 24 (1983) 151-80.

⁴ *IG* II² 34.36-37 (Alopekethen, Phrearrios); 140.7 (Eleusinios); 157.5 (Porios); 175.4 (Acharneus); 204.84 (Lamptreus); 205.9, cf. *SEG* XIV 51 (Steirieus); 207.27 (Euonymeus, Acharneus); 220.4-5 (Rhamnousios); 223B.10 (Pambotades); 229.7 (Phrearrios); 244.1 (Aphidnaios); 253.2 (Sphettios); 263.5 (ek Kedon); 276.3 (Potamios); 336.6 (Lakiades); 343.3 (Anagyrasios); 358.8 (307/6?) (Kydathenaieus); 361.7 (Alopekethen); 367.9 (Meliteus); 403.5 (Lakiades); 410.1-2, cf. *SEG* XXII 94 (Skambonides); 800, cf. *SEG* XXI 289 (Sybarides or Sypalletios); 1128.40 (Phlyeus); 3207.4 (Myrrhinousios); *Hesperia* 3 (1934) 3-4 no. 5 (Thriasios); 8 (1939) 26-27 no. 6 (Anagyrasios); 9 (1940) 327-28 no. 36 (Paianieus). Some of these may be identical with some of the persons for whom we know the full name. The spokesman of *IG* II² 244.1, for example, may be either Kephisophon Kephalionos or Demetrios Euktemonos.

⁵ This is apparent from a survey of attested *rhetores* and *strategoi* from some of the major demes (with five or more *bouleutai*; Traill 67): Acharnai 13, Aphidna 9, Lamptrai (both) 7, Paiania (both) 14, Kydathenaion 5, Eleusis 6, Alopeke 10, Euonymon 5, Anaphlystos 4, Marathon 2, Peiraieus 2, Phrearrioi 2, Phaleron 2, Kephale 2, Aixone 5, Rhamnous 7, Melite 1, Phlya 2, Erchia 6, Xypete 0, Thria 2, Kephisia 5, Pallene 6, Kerameis 4, Anagyrous 6, Athmonon 0, Myrrhinous 4, Halai (both) 1, Oe 3, Aigilia 0, Sphettos 10, Thorikos 3, Ikarion 1, Hagnous 2, Probalinthos 2, Prospalta 0, Agryle (both) 0.

⁶ If we split up *rhetores* and *strategoi* and record the various activities separately, we get the following percentages. *Rhetores* in the *ecclesia* and in the *boule* (total 132): Asty 23%, Paralia 34%, Mesogaios 43%. Prosecutors, defendants, and *synegoroi* in political public actions (44): Asty 25%, Paralia 43%, Mesogaios 32%. Ambassadors (66): Asty 27%, Paralia 41%, Mesogaios 32%. *Strategoi* (53): Asty 23%, Paralia 47%, Mesogaios 30%.

⁷ See the fundamental study by J. H. Kroll, *Athenian Bronze Allotment Plates* (Cambridge [Mass.] 1972), with the seven more he adds in an article forthcoming in *GRBM* 10.

of jurors and the annual sortition of magistrates. Bronze *pinakia* were used for the sortition of jurors in the second quarter of the fourth century, and for sortition of magistrates in the second and third quarters. I leave out of account the *pinakia* used exclusively for the sortition of magistrates and focus on those dicastic *pinakia* which still attest the deme membership of the jurors: for 86 *dikastai*, recorded on 52 different *pinakia*, the demotic can be read or restored, revealing the following distribution over the three districts:[8]

District	Total	Percentage
Asty	20	23%
Paralia	36	42%
Mesogaios	30	35%

For a proper evaluation of the percentages recorded in these two tables it is important to keep in mind that the three districts were unequal in size and population, as is demonstrated by the bouleutic quotas. If we add up the quotas for the various demes as attested in the fourth century and later, the figures are: Asty 130, Paralia 196, Mesogaios 174 (*cf.* Traill 71). A comparison of all three types of source gives the following percentages for the three districts:

District	*Bouleutai*	*Rhetores* and *Strategoi*	*Dikastai*
Asty	26%	26%	23%
Paralia	39%	36%	42%
Mesogaios	35%	38%	35%

It is significant that the three different types of evidence give almost the same percentages. The correspondence among the figures becomes even more remarkable when we realize that the bouleutic quotas, as a source, differ from the other two in important respects. The bouleutic quotas, we are told, were fixed by Kleisthenes and do not necessarily reflect the actual political participation in the age of Demosthenes. And in fact quite a number of councillors did not attend the meetings (Dem. 22.36). It is a fair guess that many of those absent were councillors belonging to the Paralia or the Mesogaios and still living in their demes. Hence the bouleutic quotas were, in a way, artificial, and the *bouleutai* attending the meetings may have

---

[8] The dicastic *pinakia* are those of Classes I–II (19 *pinakia* with 46 uses as dicastic *pinakia*), IV (17 *pinakia* with 44 uses), and V (36 *pinakia* with 71 uses). The sum is 72 *pinakia* with 161 uses. Of the seven new *pinakia*, 3 are dicastic with 11 uses. The sum of uses is not beyond doubt since some *pinakia* of Classes IV and V were reused as Class VI.

betrayed a very different representation from the three districts. The two other types of source are of a different kind. Both the *rhetores* and *strategoi* and the dicasts were volunteers, and the percentages listed above must reflect the actual political participation of citizens from the three districts (the percentages of course represent deme membership and give no information about residence).

We may assume that in the fourth century the distribution of active *bouleutai* over the three districts was similar to the distribution of *rhetores* and *strategoi* and of dicasts.[9] Accordingly, as the percentages suggest, the actual distribution of those *bouleutai* who attended a session was probably not very different from the composition of the entire *boule* and the bouleutic quotas that were allegedly set by Kleisthenes.

Thus, comparison of the bouleutic quotas with the two other types of source indicates that Kleisthenes' political reform was so successful that it insured, for the next 200 years, the same balance among citizens belonging to the three districts. There is an alternative, however: we have no unquestionably attested bouleutic quotas earlier

---

[9] In my inventory of *rhetores* and *strategoi* I recorded 29 *rhetores* (with known demotic) either as addressing the *boule* or as proposers of decrees in the *boule*. To this figure I can add four men known only by the demotic of the proposer: *IG* II² 157.5 (Porios), 223B.10 (Pambotades), 361.7 (Alopekethen), 3207.4 (Myrrhinousios). Furthermore, proposers of probouleumatic decrees were probably all *bouleutai* and so to be registered as *rhetores* active in the *boule*. The inventory does not distinguish between probouleumatic and non-probouleumatic decrees; accordingly proposers of probouleumatic decrees whose demotic is known may be listed here (for a full list of the decrees see P. J. Rhodes, *The Athenian Boule* [Oxford 1972] 247–50): Archedemos Archiou Paionides (*IG* II² 208); Aristophon Aristophanous Azenieus (121, 130); Astyphilos Halaieus (42); Demetrios Euktemonos Aphidnaios (*Syll.*³ 287); Diophantos Thrasymedous Sphettios (*IG* II² 106); Diophantos Phrasikleidou Myrrhinousios (243); Euboulides Antiphilou Halimousios (218); Gnathios Probalisios (16, ἔδοξε τῇ βουλῇ); Gnathon Lakiades (*Hesperia* 26 [1957] 207 no. 53); Hegesandros Hegesiou Sounieus (*IG* II² 123); Hierokleides Timostratou Alopekethen (206); Hieronymos Oikophelous Rhamnousios (415); Hippochares Alopekethen (330); Kallikrates Charopidou Lamptreus (215); Kallistratos Kallikratous Aphidnaios (107); Kephisodotos ek Kerameon (*Hesperia* 8 [1939] 5ff no. 3); Kephisophon Paianieus (*IG* II² 1); Lykourgos Lykophronos Boutades (328); Melanopos Lachetos Aixoneus (145); Menites Menonos Kydathenaieus (*ArchEph* 1971, 137ff); Nothippos Lysiou Diomeieus (*IG* II² 349); Pandios Sokleous ex Oiou (?) (103); Philotades Philostratou Palleneus (136); Polyeuktos Kydantides (410); Polyeuktos Sostratou Sphettios (128); Telemachos Theangelou Acharneus (*SEG* XVI 52); ... Aristyllou Keiriades (*IG* II² 205); ... Phrearrios (229); ... Lakiades (403). Of these 29 *rhetores* one is also known as the proposer of a decree of the *boule* (Diophantos Phrasikleidou), and we do not know whether Pandios belonged to Oion Kerameikon or Dekeleikon. Hence we have 27 names and demotics. All 60 attested *rhetores* in the *boule* grouped according to the three districts show: Asty 19 (32%), Paralia 16 (27%), Mesogaios 41%). These figures suggest a good distribution over the districts but indicate, if they are reliable, an underrepresentation of the Paralia.

than 403/2,[10] and the ascription of the fourth-century quotas to Kleisthenes rests on an argument from silence. The correspondence between the bouleutic quotas and actual political participation in the fourth century may rather support the opposite view: that the bouleutic quotas were adjusted, say in 403/2, to fit the existing citizen population which differed both in size and in geographical distribution from that of the age of Kleisthenes.

A study of the connection between the bouleutic quotas and the number of citizens in fourth-century Athens may throw more light on this problem. The number of citizens eligible for the *boule* was probably so small that it was only just possible to run the council constitutionally.[11] Accordingly citizens were allowed, exceptionally, to serve in the *boule* twice in their lifetime (Arist. *Ath.Pol.* 62.3), but the evidence we have indicates that only a small fraction did so.[12] Thus almost all citizens over thirty years of age served one year in the *boule*,[13] and a fraction of them two years. Now if the number of

---

[10] Two inscriptions may provide information on quotas in the fifth century. (1) *Agora* XV 1 is a dedication set up by the *prytaneis* of Erechtheis in 408/7. The number of names preserved differs in most cases from the known deme quotas: only Kedoi (2) and Upper Agryle (1) agree with the fourth-century quotas. According to the prevailing view, however, no more than 37 names (from the 14 demes) were inscribed on the stone, which thus records only *some prytaneis* and therefore gives no information about quotas. (2) K. J. Davies, *LMC* 4 (1979) 151–55, has argued that *IG* I³ 1040 may be a fragment of a list of all 500 *bouleutai*, serving *ca* 420 or earlier. Moreover, he restores the fragment to give four *bouleutai* to Gargettos (Aigeis) and 9 (or 9+?) to (?) Phrearrhioi (Leontis). If Davies is right in all his assumptions, this is evidence that the quota of Gargettos was the same in the fifth century, and possibly also that of Phrearrhioi. In my opinion, however, it is an overstatement that the inscription as restored "strongly suggests that the deme-quotas in the Council did indeed remain unchanged from the fifth century into the fourth" (155). If we take *Agora* XV 1 to give the bouleutic quotas of the demes recorded in the fragment, two are the same (Kedoi and Upper Agryle) but the others are different. One or perhaps two known quotas is too small a basis for a general conclusion, especially when both figures require considerable restoration in the fragment.

[11] E. Ruschenbusch, "Die soziale Zusammensetzung des Rates der 500 in Athen im 4. Jh.," *ZPE* 35 (1979) 177–80; "Epheben, Bouleuten und die Bürgerzahl von Athen um 330 v. Chr.," *ZPE* 41 (1981) 103–05; "Noch einmal die Bürgerzahl Athens um 330 v. Chr.," *ZPE* 44 (1981) 110–12. For the replies of P. J. Rhodes *cf.* n.12 *infra*.

[12] See P. J. Rhodes, *A Commentary on the Aristotelian* Athenaion Politeia (Oxford 1981) 531, 696, 769; "Ephebi, Bouleutae and the Population of Athens," *ZPE* 38 (1980) 193 with n.9.

[13] I make the following assumptions: (a) 21,000 citizens; (b) life expectancy at birth of 20–30 years; (c) annual grown rate of 0–1%. In a population of this type the number of thirty-year-old males constitutes 2.5–2.9% of all males over eighteen; *cf.* A. J. Coale and P. Demeny, *Regional Model Life Tables and Stable Populations* (Princeton 1966), Model West, Mortality levels 2–6, Males. Accordingly the number of male citizens who each year turn thirty in the later fourth century will be 525–610. In order to run the *boule* constitutionally, 500 new candidates are needed each year if all serve once, 250 if all serve twice. As stated *supra*, most probably served only once, and many not

citizens eligible for the *boule* was only slightly larger than the minimum number required to run it, then it follows that the number of citizens in any of the 139 demes was only just sufficient to fill the number of seats in the *boule* assigned to the deme. For a considerable surplus of citizens in one deme would mean that another was underpopulated and could not provide the prescribed number. The epigraphical evidence shows, however, that virtually all the demes did furnish the required number of *bouleutai* each year.[14] It follows that in almost all the demes the number of eligible *demotai* must have closely matched the bouleutic quotas.[15] This perfect correspondence between population and representation in the *boule* in the fourth century would be a miraculous coincidence if the bouleutic quotas had been fixed by Kleisthenes in the late sixth century, and so I conclude that the quotas were probably revised and that those known from fourth-century inscriptions were fixed in connection with the restoration of the democracy in 403/2. It is worth noting that the only prytany inscription extant from the fifth century has different quotas for the demes of Erechtheis, and the figures recorded for the single demes may be the quotas, although probably only two-thirds of the fifty *prytaneis* were inscribed on the stone. But again there is an alternative: the view that the adult male citizens in the fourth century numbered 21,000 is not undisputed,[16] and so it is still possible to ascribe the known bouleutic quotas to Kleisthenes if we presuppose a male citizen body (aged eighteen and over) of 31,000 or even more, eligible as *bouleutai* when they had passed the age of thirty.[17]

---

immediately upon turning thirty but later in life. Given a considerable mortality of men of all ages, a yearly 'class' of 525-610 new thirty-year-old citizens must be very close to the minimum required.

[14] See Traill's *Tables of Representation*.

[15] The only deme whose size is known is Halimous with three seats in the *boule* (*Agora* XV 13.10-16, 42.232-35, 43.82:88). In 346/5 the number of *demotai* was 80+, and probably not more than 100 (Dem. 57.10, 15). Consequently, Halimous could fill its three seats only if all *demotai* served once (of 100, three will be aged 30) or if 2/3 served once and 1/3 twice (of 80, two will be aged 30).

[16] This figure is based on Ath. 272c (Ktesikles *FGrHist* 245F1) and Plut. *Phoc.* 28.7 supplemented with Diod. 18.13.4-5 (where δισμυρίων has been emended to μυρίων). The number 31,000 is based on the MS. reading of Diodoros. See *infra* n.17.

[17] Scholars who follow Gomme in assuming a citizen population of 31,000, of whom *ca* 14,500 belonged to the 'hoplite class', regularly believe that the *boule* was dominated by citizens of 'hoplite status': A. W. Gomme, *The Population of Athens in the Fifth and Fourth Centuries B.C.* (Oxford 1933) 26; J. A. O. Larsen, *Representative Government in Greek and Roman History* (Berkeley/Los Angeles 1966) 10-11; Rhodes (*supra* n.9) 4-6. But this position is equally difficult to combine with the view that the known bouleutic quotas were fixed by Kleisthenes. If we assume that the 'hoplite class' filled, say, 3/4 of the seats in the *boule*, then the number of candidates required each year is

Apart from the significant correspondence between the bouleutic quotas and political activity, the percentages tabulated above reveal another surprising phenomenon: a significant underrepresentation of citizens from the Asty. If we follow the common view that most of the politically active citizens lived near the Agora and the Pnyx and that most citizens still lived in their demes, then more than half, not just a quarter, of the politically active would be members of city demes. This leads us from the question of deme membership to that of deme residence. Why do only about one fourth of all active citizens belong to the city demes? The growth of political activity in the course of the classical period must have led to an increasing overrepresentation in the political assemblies of citizens from the Asty by comparison with the other two districts. In the age of Kleisthenes, when the people and the council met only infrequently, it may have been possible even for citizens of the more remote demes to fulfil their civic duties as councillors and members of the *ecclesia*. In the later fourth century, however, when the *ecclesia* met forty times in a year, the *boule* ca 250, and the *dicasteria* 150–200, it was simply impossible for an Athenian who lived in the Paralia or the Mesogaios to attend more than a few of all the political meetings. No deme in the Paralia and the Mesogaios is closer to the Agora and the Pnyx than *ca* 12 km., a walk of at least two hours. Consequently, if we assume that most citizens in the age of Demosthenes still lived in their demes, the increasing political activity would necessarily have led to a massive overrepresentation of Athenians belonging to the city demes and to the destruction of the balance in political representation among the three districts. Now the sources testify to a small representation of citizens enrolled in the city demes, and so we must infer (a) that many citizens in the course of the classical period had moved from the countryside to Athens, and (b) that the citizens still living in their ancestral demes came to the city more often than we are used to believe and took an active part in the running of the democratic institutions, both the *ecclesia*, the *boule*, and the *dicasteria*.

375, whereas the number of thirty-year-olds of hoplite status is *ca* 360–420 (*supra* n.13). Again, if most *bouleutai* served only once, there must have been in almost all the demes an unbelievable correspondence between the quotas fixed by Kleisthenes and the number of eligible *demotai* of hoplite status in the fourth century. The view that Kleisthenes introduced the known bouleutic quotas can, in my opinion, be upheld only if we assume (a) that the adult male citizens numbered 31,000 and (b) that all served on the *boule* irrespective of their social status. On this view some demes may have been 'overpopulated' and others 'underpopulated' but still large enough to fill their quotas.

Especially for the *rhetores* and *strategoi* the constant involvement in politics must have necessitated permanent or at least long-term residence in the urban district from Athens down to the Peiraieus, or in the rural district belonging to the Asty. This *a priori* assumption receives some support from information about individual political leaders: Demosthenes of Paiania had a house in Peiraieus and one in Athens (Din. 1.69, Aeschin. 3.209); Phokion of Potamos (?) a house in Melite (Plut. *Phoc.* 18.8); Timotheos of Anaphlystos a house in Peiraieus (Dem. 49.22, *cf. APF* 510); and Timarchos of Sphettos a house behind the Akropolis (Aeschin. 1.97). Moreover, there is much less evidence to the contrary—that citizens recorded as politically active lived far from Athens, in the Paralia or the Mesogaios.[18] The dicastic *pinakia* point to the same conclusion: most of those for which the provenience is attested come from graves in the immediate environs of the city, while only a few have been found in the remote demes. Moreover, the last owner of a *pinakion*, buried e.g. in Peiraieus, is sometimes a demesman from the Paralia or the Mesogaios.[19] Concerning *rhetores* and *strategoi* and jurors, however, the prosopographical evidence is too scarce to be of much value for investigating the relation between political activity, deme membership, and deme residence. Far more important are hundreds of tombstones, which however do not testify to political activity but only to the relation between deme membership and residence for the citizen population as a whole. Gomme's is the only published discussion of this type of evidence, based on the inscriptions in *IG* II; in an unpublished paper, Aksel Damsgaard-Madsen has brought the evidence up to date by including the new material in *IG* II² and *SEG* I–XXV.[20] Gomme examined 404 citizens of the fourth and third centuries for whom the tombstone and its provenience are known; Damsgaard-Madsen has added 412 more, and his study corroborates the inference drawn by Gomme: tombstones found in the Mesogaios or the Paralia commemorate almost invariably citizens buried in their ancestral deme, whereas tombstones found in or near Athens record more citizens

---

[18] *E.g.* Astyphilos Philagrou Halaieus, a proposer of two decrees of the people but also active in his deme (*IG* II² 1175). There are surprisingly few citizens active both in their deme and in the city as *rhetores* or *strategoi*. Apart from Astyphilos I can cite only Euboulides Antiphilou Halimousios (Dem. 57.8) and Moirokles Euthydemou (?) Eleusinios (*Hesperia* 8 [1939] 180). This problem will be dealt with by David Whitehead in a forthcoming publication; I should like to thank him for letting me see his typescript.

[19] *Cf.* Kroll (*supra* n.7) 9 with n.2, 83 with n.21.

[20] Gomme (*supra* n.17) 44–45; A. Damsgaard-Madsen, *Befokningbevaegelser pa Attika i klassisk Tid belyst ud fra person-demenavnene pa attiske gravsten fra 4 & 3 arhundrede*, unpublished paper (Arhus 1980).

belonging to the Paralia and the Mesogaios than to the Asty itself. Thus Gomme's and Damsgaard-Madsen's figures illustrate a migration from the country to the town. A quantification is impossible today, but may perhaps be attempted when the numerous tombstones found all over Attica in the last decades and stored in the museums have been made accessible by publication. A tombstone (with known provenience) is preserved for only a dozen or so of the politically active citizens, but again we have some evidence of *rhetores* and *strategoi* from coastal or inland demes buried in or near Athens,[21] much less evidence of political leaders buried in their ancestral coastal or inland deme,[22] and no evidence of politically active citzens from the Asty buried outside the Athens-Peiraieus area.

Another important aspect is the daily mobility of citizens of an ancient *polis*. In our age of rapid transportation we tend to forget that people in preindustrial societies commonly walked long distances almost daily. As late as *ca* 1900, many workers were accustomed to walk as much as fifteen km. to their place of work, and the same distance back home after a working day of ten hours. Likewise in many agricultural societies a peasant had to walk similar distances between dwelling and field, unless in summer he spent the night in a shed near the field. On this analogy it is easy to believe that Athenian citizens might willingly walk between two and three hours twice a day in order to attend an important political meeting, which normally lasted only a few hours. Moreover, a citizen might combine participation in politics with other activities. Athens was not only the political but also the religious and economic centre of the *polis*. The major festivals must have attracted citizens from all over Attica, and in the Agora the Athenians bought not only manufactured goods but also their daily provision. The diet was based on barley supplemented by wheat; but in the fourth century local production of grain constituted

[21] Astyphilos Halaieus (*IG* II² 5497 and 5498, found in the 'Theseion'); Epikrates Kephisieus (*IG* II² 6444, found in the Kerameikos); Kallippos Philonos Aixoneus (*IG* II² 5432 and 5433, found in Peiraieus); Kephisophon Paianieus (*IG* II² 7062, found in the 'Theseion'); Melantes Potamios (*IG* II² 7268, found in Athens); Moirokles Kallippou Eleusinios (*IG* II² 6043, found near the Dipylon; the Moirokles referred to by Demosthenes [*PA* 10400] should perhaps be identified with the M. Kallippou Eleusinios recorded on this tombstone rather than with M. Euthydemous Eleusinios [*PA* 10401, *Hesperia* 8 (1939) 180] as I suggested in my inventory); Philon Kallippou Aixoneus (*IG* II² 5450, found near Peiraieus). In some cases a tombstone records the name of an ascendant or descendant of a *rhetor* or *strategos*, *e.g.* Proxenos Harmodiou Aphidnaios, the grandfather of Proxenos *PA* 12270 (*IG* II² 5765, found near the Akropolis); the son of Rhinon Charkleos Paianieus (?) (*Agora* XVII 968).

[22] Alkimachos Kephisiou Angelethen (*IG* II² 5228, found in Angele, near Markopulon); Kleoboulos Glaukou Acharneus (*SEG* XVI 193, found in Acharnai).

only a fraction of the grain consumed by the population of Attica. Hence most grain was imported and sold to citizens, metics, and slaves coming from all over Attica. Again quantification is impossible, but the importing of grain to Athens is incompatible with the view that the prevailing economic pattern was a kind of subsistence farming. Now meetings of the *ecclesia* were often held before or after a major festival, and a citizen coming from a remote deme may have combined political participation with attending the festival and trading in the market.

The question of daily mobility in *Greek* society needs a proper investigation, but on the basis of these rudimentary observations I may offer a sketch of the possible participation in political life by citizens residing in their ancestral demes. The Asty covers most of the plain between Aigaleos to the northwest and Hymettos to the southeast of Athens. The distance to the Agora or Pnyx from any locality within the Asty district is never more than *ca* eight km. If we draw a circle with the centre in the Pnyx and a radius of 12 km., some of the populous demes in the Mesogaios and Aixone in the Paralia fall within it.[23] If we extend the radius to 18 km., we include most of the demes of the Paralia to the northwest of Aigaleos and to the south of Hymettos and also the Mesogaios demes south and west of Pentelikon.[24] In the area delimited by the smaller circle one might walk to the Pnyx in at most two to three hours; from the demes within the 18 km. radius, the walk will take no more than 3–4 hours, depending on the routes followed. A tabulation of the bouleutic quotas with the attested *rhetores* and *strategoi* whose demes fall within these limits will give a rough idea of the proportion of citizens who could in one day walk to Athens, attend a meeting, and return home:

Region	Bouleutic Quotas		*Rhetores* and *Strategoi*	
Asty	130	26%	62	26%
12 km.	186	37%	89	38%
18 km.	308	62%	164	70%

Thus about two thirds of all politically active citizens lived either in Athens or no more than four hours' walk distant. But a third or so of

---

[23] The Mesogaios demes are Acharnai, Athmonon, Eupyridai, Kropidai, Pallene, Phlya, and Sypalettos.

[24] The Paralia demes in question are Anagyrous, Eleusis, Halai Aixonides, Kopros, Kothokidai, Lamptrai, Oe, and Thria. The Mesogaios demes are Cholleidai, Erchia, Gargettos, Ionidai, Kephisia, Kikynna, Kolonai, Konthyle, Kydantidai, Myrrhinoutta, Oa, Paiania (both), Paionidai, Pelekes, Pergase, Sphettos, Teithras, and Trinemeia.

all fourth-century *rhetores* and *strategoi* belonged to demes outside the larger circle.[25] Some of them undoubtedly had moved to Athens, but others were probably still living in their ancestral demes.

How can political activity be combined with residence far from the political centres? This is a complex question, and here I will confine myself to discussing membership in the *boule* for *demotai* from a remote deme, e.g. Anaphlystos. Every year the Anaphlystioi had ten *bouleutai* appointed. Some of the candidates doubtless resided in Athens, such as Konon II, Timotheos II, and Konon III. But given that most and perhaps all citizens had to serve on the *boule* at least once, some of the *bouleutai* representing Anaphlystos, perhaps even a majority of them, must have been local. How did they fulfil their civic duties during their year in office? The Anaphlystioi residing in Athens could of course attend as many of the *ca* 250 meetings of the *boule* as they wished, but those living in Anaphlystos probably stayed away from most meetings, attending only when they happened to be in Athens for other reasons, such as a festival or trade in the Agora. But their uninterrupted presence in Athens may have been requested during the prytany of Antiochis, the tribe to which Anaphlystos belonged. The *prytaneis* were on duty every day. A *trittys ton prytaneon* stayed in the Tholos all the time. The *prytaneis* had common meals, and two-thirds (in ordinary years) or four-fifths (in intercalary) of them had to serve for twenty-four hours as the *epistates ton prytaneon* (Arist. *Ath.Pol.* 44.1–3). That the principal duty for a *bouleutes* was to serve as a *prytanis* is indicated both by an illuminating passage in Plato's *Laws* relating to his ideal city Magnesia,[26] and by the fact that most of the bouleutic inscriptions are dedications set up by *prytaneis*. I believe that a *prytanis* living in a remote deme probably had to move to Athens and stay with a relative or *demotes* during the prytany allotted to his tribe. During the other nine prytanies his deme was probably represented in the *boule* mostly by *demotai* who had moved to Athens permanently.

Two conclusions can be drawn in summation concerning politically active citizens in fourth-century Athens. (1) Their official distribution

---

[25] In *Folkeforsamlingen* (Copenhagen 1977) 70f I accepted a circle of 20 km. radius, which however gives almost the same figures. For a judicious treatment of the problem cf. R. Osborne, *Town-Country Relations in the Athenian Polis* (Diss.Cambridge 1981) 144–50. See also P. Harding, "In Search of a Polypragmatist," *Classical Contributions: Studies . . . McGregor* (New York 1981) 46–47, and E. Kluwe, "Die soziale Zusammensetzung der athenischen Ekklesia," *Klio* 58 (1976) 298. Harding believes that the Athenians were capable of walking long distances in order to attend political meetings, while Kluwe is more pessimistic; I am inclined to follow Harding.

[26] *Leg.* 758B, cf. Rhodes (*supra* n.9) 39.

over the three districts of Asty, Paralia, and Mesogaios matches the distribution of bouleutic quotas so well that it is difficult to believe that the quotas are those fixed by Kleisthenes, and not revised later, say in 403/2. Likewise, if we accept that most citizens above thirty had to serve at least once in the *boule*, then the bouleutic quota assigned each deme must in most cases have matched almost exactly the number of citizens actually eligible, and again it is almost unbelievable that the distribution of eligible citizens over the demes was unchanged from the late sixth century to the late fourth, or that Kleisthenes anticipated the inevitable changes. Either the bouleutic quotas were revised (*e.g.* in 403/2) to match the actual fourth-century population, or there must have been considerably more eligible citizens than we are used to believe, so that all demes, even after considerable changes in population, were still populous enough to fill their number of seats in the *boule*. (2) The number of known *rhetores* and *strategoi* and of jurors attested on dicastic *pinakia* indicates that only a fourth or so of all politically active citizens belonged to the demes in the Asty. This is a strong indicaton that there had been a considerable migration from country to city and that many citizens still living in the Paralia and Mesogaios demes not too far from Athens were willing to walk long distances to attend the political assemblies.

THE INSTITUTE FOR ADVANCED STUDY AND
THE UNIVERSITY OF COPENHAGEN
July, 1983

ADDENDA

73: Since this article was published in 1983 considerable progress has been made in two different fields: (A) the political organization of Attica and (B) the history of the Attic demes.

(A) In *Demos and Trittys* (Toronto 1986) J.S. Traill updated and revised his *The Political Organization of Attica* (*Hesperia* Suppl 14 [1975]) and now presents a map of Attica which in some respects is very different from the famous and almost universally accepted map he published in 1975. The new map is based on a different interpretation of a central aspect of Kleisthenes' reforms: the *trittyes* of either 17 or 16 councillors attested in the fourth-century bouleutic inscriptions reflect the original Kleisthenic *trittyes* and are not (as argued by Wesley Thompson)[1] a specific system of *trittyes ton prytaneon* superimposed on the Kleisthenic territorial *trittyes* (persisting for all other purposes than the organization of the *boule*).[2] From Traill's new position it follows that the Kleisthenic *trittyes* were not strictly territorial and that some *trittyes* were composed of demes from different districts of Attica. Most conspicuous are some *trittyes* composed of city demes combined with demes located in north east Attica some 25 miles away from Athens, i.e. Ikarion & Plotheia (II), Probalinthos (III), Rhamnous (IX) and Eitea & Semachidai & Kolonai (X), each belonging to the »city« *trittys* of their tribe.

I follow Traill and others, e.g. P. Siewert and K. Kinzl, in believing that there was only one system of *trittyes* and not a separate system of *trittyes ton prytaneon* superimposed on a persisting system of strictly territorial *trittyes*. On the other hand, I cannot believe that the system of *trittyes* attested in the 4th century bouleutic inscriptions was the original Kleisthenic system. A comparative study of sepulchral, bouleutic and ephebic inscriptions spanning the period ca. 400 B.C. to ca. 250 A.D. shows that the relative size of the demes changed considerably throughout the period covered by the sources. Xypete, for example, was a fairly large deme in the 4th c. B.C. but dwindled and became a very small deme in the course of the Hellenistic and Roman periods, whereas the (originally) tiny deme Azenia grew to become one of the twelve largest demes in

---

[1] W. Thompson, 'Τριττὺς τῶν Πρυτάνεων,' *Historia* 15 (1966) 1-10. It is Thompson's brilliant article that has revolutionized our understanding of the *trittys*, and his study is still the indispensable starting point for all investigations of the Attic *trittyes*.

[2] Traill's new view of the Kleisthenic *trittyes* was first aired in *Hesperia* 47 (1978). It was developed by P. Siewert in *Die Trittyen Attikas und die Heeresreform des Kleisthenes* (München 1983) and has been further developed by K. Kinzl, 'On the consequences of Following *AP* 21.4 (on the *Trittyes* of Attika),' *The Ancient History Bulletin* 1 (1987) 25-33 to be followed by an article in *Chiron* 19 (1989).

ADDENDA

the Roman period. The epigraphical evidence shows that the population of a dozen demes changed drastically and noticeable fluctuations are attested for several scores of demes.³ I do not believe in a demographic system that was static during the first century where we have no sources (507-ca. 400 B.C.) but then dynamic during the next 650 years covered by the sources we have. Furthermore, in the course of this first century the Athenians suffered a disaster in Egypt in the 450s, several wars with Sparta and allies culminating in the Peloponnesian War, three attacks of plague in the years 430-26, and a crippling siege during the winter of 405/4. The conclusion is that the relative size of the demes in the Kleisthenic period must have been different — in some cases very different — from what is attested in the fourth-century sources. Next, bouleutic quotas were by necessity related to the relative size of the demes; and unless one is prepared to accept an incredibly large number of Athenian citizens ca. 500 B.C., very few demes can have been substantially more populous than required to fill their seats in the *boule*. It follows that the bouleutic quotas in the time of Kleisthenes must have been different from what is attested a century and a half later. A further inference is that the fourth century *trittyes*, which had all the same size, must be different from the original *trittyes* formed by Kleisthenes.⁴ If the organization of the *trittyes* and the bouleutic quotas were revised after Kleisthenes and before the fourth century a probable date of the reform is 403/2, but other dates are possible and the system may well have been revised more than once. Furthermore, if Arist *Ath. Pol.* 21.4 is right in describing the Kleisthenic *trittyes* as subdivisions of the three districts: Asty, Mesogeios and Paralia, it follows that the allocation of north-eastern demes to city *trittyes* attested for tribes II, III, IX and X was a result of the reform and not a part of the Kleisthenic organization of Attica. Finally, it is much easier to explain why one deme, Acharnai, had no less than 22 seats in the *boule*: instead of breaking up this oversized local community (which must have grown considerably between 507 and 403), the Athenians preferred to allow one *trittys* to be larger than the arithmetical third of the tribe's quota of 50 councillors.⁵

---

³ Cf. M.H. Hansen, L. Bjertrup, Th. Heine Nielsen, L. Rubinstein & T Vestergaard, 'The Demography of the Attic Demes. The Evidence of the Sepulchral Inscriptions,' forthcoming in *Analecta Romana Instituti Danici* 18 (1990).
⁴ Cf Hansen, Bjertrup, Nielsen, Rubinstein & Vestergaard (*supra* n. 3).
⁵ I cannot follow Traill (*supra* n. 2) 142-44 who, on a very slender evidence, suggests that Acharnai was a divided deme, belonging partly to the inland and partly to the city *trittys* of Oineis.

ADDENDA

No matter whether the fourth century *trittyes* were the original or the result of a later reform, we will have to admit that an investigation of the geographical distribution of the politically active citizens can no longer be based on the three regions: Asty, Mesogeios and Paralia, each composed of 10 territorial *trittyes*. We must instead, as suggested *supra* p. 82, group all the located demes in concentric zones with Athens in the centre: first we have the urban demes (within the city walls) as well as the demes south east of Aigaleos and north west of Hymettos, all five miles or less away from the Agora and the Pnyx.[6] Then follows all the demes outside the city district, but not further away from Athens than ca. 10 miles (as the crow flies):[7] thirdly, we can group together all the demes outside the 10 miles zone,[8] and finally we are left with a number of unlocated demes and homonymous demes located in two different zones. Of the 373 *rhetores kai strategoi* the demotic is known for 213, and if we arrange them according to the zones described above and compare them with councillors (the quotas attested in the fourth-century bouleutic inscriptions) and with jurors (known from the preserved *pinakia*) the following picture emerges

	R&S	Boul.	Dik.
City	57	131	21
5-10 miles	71	131	27
> 10 miles	73	198	31
Unlocated	12	40	11
Total	213	500	90

The percentages are as follows:

city	27	26	23
5-10 miles	33	26	30
> 10 miles	34	40	35
unlocated	6	8	12
Total	100	100	100

[6] The demes in question are: Agryle, Alopeke, Ankyle, Bate, Boutadai, Cholargos, Daidalidai, Diomeia, Eiresidai, Epikephisia, Erikeia, Euonymon, Halimous, Hermos, Hestiaia, Kedoi, Keiriadai, Kettos, Koile, Kollytos, Kolonos, Korydallos, Kydathenaion, Lakiadai, Leukonoion, Lousia, Melite, Oion Keramaikon, Peiraieus, Perithoidai, Phaleron, Potamos, Ptelea, Skambonidai, Thymaitadai and Xypete.

[7] The demes in question are: Acharnai, Aixone, Athmonon, Eleusis, Eupyridai, Gargettos, Halai Aixonides, Hybadai, Iphistiadai, Kephisia, Kikynna, Kopros, Kydantidai, Oai, Oe, Paiania, Paionidai, Pallene, Pelekes, Pergase, Phlya, Sphettos, Sypalettos, Thria, and Trinemeia.

[8] The demes in question are: Aigilia, Amphitrope, Anagyrous, Anakaia, Anaphlystos,

ADDENDA

All three types of source indicate that only a quarter of the politically active citizens came from demes in the city district and that over a third belonged to demes outside the 5-10 miles zone. What are the implications? The generally accepted view is that most meetings of the *ekklesia* and the courts tended to be dominated by the townspeople.[9] If we assume that, in the fourth century, most Athenians were still living in their ancestral deme, the figure above indicates that the accepted view is wrong. The assembly and the courts were *not* dominated by the urban population, but obviously by citizens coming from the countryside, often from very remote demes. I prefer, however, to believe that the accepted view is basically right. Although undoubtedly many citizens living in the countryside were willing to walk long distances to attend a political meeting held in Athens, cf. *supra* pages 81-82, the core of the audience at an ordinary session of an *ekklesia* or a *dikasterion* must have lived in Athens itself or not longer away than the Peiraeus. It follows that many of the citizens belonging to demes in the countryside did not live in their ancestral deme any longer but had moved to Athens and taken up residence in Athens. And this inference seems to be corroborrated by the numerous sepulchral inscriptions, cf. page 80 above.

(B) Recently, however, two major studies of the Attic demes have appeared, i.e. R. Osborne, *Demos. The Discovery of Classical Attika* (Cambridge 1985) and D. Whitehead, *The Demes of Attica 508/7 - ca. 250 B.C.* (Princeton 1986). Both Osborne and Whitehead believe that, at least to the end of the classical period, Athenians tended to live in their ancestral deme and that the alleged migration from the countryside into Athens and the Peiraeus has been grossly overrated. Osborne takes it for granted that the citizens mostly lived in the deme to which they belonged and has no discussion of the problem. Whitehead has a long and profound discussion (352-60) in which he takes issue with i.a. my 1983 article. He argues that grave stones give evidence only about the residence of men of sufficient means to have a grave monument at all, and that the

---

Angele, Aphidna, Araphen, Atene, Azenia, Besa, Deiradiotai, Dekeleia, Elaious, Erchia, Hagnous, Halai Araphenides, Hekale, Ikarion, Ionidai, Kephale, Kolonai IV & X, Konthyle, Kothokidai, Kytheros, Lamptrai, Marathon, Myrrhinous, Myrrhinoutta, Oinoe VIII & IX, Oion Dekeleikon, Phegaia, Philaidai, Phrearrioi, Phyle, Plotheia, Poros, Potamos Deiradiotai, Probalinthos, Prospalta, Rhamnous, Semachidai, Sounion, Steiria, Teithras, Thorai, Thorikos, Trikorynthos.

[9] Cf, the articles by E. Kluwe in *Klio* 58-59 (1976-77). For recent statements of the view cf. e.g. B. Strauss, *Athens after the Peloponnesian War* (New York 1986) 59: »The country was underrepresented in the assembly, courts and council,« and J. Bleicken, *Die athenische Demokratie* (Paderborn 1985) 103: Die in der stadt oder auch im Piräus wohnenden waren naturgemäss überrepräsentiert«.

ADDENDA

provenance of the stones is too rarely recorded (354). Furthermore, the *rhetores kai strategoi* formed only »the tiny minority of the politically active« and it is illigitimate from the inventory of *rhetores* and *strategoi* to make inferences about the population in general (355). Whitehead prefers to trust some references in literary sources, e.g. Dem. 57.10 that most Halimousioi still lived in Halimous (356) and first of all he stresses the *a priori* argument that »a large proportion« of Athenians must have lived in their ancestral deme, because »otherwise the internal organization of the demes themselves would have broken down« (357).

My (short) reply to Whitehead is organized into four parts in which I discuss: (a) the gravestones, (b) the politically active citizens at *polis* level, (c) the citizens active in deme politics, and (d) the *a priori* argument.

(a) The provenance of many grave stones, though insufficiently recorded in *IG* II 2, can often be established by consulting *IG* II.[10] And a closer inspection of the persons commemorated in 4th century sepulchral inscriptions seems to disprove the widespread assumption that grave monuments show a bias towards wealth.[11] On the contrary, several observations support the assumption that it was quite common for an ordinary citizen to have a (sometimes very cheap) grave stone inscribed with his name. Even slaves were not infrequently commemorated in sepulchral inscriptions.

(b) It is certainly true that many *rhetores* and *strategoi* belonged to the liturgic class and that there is a considerable overlap between the wealthy and the citizens who were politically active at the highest level. But Kroll is probably right in his assumption that »the average owner of a surviving *pinakion* came from the lower strata of the Athenian citizenry«.[12] Thus the high percentage of dikastic *pinakia* from remote demes indicates that many ordinary citizens, and not just wealthy citizens, must have moved to Athens and lived within walking distance of the *dikasteria*.

(c) Independently of each other Osborne (83-92) and Whitehead (313-26) discovered that citizens active in deme politics were different from citizens active in *polis* politics. Athenians who are attested as demarchs or proposers of deme decrees are hardly ever attested as *strategoi* or as *rhetores* moving decrees of the council or the people. Whitehead's book is appended with a prosopography of 360 Athenians who were politically ac-

---

[10] Cf. A. Damsgaard-Madsen, 'Attic Funeral Inscriptions. Their Use as Historical Sources and Some Preliminary Results,' *Studies... Rudi Thomsen* (Aarhus 1988) 62-63.
[11] Cf the forthcoming study by Th. Heine Nielsen and the other members of the Copenhagen epigraphy group (*supra* n. 3) 'Were Grave Monuments Erected by Wealthy Athenians Only or by Most Athenians Irrespective of Wealth?'.
[12] J. Kroll, *Athenian Bronze Allotment Plates* (Princeton 1972) 262.

tive at deme level (408-54); but only three of these reappear as politically active at *polis* level, cf. *supra* page 81.

Whitehead and Osborne have made an extremely important observation but have some difficulty in explaining it. They assume that some Athenians — for reasons we no longer know — restricted themselves to deme politics whereas other (and more ambitious) *demotai* preferred to meddle in city politics. I believe that a better explanation can be offered if we assume that, by the fourth century, a considerable number of Athenians had moved from the countryside into Athens. The missing overlap between *demotai* in deme politics and in city politics would be an inevitable result of such a migration: *demotai* who lived in their deme tended to concentrate on political activities at deme level, whereas *demotai* who had moved to the city participated in *polis* politics and were too far removed from their deme to be active in municipal affairs, cf. the sketch of the working of the *boule, supra* p. 83. On this explanation, however, we should expect a distinction between city demes as against inland and coastal demes to be apparent in our sources. The distinction between local and central political leaders should be attested for inland and coastal demes only, whereas citizens belonging to urban demes and living in their deme may well have been politically active both at deme level and at city level. Of the three fourth-century Athenians attested as politically active at both levels one belonged to a city deme (Halimous) the other two to coastal demes (Eleusis, Halai); but it is worth noting that city demes are poorly attested in Whitehead's prosopography. Of the 360 Athenians recorded, 310 belong to inland and coastal demes, only 50 to city demes, and of these 50 no more than 25 come from the urban demes (Kerameis, Koile, Kollytos, Kydathenaion, Melite, Peiraieus and Skambonidai). Thus, Athenians belonging to and living in urban demes may well have been politically active at both levels. The evidence is too small to allow any conclusion. What is securely attested is that, in the coastal and inland demes, there is a remarkable separation between citizens active in local and in national politics. This significant observation, made by Osborne and Whitehead, seems to run counter to their basic assumption that, in the fourth century, most Athenians still lived in the deme to which they belonged.

(d) The view that »a large proportion« of Athenians must have lived in their deme is rather vague. The emigration of, say, a third of all citizens from coastal and inland demes to the Athens-Peiraieus area is sufficient to produce a heavy concentration of citizens within or near the city walls, but not large enough to impair »the internal organization of the demes«. Whitehead's *a priori* argument is only valid if, say, two thirds or more

ADDENDA

migrated to Athens. But, on my view, the migration of a third or so is what we should expect. Accordingly, I can have my cake and eat it too.

74: Cf. *supra* page 65.

74: Cf. *infra* pages 106-10 and P. Bicknell, 'Athenians Politically Active in Pnyx II,« forthcoming in *GRBS*.

75: Cf. *infra* page 164-65.

76: Cf. the list on pages 70-72.

77: Cf. M. H. Hansen, *Demography and Democracy* (Herning 1985) 65-69 (ca 30,000 citizens living in Attica, not 21,000) 51-64 (the population required to run the *boule* constitutionally).

78: Even with a total of 31,000 citizens we will still have to assume a revision of the bouleutic quotas in e.g. 403/2, cf. *supra* pages 85-86.

80: Cf. Osborne (*supra* page 88) 47-63 and Hansen *Ath. Ass.* 64 with note 413.

80: Damsgaard-Madsen's important inmvestigation of the provenance of Attic gravestones was published in 1988, cf. *supra* page 89 note 10.

81: Add: Euegoros Philoinou Paianieus (*IG* II^2 7045, found at Dipylon); Timotheos Kononos Rhamnousios (*Agora* XVII 71, found in the Agora).

81: On Moirokles Eleusinios cf. *supra* page 68.

81: Add Kephisodotos Archippou Acharneus (*IG* II^2 5787a, found in Acharnai). Some gravestones have no known provenance, i.e. Dikaiogenes Menexenou Kydathenaieus (*IG* II^2 6569), Euboulos Spintharou Probalisios (*IG* II^2 11370) and Philochares Rhamnousios (*IG* II^2 7374).

The Number of *Rhetores* in the Athenian *Ecclesia*, 355-322 B.C.

Mogens Herman Hansen

POLITICAL PARTICIPATION in ancient Athens is a complex problem, encompassing both the various forms of participation, the degree of participation, and the number of participants. Broadly speaking we can distinguish three kinds:[1] (a) an Athenian citizen might be a member of the *ecclesia* or of the panel of jurors who manned the courts and the legislative committees (the *nomothetai*); (b) he might fill an office (*arche*), either through election or sortition; (c) he might take an initiative and, as a *rhetor*, address the *ecclesia*, *boule*, *nomothetai*, or *dicasteria*. As to (a), as an *ecclesiastes* or a juror the average Athenian citizen would have only to listen and vote. He was anonymous and could not be held responsible for how he voted, and he was paid for his participation. As to (b), as a magistrate selected by lot the citizen would have little or no power to make decisions, but on the other hand he would have administrative duties for which he could be held responsible both when he was in office and when he resigned at the turn of the year. In most cases, however, he would share the responsibilities with his colleagues: he would be one of the five hundred *bouleutai* or a member of one of the numerous boards of ten. The elective offices (most of them military) are a case apart. To stand for election is more demanding than to take part in a sortition, and the elected *archai* had more powers than other magistrates. This applies especially to the *strategia*. As a commander-in-chief a *strategos* might often be personally responsible for the conduct of a campaign or some diplomatic activity, and, if unsuccessful, his risk of being prosecuted and convicted was considerable. In the fourth century most of the magistrates were probably unpaid, but some of them, and especially the *strategoi*, might profit by gifts and various kinds of perquisites. As to (c), as a *rhetor* an Athenian citizen was always responsible for his initiative, and this applies especially to proposers (of *nomoi* or *psephismata*) and

[1] I discuss only political activity based on volunteering, and do not include civic duties such as military service, performance of liturgies, or the duty to serve as an arbitrator in one's sixtieth year.

to prosecutors bringing an action. With a few notorious exceptions,[2] the *rhetor* was (in principle) unpaid, and any profit he made might easily be interpreted as a bribe and result in a criminal action.

Membership in the decision-making bodies was in the thousands; officeholding demanded the annual participation of more than one thousand citizens. But how many Athenians took it upon themselves to act as *rhetores*? Traditionally they are counted by the score and not by the hundred,[3] and this narrowing down of political participation when we come to its highest level is sometimes viewed as an oligarchic element of Athenian democracy.[4] In this paper I will argue that an astonishing number of Athenian citizens must have acted as *rhetores* and that active participation in the debate and in the formulation of proposals, though restricted to a minority of the attendants, must have been far more widespread than is usually assumed.[5] By way of introduction I should state the limits of my investigation. (a) I confine my study to the period 355–322 B.C. (b) I examine only the *rhetores* in the *ecclesia* to the exclusion of those addressing the *boule*, the *nomothetai*, or the *dicasteria*. (c) Of the *rhetores* in the *ecclesia* I concentrate on the proposers of decrees (*psephismata*) and do not discuss *rhetores* who addressed the people supporting or opposing decrees proposed by other *rhetores*.

Re (a): lack of sources, both literary and epigraphical, is the principal reason for examining only the period 355–322. First the literary

[2] In a few types of public action, *e.g. apographe* and *phasis*, the prosecutor, if successful, received respectively 3/4 and 1/2 of the property at issue.

[3] *Cf.* G. Busolt and H. Swoboda, *Griechische Staatskunde* II (Munich 1926) 999; G. Glotz, *The Greek City* (London 1929) 159; R. J. Bonner, *Aspects of Athenian Democracy* (Berkeley/Los Angeles 1933) 49, 63–64; A. H. M. Jones, *Athenian Democracy* (Oxford 1957) 128–33; S. Perlman, "The Politicians in the Athenian Democracy of the Fourth Century B.C.," *Athenaeum* 41 (1963) 328–30, 340; M. I. Finley, *Economy and Society in Ancient Greece* (London 1981) 83. Of more special studies I may cite three examples. In "Callistratus of Aphidna and His Contemporaries," *Historia* 5 (1956) 202f, R. Sealey assumes that Athenian politics were conducted by a small number of small political groups. In "Les hommes politiques et la justice populaire dans l'Athènes du IVe siècle," *Historia* 9 (1960), P. Cloché discusses "la carrière des quarante ou cinquante Athéniens qui s'occupèrent alors des affaires publiques" (81). And in "*Isegoria* in the Assembly at Athens," *Ancient Society and Institutions* (Oxford 1966), G. T. Griffith states, "no one will suppose that the invitation in the Assembly to *all* to speak ... gave rise at any time to hundreds of ordinary Athenian citizens trying to accept it in turn" (124); *cf. infra* n.53.

[4] *Cf. e.g.* W. Nippel, *Mischverfassungstheorie und Verfassungsrealität in Antike und früher Neuzeit* (Stuttgart 1980) 106–07.

[5] A few historians take a more optimistic view of the use of *isegoria* than those mentioned *supra* n.3. They include A. G. Woodhead, "Ἰσηγορία and the Council of 500," *Historia* 16 (1967) 129; and W. Connor, *The New Politicians of Fifth-Century Athens* (Princeton 1971) 68: "There were many politicians in Athens and only the most prominent are well known to us."

sources: names of many Athenian generals and ambassadors appear in Xenophon's *Hellenica* (III–VII) and in Diodoros (XIV–XV), both covering the first four decades of the fourth century. But the historians refer only infrequently to named *rhetores* and debates in the *ecclesia*. Some names can be found in Xenophon and in the *Hell. Oxy.*, but not many. For information about Athenian domestic policy and the democratic institutions we must, for the first two decades of the fourth century, turn to Andokides, Isokrates, and Lysias. Then we are faced with a deplorable gap in the literary sources between ca 380 and 355. The only speeches from this period are some by Isokrates (not dealing with Athenian politics) and Isaios (relating to private law and giving very little information about public affairs). In 355 the greatest period of Attic rhetoric begins. For the next thirty-four years we have an unparalleled number of good sources relating to Athenian public life, primarily the speeches by Demosthenes, Aischines, Hypereides, Lykourgos, and Deinarchos, but also the late speeches of Isokrates. On the other hand, not a single speech is later than Antipatros' abolition of the democracy in 322/1. Lykourgos died in 324, Demosthenes, Hypereides, and Aischines (?) in 322, and of Deinarchos the three preserved speeches and most of the fragments antedate the Macedonian occupation of Athens. Of historians we have, apart from Diodoros XVI–XVIII, some valuable fragments of Philochoros, quoted by Didymos and Dionysios in their treatises on Demosthenes. And Plutarch provides some information in his lives of Phokion and Demosthenes. The abundance of literary sources is matched by a similar increase in the number of decrees of the people preserved on stone. In the epigraphical sources there is of course no gap between 380 and 355, but the number of preserved *psephismata* is remarkably higher for the period 355–321 than for the period 403–355. For the first forty-eight years we have some 175 decrees and fragments of decrees, for the following thirty-four years some 300. Furthermore, for our purpose the crucial piece of information is the name of the proposer of the decree, and in this an important reform took place in 354/3. Down to 355/4 the name of the proposer is always recorded without the patronymic and demotic.[6] From the

---

[6] Before 354/3 all proposers lack *patronymicon* and *demoticon*. The last unquestionable example of this practise is *IG* II² 134, passed in the third prytany of 354/3. The first examples of the new style are *IG* II² 136 and 137, both passed in the same year. Of possible exceptions to the new procedure I can mention *IG* II² 214, but Pečírka suggests 356/5 instead of 347/6 (*SEG* XXIV 88); *IG* II² 216, but Lewis suggests 365/4 instead of 346/5 (*SEG* XIV 47); *IG* II² 248, but Johnson suggests 358/7 instead of *ante a.* 343/2 (*CP* 9 [1914] 424); *IG* II² 265, but Johnson suggests a date before 354 (*SEG* XXIV 84). The only really problematic example is *IG* II² 366 passed in the archonship

autumn of 354/3 the patronymic and demotic are almost invariably added. The new style in the prescripts makes it much easier for us to identify the *rhetores* in the *ecclesia*. So both the constitutional development and the preservation of the sources mark off the years 355-322 as a well defined period: the democratic constitution was reformed after the end of the Social War in 355, and democracy was abolished in 322/1. The sources become much more abundant and precise after 355, but the literary sources dry up abruptly after 322. For the Hellenistic period we are left with epigraphical sources which (as usual) are insufficient for a proper understanding of how a constitution works.

Re (b): the council of five hundred was probably convened *ca* 250 times in a year, but we have no idea of the number of decrees passed in a session, and very few *psephismata tes boules* are preserved. Consequently it is impossible to estimate how many of the five hundred councillors took it upon themselves to act as *rhetores*.[7] Similarly, the number of court days can be estimated at *ca* 150-200, but we do not know the number of political public actions heard by the *dicasteria*. In previous publications I argued that especially the *graphai paranomon* and the *eisangeliai eis ton demon* were numerous and may have been heard by the *dicastai* every prytany, but a quantification of trials and so of *rhetores* addressing the *dicasteria* is impossible.[8] In 24.142 Demosthenes is probably exaggerating when he states that the Athenians passed new laws every month. There can be no doubt that the number of *nomoi* passed in a year was negligible compared with the number of *psephismata*, and very few proposers of laws are attested. The literary sources often refer to laws, but mention the proposer of the law only infrequently, and few *nomoi* are epigraphically preserved, presumably because new *nomoi* were recorded in the Metroon and not regularly published on *stelai* as many *psephismata* were.[9] For the *ecclesia*, however, we have much better sources (*cf. infra* 132-34).

---

of Kephisodoros (366/5 or 323/2). Because of the letter forms Kirchner prefers the later year, but Johnson (425) suggests that the inscription is a republication of a decree passed in 366/5. The reform is briefly mentioned by A. S. Henry, *The Prescripts of Athenian Decrees* (Leyden 1977) 32.

[7] For decrees of the *boule* see P. J. Rhodes, *The Athenian Boule* (Oxford 1972) 82-87, 271-72. Decrees of the *boule* only referred to in inscriptions or mentioned in literary sources are recorded in M. H. Hansen, *Initiative und Entscheidung* (Xenia 6 [Konstanz 1983] 31-32 n.39 (= *GRBS* 22 [1981] 353 n.24, but with some additions).

[8] *Cf.* M. Hansen, "How Often Did Athenian *Dicasteria* Meet?" *GRBS* 20 (1979) 243-46; *The Sovereignty of the People's Court* (Odense 1974) 25-26; *Eisangelia* (Odense 1975) 58-65.

[9] *Cf.* Dem. 25.99, Lycurg. 1.66, Harp. *s.v.* Μητρῷον.

Re (c): the term *rhetor*, when used with reference to the *ecclesia*, denotes both the citizen who addresses the people and the citizen who moves a decree.[10] The two types of *rhetor* are overlapping but not identical groups. It is well known that an Athenian who delivered a speech in the *ecclesia* did not have to move a proposal. He might support or oppose a proposal moved by another *rhetor*, or he might simply join a debate.[11] Historians never mention the reverse type of *rhetor*, an Athenian who moved a decree without addressing the *ecclesia* in support of his proposal. We do not know how common this type of *rhetor* was, but several sources testify to the existence of such *rhetores*, *e.g.* Dem. 59.43: οὔτε γὰρ ἀπὸ τῆς πολιτείας προσῄει Στεφάνῳ τουτῳὶ ἄξιον λόγου· οὐ γάρ πω ἦν ῥήτωρ, ἀλλ' ἔτι συκοφάντης τῶν παραβοώντων παρὰ τὸ βῆμα καὶ γραφομένων μισθοῦ καὶ φαινόντων καὶ ἐπιγραφομένων ταῖς ἀλλοτρίαις γνώμαις, ἕως ὑπέπεσε Καλλιστράτῳ τῷ Ἀφιδναίῳ. In this passage *rhetor* denotes the citizen who delivers a speech, and Stephanos was accordingly, in his first years, a man who did not address the assembly but was paid for moving decrees on behalf of other citizens.[12] Some general observations also point to the existence of *rhetores* who moved proposals without addressing the assembly. Many probouleumatic decrees were probably passed in the *procheirotonia*, and so there was no debate.[13] If a decree was debated, the proposer would probably speak in support of his proposal, but not necessarily:[14] the debate of a proposal was

---

[10] See Perlman (*supra* n.3) 341–46, and M. H. Hansen, "The Athenian 'Politicians', 403–322 B.C.," *GRBS* 24 (1983) 39–42.

[11] In several of his symbouleutic speeches Demosthenes says explicitly that he does not intend to to move a decree: Dem. 1.19; 3.10–13; 8.68, 73; 13.13–14.

[12] Other sources showing that some citizens were persuaded or paid to move decrees on behalf of others are: Dem. 20.132; 23.146–47, 201; 24.66, 201–03; 25.40–41; Aeschin. 3.125, 159, 242. For ἐπιγράφεσθαι in the sense 'inscribe one's name on a proposal' see Aeschin. 1.188.

[13] For this view of the *procheirotonia* (stated by Busolt and others) *cf.* M. H. Hansen, *The Athenian Ecclesia* (Copenhagen 1983) 123–30, 215–16. For a different view (taken by Wilamowitz and others) *cf.* P. J. Rhodes, *A Commentary on the Aristotelian Athenaion Politeia* (Oxford 1981) 529–31. At the annual Normal Baynes Meeting of Ancient Historians, held in Birmingham on 25–26 September 1984, David Lewis read a paper, "M. H. Hansen on the Athenian *Ecclesia*." Both Lewis and now Peter Rhodes (with reservations) accept my interpretation of the *procheirotonia*.

[14] The formula used in all decrees about the proposer, ὁ δεῖνα εἶπεν, indicates that a proposal was originally read out to the people by the man who moved it. The formula cannot be taken to mean that he also delivered a speech in support. In the fourth century proposals were read out by the γραμματεὺς (τῇ βουλῇ καὶ) τῷ δήμῳ, *cf.* Arist. *Ath.Pol.* 54.5 with Rhodes' note (*supra* n.13). A somewhat similar reform in the *dicasteria* took place around 380: earlier a witness gave evidence orally in court, but after *ca* 380 his testimony was submitted in writing and read out by a clerk, *cf.* D. M. MacDowell, *The Law in Classical Athens* (London 1978) 242–43 with literature in n.545.

opened by the herald's invitation, τίς ἀγορεύειν βούλεται; There is no sign of an initial statement by the proposer.[15] The literary sources mention *rhetores* of both types, speakers and proposers, but the numerous inscriptions record only proposers. So, once more, the nature of our sources forces us to concentrate on proposers to the exclusion of those who are only attested as speakers.

The Number of Proposals Moved in the *Ecclesia*, 355-322

After these introductory remarks on limitations I can define my investigation positively: I will attempt to estimate the (minimum) number of proposers of decrees in the Athenian *ecclesia* in the period 355-322 and to relate this figure to the total number of adult male citizens. The first problem is to calculate the total number of decrees passed by the Athenians in this period. In the period down to *ca* 350 I believe that the Athenians held 30 *ecclesiai* in a year, and in the following period 40 (no less but probably also no more).[16] So in the 34 years from 355/4 to 322/1 the Athenians must have held a total of 1300 meetings of the assembly: and this is a minimum. Some historians prefer to believe that 40 *ecclesiai* were held already in the fifth century and that an *ecclesia synkletos* was an additional meeting and not one of the three (later four) meetings, convened in an emergency.[17] They will have to assume a minimum of 1400 *ecclesiai*.

How many proposals were moved and how many decrees were passed in the course of a meeting of the *ecclesia*? According to the *Ath.Pol.*, two *ecclesiai* out of four had nine items on the agenda, three on sacred matters, three on heralds and envoys, and three on secular

---

[15] The original invitation to speak was τίς ἀγορεύειν βούλεται τῶν ὑπέρ πεντήκοντα ἔτη γεγονότων; This formula was still in use in 346/5 (Aeschin. 1.23, *cf.* 2.47), but by 330/329 it had been replaced by the simple question τίς ἀγορεύειν βούλεται; (Aeschin. 3.4). The shorter formula may have been in (common?) use already in the fifth century, see Ar. *Ach.* 45, *Eccl.* 130, Dem. 18.170; *cf.* Griffith (*supra* n.3) 119. The older formula precludes, and the later formula does not indicate, that the debate was opened by a statement of the proposer.

[16] See M. H. Hansen and F. Mitchel, "The Number *Ecclesiai* in Fourth-Century Athens," *SymbO* 59 (1984) 13-19; Hansen (*supra* n.13) 37, 42-43, 57-59, 61-62, 83-84, 101-02. For a fuller treatment of this problem see M. H. Hansen, *Die athenische Volksversammlung im Zeitalter des Demosthenes* (Xenia 10 [Konstanz 1984]). Lewis (*supra* n.13) rejects the reconstruction suggested by Hansen and Mitchel. He admits that Dem. 24.21 and 25 point to no more than three *ecclesiai* in prytany I, but holds that it is illegitimate, on this evidence, to assume only three *ecclesiai* in prytanies II-X.

[17] This is the traditional view, stated *e.g.* by Busolt (*supra* n.3); C. Hignett, *A History of the Athenian Constitution* (Oxford 1952) 233; Jones (*supra* n.3) 108-09. It is still maintained (without argumentation) by Rhodes (*supra* n.13) 521-22.

matters.[18] Do the 3 × 3 items constitute a maximum (so that regularly, say, only 4–5 items were debated) or a minimum (so that sometimes even more than 9 items were debated)? We have no evidence, but I prefer the second alternative for the following reason: about 350 B.C. the number of *ecclesiai* was probably raised from three to four in a prytany. The most reasonable explanation is that three *ecclesiai* in a prytany = thirty in a year did not suffice; there was too much business to be transacted. The inference seems to be that the agenda regularly comprised nine or more items. The agenda for the *ecclesia kyria* was considerably longer. We have no precise information about the number of items on the agenda for the fourth *ecclesia*,[19] but from the *per diem* paid out we may infer that the three *ecclesiai* for which the allowance was 1 drachma were of the same duration whereas the *ecclesia kyria* was longer, compensated by an allowance of 1½ drachmas (*Ath.Pol.* 62.2). So a total of thirty-six to forty items on the agenda to be debated in the four *ecclesiai* held in a prytany is probably a minimum rather than a maximum. Some other historians, e.g. P. J. Rhodes, also take the 3 × 3 items to be a minimum, but for a reason I cannot accept: following Wilamowitz, Rhodes believes the *procheirotonia* to be a vote on the fixing of the agenda whereby the people decided how many items to put on the agenda, and which to accept in addition to the 3 × 3 items prescribed by law (*cf. supra* n.13).

What is the relation between the number of items on the agenda and the number of proposals moved by the *rhetores* and voted on by the people? First, one item on the agenda might lead to the passing of several decrees. We have preserved, for example, no less than four decrees passed by the people at the *ecclesia* held in the precinct of Dionysos on 19 Elaphebolion 332/1.[20] All are honorary decrees for

---

[18] Arist. *Ath.Pol.* 43.6 with Rhodes' note (*supra* n.13) 529.

[19] The agenda for the *ecclesia kyria* is described in *Ath.Pol.* 43.4, and the long list of items recorded here is not even complete: it does not, for example, include citizenship decrees and honorary decrees, which, however, as the epigraphical evidence shows, were often passed in an *ecclesia kyria* (*cf. e.g. IG* II² 336, 448). In the fourth *ecclesia* the people debated and voted on supplications (*Ath.Pol.* 43.6), but again Aristotle probably records only the obligatory item on the agenda for this meeting. On the other hand, we know that the people were not allowed to debate any matter at all at any (ordinary) meeting. According to Dem. 19.185, foreign policy could be debated only in some *ecclesiai* and not in others (unless the meeting was transformed into an *ecclesia synkletos*, *cf.* Hansen [*supra* n.13] 71).

[20] *IG* II² 345 (moved by Lykourgos Lykophronos of Boutadai), 346 (moved by Demades Demeou of Paiania), 347 (moved by Aristoxenos Kephisodotou of [?] Peiraieus), *Hesperia* 8 (1939) 26–27 no. 6 (moved by E– – –, *cf. infra* 140 no. 28). This meeting must have been one of the three *ecclesiai* and not the *ecclesia kyria*; the only example of ἐκκλησία κυρία ἐν Διονύσου is totally restored, *Hesperia* 4 (1935) 35–37 no. 5. Furthermore, in the preceding year (333/2) the *ecclesia* reserved for supplications was held

foreigners, they are all non-probouleumatic, and they were proposed and carried by four different *rhetores*. Probably they were all moved in response to an open *probouleuma* inviting any Athenian who so wished to propose honours for foreigners of great merit. It is unlikely that the *boule* for this purpose presented four different open *probouleumata* (= four items on the agenda) or that the four decrees passed are alternatives to four detailed *probouleumata* submitted for ratification but all rejected and replaced with the decrees we have preserved.[21] Similarly, "peace and alliance with Philip of Macedon" was probably one item on the agenda for the *ecclesiai* in Elaphebolion 347/6, but we know that this matter entailed the passing of several decrees in each of the *ecclesiai*.[22]

Furthermore, several proposals might result in the passing of only one decree. About 10% of all decrees preserved on stone have a rider appended which was proposed and carried either by the *rhetor* who moved the principal proposal or by another *rhetor*.[23] And of the non-probouleumatic decrees some were passed in response to an open *probouleuma*, but others must be counterproposals to detailed *probouleumata*, and in this case the vote of the people was a choice between two or more proposals.[24]

On the other hand, an item on the agenda introduced by an open *probouleuma* might result in a debate but not in the proposal of any decree. In several of his symbouleutic speeches Demosthenes emphasizes that he has no intention of moving a *psephisma* on the subject, but will simply advise the people (*cf. supra* 127 with n.11). Demosthenes' speech may have been followed by a *psephisma* moved by another *rhetor*, but the impression is that a political debate was sometimes conducted in the *ecclesia* without any proposal being made and without any vote being taken.

---

on the last day of Elaphebolion (*cf. IG* II² 336b and *SEG* XXI 278). So the ἐκκλησία ἐν Διονύσου held *ca* 16–22 Elaph. was presumably one of the two *ecclesiai* with 3 × 3 items on the agenda, and the debate on the festival was probably one of the three items relating to sacred matters (*hiera*). The four honorary decrees listed above may have been passed in connection with one of the three items on the agenda relating to secular matters (*hosia*) or in consequence of an extra item on the agenda.

[21] For the definition of probouleumatic and non-probouleumatic decrees see Rhodes (*supra* n.7) 67–68. In his *Commentary* (*supra* n.13) 529 Rhodes seems to assume that each of the four honorary decrees required a separate item on the agenda.

[22] For the numerous decrees on the conclusion of peace with Philip in Elaph. 347/6 see Hansen (*supra* n.13) 70–71.

[23] *Cf.* Rhodes (*supra* n.7) 65 and tables C (247–50) and D (259–62). It is worth noting that almost all the riders are to *probouleumata*, whereas a rider to a non-probouleumatic decree occurs only twice after 403/2 (71–72).

[24] *Cf.* Rhodes (*supra* n.7) 81.

In conclusion, I assume that each item on the agenda would, on average, result in the passing of one decree and that the number of proposals voted on, including riders, must have been somewhat higher than the number of decrees. So in an *ecclesia* the Athenians would pass no fewer than nine decrees and vote on more proposals. This is, I believe, a cautious estimate, and the total number of decrees passed in a session of the *ecclesia* was probably above rather than below this figure. In support, I may refer to an analogous institution. A Swiss *Landsgemeinde* is attended by 2000–6000 citizens who, in addition to elections, have to debate and vote on 15–20 laws and decrees during a meeting which usually lasts for 2–3 hours.[25]

The result of the first part of my investigation is that the Athenians, in the period 355–322, convened no fewer than 1300 meetings of the *ecclesia*. In an *ecclesia* no fewer than 9 decrees were regularly passed, and the vote taken on more proposals. If we count riders separately, the minimal number of decrees passed in these thirty-four years must be 13,000. To suggest a maximum is impossible.

How many of these 13,000 or more decrees are known to us, and what is the relation between the number of decrees passed and decrees preserved? About 300 decrees are preserved on stone; *ca* 50 more are referred to in inscriptions, some in other decrees and some in inventories. The literary sources quote, paraphrase, or mention *ca* 150 more decrees.[26] A decree attested in the literary sources is hardly ever preserved on stone or referred to in inscriptions, and *vice versa*. The overlap between the different types of source is insignificant,[27] and so the total number of known decrees of the period 355–322 comes close to 500. The conclusion is that fewer than 4% of all decrees passed are preserved or referred to in our sources. And even this is a very optimistic figure. Most of the decrees preserved on stone are fragmentary. In several cases only a few letters of a standard formula is all we have. Most of the references in inscriptions to other decrees are of the type κατὰ ψήφισμα δήμου, sometimes with the addition: ὃ ὁ δεῖνα εἶπεν. In the literary sources references to decrees are often short and casual and give insufficient information

---

[25] *Cf.* Hansen (*supra* n.13) 209.

[26] For a survey of decrees of the fourth century see Hansen (*supra* n.13) 163–65 with nn.6 and 15, which covers the entire period from 403 to 322. My survey is no longer up to date, and minor corrections and additions will appear in a future article. Furthermore, the survey does not include decrees referred to in other decrees and in the inventories published by the various boards of magistrates. For a short survey of such references see my *Die athenische Volksversammlung* (*supra* n.16).

[27] Six decrees known from both epigraphical and literary sources are listed in Hansen (*supra* n.13) 188 n.16.

about the form and content of a decree. For our purpose the crucial piece of information is the name of the proposer, which is recorded for only 181 decrees (including riders).

Known Proposers of Decrees of the People, 355-322

In 69 decrees preserved on stone the name of the proposer can be read or confidently restored. For decrees only referred to in inscriptions the number is 16. Literary sources mention 98 decrees proposed by a named citizen. The sum is 183 decrees, but in two cases (only), a literary source refers to a decree preserved on stone,[28] and the total is accordingly 181 decrees moved by 82 citizens. I list here the known proposers:[29]

Ἀγνωνίδης Νικοξένου Περγασῆθεν, 325/4 (*IG* II² 1629.13-15)
Ἀλεξίμαχος Πήληξ, 347/6 (Aeschin. 2.83, 85)
Ἀλκίμαχος ...⁶... οἱ ἐγ Μυρρινούττης, 335/4 (EM 13067)
Ἀνδροτίων Ἄνδρωνος Γαργήττιος, 347/6 (*IG* II² 212.8)
Ἀντιμέδων, before 342 (Dem. 58.35)
Ἀπολλόδωρος Πασίωνος Ἀχαρνεύς, 349/8 (Dem. 59.4)
Ἀριστογείτων Κυδιμάχου, 335-330 (Dem. 25.87, hypoth. 1; Din. 2.12)
Ἀριστοκράτης, 353/2 (Dem. 23.1, 14)
Ἀριστόνικος Ἀριστοτέλους Μαραθώνιος, 335/4 (*IG* II² 1623.280-83)
Ἀριστόνικος Νικοφάνους Ἀναγυράσιος, 341/0 (Dem. 18.83, Plut. *Mor.* 848D)
Ἀριστόξενος Κηφισοδότου Πειραιεύς (?), 332/1 (*IG* II² 347.9-11)
Ἀριστοφῶν, 324-322 (*AthMitt* 72 [1957] 156-64 no. 1)
Ἀριστοφῶν Ἀριστοφάνους Ἀζηνιεύς (5 decrees: 2 in epigraphical, 3 in literary sources)[30]
Ἀριστώνυμος Ἀριστονίκου, 345/4 (*IG* II² 220.7-8, 28-29)
Ἀρχέδημος Ἀρχίου Παιονίδης, 349/8 (*IG* II² 208.5-6)
Βλέπυρος Πειθάνδρου Παιονίδης, 354/3 (*IG* II² 189.7)
Βράχυλλος Βαθύλλου Ἐρχιεύς, ca 330 (*IG* II² 408.5)
Δημάδης Δημέου Παιανιεύς (21 decrees: 11 in epigraphical, 10 in literary sources)
Δημέας Δημάδου Παιανιεύς, before 321 (*Hesperia* 13 [1944] 231-33 no. 5)
Δημήτριος Εὐκτήμονος Ἀφιδναῖος, 332/1 (*Syll.*³ 287.9)
Δημομέλης Δήμωνος Παιανιεύς, 339/8 (Dem. 18.222-23)

---

[28] Philokrates' decree concerning the *hiera orgas* in 352/1 (Androt. *FGrHist* 324F30, Philoch. 228F155; *IG* II² 204.54-55). Demades' citizenship decree for Alkimachos in 337/6 (Harp. *s.v.* Ἀλκίμαχος; *IG* II² 239, *cf.* Tod 180 and *SEG* XXI 267).

[29] For those who moved more than three decrees I refer to the documentation given in my inventory of *rhetores* and *strategoi* in *GRBS* 24 (1983) 159-79.

[30] In my catalogue (*supra* n.29) 161 last line, delete no. 13, *IG* II² 289, which I now take to have been moved by an unknown *rhetor* (*cf. infra* 138 no. 13).

Δημοσθένης Δημοκλέους Λαμπτρεύς, 329/8 (Syll.³ 298.9-10), 325/4 (IG II² 360.5)
Δημοσθένης Δημοσθένους Παιανιεύς (39 decrees: 1 in epigraphical, 38 in literary sources)
Δημόφιλος, 346/5 (Aeschin. 1.86, schol. Aeschin. 1.77)
Δημόφιλος Δημοφίλου Ἀχαρνεύς, 324/3 or earlier (IG II² 1631.655-58), before 318 (IG II² 421.3-4)
Δήμων Δημομέλους Παιανιεύς, 323/2 (Plut. Dem. 27.6, Mor. 846D)
Διοπείθης Διοπείθους Σφήττιος, 346/5 (IG II² 218.22-23), 346-340 (Dem. 18.70)
Διόφαντος Φρασικλείδου Μυρρινούσιος, 337/6 (IG II² 242.6-7), 337/6 (IG II² 243.6-7)
Διόφαντος Θρασυμήδους Σφήττιος, 353/2 (Dem. 19.86)
Ἐμμενίδης ἐκ Κοίλης, 332/1 or earlier (IG II² 1544.30, cf. 208.4-5)
Ἐπικράτης ....οτήτου Παλληνεύς, 353/2 (Dem. 24.27)
Ἐπιτέλης Σωνόμου Περγασῆθεν, 323/2 (IG II² 365.6)
Ἐπιχάρης Κολλείδης, before 342 (Dem. 58.30-34)
Εὐβουλίδης Ἀντιφίλου Ἁλιμούσιος, 346/5 (IG II² 218.6-7)
Εὔβουλος Σπινθάρου Προβαλίσιος, 348/7 (Dem. 19.304), 346-340 (Dem. 18.70, 75)
Εὐθύμαχος ....¹⁸........, 353/2 (IG II² 138.4)
Εὐκτήμων, 354/3 (Dem. 24.11-14)
Εὐφίλητος Εὐφιλήτου Κηφισιεύς, 323/2 (IG II² 448.6)
Ἡγήσιππος Ἡγησίου Σουνιεύς (4 decrees: 1 in epigraphical, 3 in literary sources)
Θεόδωρος Ἀντιφάνου Ἀλωπεκῆθεν, 335/4 (IG II² 330.5)
Θεομένης Ὀῆθεν, before 324 (IG II² 3207)
Θουκυδίδης, before 342 (Dem. 58.36-38)
Ἱεροκλείδης Τιμοστράτου Ἀλωπεκῆθεν, 349/8 (IG II² 206.5-7, 26-27), 349/8 (IG II² 209.5)
Ἱερώνυμος Οἰκωφέλους Ῥαμνούσιος, ca 330 (IG II² 415.11)
Ἱππόστρατος Ἐτεαρχίδου Παλληνεύς, 341/0 (IG II² 228.7-8)
Ἱπποχάρης ....?.... Ἀλωπεκῆθεν, 336/5 (IG II² 330.26, 50)
Καλλικράτης Χαροπίδου Λαμπτρεύς, 346/5 (IG II² 215.5-6), 340/339 (IG II² 233.5)
Καλλισθένης, 347/6 (Dem. 18.37, 19.86 with schol.)
Κηφισόδοτος, 336/5 (Lex.Patm. 149f)
Κηφισοφῶν Καλλιβίου Παιανιεύς (4 decrees: 2 in epigraphical, 2 in literary sources)
Κηφισοφῶν Λυσιφῶντος Χολαργεύς, 325/4 (IG II² 1629.170)
Κρατῖνος, 354/3 (IG II² 134.6), before 353 (IG II² 172.3-4)
Κτησιφῶν, 337/6 (Aeschin. 3.12)
Λυκοῦργος Λυκόφρονος Βουτάδης (11 decrees: 10 in epigraphical, 1 in literary sources)
Μειδίας Μειδίου Ἀναγυράσιος, before 322 (Hyp. fr.150)
Μοιροκλῆς Εὐθυδήμου Ἐλευσίνιος, before 342 (Dem. 58.53, 56)

Ναυσικλῆς Κλεάρχου Ὀῆθεν, 334/3 (*IG* II² 1623.313)
Νόθιππος Λυσίου Διομειεύς, 331/0 (*IG* II² 349.9-10)
Πάμφιλος Εὐφιλήτου Κηφισιεύς, 323/2 (*IG* II² 448.31)
Πολύευκτος Τιμοκράτους Κριωεύς, 347/6 (*IG* II² 212.65-66)
Πολύευκτος Κυδαντίδης, 326/5 (*IG* II² 1628.38-39), 330-324 (Hyp. 3.13-15)
Πολύευκτος Σωστράτου Σφήττιος, 332/1 (*IG* II² 344.11-12), 332/1 (*IG* II² 368.8), 324/3 (*IG* II² 363.7-8, *SEG* XII 89)
Πολυκράτης Πολυεύκτου Φηγαιεύς, 349/8 (*IG* II² 207a.2)[31]
Προκλείδης Πανταλέοντος ἐκ Κεραμέων, 328/7 (*IG* II² 354.8-9)
Σκίτων, before 347 (Dem. 21.182)
Σμίκρος, before 347 (Dem. 21.182)
Στέφανος, before 336 (Din. fr. xviii)
Στέφανος Ἀντιδωρίδου Ἐροιάδης, 347/6 (*IG* II² 213.5)
Τηλέμαχος Θεαγγέλου Ἀχαρνεύς, 339/8 (*Hesperia* 7 [1938] 291-92 no. 18), 330-328 (*IG* II² 360.28), 330-328 (*IG* II² 360.46)
Τίμαρχος Ἀριζήλου Σφήττιος, 347/6 (Dem. 19.286-87), 347/6 (Aeschin. 1.81)
Τιμωνίδης . . . . .¹². . . . . , 353/2 (*IG* II² 139.6)
Ὑπερείδης Γλαυκίππου Κολλυτεύς, 339/8 (Dem. 18.223), 338/7 (Dem. 26.11, Hyp. frr.32-33)
Φανόδημος Διύλλου Θυμαιτάδης, 332/1 (*IG* VII 4252.9-10)
Φιλέας Ἀντιγένου Παιονίδης, 331/0 (*IG* II² 348.6)
Φιλιππίδης, 336/5 (Hyp. 4.4-6)
Φιλόδημος Αὐτοκλέους Ἐροιάδης, 340/339 (*IG* II² 232.18-19)
Φιλοκλῆς Φορμίωνος Ἐροιάδης, 325/4 (Din. 3.2, 5)
Φιλοκράτης Πυθοδώρου Ἁγνούσιος (7 decrees: 1 in epigraphical, 6 in literary sources)
Φιλωτάδης Φιλοστράτου Παλληνεύς, 354/3 (*IG* II² 136.10-11)
Φρύνων Ῥαμνούσιος, 348/7 (Aeschin. 2.12)
Χαιρωνίδης Λυσανίου Φλυεύς, 333/2 (*IG* II² 338.6-7)
Χαρικλείδης, 327/6 or earlier (*IG* II² 1673.9)

These 181 decrees moved by 82 citizens are what we have left of a total of probably 13,000+ proposals moved in the period 355-322. So the preserved decrees constitute less than 1.5% of all proposals. Let us imagine that we had perfect sources. The number of proposals with the name of the proposer attested would probably rise from 181 to 13,000+, but by multiplying the number of decrees by 75 or more, what will be the effect on the number of proposers? The multiplier to be used is of course less than 75, but is it 15, or 10, or 5, or only 2? Theoretically there is a continuum of possibilities be-

---

[31] M. J. Osborne, *Naturalization in Athens* (Brussels 1981) at D 12, suggests an earlier date (*ca* 361), but the recording of the patronymic (and the demotic) of the proposer shows that the decree cannot be earlier than 354/3 (*cf. supra* 125 with n.6).

tween extremes which can be described thus: (a) We know already a good many (perhaps even the majority) of the citizens who proposed decrees between 355 and 322, and access to more than 12,800 new decrees would probably give us only twice as many names, so that the total would be some 150-200 proposers for the entire period. (b) Political initiative was so widespread among the Athenian citizens that the discovery of 75 times as many decrees would provide us with the names of hundreds of new proposers, perhaps even more than a thousand. *A priori*, both positions are tenable (*cf. infra* 141-44), but in what follows I shall apply some tests and adduce some other sources which, I believe, will force us to move away from position (a) and towards position (b). Exact figures are of course impossible, but the general trend is significant: in fourth-century Athens proposers of decrees of the people must be counted by the hundred and not by the score.

Broken Names of Proposers Attested in Inscriptions

In the 85 decrees on stone listed above, the name of the proposer is either completely recorded or confidently restored.[32] But we have also 30 more fragmentary preambles of popular decrees passed between 355 and 322 in which a few letters of the name of the proposer are still to be seen on the stone, but not enough to allow an identifi-

---

[32] In my catalogue (*supra* n.29) I accepted most of the restorations printed in *IG* II² and not questioned in later epigraphical publications. I admit, however, that "confidently restored" in some cases is a very optimistic description of what Kirchner and his predecessors have done to broken names. Occasionally other attested names fit the lacuna as well as that suggested by the editor, not to speak of the possibility that the proposer is a hitherto unknown man. Most restorations in the Corpus are made on the (tacit) assumption that the proposer is more likely to be a citizen who is already attested as proposer *vel sim.* than a citizen whose name fits the open spaces but who is not (yet) known as politically active (in the *ecclesia*). But this assumption is questionable. Half of the decrees preserved on stone and listed above (42 out of 85) are moved by citizens attested only this once as a proposer and often completely unknown otherwise. So, whenever there is a choice between two or more names which equally well fill the gap, the name of the proposer would, in my opinion, better be left as a broken name and not restored to give the name of the most active citizen. The most important examples are the following. *IG* II² 172.3-4 [Κρατῖ]νος: alternatives are *e.g.* Φυρκῖνος (*PA* 15051), Εὔθοινος (*PA* 5505, 5508, 5509). *IG* II² 207a.2 Πολυκράτης Πολυ[εύκτου Φηγαιεύς]: an alternative is Πολυκράτης Πολυαράτου Κρωεύς, *IG* II² 6551 (*PA* 12022), which is one letter shorter, but *IG* II² 207 is not *stoichedon* and some 44 letters are missing after Πολυ- (*cf.* now Osborne [*supra* n.31]). *IG* II² 209.5 ['Ιεροκλείδης Τιμοσ]τράτου Ἀλωπεκῆθεν: an alternative is - - -στράτου Ἀλωπ[εκῆθεν, *IG* II² 5584. *IG* II² 237.5-6 ['Ηγή]σιππος ['Ηγησίου Σουνι]εύς: an alternative is Κτήσιππος Χαβρίου Αἰξωνεύς (*PA* 8885). *IG* II² 330.5 Θεόδωρ[ος Ἀντιφάνου Ἀλωπεκῆθεν]: an alternative is Θεόδωρος Δημοτίωνος Φηγούσιος, *IG* II² 7642 (*PA* 6909). *IG* II² 344.11-12 [Πολύευκτος Σωστράτου Σφήττιος]: the identification of the proposer is questionable in light of M. B. Walbank, *ZPE* 48 (1982) 264-66.

cation.³³ Sometimes we can establish only the number of spaces to be filled by the name of the proposer. Even broken names, however, can be valuable pieces of information. Although we cannot identify the proposer, we can often state that the letters preserved and the spaces to be filled do not fit any of the 82 known proposers. In other cases we can state that an identification is possible but unlikely. The 30 preambles are:

1. *IG* II² 131.5 (*SEG* XXII 89): ἔ[δοξεν τῶι δήμωι ....⁸.... ε]ἶπεν (355/4). Citizens with eight-letter names who in the period 355-322 proposed decrees are: Βλέπυρος Πειθάνδρου Παιονίδης, Ἐπιχάρης Χολλείδης, Εὔβουλος Σπινθάρου Προβαλίσιος, Εὐκτήμων, Θεόδωρος Ἀντιφάνου Ἀλωπεκῆθεν, Κρατῖνος, Κτησιφῶν, Νόθιππος Λυσίου Διομειεύς, Στέφανος, Στέφανος Ἀντιδωρίδου Ἐροιάδης, Τίμαρχος Ἀριζήλου Σφήττιος. *IG* II² 131 may have been moved by any of these, or by any of those who are recorded as proposers between 380 and 355: Ἀριστίων, Ἐπιχάρης, Εὐξίθεος, Στέφανος, Φίλιππος.

2. *IG* II² 132.2 (*SEG* XXIV 86): ἔδ]οξ[εν τῶι δήμωι ......]ης εἶπ[εν (355/4). Of the 82 known proposers only four have names that can fill the six spaces before –ης: Ἐπιχάρης Χολλείδης, Ἐπιτέλης Σωινόμου Περγασῆθεν, Θεομένης Ὀῆθεν, Φιλοκλῆς Φορμίωνος Ἐροιάδης. But the last three are attested as spokesmen in the late 320's and were probably too young in 355/4 to move a decree. If this decree was moved by a known *rhetor* the most likely candidate is Ἐπιχάρης Χολλείδης. Of the proposers active in the decades before 355 the only known candidate is Ἐπιχάρης.

3. *IG* II² 132.22 (*SEG* XXIV 86): ἔ[δοξεν τῶι δήμωι ...]ΟΙ[... εἶπε]ν (355/4). Either οι or οκ may be read. Following Kirchner, Pečírka³⁴ prefers οκ and, on the assumption that the proposer is identical with that of the first decree on the stele (*cf. supra*), suggests a name of the type -οκλῆς. So Φιλοκλῆς Φορμίωνος Ἐροιάδης would be the only known *rhetor* of our period to

---

³³ *IG* II² includes several more examples of broken names than the 30 I record, but they are probably all earlier than 354/3 and fall outside the period discussed here. On *IG* II² 214, 216, 248, 265, and 366 see *supra* n.6. 263.4-5 is restored by Kirchner: - - - ἐγραμμ[άτευεν ......¹⁴...... ἐκ Κήδ]ων εἶπεν. But the sequence secretary–proposer is otherwise attested only in decrees from the beginning of the century (*cf. e.g. IG* II² 31, 72, 106). Furthermore, Kirchner allows only 23 spaces for the demotic of the *proedros* plus the name with patronymic and demotic of the secretary, which is barely possible. A preferable solution is to bring the decree back to the period before 354/3 and restore ἐγραμμ[άτευε ...... ἐπεστάτει ..^{ca.4}.]ων εἶπεν (cf. e.g. *IG* II² 110, 112) or perhaps ἐγραμμ[άτευε(ν) ἔδοξεν τῶι δήμωι ..⁵⁻⁶..]ων εἶπεν (cf. e.g. *IG* II² 96). In *Hesperia* 29 (1960) 1-2 no. 2 Meritt restored a fragmentary preamble: [ἐπὶ - - - ἄρχον]τος ἐπὶ [τῆς - - - πρυτανείας - - -]ων Λεωσ[- - - εἶπεν] (ca 350). Even if we assume that the prescript is short and several formulae are omitted (*cf. e.g. IG* II² 212, 215), the restoration of the name of the proposer in the line following the archon presupposes a line of some 100 letters, which is excessive for a decree. So the restoration of εἶπεν in line 2 is questionable.
³⁴ *The Formula for the Grant of Enktesis* (Prague 1966) 37.

fill the lacunae. Because by 324 he had served on the board of generals more than ten times, he may have been born in 375 or earlier, and so there is a remote possibility that he was the proposer of this (and the previous) decree. I tend to doubt it.

4. *IG* II² 133.8-9: ἔ[δοξεν τῶι δήμωι .....]ίδης εἶπε[ν (355/4). This decree may have been moved by one of four citizens already attested as proposers: Εὐβουλίδης Ἀντιφίλου Προβαλίσιος, Θουκυδίδης, Προκλείδης Πανταλέοντος ἐκ Κεραμέων, Φιλιππίδης.

5. *IG* II² 137.4-5: [ἐπεστάτει ....⁹....]ης εἶπεν (354/3). This decree may have been moved by one of four attested proposers: Ἱεροκλείδης Τιμοστράτου Ἀλωπεκῆθεν, Καλλισθένης, Χαιρωνίδης Λυσανίου Φλυεύς, Χαρικλείδης.

6. *IG* II² 205.8-9 (*SEG* XIV 51): [ἔδοξε]ν τῆι βουλῆι καὶ τῶ[ι δήμωι ....⁸....]ς Ἀριστύλλο Στειριε[ὺς εἶπεν] (351/0). This decree may have been moved by Δημόφιλος or Εὐθύμαχος. The inclusion of the last requires a note: Euthymachos is recorded as proposer of *IG* II² 138: Εὐθύμα[χος ....¹⁸........ εἶπεν]. So the identification with the proposer of *IG* II² 205, hence Εὐθύμαχος Ἀριστύλλου Στειριεύς, presupposes that the patronymic, not only in *IG* II² 205 but also in 138, ended in -o instead of -ου, which is indeed possible since 138.3 shows a patronymic in -o for the secretary. It is more likely, however, that *IG* II² 205 was moved by a citizen not yet known as a proposer. One attested proposer of the 370's and 360's has a nine-letter name ending in -ς, Μενέξενος.

7. *IG* II² 219.8-9 (*Hesperia* 8 [1939] 172-73 no. 3): [ἔδοξεν τῆι β]ουλ[ῆι καὶ τῶι δήμωι ....¹⁷........]εα[- - - εἶπεν] (345/4). No proposer whose patronymic and/or demotic is known has a name that fits. If we accept the restoration proposed by Schweigert (in *Hesperia*), the letters -εα- probably belong to the demotic, in which case we have a choice between [......¹⁵...... Φρ]εά[ρριος and [......¹⁴...... Εἰτ]εα[ῖος.

8. *IG* II² 220.3-4: ἐπεψήφ]ιζε Ἱπποχ[.........¹⁷.........] Οἰνοβίο Ῥα[μνου εἶπεν] (344/3). The proposer may be identical with one of the seventeen proposers for whom neither patronymic nor demotic is known.

9. *IG* II² 229.6-7: ἔ]δοξεν τῆι β[ολ]ῆι κα[ὶ τῶι δήμωι ....¹⁴........]ο Φρε[ά]ρρι[ο]ς εἶπεν (341/0). This proposer must have a name of max. ten letters. Accordingly we can rule out: (a) all proposers whose patronymic and/or demotic we know; (b) all other proposers with names of eleven or twelve letters; (c) Euthymachos ....¹⁸......... and Timonides ......¹²......; (d) Skiton and Smikros, who had both, before 347, been fined ten talents (Dem. 21.182) and are unlikely to appear as proposers in this period. We are left with nine possible candidates: Ἀντιμέδων, Ἀριστοφῶν, Δημόφιλος, Εὐκτήμων, Θουκυδίδης, Κρατῖνος, Κτησιφῶν, Στέφανος, Φιλιππίδης. But the proposer was probably a citizen not yet recorded as spokesman, *e.g.* Ἀντίβιος Ἰσχυρίου Φρεάρριος (*PA* 982).

10. *IG* II² 235.4-5: ἔδοξεν τῶ[ι δήμωι .... κρ]άτης Ἀθην[.....¹¹.....ε]ὖς εἶπεν (340/339). The only known proposers having a ten-letter name ending in -κράτης are Πολυκράτης and Φιλοκράτης, but neither was son of Ἀθην-. Accordingly this rider must have been moved by a citizen not yet recorded as a proposer in our period.

11. *IG* II² 253.1-2: - - -]υς Σ[φ]ήττ[ιος εἶπεν (before 336/5). This decree may be ascribed either to Διοπείθης Διοπείθους Σφήττιος or to Διόφαντος Θρασυμήδους Σφήττιος or to one of the proposers whose patronymic and demotic are unknown.

12. *IG* II² 276.2-3 (*Hesperia* 9 [1940] 342): ἐπεψήφιζεν Εὐθυκράτη[ς Ἀφιδναῖος ....¹⁵...... Π]οτάμιος ε[ἶπεν] (337/6). This decree may have been moved by one of the eleven known proposers who have a name of max. ten letters and for whom neither patronymic nor demotic is known.

13. *IG* II² 289.6 (*SEG* XXI 300, XXIII 60): [.......¹⁹ ᵒʳ ²⁰......]ο[υ Ἀ]ζηνιε[ὺς εἶπε] (*ca* 352-336). Kirchner, following Wilhelm, suggested [Ἀριστοφῶν Ἀριστοφάν]ο[ς Ἀ]ζηνιε[ύς, but Pečírka doubts the older spelling of the patronymic and shows that the line may have had 27 letters instead of 26. So the proposer of this rider is probably unknown and may be identified with one of the known proposers for whom neither patronymic nor demotic is recorded, or rather with a citizen not yet recorded as proposer. Note, however, the older spelling εἶπε, which apart from *IG* II² 212.66 (347/6) is not attested after 375/4 (*IG* II² 96). So there may still be a case for accepting Aristophon as the proposer (*cf.* the catalogue [*supra* n.29] 161 no. 13), but I prefer now to follow Pečírka in questioning the identification.

14. *IG* II² 336a.5-6: ἔδοξεν τῶ[ι δήμωι ....⁸....]όφρονος Λακι : εἶπεν (334/3). None of the 60 proposers with known demotics is of Lakiadai. In Athens the shortest name ending in -όφρων is Θεόφρων, and so the name of the proposer filled max. six spaces. Of the seventeen proposers whose patronymic and demotic are unknown, only Σκίτων fits the lacuna, but he is most unlikely to have been a proposer of a decree in 334/3 (*cf. supra ad* no. 9). This decree must have been moved by a citizen not yet recorded as proposer.

15. *IG* II² 336b.13-14 (*SEG* XXI 278, Osborne D 23): Νῖκις [........¹⁸........]ης Ἀριστάρχου Φ[...⁷... εἶπεν] (333/2). This decree may have been moved by any of the already known proposers whose names end in -ης and whose patronymic and demotic are unknown: Ἀριστοκράτης, Θουκυδίδης, Καλλισθένης, Τιμωνίδης, Φιλιππίδης, and Χαρικλείδης. I am inclined to believe that the decree was moved by a citizen not yet recorded as a proposer.

16. *IG* II² 339b.1-2 (*SEG* XVI 54): - - -]Ν[.....¹¹..... εἶπεν] (*ca* 335-330?). At least three known proposers are possible: Ἀριστοφῶν Ἀριστοφάνους Ἀζηνιεύς, but he was probably dead by the 330's; Δημήτριος Εὐκτήμονος Ἀφιδναῖος; Φιλέας Ἀντιγένου Παιονίδης. Moreover, the decree

may have been proposed by one of the seventeen proposers of unknown patronymic and demotic.

17. *IG* II² 343.2-3 (*SEG* XXIV 103): [ἐπεψήφιζε]ν Ἐπαμεί[νων .....¹¹....] ΚΕΡΔΗ[Σ?....⁸.... Ἀναγυράσιο[ς εἶπ]ε[ν (333/2?). None of the 82 known proposers has a name ending in -κέρδης.

18. *IG* II² 366.9-10: [ἔδο]ξεν τῶι δή[μ]ωι Ἀρι[......] εἶπεν (323/2). The proposer of this decree may well have been the Ἀριστοφῶν who in 324-322 moved a decree relating to Samos, or his name may have been, *e.g.*, Ἀρίγνωτος, Ἀρισταῖος, or Ἀριφράδης.

19. *IG* II² 367.9-10: ἔδοξεν τῶι δ[ήμωι ....⁹....]δώρου Μελιτεὺς [εἶπεν (323/2). In Athens the shortest name in -δωρος is Θεόδωρος, which however is very common in all periods. So the proposer was presumably the son of Theodoros. In this case, he has a name of max. six letters. Among the known proposers, only Σκίτων can fill the lacuna, and he is most unlikely to appear as proposer in 323/2 (*cf. supra ad* no. 9). Alternatively, we cannot rule out the possibility that the patronymic was Δώρου (*cf. IG* II² 1751.62), in which case the proposer had a nine-letter name and may have been Ἀντιμέδων, Ἀριστοφῶν, or Δημόφιλος. But Δῶρος seems to have been an extremely rare name, so I prefer to believe that this decree was moved by an unknown prosposer.

20. *IG* II² 403.4-5: [ἐπεψήφιζε ....⁸....]ς ἐκ Κε[ρ]αμέ[ων.......¹⁵.......]ς [Λα]κιάδης [εἶ]πε[ν] (*ca* 350-320). This decree may have been moved by one of the proposers for whom neither patronymic nor demotic is known.

21. *IG* II² 410.1-2 (*SEG* XXII 94): [- - -]κτο Σκ[αμβωνίδης εἶπεν] (*ca* 330). This decree may have been moved by one of the proposers for whom neither patronymic nor demotic is known.

22. *IG* II² 420.5-6 (*SEG* XXII 93): [ἐπεψήφιζεν .....¹².... ἔδοξεν τῶι δήμωι Εὐ]ρυκράτ[ης ....^{ca 16}...... εἶπεν] (332/1). If we accept the restorations suggested by Meritt, this fragmentary decree gives us the name of a citizen who is not otherwise attested as proposer.

23. *IG* II² 436.2-5: [ἔδο]ξεν τ[ῶι δήμωι - - -]ου Ἀν[- - -]εἶπεν - - - φυλ - - - (*post* 336/5). If we accept Koehler's restoration of line one to give 23 letters to the line, a possible restoration of the preamble is [ἔδο]ξεν τ[ῶι δήμωι Μειδίας Μειδί]ου Ἀν[αγυράσιος εἶπεν· ἐπειδὴ] Φυλ[- - -.

24. *IG* II² 454.8-9 (*SEG* XXI 293): [- - - ἔδοξεν τῶι δήμωι - - - Θ?]ηρι[- - -] (324/3). "The three letters of line 8 come at or near the place where the patronymic or the name of the spokesman should fall. The first two letters are clear; the third looks like *rho* corrected to *iota*, thus HPP to HPI, as in *e.g.* Θ]ηρι[κλέους, Θ]ηρι[ππίδου" (S. Dow, *Hesperia* 32 [1963] 350). The combination -ηρι- does not occur in any demotic, and probably belongs to the patronymic as Dow suggests. None of the 57 attested patronymics of known proposers will fit -ηρι-, but the proposer may have been one of the 25 other citizens listed above.

25. *IG* II² 547 (*SEG* XXI 292.13-14): [ἔδοξεν τῶι δήμωι ...]πρ[....⁹....
- - - εἶπεν - - -]δρ[...⁹.... (324/3). The name of the proposer may have been e.g. Θεόπροπος, Λαμπροκλῆς, Λαμπρίας, vel sim. A short name is preferable since the entire name must have filled max. 26 spaces. None of the 82 known proposers has a name of which the fourth and fifth letters are πρ.
26. *IG* II² 1623.240-42: κατὰ [ψήφ]ισμα δήμου [ὃ ...^ca 8...] εἶπεν (334/3 or earlier). Some 50 of the 82 known proposers have names of 7-9 letters.
27. *Hesperia* 3 (1934) 3-4 no. 5: [ἔδοξεν τῶι δήμ]ωι [........¹⁷........] Θριά[σ]ιος εἶπ[εν (327/6). The proposer was not one of the 65 spokesmen whose patronymic and/or demotic are known; he may be one of the twenty for whom neither is attested.
28. *Hesperia* 8 (1939) 26-27 no. 6: [ἔδοξεν τῶι δ]ήμωι Ε[............²³...........]άσιος εἶ[πεν (332/1). Schweigert restored Ε[ὔβοιος Κρατιστολέω Ἀναγυρ]άσιος (*PA* 5313), and this may well be right, giving evidence of a new proposer. If we leave the 23 spaces open, there is a remote possibility that the proposer was Εὐκτήμων.
29. *Hesperia* 9 (1940) 327-28 no. 36: [....⁹....]Ν[....] Παιανιε[ὺς εἶπεν] (335/4). The proposer is of Paiania and cannot be identified with any of the 63 proposers whose demotic is known. Moreover, there is no attested patronymic Ν[....]. So the patronymic must have filled at least one of the nine spaces to the left of the N, e.g. ᾽Ε᾽ν[δίου. The inference is that the name of the proposer filled max. eight spaces. Of the twenty proposers for whom neither patronymic nor demotic is known, six have names of 6-8 letters: Εὐκτήμων, Κρατῖνος, Κτησιφῶν, Σκίτων, Σμικρος, Στέφανος. But Skiton and Smikros are unlikely to appear as proposers in 335/4 (*cf. supra ad* no. 9). There is a remote possibility that the proposer is cne of the four others, but this decree was in all probability moved by a citizen who is not yet recorded as a proposer.
30. *Hesperia* 9 (1940) 332-33 no. 39: - - -]μο[.....¹¹.....εἶπεν] (*ca* 330). The proposer may have been [Μοιροκλῆς Εὐθυδή]μο[υ Ἐλευσίνιος] or one of the seventeen proposers for whom neither patronymic nor demotic is known.

* Thus, of these 30 decrees, seven must have been proposed by citizens not yet recorded as proposers (nos. 10, 14, 17, 19, 22, 25, 28). And in seven more cases the decree was probably moved by someone other than the eighty-two attested proposers (nos. 2, 3, 4, 5, 6, 15, 29). The proposer of nos. 2 and 3 may have been the same man, but in any case, by a study of the preambles recording broken names we can increase the total number of attested proposers of decrees of the people from 82 to at least 90 citizens.

New Proposers Attested in the Epigraphical Sources

If it were true that we have the names of at least half of the Athenians who proposed decrees in the period 355-322 and that only a few scores of new names would be added if we had the 12,800+ decrees now lost, then almost every new decree found in future will give us the name of a citizen who is already known as a proposer, and only exceptionally will a new decree moved by an unknown proposer add a name to our list of 82. This hypothesis can be tested by an examination of the new sources recovered over the last hundred years. There has been no significant addition to our literary sources for decrees of the people of the period 355–322,[35] but the epigraphical evidence has grown every year, and a survey of the publications since the late nineteenth century will indicate what is to be expected as more decrees are found. For my investigation I presuppose information about all proposers mentioned in literary sources and move forward by three steps: the publication of *IG* II in 1877–83; the publication of *IG* II.5 in 189͜,[36] and later publication up to 1983.[37] The evidence is best presented in a diagram:

	Number of decrees	Number of proposers	New proposers (epigr. sources)	New proposers (all sources)	Percentage
IG II	40	25	25	17	17:40 = 43%
IG II.5	32	28	22	20	20:32 = 63%
Later	13	11	7	6	6:13 = 46%

It is impossible to draw a graph on the basis of these figures, but they do show beyond dispute that it would be absurd to assume that new decrees will provide mostly new attestations of proposers already known from other decrees. On the contrary, we have every reason to infer that on average every second decree found in the future will reveal a citizen not yet known as a proposer (but perhaps as a trierarch or *bouleutes* or *diaitetes*, etc.). It is impossible to say when and how the proportion of new proposers will begin to drop drastically. The next 100 decrees may give the names of 40 new proposers, but the next 1000 decrees, if found, would undoubtedly reveal fewer than 400 new names. The only conclusion is that the epigraphical evidence, according to this test, favours the view that perfect sources would give us the names of many more proposers than are now recorded.

[35] The only additions are Kephisodotos' honorary decree for Demades (*Lex.Patm.* 149 *s.v.* ἑκατόμπεδον) and Philokrates' decree on the ἱερὰ ὀργάς (Didymos *In Dem.* coll. 13.57 [Philoch. F155]) and 14.48 [Androt. F30]).

[36] With *IG* II.5 I group three inscriptions from the Oropos district first published in 1891 and included in *IG* VII (1892), *viz.* 4252, 4253 (*Syll.*[3] 287), 4254 (*Syll.*[3] 298).

[37] This group comprises: *IG* II[2] 218.6–7; 218.22–23; 220.7–8, 28–29; 276.23–24; 408.5–6; 452.11 (*cf.* *SEG* XXI 284); *Hesperia* 4 (1935) 169–70 no. 32 (*cf.* 9 [1940] 339–40); 7 (1938) 291–92 no. 18; 9 (1940) 325–27 no. 35; 13 (1944) 231–33 no. 5; 43 (1974) 322–24 no. 3; *AthMitt* 72 (1957) 156–64 no. 1; EM 13067, unpublished but *cf.* *SEG* XXI 272.

The Distribution of Decrees among Proposers

The next test is also based on statistics, focused again on the epigraphical evidence. Let me say in advance that the test is inconclusive—which in itself, however, is an interesting conclusion. I presuppose that the epigraphical evidence gives us a fairly random sample of decrees moved by named citizens. Of the *ca* 13,000 decrees passed in the years 355–322, perhaps only a few thousand were inscribed on stone, primarily honorary decrees as is evident from the 85 extant which record the name of the proposer. In eight cases only the preamble is preserved and the content of the decree is unknown. Of the remaining 77 decrees, 54 are honorific (including citizenship decrees), and no more than 23 relate to other matters (*e.g.* the navy, cult, public works, and, occasionally, foreign affairs). The paucity of really important decrees preserved on stone is indeed significant, and it would be foolish to write a treatise on the powers of the *ecclesia* based on epigraphical sources. But this investigation is limited to the identity of the proposers, and for this purpose I believe that the decrees on stone are more representative. The *a priori* assumption that the moving of honorary decrees was usually left to minor *rhetores* is contradicted by the fact that, *e.g.*, Androtion, Aristophon, Demades, Demosthenes, Diopeithes of Sphettos, Hegesippos, Lykourgos, and Polyeuktos of Sphettos are attested as proposers of honorary decrees. Conversely, we find otherwise unattested citizens as proposers of rather important decrees, *e.g.* the dispatch of a squadron (Aristonikos of Marathon and Kephisophon of Cholargos). So I presume that the preserved decrees record political leaders and minor *rhetores* indiscriminately. I will go no further than that. The preservation of eleven decrees on stone moved by Demades and ten by Lykourgos as against only one by Demosthenes and none by Hypereides is a sufficient warning that no far-reaching conclusions can be drawn, but is in no way incompatible with a random transmission of decrees inscribed on stone (*cf.* n.39 *infra*).

The following table shows decrees distributed among proposers. The first column gives the number of proposers, the second the number of decrees moved by each, the third the total:

$$\begin{aligned} 42 \times 1 &= 42 \\ 8 \times 2 &= 16 \\ 2 \times 3 &= 6 \\ 1 \times 10 &= 10 \\ 1 \times 11 &= 11 \end{aligned}$$

54 proposers move 85 decrees

Is it possible on the basis of this small sample (less than 1% of all decrees) to say anything about the number of proposers involved? For my test I will suggest two models: (a) all 13,000 decrees were moved by 90 citizens of whom 10 moved 400 decrees each (= 4000 decrees), 20 moved 150 decrees each (= 3000), and 60 moved 100 decrees each (= 6000). (b) All 13,000 decrees were moved by 620 citizens of whom 10 moved 600 decrees each (= 6000 decrees), 10 moved 100 decrees each (= 1000), and 600 moved 10 decrees each (= 6000). In model (a) I suppose that we already know every proposer, from our literary and epigraphical sources (broken names included), and that the next 12,800 would not give us a single new name but only allow us to restore the minimum seven or eight broken names we have. In model (b) I suppose that the recovery of 150 times as many decrees as we have will reveal *ca* seven times as many named proposers. In order to test these two models against the 85 preserved decrees moved by 54 citizens, I have devised an experiment by which 85 random decrees can be drawn from a total of 13,000. All decrees are numbered 1–13,000 and all proposers are also numbered. In model (a) proposer 1 moves decrees 1–400, proposer 2 moves decrees 401–800, proposer 11 moves decrees 4001–4150, etc. In model (b) proposer 1 moves decrees 1–600, proposer 2 moves decrees 601–1200, proposer 11 moves decrees 6001–6100, etc. The drawing of 85 random numbers among 13,000 (one experiment) has been simulated by a calculation based on five-digit random numbers.[38] The results for the two models are as follows (the number of proposers, the decrees of each, and the total):

(A) $31 \times 1 = 31$
$14 \times 2 = 28$
$2 \times 3 = 6$
$2 \times 4 = 8$
$1 \times 5 = 5$
$1 \times 7 = 7$
51 proposers move 85 decrees

(B) $40 \times 1 = 40$
$3 \times 2 = 6$
$3 \times 3 = 9$
$2 \times 4 = 8$
$1 \times 5 = 5$
$1 \times 8 = 8$
$1 \times 9 = 9$
51 proposers move 85 decrees

The striking similarity between the results obtained for (a) and (b) strongly indicates that the experiment need not be repeated. So far as the total number of proposers is concerned, there is no difference between (a) and (b), and both models come very close to the 54 proposers actually attested in the decrees preserved on stone. An-

---

[38] Detailed information about the procedure can be obtained from the author. I should like to thank Lic. Scient. Niels Herman Hansen for his assistance.

other experiment based on the same models or a slight revision of them might easily give us 54 proposers instead of 51. As to the distribution of decrees among proposers, model (a) seems inferior to model (b), but even within a total of 90 proposers model (a) can easily be revised to give as good results as (b).[39]

In conclusion: the hypothesis that the 85 preserved decrees moved by 54 citizens are a random sample of 13,000 decrees is compatible both with the hypothesis that we already know every single proposer, 90 citizens in all, and with the hypothesis that we know only a seventh of all proposers active between 355 and 322, *i.e.* 90 out of more than 600.

Circumstantial Evidence for Named Proposers

In addition to our direct evidence for *rhetores* who moved decrees of the people, we have a substantial amount of indirect evidence for politically active citizens who probably moved decrees between 355 and 322, but are not (yet) attested as proposers of known decrees passed within the period. The weightiest indirect evidence can be grouped under four headings: (1) citizens who were politically active in the period 355–322 but are attested as proposers of decrees only before 355 or after 322; (2) citizens attested in the period 355–322 as speakers in the *ecclesia* but not as proposers of decrees; (3) citizens attested as proposers of decrees of the *boule* during 355–322 but not as proposers of decrees of the people; (4) citizens attested as proposers of *nomoi* passed by the *nomothetai* but not as proposers of *psephismata* passed by the *ecclesia*.

1. Proposers of decrees attested before 355 and after 322

Some of the Athenian citizens who proposed and carried decrees before 355 were still politically active after 355/4 and are attested in this period as (*e.g.*) ambassadors or prosecutors. But my list of 82 proposers includes only citizens whose attested decrees fall within 355–322. Yet it is a fair assumption that a proposer of decrees before 355 who was still politically active after 355 would also continue to propose decrees. Similarly, some of the citizens attested as proposers only after 322 were already politically active before the overthrow of the democracy in 322/1 and may well have moved decrees in the last

[39] In (b) the ten most active citizens (600 proposals each) showed up as proposers of the following numbers of decrees: proposer no. 1, three decrees; no. 2, three; no. 3, eight; no. 4, one; no. 5, two; no. 6, four; no. 7, nine; no. 8, three; no. 9, five; no. 10, four. So the fact that the epigraphical evidence gives us eleven decrees by Demades, ten by Lykourgos, as against one by Demosthenes, is not necessarily incompatible with the hypothesis that the 85 decrees constitute a random sample of the 13,000 decrees.

years of our period. So in addition to the 82 attested proposers for 355-322, we can draw up a list of citizens attested as proposers only before 355 or after 322, but probably also active in the *ecclesia* in the period 355-322:[40]

ante 355:
Αὐτόλυκος (*IG* II² 107.30)
Ἐξηκεστίδης Χαρίου Θορίκιος (*IG* II² 116.8)
Ἡγήσανδρος Ἡγησίου Σουνιεύς (*IG* II² 123.7)
Κηφισόδοτος ἐκ Κεραμέων (Xen. *Hell.* 7.1.12-14; *Hesperia* 8 [1939] 5-12 no. 3; *IG* II² 141.30; Arist. *Rh.* 1411a6-11)
Μελάνωπος Λάχητος Αἰξωνεύς (*IG* II² 145.13)
Μενίτης Μένωνος Κυδαθηναιεύς (*ArchEph* 1971, 137-45)
Πάνδιος Σωκλέους ἐξ Οἴου (*IG* II² 103.6, 105.6, *cf.* 130-33)
Πύρρανδρος Ἀναφλύστιος (*IG* II² 44.7)

post 322:
Δημοχάρης Λάχητος Λευκονοεύς (*IG* II² 1492.126-27)
Ἡγήμων (*IG* II² 1469.121-22)
Στρατοκλῆς Εὐθυδήμου Διομειεύς (*cf.* Rhodes [*supra* n.7] 270)

If all the 13,000+ proposals were preserved, I do not doubt that we would find many of these citizens recorded as proposers of decrees in the period 355-322.

2. Speakers in the *ecclesia*

Not infrequently a literary source mentions a citizen who addressed the *ecclesia* during a debate but did not move a proposal. Some of these Athenians are well attested in other sources as proposers of decrees of the people, but the following twenty are known only as speakers and not as proposers:

Αἰσχίνης Ἀτρομήτου Κοθωκίδης (Dem. 18.136, 140, 285; 19.10, 35, 113, 209, 304, 310, etc.)
Ἀμεινιάδης (Aeschin. 3.130)
Ἀριστόμαχος Κριτοδήμου Ἀλωπεκῆθεν (Dem. 23.13, 110)
Αὐτόλυκος (Aeschin. 1.81ff)
Ἀφαρεύς Ἰσοκράτους Ἐρχιεύς (Plut. *Mor.* 839c)
Γλαυκέτης (Dem. 24.13)
Δημοκράτης Δημοκλέους Ἀφιδναῖος (Plut. *Mor.* 803d)
Δημοχάρης Λάχητος Λευκονοεύς (Plut. *Mor.* 847d)

---

[40] For the political activity attested between 355 and 322 *cf.* the inventory (*supra* n.29). But for two of the men listed here the activity is not of the type recorded in the inventory: Exekestides was eponym of a naval symmory between 356 and 340 (*IG* II² 1617.40-41, *cf.* Davies, *APF* p.175), and Menites is probably the taxiarch mentioned at Aeschin. 2.169-70, *cf.* D. M. Lewis, *BSA* 50 (1955) 31.

Δίφιλος Διοπείθους Σουνιεύς (Din. fr. xli)
Εὐξένιππος Ἐθελοκράτους Λαμπτρεύς (Hyp. 3.14)
Κηφισόδωρος (Timokles fr.17)
Κτησιφῶν (Dem. 19.12)
Μελάνωπος Λάχητος Αἰξωνεύς (Plut. Dem. 13.3; Dem. 24.13)
Νεοπτόλεμος Σκύριος (Dem. 19.12, 315)
Πάταικος Ἐλευσίνιος (Dem. Ep. 3.16)
Πυθέας (Plut. Mor. 804B)
Πυθοκλῆς Πυθοδώρου ἐκ Κήδων (Dem. 18.285)
Ταυρέας (Dem. Ep. 3.16)
Φυρκῖνος (Lycurg. 1.19)
Φωκίων Φώκου Ποτάμιος (Plut. Phoc. 7.5-6)

We know that a political leader, e.g. Demosthenes, sometimes had his proposals moved by other citizens who were either paid or persuaded to act as proposers (Aeschin. 3.159). But I cannot believe that a political leader would consistently make use of others and never propose a decree in his own name. Moreover, I take a speech delivered in the *ecclesia* to be a more conspicuous and demanding political activity than the proposal of a decree or a rider. We may then assume, *a priori*, that citizens attested as speakers were also, at least occasionally, proposers of decrees. Melanopos and Autolykos, for example, who are attested as speakers in the period 355-322, are both recorded before 355 as proposers of decrees, and I find it unbelievable that Aischines never proposed and carried a decree of the people. So I suggest that most, perhaps all twenty *rhetores* listed above would also be known as proposers of decrees if we had perfect sources. On the other hand, Euxenippos, whom Hypereides describes as an *idiotes*, may be an example of an Athenian citizen who (once) had to address the *ecclesia* but never moved a single proposal.

3. Proposers of decrees of the *boule*

Proposers of decrees of the *boule* consist of spokesmen of probouleumatic decrees (decrees of the *boule* ratified by the *ecclesia*) and spokesmen of decrees of the *boule* (independent decrees of the *boule* and *probouleumata* resulting in a non-probouleumatic decree of the *ecclesia* moved by another man). Spokesmen of probouleumatic decrees are of course recorded above among the 82 proposers of decrees of the *ecclesia*. But we know also about twenty citizens who in the period 355-322 proposed and carried decrees of the *boule* in the second sense. Seven of these spokesmen are also known as proposers of decrees of the *ecclesia* (recorded above), but thirteen are attested only as spokesmen of decrees of the *boule*:

Ἀγασίας Χειριγένους (?) Ἰκαριεύς (?), 336/5 (*IG* II² 330.32)
Ἀντίδοτος Ἀπολλοδώρου Συπαλήττιος, 333/2 (*IG* II² 337.5–7), *probouleuma*
Δεινόστρατος Δεινιάδου Ἀγκυλῆθεν, 343/2 (*IG* II² 223.4)
Δημέας Σφήττιος, before 324 (*IG* II² 3207)
Διοφάνης Κηφισιεύς, before 324 (*IG* II² 3207)
Εὐετίων Αὐτοκλείδου Σφήττιος, 328/7 (*IG* II² 354.32), *probouleuma*
Ἡγέμαχος Χαιρήμονος Περιθοίδης, 334/3 (*IG* II² 1156.36)
Καλλισθένης Χαροπίδου Τρινεμεύς, 328/7 (*Agora* XV 49.41)
Καλλίστρατος Θορίκιος, 330/329 or earlier (*IG* II² 1627.380 etc.)
Κηφισόδοτος Εὐαρχίδου Ἀχαρνεύς, 329/8? (*IG* II² 360.51), *probouleuma*
Κτησικλῆς Βατῆθεν, before 324 (*IG* II² 3207)
Πολύευκτος Καλλικράτους Ἑστιαιόθεν, 324/3 (*IG* II² 1631.350–51)
Φυλεύς Παυσανίου Οἰναῖος, 325/4 (*IG* II² 360.66), *probouleuma*

Demosthenes states (22.36) that many councillors never moved any proposal and that the *boule* was in fact dominated by a comparatively small number of *rhetores*. So a citizen attested as a spokesman in the *boule* is very likely to have proposed and carried at least one probouleumatic decree during his year as a councillor. Accordingly I suggest that some of the thirteen citizens listed above, probably even most of them, were in fact proposers of probouleumatic decrees now lost. The same observation applies to the four citizens who are known as speakers in the *boule*, but not as proposers:

Δημοκράτης Δημοκλέους Ἀφιδναῖος (Aeschin. 2.17)
Εὔδοξος Θεαγγέλου Συπαλλήτιος (*IG* II² 223c.10–12)
Ἰατροκλῆς Πασιφῶντος (Aeschin. 2.16)
Λεωσθένης Λεωσθένους Κεφαλῆθεν (Diod. 17.111.3)[41]

4. Proposers of *nomoi*

Some Athenian political leaders are known as proposers of both *nomoi* and *psephismata*, viz. Aristophon, Euboulos, Demosthenes, Lykourgos, Aristonikos (of Marathon), Epikrates (of Peiraieus), and Phanodemos (of Thymaitadai). But no preserved decree of the people can be ascribed to six citizens who however are all attested as proposers of *nomoi* in the period 355–322:

Εὐκράτης Ἀριστοτίμου Πειραιεύς (*Hesperia* 21 [1952] 355–59 no. 5)
Ἡγήμων (Aeschin. 3.25; *IG* II² 1628.300)
Κηφισοφῶν Κεφαλίωνος Ἀφιδναῖος (?: *IG* II² 244.1)

---

[41] In the catalogue (*supra* n.29) 172 line 21, add: Addresses the *boule* (at a secret meeting) and applies for money and men, 324/3 (Diod. 17.111.3).

Λεπτίνης ἐκ Κοίλης (Dem. 20.95, 128)
Μειδίας Κηφισοδώρου Ἀναγυράσιος (Dem. 21.173)
Τιμοκράτης Ἀντιφῶντος Κριωεύς (Dem. 24.63; 24.39-40, 71)

To propose a law and defend it before the *nomothetai* was a much more demanding and complicated procedure than to move a decree in the *ecclesia*, and so it is reasonable to assume, *a fortiori*, that a citizen who took it upon himself to move a law is also likely to have been, at least occasionally, the proposer of a decree of the people. This assumption can be substantiated for some of the citizens listed above. In a late source Eukrates, who moved the tyranny law of 337/6, is mentioned as one of the political leaders in Athens in the 320's.[42] Kephisophon, who may have moved the law on the repair of the wall in 337/6, is attested as a member of the Theoric Board in 343/2.[43] I cannot believe that political leaders like Leptines and Meidias never acted as spokesmen in the *ecclesia*, and Demosthenes accuses Timokrates of having been paid for moving decrees in the *ecclesia* (24.66, 201-03). The allegation of bribery may well be wrong, but there can be no doubt that Timokrates was a regular proposer of decrees in the assembly. So all the citizens listed above as proposers of laws would probably also appear as proposers of decrees if we had fuller sources.

Thus the examination of four different kinds of indirect evidence has provided us with the names of 48 citizens (some recorded more than once) who are not attested as proposers of decrees of the people during 355-322, but most of whom certainly would be if we had full knowledge of the 13,000+ proposals. And the indirect evidence is by no means exhausted by the names listed above. Twenty more citizens are attested as envoys elected by the people between 355 and 322,[44] and 25 other citizens are known as prosecutors or *synegoroi* in political public actions.[45] Furthermore, eight citizens are mentioned in

[42] In Luc. *Dem.Laud.* 31 Eukrates of Peiraieus is mentioned along side Demosthenes, Himeraios of Phaleron, and Aristonikos of Marathon.

[43] *Cf.* the catalogue (*supra* n.29) 171. In the law *IG* II² 244.2 an alternative restoration of the name of the proposer is [Δημήτριος Εὐκτήμονος] Ἀφιδναῖος, *cf. Syll.*³ 287.9.

[44] Ἄνδρων, Ἀριστογείτων (*PA* 1774), Ἀριστόδημος, Ἀφόβητος, Ἀχιλλεύς, Δέρκυλος, Δημήτριος Φανοστράτου Φαληρεύς, Διόφαντος (*PA* 4421), Δρωπίδης, Εὐδίδακτος, Εὐκλείδης, Εὐφρόσυνος, Ἐφιάλτης, Θηβαγένης, Θρασυκλῆς ἐξ Οἴου, Ἰφικράτης (*PA* 7736), Κίμων, Κλειτόμαχος, Μενέλαος, Πολύξενος. For references see the inventory (*supra* n.29). Envoys who are also attested as *rhetores* in the *ecclesia* or in the *boule* are listed above and are not included in this note.

[45] Ἀρχίας, Ἀρίστων, Ἀψηφίων, Δεινίας, Διόδωρος, Διώνδας, Εὐθυκλῆς, Εὔνομος Κυδιμάχου, Θεοκρίνης, Θεόφιλος, Ἱμεραῖος, Καλλικράτης, Λυκῖνος, Μελάντης, Μενέσαιχμος, Πιστίας, Προκλῆς, Σωσικλῆς, Φανόστρατος, Φίλιππος (*PA* 14374), Φιλο-

the literary sources as political leaders, but not a single political activity can be ascribed to any of them.⁴⁶ Again, it is reasonable to assume that many citizens who were active as envoys or prosecutors in political public actions would also take an active part in the decision-making process in the *ecclesia*. So in addition to the 82 attested proposers, we know 48 citizens who probably were proposers and 53 more who may be presumed to be. Combining the direct and the indirect evidence, we can draw up a list of 183 citizens who either certainly or probably or presumably were proposers of decrees of the people during 355-322. Is this list fairly exhaustive? Or is it so defective that perfect sources would give us the names of three or five or ten times as many proposers of decrees of the people? *A priori*, it is remotely possible that the discovery of *ca* 12,800 more decrees, in addition to many more attestations of the 82 known proposers, would provide us mostly with names of the 101 who are known as having performed other forms of political activity, and that any new decree to be found only exceptionally would bring us an addition to the extended list of 183 certain, probable, and possible proposers. But this hypothesis can be ruled out by a closer inspection of the epigraphical evidence.

Over the years the recovery of documents on stone has provided us with the names of 54 citizens who between 355 and 322 proposed and carried decrees of the people. 43 names are new in the sense that these citizens are not attested in literary sources as proposers of decrees. I argued above that the future recovery of more decrees is likely to add many names to the list of 82 proposers now attested in literary and epigraphical sources. But then we have to ask the question: are these new proposers likely to be citizens already known as politically active in other fields (*i.e.* already recorded among the 101 men mentioned above)? Or will new epigraphical sources bring us the names of citizens who are either completely unknown or at least not known as politically active? Again, a glance at what has been found will indicate what to expect of future discoveries. Of the 43 new proposers attested in epigraphical sources, only seven names recur in the lists of 48 citizens recorded to have performed related forms of political activity, and if by including envoys, prosecutors,

---

κράτης Ἐπικράτου Ἐλευσίνιος, Φιλοχάρης Ἀτρομήτου Κοθωκίδης, Φορμίων (*PA* 14952), Χάρης, Χαρῖνος. For references see the inventory (*supra* n.29). Prosecutors who are also attested as *rhetores* in the *ecclesia* or in the *boule* are listed above and are not included in this note.

⁴⁶ *Cf.* the inventory (*supra* n.29) 179, where three out of the eleven men listed fall outside the period 355-322 (Kallippos, Lykon, Xenotimos).

etc., we extend the investigation to cover all the 101 politically active citizens, only four more proposers can be identified with citizens who were politically active in other fields. So for 32 out of the 43 citizens the attestation as proposer in the *ecclesia* is the only recorded political activity. In conclusion, for the years to come, every second decree to be recovered will, on average, bring us the name of a new proposer. And, again on average, in three cases out of four this new proposer will be a citizen not previously attested as having performed any political activity.[47] The total number of proposers of decrees of the people in the period 355-322 is likely to have been much larger than the 183 citizens of whom 82 are attested and 101 are likely to have been active in the *ecclesia*.

The Number of Proposers of Probouleumatic Decrees

In his careful investigation of decrees of the *boule* and the *demos*, Rhodes argued convincingly that decrees of the *ecclesia* are fairly evenly divided between probouleumatic and non-probouleumatic.[48] Accepting a total of 13,000+ decrees in the period 355-322, we must infer that some 6500 decisions made by the people were ratifications of *probouleumata* proposed and carried in the *boule* by one of the councillors. Demosthenes states (22.36) that the decrees of the *boule* (including *probouleumata*) were moved by a minority of the councillors and that most members of the *boule* only listened to and voted on the proposals moved by the *rhetores*. Let us assume that only 25-50 councillors in the course of the year took it upon themselves to be spokesmen of *probouleumata*. This is, in my opinion, a modest estimate, but the conclusion is nevertheless that some 850-1700 councillors were responsible for the probouleumatic decrees ratified by the *demos* in the period 355-322. We know, however, that an Athenian citizen might serve twice on the *boule*, and if most councillors did serve a second year, the number of proposers is reduced to some 500-1000. But again I believe that Rhodes is right in assuming that most councillors served only once.[49] So a simple calculation of the probouleumatic decrees suggests that only some 50% of all decrees of the people in 355-322 were probably moved by no fewer than 700-1400 citizens, sometimes in collaboration with a *rhetor* in the *ecclesia* who persuaded (or paid) the councillor to act as a spokesman (*cf.*

---

[47] That is, political activity of the types listed in my inventory. New proposers may of course be identified with ordinary councillors listed in the *bouleutai* inscriptions or with trierarchs listed in the naval inscriptions.

[48] Rhodes (*supra* n.7) 79.

[49] Rhodes (*supra* n.13) 596, 769, and especially *ZPE* 38 (1980) 193.

Aeschin. 3.125). But that is a different matter to be discussed elsewhere. The non-probouleumatic decrees may have been moved by a much smaller number of citizens (who were also responsible for probouleumatic decrees during their one to two years in the *boule*). The epigraphical evidence supports this assumption: 21 attested probouleumatic decrees and riders are moved by twenty citizens, whereas 36 non-probouleumatic decrees and riders are moved by 24 citizens.[50] This is still a good rotation of proposers, but less marked.

In conclusion, the rule that no citizen could serve on the *boule* more than twice and that most did only once ensured a considerable rotation of *bouleutai* and so of proposers of probouleumatic decrees. Again, the high number of probouleumatic decrees (50% of all) ensured a very high number of proposers of decrees, and so a total of, say, 700-1400 proposers in the period 355-322.

The Number of Proposers Attending an *Ecclesia*

I have argued that *ca* 13,000 decrees passed by the people in 355-322 were presumably moved by no fewer than 700-1400 citizens. How can this figure (covering 34 years) be related to the total number of citizens at any given time and to the number of citizens attending a meeting of the *ecclesia*? We have reason to believe that the adult male citizen population (in any year of this period) amounted to some 21,000 men, and that every year some 600-750 eighteen-year-old Athenians would be inscribed as full citizens in the *lexiarchika grammateia*.[51] So, in the 34 years between 355 and 322, *ca* 20,000-25,000 new citizens would be inscribed, and the total number of citizens recorded in the *lexiarchika grammateia* during 355-322 must have been *ca* 41,000-46,000, or, to strike an average, *ca* 43,500. The ratio of all citizens recorded during 355-322 to all citizens on record in any year is then 43.5:21.[52] If we apply this ratio to the number of proposers, the inference is that 700-1400 proposers in 34 years is the equivalent of 340-680 proposers in any year. In this context,

---

[50] Of the 85 epigraphically attested decrees (*cf. supra* 132) 21 proposals and riders are probouleumatic, 36 are non-probouleumatic, and in 28 cases the significant formulae are lost and the decree cannot be classified.

[51] *Cf.* A. J. Coale and P. Demeny, *Regional Model Life Tables and Stable Populations* (Princeton 1966). As a possible model for Athens I use Model West, males, mortality level II-VI, annual growth rate 0-½%. In these tables the 18-year-old men constitute min. 2.8% (Mortality level VI, annual growth rate 0%) and max. 3.6% (Mortality level II, annual growth rate ½%) of all males above 18. So the Athenian 18-year-old men must have numbered, on average, 600-750 out of 21,000 males above 18.

[52] It makes no difference for the calculation of the fraction (43.5:21) whether we use 21,000 citizens as the starting point or 31,000 citizens (still maintained by some historians as the preferable number of male citizens in the later fourth century).

of course, 'proposer' means potential proposer. The high number of proposers means a small number of decrees moved by the average proposer. Consequently, several prytanies, perhaps even several years, might pass between two decrees moved by the same man. But he was a potential proposer in the sense that, in the *ecclesia*, he might always contemplate the possibility of intervening and handing in a proposal. In this sense, the number of 'proposers' attending a meeting of the *ecclesia* must be counted by the hundred rather than by the score.[53]

Rhetores versus Idiotai as Proposers of Decrees

This very high number of proposers must now be related to the accepted view of Athenian politics, which is well stated by Jones,[54] that the Athenian assembly was dominated by a small group of full-time political leaders and a somewhat larger class of semi-professional 'politicians' who *i.a.* proposed motions in the council and in the assembly.[55] Let us spell out the consequences of this view: if we suppose that such a professional or semi-professional 'politician' would, on average, move one proposal every fourth *ecclesia* over a period of *ca* 25 years (which is indeed a moderate estimate on Jones' description of what it meant to be a 'politician' in fourth-century Athens), then in the period 355–322 slightly more than 50 *rhetores* would have moved all the 13,000 proposals discussed above. Even granted that 13,000 is probably a minimum, this picture of Athenian politics is incompatible both with the fact that access to less than two percent of all sources has already given us the names of at least 90 proposers (82 named proposers plus 8 or more others with broken names) and with the probability that more sources, if found, will bring us the names of hundreds of new proposers.

On the other hand, there can be no doubt that a few 'professional' or 'semi-professional politicians' did exist in Athens and did in fact move a considerable number of decrees in the *ecclesia*: the lexicographers report that Timarchos moved more than 100 decrees.[56] They may be exaggerating, but if the notes are based on good sources, they

---

[53] Griffith (*supra* n.3) is of course right in believing that the herald's question τίς ἀγορεύειν βούλεται; never resulted in a queue of hundreds of citizens wishing to address the *ecclesia*. According to my view there is an essential difference between the regular speaker and the occasional speaker, and therefore, in every session of the *ecclesia*, an essential difference between those who actually address the people and those who may or may not address the people.
[54] *Supra* n.3: 128–33.
[55] *Cf.* my comments on this distinction (*supra* n.10) 47 n.43.
[56] Aeschin. 1 hypoth. 1; Suda *s.v.* Τίμαρχος.

indicate that one hundred is a possible number of decrees moved by one political leader. Next, in the speech *Against Ktesiphon*, Aischines says that Aristophon was acquitted 75 times in a *graphe paranomon*. This is indeed a record, and it has recently been questioned.[57] One may suspect either a corruption of the text or a gross exaggeration. But even if we take this piece of information at face value, it is not out of proportion with the 100 decrees claimed for Timarchos. When Aischines made his remark, Aristophon had been politically active for some sixty years. If he met with much opposition and every third decree was appealed against to the *dicasteria*, he proposed 225 decrees in a period of 60 years, which is the equivalent of fewer than 100 decrees in 25 years. Third, for three named political leaders we have information about a very high number of datable decrees: Demosthenes 39, Demades 21 (+ 5 in the period 321–318),[58] Lykourgos 11. Given the fragmentary preservation of the sources, each of these three citizens was probably responsible for several hundred proposals. Furthermore, that Demosthenes was more or less a professional political leader is apparent from several sources, *e.g.* the speech *Against Zenothemis*: ἐμοὶ [Δημοσθένει] συμβέβηκεν, ἀφ' οὗ περὶ τῶν κοινῶν λέγειν ἠρξάμην, μηδὲ πρὸς ἓν πρᾶγμ' ἴδιον προσεληλυθέναι· ἀλλὰ καὶ τῆς πολιτείας αὐτῆς τὰ τοιαῦτ' ἐξέστηκα ... (the text breaks off) (Dem. 32.32). Finally, the scanty evidence we have shows that a *rhetor* sometimes proposed and carried decrees at two successive meetings of the *ecclesia*;[59] and a *rhetor* might even move two or more decrees at the same session of the *ecclesia*.[60]

Summing up. (a) Some of the political leaders were almost professional, and a *rhetor* of this type was probably responsible for several hundred decrees in the course of his political career.[61] (b) On the other hand, no fewer than 700–1400 citizens were probably active as proposers of decrees in the *ecclesia* in the period 355–322. A combination of (a) and (b) leads to two observations. (1) The average

---

[57] Aeschin. 3.194; cf. S. I. Oost, "Two Notes on Aristophon of Azenia," *CP* 72 (1977) 238–42.

[58] Cf. A. N. Oikonomides' list of Demades' decrees, *Platon* 8 (1956) 106.

[59] Philokrates of Hagnous moved the peace at the session held 19 Elaph. 347/6, and a decree about the oath on the peace at the following session held 25 Elaph. (Aeschin. 3.54, 74).

[60] E.g. Demades (*IG* II² 240, 241), Diophantos of Myrrhinous (242, 243), and Demosthenes, who at the two sessions held in the beginning of Elaphebolion 347/6 moved at least four decrees (*cf.* Hansen [*supra* n.13] 70).

[61] In model (b) (*supra* 143) I suggested that 600 decrees were moved by each of the 10 most active political leaders. For Demosthenes (who was active throughout the period 355–322) a total of 600 decrees would mean that he, on average, moved a decree every second *ecclesia*, which is an impressive effort, but not impossible.

proposer must have moved very few decrees, probably fewer than ten and many citizens only one or two. (2) The number of 'professional' and 'semi-professional' politicians must have been very small, perhaps only some ten to twenty citizens. If we move from twenty to thirty or even forty political leaders, we will have great and increasing difficulties in finding room for the very high number of occasional proposers indicated by the sources. Thus, to Jones' two groups of professional and semi-professional 'politicians' we must add a third important group, mentioned neither by him nor by any other historian: the ordinary politically active citizen who occasionally took it upon himself to hand in a proposal and who took a pride in being an *idiotes* and a *rhetor* only in the legal but not in the political sense of this term.[62] At any meeting of the *ecclesia* some 300–600 citizens out of more than 6000 attending may have been prepared, if necessary, to move a proposal, which is an indication that participation in politics, even at the highest level, was more widespread than assumed by most historians. On the other hand, the number of speakers who *regularly* addressed the people was probably much smaller. In this respect there seems to be an important contrast between the ideal democratic *isegoria* inviting any citizen to take an active part in the debate and a rather narrow group of *rhetores* in the political sense who tended to dominate the debate. But the unquestionable existence of a small group of political leaders has led many historians to draw a much too clear-cut distinction between 'politicians' (who addressed the people and moved the proposals) and ordinary citizens (who listened and voted). This dichotomy obliterates the very important and rather numerous group of citizens who sometimes acted as *rhetores* (in the legal sense) and who, combined, must have been responsible for a very high number of all decrees passed by the people, often perhaps on routine business (*e.g.*, honours) but sometimes at least on important matters. Some ordinary citizens collaborated with the political leaders, but some may also have been acting on their own initiative. Furthermore, it is wrong to draw sharp lines between the groups. The sources indicate instead a continuum with no rigid distinctions between the political leader, the minor *rhetor* (often attached to a political leader), the citizen who only occasionally acted as a *rhetor*, the citizen who only once or twice in his life proposed a decree, and the citizen who only listened and voted. Especially membership of the *boule*, involving the participation of almost all citizens older than thirty, secured a considerable rotation of pro-

[62] *Cf.* my notes on political participation (*supra* n.10) 43–49, esp. 48.

posers of probouleumatic decrees which probably constituted about 50% of all decrees passed in the period.

Conclusion

Studies of 'politicians' in classical Athens and reconstructions of political groups are mostly based on three assumptions: (a) politics in Athens were in the hands of a group of 'professional' and 'semi-professional' politicians; (b) the number of 'politicians' involved was relatively small; (c) we know many and perhaps even most of the 'politicians' involved.[63] The evidence presented in this article points to three different assumptions: (a) in addition to the political leaders there was an important group of politically-minded citizens who were active, even as proposers, but only occasionally and not professionally; (b) the number of citizens involved in politics as proposers (and not only as voters) was much larger than usually believed, and there was no sharp distinction between the professional, the semi-professional, and the ordinary citizen; (c) hundreds of minor and probably also some major political figures are completely unknown to us, and several of those who are attested only once or twice and appear only as minor figures may well have been political leaders responsible for numerous important proposals, now lost.[64]

THE UNIVERSITY OF COPENHAGEN
April, 1984

---

[63] These three assumptions are made by almost all historians who have written in detail on politics and political groups in fourth-century Athens. See most notably K. J. Beloch, *Die attische Politik seit Perikles* (Leipzig 1884); P. Cloché, *La politique étrangère d'Athènes de 404 à 338 avant Jésus-Christ* (Paris 1934); and the very interesting studies by R. Sealey (*supra* n.3).

[64] This article and its predecessors on Athenian political leaders, *GRBS* 24 (1983) 33–55, 151–80, 227–38, all stem from a seminar held in March 1983 at the Institute for Advanced Study in Princeton. I should like to thank the Institute for appointing me a visiting member for spring 1983, the Commission for Educational Exchange between Denmark and the United States for appointing me a Fulbright Scholar for the same period, and the Danish Research Council for the Humanities for supporting me with a grant-in-aid. I should also like to thank the other members of the informal B-Building seminars, held every evening after 10 p.m. over a bottle of wine, and attended by Fordyce Mitchel, Gerhard Thür, Bruce Frier, Egon Verheyen, and myself. Finally, I should like to thank David Lewis for some very helpful notes, especially on my lists of proposers (*supra* 132–40).

ADDENDA

95: On *IG* II² 157 cf. Develin (*supra* page 65) 295 with the note by D.M. Lewis. On *IG* II² 207 cf *supra* page 67.

97: Cf. *infra* page 164.

99: Cf. *infra* pages 167-75.

101: Cf. M.B. Walbank, *AHB* 2 (1988) 57-9.

102: The updated inventory of *rhetores* and *strategoi* (*supra* pages 34-64) entails the following addenda and corrigenda of the list of proposers of decrees: Ἀλεξίμαχος: add the patronymic Χαρίνου; Ἀριστόξενος: delete the demotic; Δημάδης: moved 22 decrees, 11 in epigraphic sources; Διόφαντος: for 353/2 read: 352/1; Ἐμμενίδης: delete the demotic; Ἐπικράτης; for 353/2 read: 354/3; Ἐπιτέλης: for Σωνόμου read: Σωναύτου; Εὐκτήμων: for 354/3 read 355/4; Κηφισόδοτος: for 149f read 159f; Μοιροκλῆς: delete the patronymic; Πολυκράτης: for Πολυεύκτου Φηγαιεύς read: Πολυκράτους; Φιλοκλῆς: for 325/4 read: 324/3; Χαρικλείδης: for 327/6 or earlier read: 333/2(?).

105: Cf., however, C.J.Schwenk, *Athens in the Age of Alexander* (Chicago 1985) 177-81 no. 33.

109: Schwenk (*supra* ad page 105) 184 no. 35 restores Εὐ]θυκράτ[ης, in which case possible restorations are: Εὐθυκράτης Χαρίου Κυδαθηναιεύς (*IG* II² 1629.643f) or Εὐθυκράτης Δημάρχου Κειριάδης (*SEG* 32.279).

110: Another broken name of a proposer of a decree is attested in W. Peek, *Kerameikos* III (Berlin 1941) no 1 lines 4-5: name --]οσΑρις[---. Peek suggests (hesitatingly) a date around 360.In *ClMed* 38 (1987) 75-79 I date the decree 347/6, but an alternative (later) date is suggested by D.M. Lewis cf. page 79.

114: as a possible explanation of the disproportion between the numerous decrees on stone moved by Demades or Lykourgos and the preservation of one decree only by Demosthenes I suggest that Demades and Lykourgos regularly appended their decrees with the publication formula, whereas Demosthenes was not in the habit of adding any provision that the decree be published on stone.

121: In accordance with my views in *Demography and Democracy* (*supra*

ADDENDA

page 91) I now suggest that the Athenian citizen population in the fourth century totalled ca. 30,000 adult males (living in Attica). Thus, ca. 1,000 young citizens must have been inscribed in the demes every year, and the total number of citizens inscribed in the *lexiarchika grammateia* during the 34 years from 355 to 322 must have been ca. 64,000 (30,000 + 1,000 x 34). The ratio is the same.

Two Notes on the Pnyx

Mogens Herman Hansen

In memory of Fordyce W. Mitchel

1. Fencing-Off of the Auditorium

Of the scanty sources describing the opening of an *ecclesia*, two enigmatic passages refer to γέρρα, *viz.* the famous passage in Demosthenes' speech *On the Crown*, describing the *ecclesia* held after Philip's capture of Elatea in 339, and a passage from the Neaera speech describing the procedure adopted for ratification of citizenship decrees:

> Dem. 18.169: ἑσπέρα μὲν γὰρ ἦν, ἧκε δ' ἀγγέλλων τις ὡς τοὺς πρυτάνεις ὡς Ἐλάτεια κατείληπται. καὶ μετὰ ταῦθ' οἱ μὲν εὐθὺς ἐξαναστάντες μεταξὺ δειπνοῦντες τούς τ' ἐκ τῶν σκηνῶν τῶν κατὰ τὴν ἀγορὰν ἐξεῖργον καὶ τὰ γέρρ' ἐνεπίμπρασαν, οἱ δὲ τοὺς στρατηγοὺς μετεπέμποντο καὶ τὸν σαλπιγκτὴν ἐκάλουν· καὶ θορύβου πλήρης ἦν ἡ πόλις. τῇ δ' ὑστεραίᾳ, ἅμα τῇ ἡμέρᾳ, οἱ μὲν πρυτάνεις τὴν βουλὴν ἐκάλουν εἰς τὸ βουλευτήριον, ὑμεῖς δ' εἰς τὴν ἐκκλησίαν ἐπορεύεσθε, καὶ πρὶν ἐκείνην χρηματίσαι καὶ προβουλεῦσαι πᾶς ὁ δῆμος ἄνω καθῆτο.

> Dem. 59.89f: ἔπειτ' ἐπειδὰν πεισθῇ ὁ δῆμος, καὶ δῷ τὴν δωρεάν, οὐκ ἐᾷ κυρίαν γενέσθαι τὴν ποίησιν, ἐὰν μὴ τῇ ψήφῳ εἰς τὴν ἐπιοῦσαν ἐκκλησίαν ὑπερεξακισχίλιοι Ἀθηναίων ψηφίσωνται κρύβδην ψηφιζόμενοι. τοὺς δὲ πρυτάνεις κελεύει τιθέναι τοὺς καδίσκους ὁ νόμος καὶ τὴν ψῆφον διδόναι προσιόντι τῷ δήμῳ πρὶν τοὺς ξένους εἰσιέναι καὶ τὰ γέρρα ἀναιρεῖν, ἵνα κύριος ὢν αὐτὸς αὑτοῦ ἕκαστος σκοπῆται πρὸς αὑτὸν ὅντινα μέλλει πολίτην ποιήσεσθαι, εἰ ἄξιός ἐστι τῆς δωρεᾶς ὁ μέλλων λήψεσθαι.

Discussion has focused on the first passage,[1] while the second has mostly been adduced in attempts to emend the phrase τὰ γέρρ' ἐνεπίμπρασαν in 18.169. I will instead concentrate on the Neaera passage: it gives valuable information about the *gerra* and, apart from

---

[1] S. Karsten, "Over Demosthenes, De Corona § 169 p. 284," *SitzAmst* (1857) 38–65; P. Girard, "Conjecture à propos de Démosthène Disc. sur la Couronne, 169," *RevPhil* 11 (1887) 25–32; R. E. Wycherley, *The Athenian Agora* III *Literary and Epigraphical Testimonia* (Princeton 1957) 190f nos. 623–24; H. Wankel, *Demosthenes. Rede über den Kranz* (Heidelberg 1976) 849–54; M. Valozza, "Demosth. Cor. 169," *MusCrit* 15–17 (1980–82) 135–41.

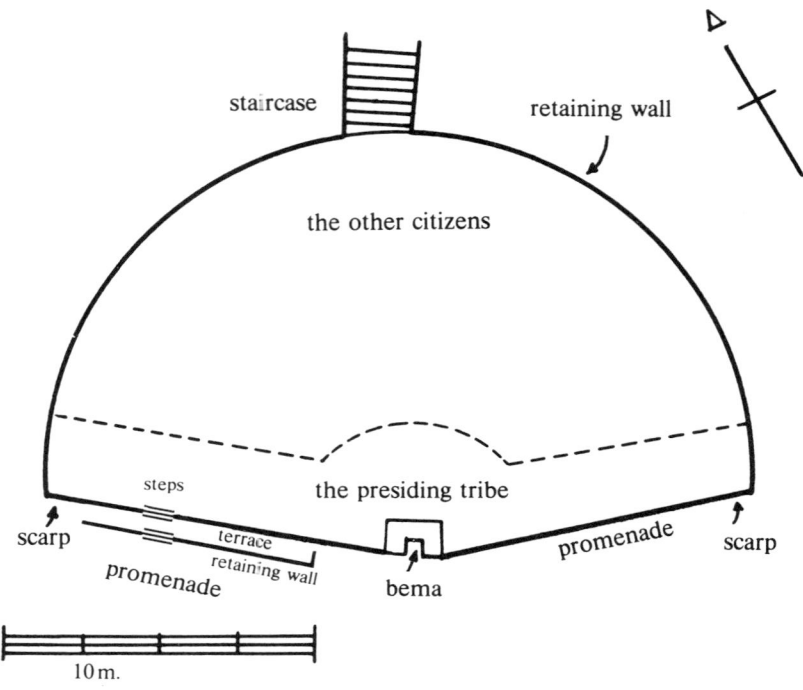

Figure 1

a transposition of the two infinitives εἰσιέναι and ἀναιρεῖν,[2] the text has never been questioned.

From Dem. 59.89f. as well as from other sources,[3] we learn that sessions of the *ecclesia* were regularly attended by foreign spectators. Moreover, when an *ecclesia* was preceded by a ratification, requiring a quorum of 6,000 voting by ballot, foreigners were not admitted until the *psephophoria* was over. They were kept out by *gerra*, which were removed when the ballot was over and the session was opened. Where were the foreigners seated during the session? Here a plan of the Pnyx will be helpful, and since the Neaera speech was delivered *ca* 342–340,[4]

---

[2] Karsten (*supra* n.1) 44, note.
[3] Aeschin. 3.224, Ar. *Eccl.* 243f.
[4] *Cf.* L. Gernet, *Démosthène, plaidoyers civils* IV (Paris 1960) 69. Gernet's assumption (98 n.1) that these meetings of the *ecclesia* took place in the Agora and not on the

Fig. 1 shows Pnyx III, which, following Thompson,[5] I take to have been constructed in the 340's. The foreigners were probably not seated in the northern part of the auditorium with the other citizens, nor is it likely that they were admitted to the front part of the auditorium, which, I have argued previously,[6] was probably occupied by the presiding tribe (ἡ προεδρεύουσα φυλή). Because of the high semi-circular retaining wall, spectators cannot have watched the *ecclesia* from the area to the west, north, and east of the auditorium. So the only possible location for spectators is the open area with promenades above the scarps that bound the auditorium to the south. The narrow terrace (of *ca* 40 × 4 m.) to the southwest between the scarp (north) and a retaining wall (south)[7] is an obvious location for (some) spectators and (perhaps) foreign ambassadors as well as *xenoi* to be honoured. The steps leading down from the terrace into the auditorium may have been used by ambassadors and *xenoi* when called to the platform. Similarly, the small stairway from the promenade down to the terrace (probably to be closed by a two-leaved gate) is too narrow (*ca* 1.5 m.) to have served as an entrance to the auditorium used by a great number of citizens, but may well have been used by a smaller number of foreigners descending from the promenade to the terrace.

Now, in Dem. 59.89f Apollodorus tells us that, before the *ecclesia* was opened, spectators were kept out by *gerra*, which were then removed. What are *gerra*, where were they set up, and why were they removed before the *ecclesia*? Γέρρον is wickerwork,[8] and in this passage the reference must be to some kind of fence; but *gerron* can also be used of e.g. a shield made of wickerwork, which suggests that fences made of *gerron* could well be so closely plaited that spectators would not be able to watch the *ecclesia* from behind.

Where were the *gerra* set up? We know that admission to the assembly was checked by thirty συλλογεῖς τοῦ δήμου and that every

---

Pnyx is refuted in my article, "How Many Athenians Attended the *Ecclesia*?" *GRBS* 17 (1976) 117–21 (= *The Athenian Ecclesia* [Copenhagen 1983] 3–7 with addendum 21).

[5] H. A. Thompson, "The Pnyx in Models," *Hesperia* Suppl. 19 (1982) 144f. Let me point out, however, that the reconstruction I suggest here is equally compatible with the period of Pnyx II (*ca* 400–345), in which citizens entered the auditorium not by one central stairway, but by two narrower stairways, one to the west and one to the east of the axis.

[6] M. H. Hansen, "The Athenian *Ecclesia* and the Assembly-Place on the Pnyx," *GRBS* 23 (1982) 246–48 (= *The Athenian Ecclesia* [supra n.4] 30–32).

[7] K. Kourouniotes and H. A. Thompson, "The Pnyx in Athens," *Hesperia* 1 (1932) 169–72.

[8] Eust. *Od.* 1924.3; *Lex.Seg.* 33.25; Hesych. *et al.*; Hdt. 7.61.1; Xen. *Cyr.* 2.1.21; Strab. 7.2.3; *cf.* P. Chantraine, *Dictionnaire étymologique de la langue greque* (Paris 1968) 217.

citizen approaching the auditorium was issued a *symbolon* (probably to be exchanged for *misthos* when the meeting was over).[9] This practice suggests that only one entrance to the Pnyx was kept open. If citizens had been allowed to enter the auditorium both from the staircase to the north and from around the ends of the scarps to the southeast and southwest, control of admission and distribution of *symbola* would have had to be conducted at different places, and the procedure would be unreasonably complicated. First, the πίναξ ἐκκλησιαστικός was kept locally in the demes (Dem. 44.35), and there is no evidence for a central register of citizens entitled to attend the *ecclesia*. The checking of attendants was probably based on the idea that any citizen approaching the auditorium would be known to at least one of the thirty *syllogeis*, so that an *atimos*, for example, who attempted to sneak in could be recognized and refused admission. But this form of control can only have been effective if all the *syllogeis* were grouped together and could inspect all the prospective attendants. Second, when an *ecclesia* was preceded by a vote by ballot, admission to the auditorium through several entrances would have required that urns be set up and *psephoi* dispensed at several different places, which, again, is most unlikely. Accordingly, the reasonable assumption seems to be that *all* citizens had to enter the auditorium by ascending the staircase to the north. But in that case the free entrance to the auditorium from the south around the ends of the scarps must have been blocked, probably by fences set up along the south side of the auditorium above the scarps from the western to the eastern end of the retaining wall.

Furthermore, it is apparent from the Neaera speech that, in order to exclude foreigners, *gerra* were placed in the area where the ballot took place, and that the ballot was conducted while the citizens were approaching the Pnyx. If, as argued above, all citizens entered the auditorium by ascending the staircase, these *gerra* must have been set up either (a) in the area in front of the staircase (if the vote was taken before ascending) or (b) in the northern part of the auditorium (if the vote was taken after the citizens had mounted the steps and entered the auditorium). If we accept (b), it follows first that foreigners were allowed to mount the steps and stand in the auditorium, but outside the *gerra*, when the ballot took place; and second, that when the *gerra* had been removed and the session was opened, there would no longer be any clear separation of foreigners from citizens in this part of the auditorium. Both consequences are open to objection

---

[9] *IG* II² 1749.75–79 (*Agora* XV 38.78–82); Poll. 8.104. *Cf.* 249 *infra*.

and force us to accept (a) as the more plausible reconstruction of where the ballot took place.

To sum up, before an *ecclesia* was opened the auditorium was fenced off by a set of *gerra* running from the western to the eastern ends of the retaining wall along the promenade above the scarps. Another set of *gerra* was put up in the area in front of the staircase to the north. But why were these *gerra* removed before the meeting and not simply left to be taken down when the session was over? Moreover, why, as reported by Apollodorus, is the sequence (1) admission of foreigners, (2) removal of *gerra*? The explanation may be that the speaker adopts the figure *hysteron-proteron*. But the passage is otherwise straightforward, and we expect the various stages in the procedure to be reported in chronological order. I suggest the following reconstruction: when the control (and, occasionally, the ballot) was over and the citizens had all ascended the staircase and taken their seats, the foreign spectators standing outside the *gerra* around the staircase were allowed to come forward through the fence to walk along the retaining wall and to go to the area above the scarps (where other foreigners are perhaps already waiting behind the fence); then the *gerra* along the top of the scarps were removed so that spectators could have a full view of the auditorium in front of them. On this reconstruction we can explain both why the spectators were admitted to their place before the *gerra* were taken down and why the *gerra* (above the scarps) had to be removed before the meeting was opened, and could not simply be left till after the *ecclesia* was over: they would have obstructed the view for spectators watching the *ecclesia* from above the scarps.

To judge from the Neaera passage alone, the fence in front of the staircase may have been left in place from *ecclesia* to *ecclesia*; but, on my interpretation, at least the *gerra* above the scarps had to be put up in advance of an *ecclesia* and taken down again just before the session was opened. Since a session of the *ecclesia* started early in the morning,[10] it is a fair assumption that the *gerra* were set up the evening before, and with this in mind we can now turn to our other passage (Dem. 18.169),[11] describing the notorious events in 339 when

---

[10] Ar. *Eccl.* 740f, *cf.* 283f, 291, 390f; *Thesm.* 376.

[11] Schol. Ar. *Ach.* 22 is another source in which *gerra* are connected with the opening of an *ecclesia*. For its discussion of *gerra*, however, this scholium is probably based on Ar. *Ach.* 21f, Dem. 18.169, and Dem. 59.89f combined. Consequently, it is not an independent source and, *pace* Girard (*supra* n.1), I reject it as a source for the meaning and use of *gerra*. It is a valuable source for τὸ μεμιλτωμένον σχοινίον, but that is a different problem, not to be discussed in this note.

Philip's capture of Elatea was reported to Athens in the evening and an *ecclesia* (σύγκλητος) was held the next morning.

In the phrase τὰ γέρρα ἐνεπίμπρασαν, the noun has never been doubted and, following several commentators both ancient and modern, I take these *gerra* to be identical with the *gerra* mentioned in the Neaera speech. On the other hand, I agree with most editors and commentators that ἐνεπίμπρασαν must be corrupt.[12] It does not make sense to set fire to the *gerra* needed the very next morning to fence off the auditorium when the citizens approaching from the Agora had to be checked and foreigners kept out of the auditorium.[13] Since we can infer from the Neaera passage alone that the *gerra* had to be put up before an *ecclesia*, a verb meaning 'erect' will give the required meaning, and ἐνεπετάννυσαν or ἀνεπετάννυσαν suggested by Karsten, Girard, and others must be on the right lines.[14]

But the phrase τοὺς τ' ἐκ τῶν σκηνῶν τῶν κατὰ τὴν ἀγορὰν ἐξεῖργον still has to be explained. Note first that Demosthenes refers to σκηναὶ κατὰ τὴν ἀγοράν, not ἐν τῇ ἀγορᾷ. The preposition κατά + acc. may well indicate that these *skenai* are 'in the neighbourhood of the Agora' rather than 'in the Agora' itself.[15] Next, I follow Thompson and Wycherley in their interpretation of σκηναί: "A distinction should be made between the booths (*skenai*), light wooden structures flimsily covered, and more permanent shops or small factories (*ergasteria*), built of stone or brick."[16] Third, the τε ... καί construction suggests that τοὺς ... ἐκ τῶν σκηνῶν ἐξεῖργον and τὰ γέρρα ἐνεπίμπρασαν (read: ἐνεπετάννυσαν) should be taken together and interpreted in the light of each other. Now, if the area between the Pnyx and the Agora itself was regularly filled with

---

[12] The corruption must, however, be early, since ἐνεπίμπρασαν is both attested in *P.Ryl.* I 57 (early third century A.D.) and is the reading of all scholiasts and lexicographers.

[13] Valozza (*supra* n.1) 137–41, rejecting the parallel between Dem. 18.169 and 59.89f, takes γέρρα to be the roofs of the σκηναί and, emphasizing the θόρυβος, defends ἐνεπίμπρασαν. For a system of beacons lit first in the city and then spreading over the countryside, she refers to Aen. Tact. 6f and Onosander 25.2f. I am not persuaded and insist that the *gerra* in Dem. 18.169 must be the same as those referred to in Dem. 59.89f.

[14] *Cf.* Wankel's lucid *Forschungsbericht* (*supra* n.1). Wankel's own position (849–52) is that ἐνεπίμπρασαν is probably corrupt, but he rejects all emendations proposed. He is skeptical about the value of the Neaera passage and does not believe that it can shed any light on Dem. 18.169. Karsten's emendation and interpretation (*supra* n.1) are based on the parallel between Dem. 18.169 and 59.89f; in my opinion his account, presented in 1857, surpasses all later treatments of the problem.

[15] *Cf.* Kühner-Gerth, *Ausführliche Grammatik der griechischen Sprache* II.1 (Leipzig 1898) 477f, §433.

[16] *The Athenian Agora* (Princeton 1972) 170.

booths,[17] these booths had to be taken down before a session of the *ecclesia* in order to make room for the *gerra* that fenced off the area in front of the staircase leading up to the auditorium of the Pnyx. The checking of some 6,000 citizens by the thirty *syllogeis* will have required a free space of several thousand square meters surrounded by *gerra*.

On this interpretation of the two passages, Dem. 19.169 and 59.89f can be combined to give a coherent and perfectly intelligible picture of the preparations for a session of the Athenian *ecclesia*: on the day preceding the session all booths (*skenai*) were removed from the area to the north of the central staircase leading up to the auditorium of the Pnyx. Next, *gerra* were set up to fence off the area in front of the staircase where citizens the next morning would be checked by the *syllogeis* and sometimes would have to take a vote by ballot on the ratification of e.g. a citizenship decree. *Gerra* were also put up along the scarps to the south of the auditorium to prevent foreigners and *atimoi* from sneaking into the auditorium. When all the citizens attending the session were seated in the auditorium, foreigners were admitted and the *gerra* along the scarps were removed to allow spectators to have a clear view of the session from the area behind the scarps. Then the meeting was opened by sacrifice and prayer.

2. Trittys Divisions in the Auditorium?

Over the years it has often been discussed whether the Athenians were organized into *phylai* during an *ecclesia* or whether they were seated in the auditorium as they pleased, irrespective of tribal divisions. I have adopted the latter view,[18] but in a fascinating recent study P. Siewert has argued that Athenians attending an *ecclesia* were, in some way, organized into *trittyes*. In support of his view Siewert invokes a group of fifth-century *horoi* inscribed with the names of *trittyes*.[19] He notes that, of the ten *horoi* found in Athens, six are made of *poros* stone and four of marble. Of the four marble *horoi*, one was found in the Pnyx "not far from the *bema*" of Pnyx III (*IG* I² 884), another was found on the western slope of the Areopagus (*IG* I² 883) and the other two were discovered in the southeastern corner of the Agora (*SEG* 10.370, 21.109). Insofar as the original size of these *horoi* can be measured, Siewert believes that

---

[17] That σκηναί were set up in the neighbourhood of the Pnyx is strongly indicated by Ar. *Thesm.* 658.
[18] *Cf.* Hansen (*supra* n.6: 1983) 29, 105, 115f, 228.
[19] P. Siewert, *Die Trittyen Attikas und die Heeresreform des Kleisthenes* (Munich 1982) 10–13.

they may fit some stele beddings cut in the rock surface of the Pnyx and uncovered by the excavators in the 1930's. Siewert suggests that the four marble *horoi* belong to a series of originally thirty *horoi* set up on the Pnyx to indicate subdivisions of the auditorium.

What are the consequences of this view? Were the Athenians seated *trittys* by *trittys* in the auditorium? This is, *a priori*, most unlikely for Pnyx I, with which Siewert associates the *horoi*. (a) The auditorium of Pnyx I (*ca* 2,400 m.²) could accommodate no more than 6,000 citizens, *i.e.* the quorum required for the ratification of certain decrees.[20] (b) The theory that *ecclesiai* attended by 6,000 or more citizens were held as *Vollversammlungen* in the Agora has no foundation in the sources and must be rejected as a fantasy.[21] Apart from occasional meetings held in the Piraeus or in the precinct of Dionysus, all *ecclesiai*, down to the end of the fourth century, were probably held on the Pnyx. (c) Let us assume, for the sake of argument, that the auditorium of Pnyx I was subdivided into thirty sections of the same size. It is unbelievable that the citizens attending an *ecclesia* were evenly distributed over the thirty *trittyes*. On the contrary, we must assume that citizens belonging to one *trittys* (*e.g.* Kydathenaion) usually outnumbered citizens belonging to another (*e.g.* Phrearrhioi). Moreover, the number of attendants coming from any of the thirty *trittyes* could probably vary from *ecclesia* to *ecclesia*. On Siewert's reconstruction some *trittys* sections may have been filled to the last man, while in other sections considerable space must have been left open. But Pnyx I could hold only 6,000 attendants if they were evenly distributed over the entire auditorium without interspersed open areas. So, *a priori*, the grouping of attendants into well-defined *trittys* sections is most unlikely; and a closer inspection of the *horoi* seems to disprove Siewert's reconstruction.

Siewert had not had the opportunity to study the marble *horoi* themselves.[22] Neither have I, but in Athens John Camp and Judith Binder have been kind enough to examine the stones for me, and they report that no two of the marble *horoi* would seem to be associated (PLATES 1-2).[23] Siewert's suggestion that they belong to the

[20] *Cf.* Hansen (*supra* n.5: 1983) 25f.
[21] *Cf.* Hansen (*supra* n.6: 1983) 7f, 13. Siewert (*supra* n.19) 58f repeats the traditional view of *Vollversammlungen* held in the Agora.
[22] Siewert (*supra* n.19) 12 n.61.
[23] "The four stones would not seem to be of the same series; they display differences of stone, letter height and forms, and disposition of text on the stone. In fact, no two seem to be associated. Agora I 5053 (*SEG* 10.370): Pentelic marble, letter height *ca* 0.017-8 m., deeply-cut careful letters. Agora I 6699 (*SEG* 21.109): Hymettian marble, fairly shallow, slight serifs? EM 10634 (*IG* I² 884): the most interesting since it is still

HANSEN PLATE 1

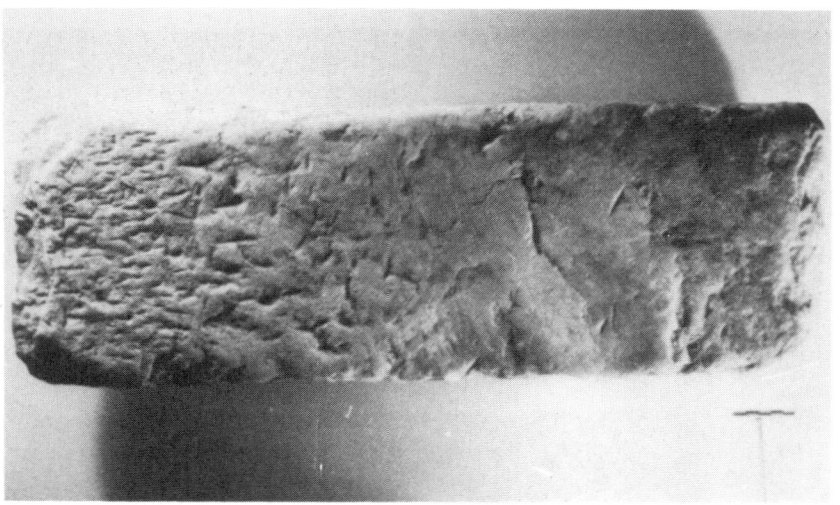

B *SEG* 21.109 (= *Agora* I 6699)

A *SEG* 10.370 (= *Agora* I 5053)

PLATE 2   HANSEN

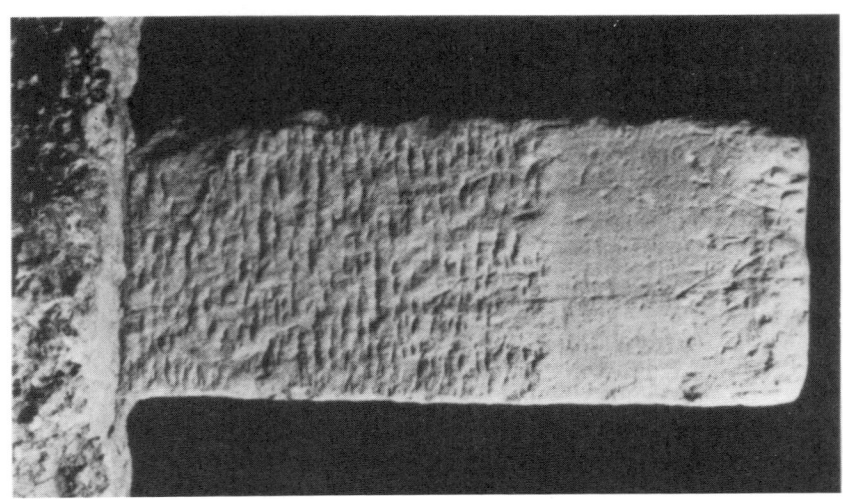

A   *IG* I² 884 (= *EM* 10634)

B   *IG* I² 883 (= *EM* 10072)

same series must therefore be discarded, and the only *horos* to be connected indisputably with the Pnyx is *IG* I² 884, inscribed Λακιαδῶν τριττύς. As Thompson suggested in 1932, it may simply indicate the border line of the city *trittys* of the Oineis tribe, *vel sim.*[24] We do not know. In any case, no *trittys horos* from a coastal or inland *trittys* can any longer be associated with the Pnyx.

Siewert does not explicitly discuss the fourth-century *ecclesia*, but he notes, correctly, that Aristophanes' *ecclesiazousai* are all seated in the front of the auditorium,[25] which is impossible if the citizens in the auditorium had been organized into thirty separate *trittys* sections. Siewert might have added Aeschin. 2.64-68, where we learn that Demosthenes of Paiania (Pandionis III) was sitting next to Amyntor of Erchia (Aigeis II). In the light of Aristophanes Siewert will not argue that the Athenians in the fourth century were seated by *trittyes*. But as an alternative, he suggests that *trittys* divisions were applied when the citizens were controlled by the thirty συλλογεῖς τοῦ δήμου. He assumes, accordingly, that the board of *syllogeis* was made up of one councillor from each of the thirty *trittyes*.[26] But the only prosopographical evidence we have for the *syllogeis* is *Agora* XV 38.78-82, an honorary decree for three *prytaneis* from the Aigeid tribe. They are rewarded for their careful control of the συλλογὴ τοῦ δήμου and the διάδοσις τῶν συμβόλων, and they are undoubtedly the *syllogeis* of the Aigeid tribe. But all three *prytaneis* represent only one of the 'territorial *trittyes*' traditionally assumed, *viz.* the Mesogaios *trittys*, and only two of the so-called τριττύες τῶν πρυτάνεων, the Mesogaios and the Asty *trittyes*;[27] thus, Siewert's reconstruction runs counter to the only prosopographical evidence we have. Furthermore, the marble *horoi* were, according to Siewert, set up *in* the auditorium. But the citizens were checked by the *syllogeis* as they were approaching the Pnyx and before they entered the auditorium. If the *horoi* indicating *trittys* divisions were used for initial control of attendants, they should be associated with the area in front of the stairway(s) to the north of the Pnyx, and not with the stele beddings in the auditorium of the Pnyx.

---

leaded into its base, a large irregular block of pinkish Acropolis limestone; Pentelic; letter height 0.02 m.; Vᵃ letters, 3-bar *sigma*, *omicron* for *omega*; it seems earlier than the other three. EM 10072 (*IG* I² 883): Pentelic; letter height 0.03 m. Judith Binder and I agree that all four were probably carved at different times by different masons. I note also that Agora I 5053 has the word *trittys* first, unlike all the others" (letter from John Camp).

[24] *Supra* n.7: 105 n.2.
[25] Siewert (*supra* n.19) 13 with n.62, referring to Ar. *Eccl.* 296f.
[26] Siewert (*supra* n.19) 3 and 13.
[27] *Cf.* P. J. Rhodes, *The Athenian Boule* (Oxford 1972) 129 with n.9.

We are now left with the possibility that *trittys* divisions were applied when the Athenians in the *ecclesia* voted by ballot and not by a show of hands. But again, a vote by ballot took place either before an *ecclesia* (Dem. 59.89f) or when the session was over (Xen. *Hell.* 1.7.9). In both cases the division of voters into *trittyes* would require the *horoi* to be in front of the auditorium, not in the auditorium. Furthermore, we have no evidence whatsoever for subdivisions being applied in the ratifications by ballot preceding an *ecclesia*, and the only source for voting by ballot after an *ecclesia* is the verdict passed on the eight generals in 406 in consequence of Callixenus' decree (mentioned above). But in this case the vote was taken by tribes and not by *trittyes* and, second, the procedure prescribed by Callixenus' decree was exceptional. Regularly, a sentence of death would be passed in the *ecclesia* by a show of hands and not after the *ecclesia* by ballot (Dem. 19.31).

Summing up, the theory that *trittyes* divisions were important for how the Athenians were organized in the *ecclesia* has, on the available evidence, nothing to recommend it and should be discarded.[28]

THE UNIVERSITY OF COPENHAGEN
June, 1985

---

[28] I should like to thank Peter Rhodes, Homer Thompson, and the anonymous referee for their comments on this article. Let me add, however, that both Homer Thompson and the referee are sceptical about the emendation ἐνεπίμπρασαν : ἐνεπετάννυσαν. I should like to thank the Epigraphical Museum for permission to publish photographs of *EM* 10072 and 10634, and the Agora Excavations for permission to publish photographs of *Agora* I 5053 and 6699. Further, I am most grateful to Dr. Judith Binder, Director D. Peppas-Delmouzou, and Dr. Nara Narapa-Molisani for their kind assistance and advice.

ADDENDA

131: In recent years I have lost confidence in Homer Thompson's redating of Pnyx III and I am now inclined to believe that he was right when, in his first article, he connected the magnificent auditorium of the third period with the Hadrianic building programme. The three weighty arguments against a date before or during the Lycurgan period are: (1) the megalithic masonry of the retaining wall is unparalleled in the fourth century B.C. but exceedingly common in the Hadrianic period. (2) The small sanctuary of Zeus Hypsistos (cf. *Hesperia* 1 [1932] 193-200) antedates the *bema* and the scarps of Pnyx III, but the cult of Zeus Hypsistos cannot be traced further back than the first century A.D. (3) Some Roman pottery was found behind the great retaining wall (*Hesperia* 1 [1932] 180ff); in *Hesperia* 12 (1943) 299 it was taken to be evidence of a later repair of the retaining wall. I am not persuaded and I tend to prefer Thompson & Kourouniotes' first evaluation of the pottery and its consequence for the chronology of the retaining wall. — I am grateful to Judith Binder for having drawn my attention to the persisting problem of the chronology of Pnyx III and for constantly reminding me of it in her letters. I hope that, in near future, she will publish a full account of the date of Pnyx III. Let me add that none of my theses will be invalidated by a restatement of the Hadrianic date of Pnyx III. With a few minor changes my reconstruction of the assembly and its sessions is compatible with having Pnyx II in use throughout the fourth century B.C.

134: Palaeographically, however, the corruption is not easy to explain. Comparing the forms ἐνεπετάννυσαν and ἐνεπίμπρασαν I note that the first four and the last three letters of the words are identical, and a simplification of the geminate νν should cause no problem. But in early literary hands (3rd-2nd c. B.C.) the five letters -ετανυ- are easily distinguishable from the five letters -ιμπρα-. I should like to thank Lene Rubinstein for giving her expert opinion on the papyrological aspects of the question. It may be worth noting that the detail about the γέρρα is left out in the paraphrase in P. Oxy. 858 lines 25-30.

THE CONSTRUCTION OF PNYX II AND THE INTRODUCTION OF ASSEMBLY PAY

BY
MOGENS HERMAN HANSEN

Summary: In this note I argue that the construction of Pnyx II and the introduction of assembly pay were not only contemporaneous but also connected events. Pnyx I had an auditorium which could accomodate 6,000 citizens, but it had no salient delimitation to the south. Thus more citizens could easily attend the sessions from outside the auditorium itself, and there was no restricted admission. The auditorium of Pnyx II, on the other hand, was closed on all sides and had a restricted capacity. It could easily hold 6,000 participants, bur only a limited number of citizens was admitted. The reason for the change from an open auditorium with free admission to a closed auditorium with restricted admission was probably the introduction of assembly pay. Both the rebuilding of the Pnyx and the introduction of assembly pay must be dated within the decade 403-393. I suggest that the introduction of assembly pay entailed controlled and restricted admission which again influenced the way the auditorium of Pnyx II was designed. Assembly pay, rapidly rising from one to three obols, may have been introduced as early as in 403, and the auditorium of Pnyx II may have been completed before 400. But a date in the 390s is a possibility that cannot be ruled out.

THE AUDITORIUM OF PNYX I AND II

The auditorium of Pnyx I was very simple.[1] The sloping rock was roughly dressed. High parts were cut away and hollows probably filled with earth. The northern part of the auditorium was bounded by a low retaining wall that supported an earth terrace and provided a level area at the front of

---

[1] K. Kourouniotes & H. A. Thompson, *The Pnyx in Athens, Hesperia* 1 (1932) 96-107; W. A. McDonald, *The Political Meeting Places of the Greeks* (Baltimore 1943) 68-70; H. A. Thompson & R. E. Wycherle, *The Agora of Athens, The Athenian Agora* 14 (1972) 48-49; H. A. Thompson, *The Pnyx in Models, Hesperia* Suppl. 19 (1982) 134-38.

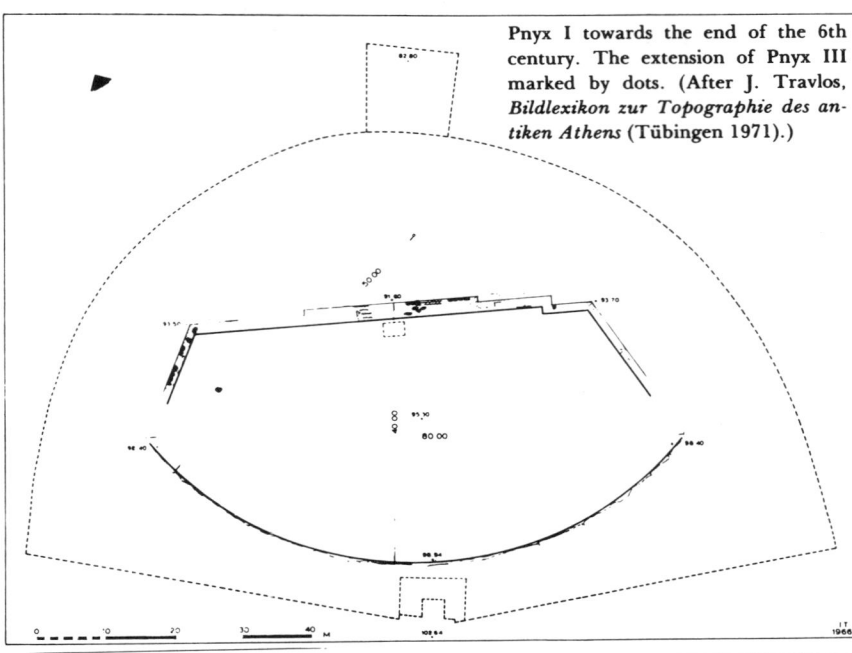

Pnyx I towards the end of the 6th century. The extension of Pnyx III marked by dots. (After J. Travlos, *Bildlexikon zur Topographie des antiken Athens* (Tübingen 1971).)

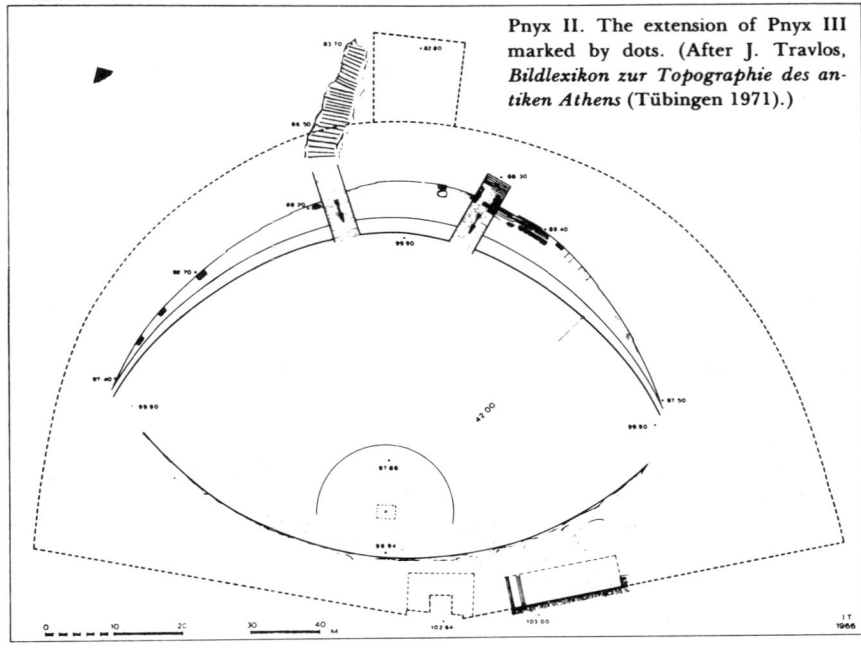

Pnyx II. The extension of Pnyx III marked by dots. (After J. Travlos, *Bildlexikon zur Topographie des antiken Athens* (Tübingen 1971).)

the auditorium. On the other hand, the southern up-hill border of the auditorium was demarcated only by the line where the dressing of the rock stopped. The resulting seating floor had an area of about 2,400 m^2 and could accomodate 6,000 seated participants, i. e. the quorum required for some types of decision made by the people.[2] Now, what happened if 7,000 or 8,000 or 9,000 citizens showed up in the morning and wished to attend the ekklesia? They could probably take their seats on the bare undressed rock to the south of the auditorium. »The naturel contours of the hillside would have permitted many citizens to sit or stand outside the dressed seating floor.« This is the observation made by Homer Thompson[3] and, in my opinion, it is supported by Aristophanes' description of the ekklesia kyria in the opening scene of the Acharnians. Just before the session is opened, the herald proclaims: πάριτ' ἐς τὸ πρόσθεν, πάριθ' ὡς ἂν ἐντὸς ἦτε τοῦ καθάρματος.[4] The katharma was a purification line indicated by the blood of a young pig which had been sacrificed and dragged around the circumference of the auditorium.[5] Undoubtedly the herald had to make this proclamation because some of the citizens were slow in crossing the purification line already drawn by the sacrificers (οἱ περιστίαρχοι). In any case, the herald's remark shows that there was no salient physical demarcation of the border of the auditorium to the south. We may assume that some citizens, if the auditorium was full, took their seats outside the dressed floor and that, on other occasions, the purification line could be drawn further uphill if the auditorium itself was not big enough to accomodate all who wished to attend. In conclusion, there was no restricted admission to the auditorium of Pnyx I. When the auditorium was full, the presidents knew that the required quorum of 6,000 was present.[6] If more showed up, they could take their seats on the slope itself to the south of the dressed floor of the auditorium. When the vote was taken by a show of hands, it would be impossible for the prytaneis, when overlooking the raised hands, to tell precisely where the purification line was and how many citizens were standing just outside the line.

---

[2] M. H. Hansen, The Athenian Ecclesia (Copenhagen 1983) 25-26, cf. 212-13.
[3] Thompson (supra n. 1) 135.
[4] 43-44. The herald's proclamation indicates that the seating floor was almost occupied. So, eventually, the session must have been well attended, and Dikaiopolis' complaint that he is all alone on the Pnyx (20) does not hold the Athenians up to ridicule because they shirk, but bacause they are late, cf. 21-25. — Suggested to me by Oswyn Murray.
[5] On the katharma, cf. Aeschin. 1.23 with the scholia; Ar Ach. 44 with the scholia; Eccl. 128-29 with the scholia; Istros (FGrHist 334) fr. 16 (= Phot. and Suid. s. v. περιστίαρχος); D. 54.39; Harp. s. v. καθάρσιον; Plut. Mor. 814 b.
[6] Cf. Hansen (supra n. 2) 26.

The auditorium of Pnyx II was very different.[7] The natural slope of the hillside was reversed by heaping up a mass of earth filling. This huge earthern embankment was supported by a semicircular retaining wall. Access to the auditorium was provided by two stairways along the retaining wall to the north east and north west. The new auditorium sloped from north east to south west. Now those attending had their backs turned to the Agora and were sheltered against the north wind, but they faced the sun. The platform was moved to the centre of the semicircle. The high semicircular retaining wall closed the auditorium to the west, north, and east. The delimitation of the front of the auditorium is more problematical. Perhaps scarps were cut in the rock a few meters in front of the exstant scarps of Pnyx III.[8] In any case, Ar. *Eccl.* 378-79 shows beyond doubt that *miltos* was used to close the auditorium on all sides: καὶ δῆτα πολὺν ἡ μίλτος, ὦ Ζεῦ φίλτατε, γέλων παρέσχεν, ἣν προσέρραινον κύκλῳ. Whether the *miltos* was used to keep latecomers from intruding, or to prevent participants from leaving the auditorium before the session was closed, we do not know.[9] Spectators may have been seated (or standing) to the south of the auditorium behind the *bema* and outside the *miltos*,[10] but when the vote was taken, the presiding *proedroi* would overlook only the hands raised in the auditorium itself, and there would probably be no difficulty in distinguishing between participants and outsiders.

Another line in the *Ekklesiazousai* calls for further comment. When the women are rehearsing the *ekklesia*, Praxagora, playing the part of the herald, exclaims: ὁ περιστίαρχος, περιφέρειν χρὴ τὴν γαλῆν. πάριτ' ἐς τὸ πρόσθεν. Ἀρίφραδες, παῦσαι λαλῶν. κάθιζε παριών (128-30). The announcement πάριτ' ἐς τὸ πρόσθεν is strikingly similar to the line from the *Acharnians* quoted above, but there are significant differences. Praxagora tells the citizens to move forward and take their seats, in order to make room for the *peristiarchos*. In the *Acharnians*, the message was to cross the purification line already made by the *peristiarchos*. Again, in the *Ekklesiazousai* the

---

[7] Kourouniotes & Thompson 113-28; Thompson & Wycherley 49-50; Thompson 138-40. (*supra* n. 1).

[8] W. B. Dinsmoor, *AJA* 37 (1933) 180-82 (reply by Kourouniotes & Thompson 652-56); McDonald (*supra* n. 1) 71-75; Thompson upholds his original reconstruction, cf. (*supra* n. 1) 138-39.

[9] R. G. Ussher, *Aristophanes' Ecclesiazusae* (Oxford 1973) 129 (note to 378-79); Hansen (*supra* n. 2) 19 with notes 69-70.

[10] On spectators cf. Aeschin 3.224 and M. H. Hansen, *Two Notes on the Pnyx*, *GRBS* 26 (1985) 242-43 (discussing Pnyx III, but the observations apply to Pnyx II as well, cf. note 5).

herald, speaking from the *bema* of Pnyx II, addresses those who stand in the upper, northern, part of the auditorium close to the retaining wall, thus obstructing the *peristiarchos'* way. In the *Acharnians*, where we are in the auditorium of Pnyx I, the herald faces south and the citizens addressed must be those who are standing on the slope above the auditorium.

To sum up, an essential difference between Pnyx I and Pnyx II was that the auditorium of Pnyx I was not a closed structure and could probably be extended uphill if necessary. The auditorium of Pnyx II, on the other hand, was closed on all sides; it had a limited capacity, and participants must have been clearly separated from spectators and outsiders.

RESTRICTED ADMISSION AND ASSEMBLY PAY

What is the purpose of changing an open auditorium into a closed one? and to have restricted admission instead of giving access to all who wish to attend? In my opinion, the change goes with the more careful checking of participants, with the handing out of *symbola* to be exchanged for assembly pay after the session, i. e. the restricted admission was probably a consequence of paying citizens for attendance. The connection is apparent from Aristophanes' description of the women's *coup d'état* in the *Ekklesiazousai*. In the *parodos* the women hurry to the assembly disguised as men. They say that if they are late the *thesmothetes* will not pay them the three obols (290-92), and so they hope to arrive in time to get a *symbolon* (296-97)[11] and to oust the men coming from the city (300-301). What matters to the women is not to snatch the three obols from the men, but to get access to the *ekklesia* themselves and to exclude as many men as possible, obviously in order to control the majority when the vote is taken. The inference must be that the *symbolon* served a double purpose: it was both a ticket to the *ekklesia* and a token to be exchanged for the fee of three obols after the session. This interpretation of the women's strategy receives additional support

---

[11] For *symbola* cf. IG^2 1749.76 (= *Agora* XV 38.79). During the excavations of the Pnyx and the Agora no tokens have been found which can unquestionably be identified as the *symbola* handed out to the *ekklesiastai*. But a collection of small lead tokens in the Numismatic Museum in Athens was published by I. N. Svoronos in 1900 (*JIAN* 3, 319-43). The tokens have a diameter of ca. 15 mm and are stamped on the one side with a head wearing a laurel crown (representing the Athenian *demos*?) and the legend ΔΗΜ or ΔΗΜΟ or ΔΗΜΟΣ. The only date given by Svoronos is the classical (4th. c.) or Hellenistic period. M. Crosby (*The Athenian Agora* X [1964] 78-80) may well be right in her suggestion that these tokens are the *symbola* which the *syllogeis tou demou* handed out to the *ekklesiastai*.

(a) from a remark made by Praxagora just before the *parodos* and (b) from the dialogue between Chremes and Blepyros after the *ekklesia*.

Re (a) In 282-84 Praxagora urges on the women telling them that usually men who arrive after dawn have to *go back home* (ὑαποτρέχειν) without pay. She does not say that they have to *attend* the *ekklesia* without pay. Here again assembly pay is connected with admission to the assembly place, and late-comers seem to be refused admission. If late-comers were simply admitted, but not paid, and if the auditorium could accommodate as many as wished to attend, Praxagora's remark makes no sense.

Re (b) Chremes states explicitly that he failed to obtain the fee because he was late (380-81), and his description of the meeting conveys the impression that he was a spectator and not a participant (e. g. 431-34).

Now, how many citizens were admitted and paid for attendance? We know that some types of decision required ratification by a quorum of 6,000 voting by ballot.[12] Thus, at least 6,000 must have been admitted. Furthermore, in the *Ath. Pol.* 41.3 Aristotle explicitly connects the introduction of assembly pay with the ratification of decrees: μισθοφόρον δ' ἐκκλησίαν τὸ μὲν πρῶτον ἀπέγνωσαν ποιεῖν· οὐ συλλεγομένων δ' εἰς τὴν ἐκκλησίαν, ἀλλὰ πολλὰ σοφιζομένων τῶν πρυτάνεων, ὅπως προσιστῆται τὸ πλῆθος πρὸς τὴν ἐπικύρωσιν τῆς χειροτονίας, πρῶτον μὲν Ἀγύρριος ὀβολὸν ἐπόρισεν, μετὰ δὲ τοῦτον Ἡρακλείδης ὁ Κλαζομένιος ὁ βασιλεὺς ἐπικαλούμενος διώβολον, πάλιν δ' Ἀγύρριος τριώβολον. In this passage we are told that the Athenians, after various coercive measures had failed, introduced assembly pay in order to ensure that enough citizens were present when a decision made by a show of hands had to be ratified — *viz*. by a quorum of 6,000 voting by ballot.[13] The presumption is that 6,000 were paid for attending the *ekklesia* and, if admission and assembly pay were closely connected, only 6,000 were admitted to the auditorium.

Alternative reconstructions must, in my opinion, be rejected as incompatible with the evidence we have. I will briefly discuss three other possibilities: (a) All who arrived before a specified time were paid whereas those who arrived later were not paid. On this interpretation, the purpose of the allowance must have been to ensure punctuality rather than to encourage more citizens to attend.[14] (b) only the first e. g. 1,000 or 3,000 were paid,

---

[12] Cf. And. 1.87; D. 24.45, 59; D. 59.89-90, cf. Hansen (*supra* n. 2) 11-12.

[13] Cf. M. H. Hansen, *Die athenische Volksversammlung im Zeitalter des Demosthenes*, Xenia 13 (Konstanz 1984) 127 note 92.

[14] P. J. Rhodes thinks it a serious possibility that fourth-century Athens did what Hellenistic

but this stimulus was sufficient to induce at least 6,000 to attend the sessions regularly. (c) Citizens were admitted (and paid) until the auditorium was full, but the auditorium could hold many more than the required quorum. Thus many more than 6,000 were admitted and paid. I have the following objections.

Re (a) That payment was conditioned by arrival before a specified time is not easy to reconcile with what we know from Aristophanes' *Ekklesiazousai*. Chremes, for example, complains that he was too late to obtain the *ekklesiastikon*, but the reason he states is not that he arrived later than usual, but that an unexpected crowd had showed up before him (380-84). The inference must be that he would have been paid if the *ekklesia* had been attended only by the usual number of participants. Similarly, although it is already morning (312), Blepyros envisages the possibility of attending the *ekklesia* and *being paid for it* (352 ff., 389). Again, the presumption is that a certain number of participants were paid for and that even latecomers might obtain the allowance if only they arrived before the fixed number of *symbola* had been handed out.

Re (b) In Athens it is unparalleled to adopt a system by which all are admitted (until the house is full) but only some are paid.[15] The regular system is to connect payment with attendance. In the *dikasteria*, for example, those who were late were refused both admission and pay whereas all who were admitted were also paid after the session. It is *a priori* likely that the same system was applied to sessions of the *ekklesia*. More important, to separate admission from payment runs counter to Aristophanes' description of the assembly in the *Ekklesiazousai*, cf, above.

Re (c) Let us suppose instead that all were admitted (and paid) until the auditorium was full. This assumption meets both the objections stated re (b), and the crucial question is then: how many citizens could be accommodated in the auditorium of Pnyx II?

According to the excavators the auditorium of Pnyx II covered ca. 2,600 m^2, some 200 more than Pnyx I. But the excavators have, somewhat arbitrarily, placed the *bema* of Pnyx II about 10 m in front of the surviving

---

Iasos was to do, and paid those arrived before a specified time (Michel 466 with Hicks, *JHS* 8 [1887] 103-11, 116-18). (Letter of June 24th 1986).

[15] In the *Politics* (1298b23-26), however, Aristotle suggests a possible way of creating a balance between rich and poor citizens attending an *ekklesia*: when the poor outnumber the rich, assembly pay is given only to a number of poor equal to the number of rich. It is not clear from Aristotle whether such a system was ever practised or is mentioned as a possibility only.

bema (of Pnyx III). Dinsmoor and McDonald, however, objected to this reconstruction and adduced several arguments in favour of the view that the *bema* was placed further south, near the *bema* of Pnyx III, and that scarps were cut along the front of the auditorium (obliterated by the deeper scarps of Pnyx III). Thus they give a full semicircular form and an area of some 3,200 m^2 to the auditorium.[16] Now, the space required for a human being attending a large meeting is 0.4 m^2.[17] On the asumption that the entire auditorium was used as seating floor for the participants, the capacity of Pnyx II was 6,500 citizens if we follow the excavator's scheme, but ca. 8,000 if we follow the reconstruction suggested by Dinsmoor and McDonald. The maximum figure of 6,500 is very close to the required quorum of 6,000, but a reconstruction allowing a (maximum) attendance of ca. 8,000 requires further comments.

According to Praxagora, it regularly happened that some citizens had to go home unpaid, i. e., on this interpretation, it regularly happened that they found the house full (*Eccl.* 282-84). Similarly, we are told in the *Ploutos* (329-31) that the citizens were willing to be closely packed in order to obtain the fee of three obols.[18] Now, if the auditorium of Pnyx II could hold as many as 8,000, and if all were admitted until the house was full, we are asked to believe that, regularly, in the mornings some 8-9,000 turned up of whom some 8,000 were admitted and paid. Such a massive participation is, in my opinion, incredible even though the citizen population living in Attica probably totalled some 25-30,000 adult males, and not ca. 20,000 as many historians tend to assume — not to speak of some 13,000 as has recently been suggested.[19]

On the other hand, an auditorium of ca. 3,200 m^2 does not necessarily entail that the seating floor covered 3,200 m^2. There may, for example, have been a passage of, say, 2-3 m running all the way along the retaining wall and the front of the auditorium beneath the scarps. In that case, the seating floor may well have covered only some 2,600 m^2 as in the reconstruction suggested by the excavators. The auditorium of Pnyx II was presumably equipped with wooden benches, whereas, during the first period, the citizens had been seated on the bare rock. A seating floor of some 2,600 m^2 is com-

---

[16] Cf. *supra* n. 8.
[17] Cf. Hansen (*supra* n. 2) 17, 212-13.
[18] Ar. *Pl.* 329-31: δεινὸν γὰρ εἰ τριωβόλου μὲν οὕνεχα ὠστιζόμεσθ' ἑκάστοτ' ἐν τῇκκλησίᾳ, αὐτὸν δὲ τὸν Πλοῦτον παρείην τῷ λαβεῖν. For the verb ὠστίζεσθαι cf *Ach.* 24 & 42.
[19] Cf. M. H. Hansen, *Demography and Democracy* (Copenhagen 1985) 68 and passim.

patible with a (maximum) attendance of 6,000, slightly more comfortably seated than previously. Further speculations serve no purpose. My conclusion is that the auditorium of Pnyx II may well have had a maximum capacity of 6,000 citizens, no matter whether we adopt the excavator's scheme or the reconstruction suggested by Dinsmoor and McDonald. On the other hand, a seating floor of 3,200 m² allowing a regular attendance of 8,000 is difficult to reconcile with what we are told in Aristophanes' comedies and with what we know about the size of the Athenian citizen population.

THE DATE OF PNYX II AND OF ASSEMBLY PAY

By interpreting the remains of Pnyx II in the light of the literary sorces, I suggest that there is a close connection between the quorum of 6,000, the capacity of the auditorium of Pnyx II, the restricted admission to the sessions, and the intioduction of assembly pay. The most reasonable explanation of the connection is, in my opinion, that the open auditorium of Pnyx I was changed into the closed auditorium of Pnyx II because the introduction of assembly pay had led to restricted admission and a stricter control of those attending. Now, this is to reverse the traditional chronology according to which the reconstruction of the assembly place is placed before 400, whereas the introduction of assembly pay is often assigned to the 390s.[20] What is the evidence for the chronology of Pnyx II and of assembly pay?

First the rebuilding of the assembly place. The archaeological evidence points to a date around 400 B. C.[21] which, as already the excavators pointed out, fits a story told by Plutarch in the *Life of Themistokles* about the Thirty Tyrants who ruled Athens in 404-403: The Thirty arranged that the *bema* of the Pnyx was turned round so that the *rhetor* now faced the inland (where the more oligarchic peasants lived) but had his back turned to the sea (which was reminiscent of democracy).[22] The account is anecdotal but may contain a core of truth, in which case the most reasonable explanation is that the oligarchs used the reconstruction as a pretext for having the assembly place

---

[20] E. g. C. Mossé, *La fin de la démocratie athénienne* (Paris 1963) 303. In his *Commentary on the Aristotelian Athenaion Politeia*, however, P. J. Rhodes notes that the introduction of payment must be dated soon after the democratic restoration (492).

[21] Kourouniotes & Thompson 128-38; Thompson 139 (*supra* n. 1).

[22] Plu. *Them.* 19.6: διὸ καὶ τὸ βῆμα τὸ ἐν Πυκνὶ πεποιημένον ὥστ' ἀποβλέπειν πρὸς τὴν θάλατταν ὕστερον οἱ τριάκοντα πρὸς τὴν χώραν ἀπέστρεψαν, οἰόμενοι τὴν μὲν κατὰ θάλατταν ἀρχὴν γένεσιν εἶναι δημοκρατίας, ὀλιγαρχίᾳ δ' ἧττον δυσχεραίνειν τοὺς γεωργοῦντας. Cf. Kourouniotes & Thompson 134-36; Thompson 140 (*supra* n. 1).

closed.²³ On this interpretation, the actual restoration was carried out and completed only after the restoration of the democracy in 403/2. When the rebuilding was finished we do not know, but since the assembly described by Aristophanes in the *Ekklesiazousai* takes place on the Pnyx,²⁴ the *terminus ante quem* must be 393 or 392.²⁵ Assembly pay was introduced after the restoration of democracy (Arist. *Ath. Pol.* 41.3, quoted above) and had risen to three obols per session when the *Ekklesiazousai* was performed (Ar. *Eccl.* 292, 308, 380, 392). Thus the *terminus post quem* is 403/2 and the *terminus ante quem* 393 or 392. If Plutarch's story is altogether rejected, it is impossible to give any further specification than within the decade 403-393. If, on the other hand, there is a historical background to the anecdote told by Plutarch, an early date is to be preferred: the Pnyx was closed by the Thirty in 404, reconstruction begun in the autumn of 403 or later and the new assembly place reopened by 400 or earlier. Assembly pay, then, was introduced in connection with the restoration of democracy in 403/2 and may well have risen to three obols before the new assembly place was finished.²⁶

---

²³ Cf. R. A. Moysey, *The Thirty and the Pnyx, AJA* 85 (1981) 31-37. The suggestion that the Thirty may have used rebuilding as an excuse for closing the assembly place is made on page 35.

²⁴ Ar. *Eccl.* 281, 283.

²⁵ For the date of the *Ekklesiazousai*, cf. Ussher (*supra* n. 9) xxv.

²⁶ I should like to thank Peter Rhodes for reading and commenting on a draft of this article.

ADDENDA

152: The only other piece of evidence that bears on the date of the *ekklesiastikon* is the grant of citizenship to Herakleides of Klazomenai. We know from Arist. *Ath. Pol.* 41.3 that Herakleides of Klazomenai moved the proposal by which assembly pay was raised from one to two obols. Again, Herakleides of Klazomenai is the person honoured on a fragmentary stele inscribed with two decrees. The second decree (*IG* I^3 227 lines 5-24 + *IG* II^2 65, cf. M.B. Walbank in *ZPE* 51 [1983] 183-84) is a grant of *enktesis ges kai oikias*, probably passed in 424/3. But the grant of *enktesis* is preceded by a later honorary decree, probably a grant of citizenship, of which only the last lines survive (*IG* I^3 227.1-4) The citizenship decree was undoubtedly passed after the restoration of democracy in 403/2. Walbank suggests 399/8, but in Plato's *Ion* 541 C-D Sokrates refers to Herakleides as having served on the board of generals, which indicates that he had been naturalized (and elected *strategos*) beore the trial of Sokrates in 399, possibly as early as 403/2, cf. J.D. Moore in *GRBS* 15 (1974) 433. Accordingly, Herakleides' proposal to raise the *ekklesiastikon* from one to two obols may have been moved ca. 400 or even before the turn of the century, more or less contemporaneously with the completion of Pnyx II.

The Organization of the Athenian Assembly: A Reply

Mogens Herman Hansen

IN SEVERAL articles and in a recent monograph,[1] I have argued against the view that, during the *ekklesiai*, the Athenians were seated in tribal groups. I have also argued against the view that they gathered together in political groups; and my position has been that the Athenians attending a session of the *ekklesia* were seated at random and as they pleased. In "Voting in Tribal Groups in the Athenian Assembly," *GRBS* 28 (1987) 51–92, G. R. Stanton and P. J. Bicknell have reopened the question and argued that, in the assembly place on the Pnyx, the Athenians were organized not only in tribes, as often maintained in this century, but also in *trittyes*, as some scholars believed in the nineteenth century, a view recently revived by P. Siewert in his seminal study of the Attic *trittyes*.[2]

I am much impressed by Stanton and Bicknell's valuable contribution to the discussion of the evidence, but I am not persuaded. A full treatment of the problem will be published in *The Athenian Ecclesia II: A Collection of Articles 1983–88*. But I would like to offer a short rejoinder in the periodical in which most of the discussion has been conducted. Like Stanton and Bicknell I will treat Pnyx I, II, and III separately and open my rejoinder with a discussion of the evidence for the first period of the assembly place on the Pnyx.

Pnyx I

According to Stanton and Bicknell the auditorium of Pnyx I was constructed by Cleisthenes and fitted out with thirty *trittys* markers, each indicating a sector in which members of the *trittys* in question were seated during sessions of the *ekklesia*. In support of their view Stanton and Bicknell adduce four fifth-century *trittys* markers of marble: *IG* I² 883 (*ca* 450?) found west of the Areopagus, [Κερ]αμέον

---

[1] M. H. Hansen, "How Did the Athenian *Ecclesia* Vote?" in *The Athenian Ecclesia* (Copenhagen 1983) 115f; "Two Notes on the Pnyx," *GRBS* 26 (1985) 247–50; *The Athenian Assembly in the Age of Demosthenes* (Oxford 1987) 39–41, 127.

[2] *Cf. e.g.* C. Schäfer, *AM* 5 (1880) 87; P. Siewert, *Die Trittyen Attikas und die Heeresreform des Kleisthenes* (Munich 1982) 10–13.

[τρ]ιττύς; *IG* I² 884 (*ante med. s. V*) found on the Pnyx, Λακιαδῶν τριττύς; *SEG* X 370 (*ca* 420?) found in the Agora, τριττ[ὺς] Σφετ[τίον]; and *SEG* XXI 109 (*ca* 450) found in the Agora, [Σκ]α[μ]βο[νιδῶ]ν τριττύς. Stanton and Bicknell (52–55) follow Siewert[3] in believing that these four marble *horoi* belong together and were used as *trittys* markers in the auditorium of Pnyx I. I have the following objections: (a) The four *horoi* belong in the period *ca* 460–420. I find it inconceivable that the thirty *trittys* markers erected on the Pnyx *ca* 500 in consequence of Cleisthenes' reforms were damaged so rapidly that, after less than two generations, several had to be replaced—so many in fact that the four we have preserved are all replacements of the period 460–420. For comparison I note that of the three preserved boundary stones set up in the Agora during the same period (*ca* 500), two were found *in situ* and must have served their purpose for almost a millennium without having been replaced.[4]
(b) Further, the four marble *horoi* "display differences of stone, letter height and form, and disposition of text on the stone."[5] Following Camp and Binder I prefer the view that the four *horoi* belong to four different series. Thus the only *trittys* marker to be connected indisputably with the Pnyx is *IG* I² 884, inscribed Λακιαδῶν τριττύς.
(c) The stele *IG* I² 884 was found by Pittakis, and in his first report he wrote: Ηὗρον αὐτὴν τὸ 1846 'Ιανουαρίου 18 οὐ μακρὰν τοῦ βήματος τῆς πυκνός.[6] A few years later Rangabé republished the stone and stated: "trouvé, d'apres M. Pittaki, dans un trou creusé dans le roche horizontal du Pnyx."[7] He believed, as do now Stanton and Bicknell, that the *trittys* marker once indicated the place where the citizens of Lakiadai were seated during the sessions of the *ekklesia*: "Je crois devoir le considerer aussi comme une borne, indiquant la place que les Laciades occupaient dans les assemblées populaires." Thus, he probably took the stele to have been found in the auditorium in front of the *bema*. In a subsequent publication, however, Pittakis objected, *inter alia*, to Rangabé's interpretation of where the stone was found: Ὁ Κ. Ῥαγκαβῆς λανθάνεται· τοιούτους λόγους δὲν εἶπον· ὃ δὲ ἔγραψα εἶναι τοῦτο. "... Ηὗρον αὐτὴν τὸ 1846 'Ιανουαρίου 18 οὐ μακρὰν τοῦ βήματος τῆς Πυκνός."[8] Pittakis' objection, if it can be trusted, indicates that he found the stone, not in the auditorium itself, as Rangabé

---

[3] Siewert (*supra* n.2) 11f.
[4] *Cf.* H. A. Thompson and R. E. Wycherly, *The Athenian Agora* XIV *The Agora of Athens* (Princeton 1972) 117–19.
[5] Report on the four *horoi* by J. Camp and J. Binder quoted in Hansen, "Two Notes" (*supra* n.1) 248f n.23.
[6] *ArchEph* (1853) 773 no. 1289.
[7] A. R. Rangabé, *Antiquités helléniques* II (Athens 1855) 586 no. 890.
[8] *ArchEph* (1856) 1357 no. 2700.

seems to assume, but probably in the area above the scarps of Pnyx III. To sum up, I find it impossible to decide whether the stele was found some meters to the north of the *bema* in the auditorium, or some meters to the south of the *bema* above the scarps. Thus, I agree with E. Meyer, who concludes: "Es ist also recht unsicher, ob der Stein zum alten Volksversammlungsplatz gehört."[9]

(d) Let us suppose with Stanton and Bicknell that the seating floor of Pnyx I was covered with thirty *trittys* markers, each indicating the gathering point for the members of a *trittys*. The auditorium could hold only 6,000 citizens. What happened if, occasionally, some 7,000 or 8,000 citizens turned up? The supernumeraries undoubtedly took their places on the undressed rock east, south, and west of the auditorium;[10] but since the *trittys* markers cannot have indicated subdivisions of the hillside outside the auditorium, the organization into *trittyes* must have broken down whenever more than 6,000 citizens attended a session.

(e) Stanton and Bicknell assume that the marble *trittys* markers set up in Pnyx I indicated gathering points, not boundaries (68), whereas the *trittys* markers of poros stone,[11] which—according to Stanton and Bicknell—served the same purpose in the assembly place in the Piraeus, clearly indicated boundary lines between the areas reserved for the individual tribes and *trittyes* (61f with *Fig.* 3). I find it disquieting to have one kind of organization used in Pnyx I but a different kind used in the contemporary assembly place in the Piraeus and again in Pnyx III.

(f) In addition to the epigraphical evidence we have one literary source that Stanton and Bicknell take to bear on the problem how the Athenians were seated and voted in the fifth-century assembly place, Xen. *Hell.* 1.7.9. During the trial of the Arginousae generals, Callixenus proposed and carried a decree that the assembly pass sentence on the eight generals collectively and that the vote be taken by ballot and according to tribes:

διαψηφίσασθαι Ἀθηναίους ἅπαντας κατὰ φυλάς· θεῖναι δὲ εἰς τὴν φυλὴν ἑκάστην δύο ὑδρίας· ἐφ' ἑκάστῃ δὲ τῇ φυλῇ κήρυκα κηρύττειν, ὅτῳ δοκοῦσιν ἀδικεῖν οἱ στραγηγοὶ οὐκ ἀνελόμενοι τοὺς νικήσαντας ἐν τῇ ναυμαχίᾳ εἰς τὴν προτέραν ψηφίσασθαι, ὅτῳ δὲ μή, εἰς τὴν ὑστέραν.[12]

---

[9] E. Meyer, *RE* 21 (1951) 1115 s.v. "Pnyx."
[10] M. H. Hansen, "The Construction of Pnyx II and the Introduction of Assembly Pay," *ClMed* 37 (1986) 91; *cf.* H. A. Thompson, "The Pnyx in Models," *Hesperia* Suppl. 19 (1982) 135: "The natural contours of the hillside would have permitted many citizens to sit or stand outside the dressed seating floor."
[11] Listed and described by Siewert (*supra* n.2) 12 with n.57.
[12] For a description of the trial of the generals *cf.* Hansen, *The Sovereignty of the*

Stanton and Bicknell cite Callixenus' *proboulema* in support of their view that "the assembly always sat in tribal groups" (71), but in my opinion the passage does not support this view. First, the other evidence we have for *psephophoria* in the assembly (relating to the fourth century) shows that the ballot took place *outside* the assembly place and before the citizens took their seats in the auditorium.[13] In the trial of the generals the vote took place *after* the *ekklesia* and, probably, *outside* the auditorium. Thus, the voting procedure described in Callixenus' decree offers no information about how the vote is to be taken *during* the session. Second, Callixenus' minute description of how the vote is to be taken shows that the ballot he prescribes is exceptional and not standard procedure. Third, other sources (*e.g.* Dem. 19.31) confirm that the *ekklesia*, when transformed into a law court, regularly voted by show of hands and not by ballot. From these three observations I infer that Callixenus' decree prescribed an exceptional form of ballot imitating the voting procedure used in an *ostrakophoria* and in the *dikasteria*; and since the vote was to be taken after the session, and probably outside the assembly place, the passage does not elucidate the problem how the citizens were organized in the auditorium.

Pnyx II

No archaeological or epigraphical evidence sheds light on how the audience was seated in the auditorium of Pnyx II, but several texts give valuable information. The principal literary sources are (a) Aristophanes' *Ecclesiazusae*; (b) a passage in Aeschines' speech *On the Embassy* (2.64-68); and (c) a passage in the Demosthenic speech *Against Neaira* (59.43).

(a) In the *Ecclesiazusae* Aristophanes describes how the women implement their scheme to sit packed together around the *bema*. The play has always been adduced in support of the view that the Athenians sat in the auditorium where they wanted and not according to tribes. Bicknell, however, advances an alternative interpretation. During the period of Pnyx II the members of the inland demes sat at the very front across the auditorium from east to west, subdivided into ten *trittys* groups (82f). Next, he argues that the disguised women pose as members of the inland demes (to be seated in the front of the auditorium: 84), and concludes that Aristophanes' play supports the

---

People's Court in Athens (Odense 1974) cat. no. 3, and *Eisangelia* (Odense 1975) cat. no. 66.

[13] Dem. 59.89f; *cf.* Hansen, *The Athenian Ecclesia* (*supra* n.1) 13.

assumption that, in Pnyx II, the audience was organized into thirty *trittyes* with the ten inland *trittyes* in the front and the ten city *trittyes* in the back of the auditorium (82f).

Bicknell's interpretation is ingenious but unconvincing. Aristophanes emphasizes that the women are in a hurry (84–87, 282ff) and that they intend to oust the men from the city (302, τοὺς ἐξ ἄστεως ἥκοντας). If inland dwellers invariably sat in the front of the auditorium and city dwellers in the back, the women cannot oust the men from the city, and they do not have to hasten. They have the lead on the men from the countryside and, as long as they arrive before them, they can have the front seats to themselves and, in any case, they will not have to mingle with the men from the city. Furthermore, the conversation between Chremes and Blepyrus at 372–477 disproves the assumption that the women posed as members of the inland demes. When Chremes reports the audience's response to Praxagora's speech he says: εἶτ' ἐθορύβησαν κἀνέκραγον ὡς εὖ λέγοι, τὸ σκυτοτομικὸν πλῆθος, οἱ δ' ἐκ τῶν ἀγρῶν ἀνεβορβόρυξαν (431–33). Obviously the front part of the auditorium was filled, not with citizens pale as city dwellers, but with pale city dwellers whom Chremes opposes to the citizens from the countryside. If we accept Bicknell and Stanton's reconstruction of how the Athenians were seated in Pnyx II, Chremes would have wondered himself, and Blepyrus would have asked him, "but how can it be that city dwellers were seated in front of the auditorium?" Thus, we are back at the traditional interpretation: Aristophanes' play strongly supports the view that the citizens were seated at random where they pleased, and not organized into tribes or *trittyes*.

(b) Bicknell and Stanton may, of course, revise their interpretation of Aristophanes and claim that the women all posed as members of the city demes and that the fifth-century organization of the auditorium was upheld in the fourth century, but then they will have difficulties in explaining the conversation between Demosthenes and Amyntor, reported at Aeschin. 2.64–68. I grant Stanton and Bicknell (81f) that a conversation between Amyntor of Erchia (inland *trittys* of Aigeïs II) and Demosthenes of Paiania (inland *trittys* of Pandionis III, regularly seated near the scarps) is possible *if the organization of the trittyes had been reversed* so that, in the auditorium of Pnyx II, the inland *trittyes* were placed near the *bema* whereas the city *trittyes* were relegated to the back along the retaining wall. But the italicized provision is crucial, and the explanation for it offered by Stanton and Bicknell is rather weak: they believe that the whole reconstruction of the Pnyx was carried out by the Thirty in 404, moving the city dwellers to the

56   ORGANIZATION OF THE ATHENIAN ASSEMBLY

back of the auditorium in order to reduce their influence on the debate and give more weight to the peasants living in the countryside (82f). Following Moysey,[14] I still hold that the Thirty may well have started the rebuilding as reported by Plutarch, perhaps as a pretext for closing the Pnyx; I refuse to believe, however, that the elaborate building up of the auditorium of Pnyx II is the work of the oligarchs. The new closed auditorium is, in my opinion, to be connected with the introduction of assembly pay and accordingly belongs in the years around 400.[15]

(c) A further argument against having the inland *tryttyes* close to the *bema* may be found in the Demosthenic speech *Against Neaira*, where we are told that Stephanus of Eroiadai was regularly to be found near the *bema* shouting at the speakers (Dem. 59.43). Now, Eroiadai is the name of two different demes: one belonged to Hippothontis (VIII) and the other to Antiochis (X). Eroiadai (VIII) was probably located in the city district,[16] whereas the location of Eroiadai (X) is unknown.[17] In a prytany inscription of 334/3, however, Eroiadai is recorded in the third column with Alopeke.[18] If we follow Traill in taking Eroiadai (X) to belong in the city *trittys*,[19] the inference is that Stephanus, though he belonged to the city *trittys* of either Hippothontis or Antiochis, nevertheless preferred to take his seat in Pnyx II near the *bema*, and not near the back. If the allocation of Eroiadai (VIII) and (X) is correct, Stanton and Bicknell's theory is disproved once and for all. But we must not forget that prytany inscriptions may not be reliable guides for assigning demes to *trittyes*, and that the relation between geographical *trittyes* and bouleutic *trittyes* is a moot point.

Pnyx III

In any discussion of the auditorium of Pnyx III two crucial problems must be addressed: (a) how are we to explain the six stele beddings running parallel to the scarps at a distance of *ca* 10.5 meters? and (b) how are we to interpret the law of 346/5 on ἡ προεδρεύουσα φυλή?

(a) On Stanton and Bicknell's interpretation of the stele beddings (60f with *Fig.* 3) the seating floor reserved for each of the five tribes in the

---

[14] R. A. Moysey, "The Thirty and the Pnyx," *AJA* 85 (1981) 31–37.
[15] Hansen (*supra* n.10) 93–98.
[16] J. S. Traill, *Demos and Trittys* (Toronto 1986) 137; Siewert (*supra* n.2) 171f.
[17] Traill (*supra* n.16) 139. There is some evidence (tombstones) that Eroiadai (X) was located inland at Charvati (Peuka) near Pallene.
[18] *Agora* XV 44.67 (334/3).
[19] *Cf.* Traill, "Diakris, the Inland Trittys of Leontis," *Hesperia* 47 (1978) 104.

western part of the auditorium of Pnyx III is: VI Oineis, 260 m.²; VII Kekropis, 360; VIII Hippothontis, 465; IX Aiantis, 435; and X Antiochis, 270. I find the disparity of seating facilities given to the various tribes suspicious, especially if a sector of no less than 435 m.² was assigned to the smallest of all tribes, *viz.*, Aiantis, whereas the members of the medium-sized tribe Antiochis has to squeeze together in a sector of no more than 270.²⁰ On this reconstruction, the huge auditorium could accommodate no more than *ca* 675 citizens belonging to Antiochis, but some 1,100 belonging to Aiantis. With a normal attendance of *ca* 6,000 citizens, the presumption is that the sector assigned to Antiochis was simply too small, whereas the citizens of Aiantis probably never filled the sector assigned to their tribe.

(b) In the law of 346/5 on the presiding tribe (Aeschin. 1.33f, 3.4; Dem. 25.90) Stanton and Bicknell suggest taking προεδρεύουσα in a metaphorical sense: "being in charge of the meeting and keeping order" (64). But at 1.34 Aeschines refers to the law as ὁ περὶ τῆς προεδρίας τῶν φυλῶν νόμος. The noun προεδρία is almost always used in a literal sense,²¹ and at Aeschines 1.34 it is explicitly stated that the law concerns what goes on around the platform (καθ' ἑκάστην ἐκκλησίαν ἀποκληροῦν φυλὴν ἐπὶ τὸ βῆμα, ἥτις προεδρεύσει). Thus, the presiding tribe must have been seated in the front part of the auditorium around the *bema*, and we know that the presiding tribe was selected by lot before a session of the *ekklesia* was opened.²² The system by which all members of one tribe had to take turns sitting in front around the *bema* is, in my opinion, irreconcilable with the view that the citizens were organized into thirty well-defined *trittys*-groups spread out over the auditorium with an open area in front.

Summing up, I find that the evidence presented by Stanton and Bicknell is insufficient to prove that the Athenians attending an *ekklesia* were seated and voted in *trittys* groups. Regarding Pnyx I, we cannot be certain that *IG* I² 884 was found in the auditorium of the Pnyx; and Xenophon *Hell.* 1.7.9 was an extraordinary measure prescribing that a ballot be taken by tribes (not *trittyes*) after the *ekklesia*. Regarding Pnyx II, Aristophanes' description of the women's coup in *Ecclesiazusae* strongly supports the view that the citizens could sit as

---

[20] On the relative size of the tribes *cf.* J. Traill, *The Political Organization of Attica* (=*Hesperia* Suppl. 14 [1975]) 32 with n.20.

[21] Hdt. 6.57; Ar. *Ach.* 42, *Eq.* 575, 702-04; Xen. *Vect.* 3.3; Pl. *Leg.* 881B, 946B; Arist. *Rh.* 1361a35; Dem. 18.91; Aeschin. 2.80, 110; 3.76, 154; Dinarchus 2.13; *cf.* the literal προεδρία at competitions commonly granted in honorific decrees. προεδρία appears in a metaphorical sense only at Arist. *Pol.* 1292a9, 1309a29.

[22] Hansen, *The Athenian Ecclesia* (*supra* n.1) 41.

they pleased in the auditorium; the conversation between Demosthenes and Amyntor (Aeschin. 2.64–68) is inconclusive; whereas Stephanus of Eroiadai's position near the *bema* upsets Stanton and Bicknell's reconstruction, if we follow Traill in taking both Eroiadai VIII and X to belong to the urban *trittys* of (respectively) Hippothontis and Antiochis. Regarding Pnyx III, the subdivisions of the auditorium suggested in their *Fig.* 3 (61) are, in my opinion, odd and do not fit what we know about the relative size of the tribes. Finally, the law on the presiding tribe (Aeschin. 1.33f) is to be taken literally and not metaphorically; and a system of rotation in which all members of one tribe were gathered around the *bema* is irreconcilable with an organization of the audience into thirty fixed *trittys* sectors.

UNIVERSITY OF COPENHAGEN
February, 1988

ADDENDA

155: For a reply to the second part of this article (Pnyx II pages 158-60) cf. P. Bicknell, 'Athenians Politically Active in Pnyx II,' *GRBS* 30 (1989).

159: Bicknell (*supra ad* page 155) offers the following elaboration of his reconstruction: »Stanton and I do not envisage that x positions in the auditorium were rigidly set aside for members of the inland demes, the same number for members of the coastal demes and the same number again for members of the city demes. It was a matter of first come first admitted, and so paid, with the proviso that those inland dwellers who gained admission were grouped up front and so on. It was theoretically possible and may actually have happened, that the red painted ropes were brought into action to exclude superfluous ekklesiasts (378-79) at a juncture when two-thirds, say, of those admitted were city dwellers. In that case such would spread from the rear quite deeply into the auditorium.« On this reconstruction, however, the Athenians from the city *trittyes* would fill the area around the ten *trittys* markers in the middle of the auditorium as well as the area around the ten *trittys* markers along the retaining wall, and only the area around the ten *trittys* markers in the front of the auditorium would be left to citizens belonging to inland and coastal *trittyes*. There would be no proper organization of the citizens into *trittyes*, and voting by tribal groups would be ruled out.

159: Bicknell takes the opposition between τὸ σκυτοτομικὸν πλῆθος and οἱ ἐκ τῶν ἀγρῶν to be a distinction between pale country-dwellers working indoors and rustics labouring in the fields. But οἱ ἐκ τῶν ἀγρῶν is idiomatic for country-dwellers opposed to city-dwellers, cf. e.g. Xen. *Hell.* 4.6.3; Lys. 31.8; Dem. 19.86; Lycurg. 1.16, and σκυτοτόμοι are regularly associated with the city, cf. Xen. *Hell.* 3.4.17; Lys. 24.20. Thus, the opposition is between a majority of pale city-dwellers sitting near the *bema*, and a minority of country-dwellers sitting in the back of the auditorium. For the proverbial paleness of shoemakers, cf. schol. Ar. *Pax* 1310. For a judicious interpretation of the passage, cf. Usher's edition (Oxford 1973) *ad loc.*

159: In his preface Bicknell writes: »After much reconsideration I have come to the conclusion that Pnyx II will have been completed by and become operational in 403/2.« I think he is right, cf. *Ath. Ass.* 13. Bicknell and I now agree that Pnyx II was opened *after* the restoration of the democracy. But, according to Bicknell and Stanton, the reason for moving the ten city *trittyes* from the front to the back of the auditorium was the oligarchs' wish to curb the influence exerted by the prodemocratic urban population. Bicknell's redating of Pnyx II leaves him without an explanation of why the citizens belonging to the city demes had to be moved from the front seats to the area furthest from the *bema*.

160: I am not convinced by Bicknell's interpretation of Dem. 59.43: »I am unable to believe that Stephanos did not speak to the resolutions concerned. Accordingly, even when he was a *sykophantes*, Stephanos' verbal contributions in the assembly were formal and directed at, not from, the audience. Their delivery was theatrical in the extreme with Stephanos exemplifying the type of speaker who ranted and raved and, like Timarchos, moved about beside the *bema*.« At Aeschin. 1.26, however, Timarchos is reported to have stripped off his *himation*, not to have moved around beside the *bema*, which would probably have made his speech inaudible. The proper parallel to Stephanos' behaviour as described at Dem. 59.43 is rather Philokrates and his supporters who obviously stand beside the *bema* (καὶ παραστὰς ὁ μὲν ἔνθεν, ὁ δ' ἔνθεν ... Dem. 19.23, 45-6) and shout at Demosthenes while he is addressing the people.

160: Bicknell lists and gives a valuable analysis of the *trittys* afilliation of citizens who addressed the people or moved proposals in the assembly compared with those who were elected *strategoi*. He shows that, of citizens active in the *ekklesia*, those belonging to city or inland demes were outnumbered by citizens from the inland demes, whereas citizens elected *strategoi* were evenly distributed over the three districts. With a few modifications Bicknell adopts Traill's revised map of the political organization of Attica and the result is as follows: of 47 *rhetores* attested as active in Pnyx II, 24 ($=51\%$) belonged to inland demes, 12 ($=26\%$) to coastal demes and 11 ($=24\%$) to city demes. During the same period 35 *strategoi* are attested of whom 12 ($=34\%$) belonged to inland demes, 11 ($=32\%$) to coastal demes and 12 ($=34\%$) to city demes. For 53 *rhetores* in the *ekklesia* during the first period of Pnyx III (ca. 345-322) the distribution is very close to that of Pnyx II: Mesogaios 25 ($=47\%$), Paralia 11 or 12 ($=23$ or 21%) and Asty 16 or 17 ($=30$ or 32%). Bicknell suggests that citizens from the Mesogaios were overrepresented among the *rhetores* in the *ekklesia* because they were seated close to the *bema* and thus had a better opportunity to address the people.

Bicknell's demonstration of the different distribution of *strategoi* and *rhetores* in the *ekklesia* is very important but I am not persuaded by his explanation of it. Instead of comparing *strategoi* with *rhetores* in the *ekklesia* I will compare the *rhetores* in the *ekklesia* with those in the *boule*. Of the 373 politically active citizens attested in my inventory no less than

ADDENDA

80 are known as *bouleutai* as well, and for 64 of these the demotic is preserved (cf. *supra* pages 70-72). Like Bicknell and with the same reservations I will adopt Traill's revised map (cf. *supra* page 85). For the sake of brevity I will treat the period of Pnyx II and Pnyx III together. Apart from (Phyleus Pausaniou) Oinaios the other 63 demotics can be assigned to one of the three districts and the distribution is: Mesogaios 32 (= 51%), Asty 20 (= 32%) and Paralia 11 (= 17%). Thus the overrepresentation of the Mesogaios district is the same as in the case of the *rhetores* in the *ekklesia*, but here the explanation cannot be the organization of the citizens in the auditorium. First, the proximity to the *bema* must have mattered less in the *boule* than in the *ekklesia*, and second we know that the seats in the *bouleuterion* were assigned to the *bouleutai* by lot (Philoch fr. 140), whereby organization into *trittyes* is ruled out; it would be absurd to assume that sortition took place within the 30 *trittyes*. Nevertheless, the distribution of the attested *bouleutai* on the three districts is remarkably similar to the distribution of the *rhetores* in the *ekklesia*. Thus, it is most unlikely that the overrepresentation in Pnyx II and III of citizens from the Mesogaios had anything to do with how the citizens were organized in the auditorium. Bicknell's study of the *rhetores* in the *ekklesia* is still very important, but a comparison with the *bouleutai* suggests that we must look for a different explanation.

160: On the date of Pnyx III cf. *supra* page 141.

THE NUMBER OF ECCLESIAI
IN FOURTH-CENTURY ATHENS

M. H. Hansen and F. Mitchel

Institute for Advanced Study, Princeton

According to *Ath. Pol.* 43.3, the *prytaneis* had an obligation to summon the *ecclesia* four times every prytany: οἱ δὲ πρυτανεύοντες ... συνάγουσιν ... τὸν δῆμον ... τετράκις τῆς πρυτανείας ἑκάστης. When was the number of *ecclesiai* in a prytany fixed at four? The traditional assumption, with no supporting evidence, is that "the likeliest time for an increase in the number of regular meetings is the half-century following Ephialtes' reform."[1] This is only one example of the common belief that fourth-century sources for Athenian institutions can be projected back into the fifth century. The view is based on three assumptions: (a) the democracy restored in 403 was, with some minor adjustments, identical with the so-called radical democracy, introduced by Ephialtes in 462 and developed in the Periclean period. (b) As assumed by *Ath. Pol.* 41.2, the fourth-century democracy was static, and there were no major constitutional reforms between 403 and the early 320s. (c) Consequently, many of the democratic institutions described in the second part of *Ath. Pol.* can be extrapolated and used as evidence for the fifth-century democracy.

We tend generally to question all three assumptions, and in this particular case, the fixed number of *ecclesiai*, we believe that the traditional extrapolation of fourth-century institutions is demonstrably wrong. There is one more source, besides *Ath. Pol.* 43.3, which refers explicitly to the number of *ecclesiai* in a prytany, *viz.*, the law on *nomothesia* quoted by Demosthenes in his speech *Against Timokrates*: ἐπὶ δὲ τῆς πρώτης πρυτανείας τῇ ἑνδεκάτῃ ἐν τῷ δήμῳ, ἐπειδὰν εὔξηται ὁ κῆρυξ, ἐπιχειροτονίαν ποιεῖν τῶν νόμων. ... ἐὰν δέ τινες τῶν νόμων τῶν κειμένων ἀποχειροτονηθῶσι, τοὺς πρυτάνεις, ἐφ' ὧν ἂν ἡ ἐπιχειροτονία γένηται, ποιεῖν περὶ τῶν ἀποχειροτονηθέντων τὴν τελευταίαν τῶν τριῶν ἐκκλησιῶν (Dem. 24.20–21). In 24–27 Demosthenes comments on the law and refers to the number of *ecclesiai* in the following

167

words: μετὰ ταῦτα δέ, ἂν χειροτονῇτ' εἰσφέρειν, οὐκ εὐθὺς τιθέναι προσέταξαν, ἀλλὰ τὴν τρίτην ἀπέδειξαν ἐκκλησίαν, ... (Dem. 24.25).

The speech *Against Timokrates* was delivered in 353/2 and, assuming that the four obligatory meetings described in *Ath. Pol.* 43.3 had been introduced long before that date, R. Schoell[2] offered the following interpretation of the passages: «Der Inhalt dieser Anordnungen ist durch die Wiederholung des Redners gesichert. Den Wortlaut hat Westermann, der zwischen Urkunde und Rede das umgekehrte Verhältniss annimmt, mit wenig Glück angefochten. Er hält die 'dritte' Ekklesia bei Demosthenes für die dritte der Prytanie: der Ausdruck 'die letzte der drei Versammlungen' soll verrathen, dass der Verfasser der Einlage nur drei ordentliche Gemeindeversammlungen der Prytanie kannte, also von der Voraussetzung der späteren Zeit ausging, da die Bürgerschaft in zwölf Phylen gegliedert war. Indess ἡ τρίτη ἐκκλησία ist im Munde des Redners die drittnächste von dem vorher angedeuteten Zeitpunkt an, wie in der bekannten Formel des Probuleuma ἡ πρώτη ἐκκλησία nicht die 'erste' schlechthin, sondern die 'nächstfolgende' (ἡ ἐπιοῦσα heisst es seit Anfang des 3. Jahrhunderts): als 'die letzte der drei (noch übrigen) Versammlungen' wird verständlich genug die vierte und letzte ordentliche Versammlung der Prytanie bezeichnet. Dass zwischen diese Verhandlung und jene erste vorbereitende mehr als eine Versammlung fiel, lässt sich auch aus der von Demosthenes anderswo berührten Vorschrift entnehmen, nach welcher die neuen Gesetzvorschläge dem Ratsschreiber einzureichen und von diesem 'in den Volksversammlungen' zu verlesen sind.»

In so far as Dem. 24.21 and 25 have been adduced in later discussions of the number of *ecclesiai* in a prytany, Schoell's interpretation has won general acceptance,[3] but we are not persuaded. First, this interpretation strains the meaning of Demosthenes' Greek in his paraphrase of the law in 24.25. Although it is correct that εἰς τὴν πρώτην ἐκκλησίαν refers to the following *ecclesia* (cf. e.g. *IG* II²152.13), there is no indication whatsoever in any source warranting the inference that ἡ δευτέρα or ἡ τρίτη ἐκκλησία could mean the second or third meeting AFTER this meeting, i.e. the third or the fourth meeting. On the contrary, the

The Number of Ecclesiai in Fourth-Century Athens 15

Athenians preferred inclusive counting, and ἡ τρίτη ἡμέρα means invariably the day after tomorrow and never the third day from tomorrow, i.e. the fourth day from today.

In the second place, the reason why Demosthenes refers to the third meeting is that he is paraphrasing the law which prescribes ἡ τελευταία τῶν τριῶν ἐκκλησιῶν. But again, the straightforward rendering of the Greek is "the last of the three *ecclesiai*," and certainly not "the last of the three (remaining) *ecclesiai*." It is perhaps just possible to follow Schoell's interpretation of the law, but then we should certainly expect that Demosthenes, in his paraphrase, would state τὴν τετάρτην ἀπέδειξαν ἐκκλησίαν, and not τὴν τρίτην. The law and the paraphrase combined strongly indicate that the Athenians, in 353/2, had three meetings of the *ecclesia* in a prytany and not four.

In support of his interpretation Schoell adduces two other passages from the orators referring to *nomothesia*: Dem. 20.94 and Dein. 1.42. In the Leptines speech Demosthenes describes the 'Solonian' *nomothesia* as follows: καὶ πρὸ τούτων γ' ἐπέταξεν ἐκθεῖναι πρόσθε τῶν ἐπωνύμων καὶ τῷ γραμματεῖ παραδοῦναι, τοῦτον δ' ἐν ταῖς ἐκκλησίαις ἀναγιγνώσκειν, ἵν' ἕκαστος ὑμῶν ἀκούσας πολλάκις .... And in his description of Demosthenes' trierarchic law of 340/9 Deinarchos states: οὐ φράσετε τοῖς πλησίον ὅτι τρία τάλαντα λαβὼν μετέγραφε καὶ μετεσκεύαζε τὸν νόμον καθ' ἑκάστην ἐκκλησίαν. According to Schoell both sources presuppose four *ecclesiai* in a prytany and are incompatible with three meetings.

The Deinarchos passage refers to a law moved by Demosthenes in 340/9 by which time the number of *ecclesiai* in a prytany had in fact been raised from three to four, cf. *infra*; and therefore the passage cannot be adduced as evidence for the procedure in 353/2. Furthermore, we have no indication whatsoever that Demosthenes' law was passed in connexion with the ἐπιχειροτονία τῶν νόμων in the first prytany. He may have availed himself of one of the other procedures for *nomothesia* described in Dem. 24.33 and in Aischin. 3.38–40.[4]

Second, the law paraphrased in Dem. 20.94 is certainly not the law quoted in Dem. 24.20–23, but either a law no longer preserved, or, probably, the law quoted in Dem. 24.33, warranting a different procedure for initiating *nomothesia*.[5] In this law there is no trace of an initial ἐπιχειροτονία τῶν νόμων, and so the procedure may have been to introduce a new *nomos* in one *ecclesia*, to have it discussed in a second *ecclesia* and to have the *nomothetai* appointed in a third *ecclesia*. So the plural ἐκκλησίαις causes no problem. Moreover, in the phrase ἕκαστος ὑμῶν ἀκούσας πολλάκις, the reference is to the jurors who are appointed *nomothetai*. Accordingly, ἀκούσας πολλάκις refers not only to the reading out of the bill in the *ecclesiai*, but also to the reading out of the bill to the *nomothetai* appointed to hear the bill and to vote on it.

* Now, there is only one argument left in support of Schoell's strained interpretation of Dem. 24.21 & 25, *viz.*, the *a priori* assumption that the four obligatory meetings mentioned in Arist. *Ath. Pol.* 43.3 were introduced before 353/2, perhaps already in the fifth century. We prefer the straightforward interpretation of Demosthenes to the unfounded *a priori* assumption and suggest that the *prytaneis* in 353/2 were instructed to summon three meetings of the *ecclesia* in a prytany = 30 meetings in a year. But this interpretation necessarily leads to the questions: when was the requirement of three meetings in a prytany introduced? and when was the number of obligatory meetings raised to four?

We tend to believe that in the later fifth century and in the first half of the fourth century there was only one fixed meeting every prytany, *viz.*, the ἐκκλησία κυρία, which is attested as early as ca. 446/5 (*IG* I³41.37) and again in ca. 440–32 (*IG* I³49.10).[6] Other meetings could be called by the *prytaneis* on their own initiative or by orders of the *boule* or the *demos* itself, and sometimes the *strategoi* might ask the *boule* and/or the *prytaneis* to summon a meeting. There was probably no restriction on the number of meetings to be summoned.[7]

In the period 362–55, and probably in connexion with the financial crisis caused by the Social War 357–55, the hearing of all political actions was transferred from the *ecclesia* to the *dicasteria*, and we suggest that, as a part of this reform, the number of business meetings of the *ecclesia* was fixed at three,
* probably one ἐκκλησία κυρία and two other meetings. If the main purpose of the reform was to reduce political pay, because the Athenian state was near bankruptcy, it is a reasonable guess that

The Number of Ecclesiai in Fourth-Century Athens

the three meetings in a prytany was the maximum number of *ecclesiai*.[8]

By the early 320s, however, when the *Ath. Pol.* was composed, the number of fixed meetings had been raised to four, as described in 43.3–6. Moreover, the information we have about meetings of the *ecclesia* called to deal with the peace of Philokrates in 347/6, strongly suggests that the Aristotelian system had been introduced before this year.[9] Probably, the three meetings did not suffice, and moreover, the financial crisis was less acute. On the other hand, the sources for the peace of Philokrates, especially Dem. 19.154, Aischin. 2.72 and *IG* II²212, indicate (a) that four meetings in a prytany was not only a minimum but also a maximum, and (b) that an ἐκκλησία σύγκλητος was not an extra meeting, but one of the four obligatory meetings summoned at short notice in an emergency, or by orders of the *boule* (and not by the *prytaneis* on their own initiative).[10]

So the period of three fixed meetings was short. The *terminus post quem* is 362/1 (the last attested case of a political action heard by the *ecclesia*), and the *terminus ante quem* is 347/6 (where the evidence points to four meetings in Prytany VIII = Elaphebolion 8–25). In 307/6, when the number of *phylai* was raised from ten to twelve, the Athenians probably returned to three fixed *ecclesiai* in a prytany (no more and no less),[11] but the number of *ecclesiai* in a year would now be 36 instead of 30. Westermann suspected that the law quoted in Dem. 24.20–23 is a forgery inserted in the speech, and that the three *ecclesiai* in a prytany mentioned in 21, only reflect the third-century constitution.[12] A third-century *nomos*, passed by the *nomothetai*, is indeed preserved on stone,[13] and it is possible that the *epicheirotonia ton nomon* was still practised in the first prytany every year, but Demosthenes' paraphrase in 24.24–27 guarantees that the inserted document is not a later forgery but a law already in force by 353/2.

Conclusion

The law on ἐπιχειροτονία τῶν νόμων, quoted by Demosthenes in 24.20–23, and paraphrased in 24–27, shows that the *prytaneis*, in 353/2, were bound to summon three *ecclesiai* in a prytany (and not four). In 21, we take the phrase τὴν τελευταίαν τῶν τριῶν ἐκκλησιῶν to be a reference to the third and last *ecclesia* of the first prytany and, accordingly, in Demosthenes' paraphrase in 25, τὴν τρίτην ἀπέδειξαν ἐκκλησίαν refers to the third *ecclesia* of the prytany, and *not* to the third following *ecclesia*, i.e. the fourth *ecclesia*. The inference is that the system of four *ecclesiai* in a prytany, as described in *Ath. Pol.* 43.3–6, was introduced as late as ca. 350, and cannot be extrapolated and used as evidence for the democratic constitution of the late fifth and early fourth centuries.

NOTES

1 P. J. Rhodes, *A Commentary on the Aristotelian Athenaion Politeia* (Oxford 1981) 521. Cf. e.g. C. Hignett, *A History of the Athenian Constitution* (Oxford 1952) 233, etc.
2 R. Schoell, "Ueber attische Gesetzgebung" *SbbMünchen* (1886) 100–01. The description in the *Ath. Pol.* of the four meetings of the *ecclesia* in a prytany was known before the recovery of the text on papyrus in 1890; cf. Arist. fr. 434–436 (ed. Rose).
3 Cf. H. Swoboda in G. Busolt & H. Swoboda, *Griechische Staatskunde* II (Munchen 1926) 987–88 with note 4. Cf., hesitatingly, D. M. MacDowell, "Law-making at Athens in the Fourth Century B.C." *JHS* 95 (1975) 68 with further references in note 17.
4 Cf. M. H. Hansen, "Οἱ πρόεδροι τῶν νομοθετῶν. A Note on *IG* II²222." *ZPE* 30 (1978) 156–57; "*Nomos* and *Psephisma* in Fourth-Century Athens," *GRBS* 19 (1978) 327–29.
5 Cf. M. H. Hansen, "Athenian *Nomothesia* in the Fourth Century B.C. and Demosthenes' Speech *Against Leptines*." *ClMed* 32 (1980) 92–93. MacDowell *op. cit.* (*supra* n. 3) 63–65 assumes that Demosthenes refers to a different law, now lost, i.e. "The Old Legislation Law."
6 For the ἐκκλησία κυρία cf. furthermore *IG* I³123.5–6; 237.13 (the term is restored in both inscriptions). A meeting of the ἐκκλησία could be summoned at ten days' notice (*IG* I³93.15) or at five days' notice (*IG* I³85.11) or overnight (*IG* I³68.30). The ἐκκλησία was summoned by the *prytaneis* (*IG* I³34.18–19; 93.17). For ἐκκλησία cf. also *IG* I³61.54; 68.11 (restored); 105.53 (restored at lines 27, 44–45); 182.21. We express our gratitude to Professor William C. West who generously made available to us the machine readable file of *IG* I³ in the Ibycus System at the University of North Carolina.
7 For a detailed discussion of the number of fixed meetings in 431, cf. J. Christensen & M. H. Hansen, "What is *Syllogos* at Thuc. ii.22.1?" *ClMed* 34 (1983) 15 with n. 3.
8 For the judicial reform and the introduction of a maximum number of meetings cf. M. H. Hansen, "How Often Did the *Ecclesia* Meet?" *GRBS* 18 (1977) 43–70, especially 69–70.

9 Cf. Hansen, *op. cit.* (*supra* n. 7) 54–67.
10 Cf. Hansen, *op. cit.* (*supra* n. 7) 44–54; "When did the Athenian *Ecclesia* Meet?" *GRBS* 23 (1982) 331–8.
11 Cf. Hansen, *op. cit.* (*supra* n. 7) 67; "'Εκκλησία σύγκλητος in Hellenistic Athens" *GRBS* 20 (1979) 149–56.
12 A. Westermann, "Untersuchungen über die in die attischen Redner eingelegten Urkunden," *Abhandlungen d. Phil. Hist. Classe d. K. Sächs. Gesellschaft der Wissenschaften* I (1850) 19–21.
13 The inscription is not yet published, but the text is easily read in the excellent photograph published by John Papademetriou in his "The Sanctuary of Artemis at Brauron," *Scientific American* 208.6 (June 1963) 110–120. The photograph is on page 118, and the third-century date is there suggested.

ADDENDA

169: P.J. Rhodes is still inclined to accept the traditional interpretation of Dem. 24.21 & 25, cf. *CQ* 35 (1985) 55 n. 4 and *CR* 38 (1988) 311. D.M. Lewis addressed the problem in 'M.H. Hansen and the Athenian *Ecclesia*' unpublished paper read at *The Noman Baynes Annual Meeting of UK Ancient Historians* on 25 September 1984. He agrees with us on the interpretation of Dem. 24.21 & 25: both passages show that, in the first prytany, only three *ekklesiai* were convened, not four. He objects, however, that it is unwarranted to generalize and assume, as we do, that only three *ekklesiai* were held in all ten prytanies. Hekatombaion was, according to Lewis, a month with extraordinarily many festival days; thus the first prytany was probably exceptional in having only three *ekklesiai* instead of four. — But the number of festival days in Hekatombaion was above the average only if the Panathenaia included all days from the 23rd to the 29th or 30th, cf. J.D. Mikalson, *The Sacred and Civil Calendar of the Athenian Year* (Princeton 1975) 34. Admittedly, there are few attestations of *ekklesiai* held in Hekatombaion, cf. *Ath. Eccl.* 136 n. 4, and so far no meetings on Hekatombaion 29 or 30 are attested, but it would be strange to have fewer meetings than usual during the first prytany of the year in which extra business, e.g. *nomothesia* had to be transacted.

169: Cf. M.H. Hansen, 'Athenian *Nomothesia*,' *GRBS* 26 (1985) 346-52.

170: Mitchel and I discussed but did not in our article argue against an interpretation which, to the best of my knowledge, has not (yet) been advanced by anybody but which, nevertheless, deserves mention and refutation. When the law stipulates the last of the three *ekklesiai* (Dem. 24.21) and when Demosthenes (in 24.25) offers the paraphrase »the third *ekklesia*«, it is just possible, but unlikely, that the reference is to the third *ekklesia*, *apart from* the *ekklesia kyria* (which is left unmentioned). In *Ath. Pol.* 43.3-4 Aristotle refers to four *ekklesiai* of which one is *kyria*. By analogy I assume that the law quoted in Dem. 24 refers to three *ekklesiai* of which one is *kyria*.

170: It is worth noting that Arist. *Ath. Pol.* 43.4-6 describes only three different types of agenda, of which one is used twice in a prytany, *viz.* the agenda which prescribed (a minimum of) three items on the cult, three on foreign policy and three on domestic policy. Three types of agenda correspond to three meetings in a prytany. I suspect that the Athenians in 355 may have underestimated the amount of business to be dealt with in this meeting of the *ekklesia*, and after a few years they preferred to have two (shorter) meetings of this type every prytany rather than a protracted

ADDENDA

meeting in which they might not have time enough for a satisfactory debate of the problems.

How Often Did the Athenian *Ekklesia* Meet? A Reply

Mogens Herman Hansen

A DECADE AGO I advanced the views (a) that, in the 350's, the Athenians put a limit on the number of *ekklesiai* to be held in a prytany and (b) that an *ekklesia synkletos* was not an extra meeting, but one of the prescribed meetings held extraordinarily, *e.g.* in an emergency with shorter notice than usual, sometimes even overnight.[1] In its fully developed form my theory is that, in the 350's, the Athenians held three meetings of the assembly in a prytany, but that the number in the early 340's was raised to four, each with a fixed agenda, as described by Aristotle in the *Ath.Pol.* (43.3–6).[2]

This new interpretation of the number and types of meeting of the Athenian *ekklesia* has sometimes been met with opposition or doubt, but the critique has been stated only briefly and vaguely in the form 'I am not persuaded', *vel sim.*[3] Recently, however, a full discussion of my views has been undertaken by Edward M. Harris,[4] who offers a clever and clearly argued restatement of the traditional views (a) that there

---

[1] In referring to my own publications I use the following abbreviations: *AE=The Athenian Ecclesia. A Collection of Articles 1976–83* (Copenhagen 1983); *AV=Die athenische Voksversammlung im Zeitalter des Demosthenes* (=*Xenia* 13 [Konstanz 1984]); *AA=The Athenian Assembly* (Oxford 1987). My views were first presented in "How Often did the *Ecclesia* Meet?" *GRBS* 18 (1977) 43–70 (=*AE* 35–72). They were further developed in "'Ἐκκλησία Σύγκλητος in Hellenistic Athens," *GRBS* 20 (1979) 149–56 (=*AE* 73–81) and "When Did the Athenian *Ecclesia* Meet?" *GRBS* 23 (1982) 331–50 (=*AE* 83–102).

[2] *Cf.* the addenda in *AE* 63–72, 81, and 102; M. H. Hansen and F. W. Mitchel, "The Number of *Ecclesiai* in Fourth-Century Athens," *SymbOslo* 59 (1984) 13–19, and *AV* 31f n.113.

[3] *Cf. e.g.* P. J. Rhodes, *A Commentary on the Aristotelian Athenaion Politeia* (Oxford 1981) 521f; K. W. Welwei, *Die griechische Polis* (Stuttgart 1983) 200; J. Bleicken, *Die athenische Demokratie* (Shöningh 1985) 105. The only argument against my view had been that of M. M. Markle, "Jury Pay and Assembly Pay at Athens," *Crux. Essays . . . G. E. M. de Ste Croix* (=*History of Political Thought* VI [Exeter 1986]) 274 n.18. Markle holds that the *ekklesiai* convened on Elaph. 18 and 19 of 347/6 must be reckoned as two meetings, thus giving five *ekklesiai* in prytany VIII instead of four; but *cf. AA* 29 with n.198, and 43 *infra*.

[4] "How Often Did the Athenian Assembly Meet?" *CQ* N.S. 36 (1986) 363–77 (hereafter 'Harris').

was no restriction on the number of *ekklesiai* to be held, and (b) that *ekklesiai synkletoi* were always extra meetings.

The greater part of Harris's article is a rejection of my interpretation of a number of passages, but he begins by stating two positive reasons for accepting the traditional view. (1) An *a priori* argument: there *must* have been extra meetings, and any restriction on the people's right to assembly is against common sense. (2) The lexicographers and scholiasts who define *ekklesia synkletos* as an extra meeting deserve to be taken seriously and should not be "tossed out without further consideration" (366). I will discuss these two essential points first, starting with the *a priori* argument that it is unbelievable that the Athenians could have had a maximum number of *ekklesiai* in a prytany.

Harris admits that "the assembly tried, especially in the fourth century B.C., to conduct its business according to set rules"; but he contends (1) that "these rules were *self-imposed*" and (2) they "did *not represent any limitation* on the powers of the assembly" (364, my italics). The sources we have tend to disprove both of Harris's assumptions.

Re (1), in 346/5, for example, the Athenians passed a law by which front-row seats in the *ekklesia* were reserved for all members of one tribe entrusted with the maintenance of order during the meeting.[5] This νόμος on the εὐκοσμία τῶν ῥητόρων was in all probability, like other *nomoi*, passed by the *nomothetai* and not by the *ekklesia*.[6] Thus the rule was *not* self-imposed.

Re (2), in or around 355 the *ekklesia* was deprived of all jurisdiction in political trials, and thereafter all major public actions opened in the *ekklesia* were referred to the *dikasteria* which heard the case and passed the verdict.[7] We do not know precisely how and when the reform was enacted, but that it took place is no longer doubted, not even by my critics,[8] who are sceptical about the limited number of *ekklesiai* I propose. *Pace* Harris, this reform unquestionably imposed an important limitation on the powers of the assembly.

Next, Harris believes that a restriction on the number of meetings per prytany "would have inhibited the ability of the assembly to re-

---

[5] Aeschin. 1.33f, 3.4; Dem. 25.9; *cf. AE* 30–32.

[6] We have a few examples of general, permanent rules which, in an emergency, were passed by the *ekklesia* and took the form of *psephismata* (*cf. AE* 183–91); but in our sources there is no example whatsoever, after *ca* 400, of the *ekklesia* passing a *nomos* (*cf. AE* 163f). Other *nomoi* regulating the assembly's powers and procedures include *e.g.* the *merismos*: *cf.* P. J. Rhodes, *The Athenian Boule* (Oxford 1972) 101–03; *AE* 191f.

[7] *Cf. AE* 60 with further references.

[8] *Cf. e.g.* Rhodes (*supra* n.3) 525.

spond to emergencies" (364). Let us suppose, for example, that an emergency occurred at the end of a prytany when all four meetings had been held. "Would the *prytaneis* have simply turned to the people and said that they could not call another meeting and that the matter would just have to wait until the beginning of the next prytany?" (364). Of course not. They would have broken the rules, as all people have done in all states throughout history. But that does not prove that there could not have been any rule as to the number of assemblies to be held constitutionally in a prytany. As a parallel, I adduce two examples from modern constitutions.

In Texas and in Montana the legislature meets only every second year. This rule is often felt to be a serious obstacle to the constant demand in modern society for new legislation. But the rule is laid down in the constitutions of both states, and all attempts to have the constitutions changed have so far failed. Here there is a clear and strongly-felt limitation on the legislature's right to assemble, and the only escape has been, very exceptionally, to ask the governor to call an extra session.[9] Again, in many states of the United States and also in the United Kingdom, sessions of the legislature or Parliament or their committees can run for a fixed number of days only. What happens if important business has not yet been transacted when the time is running out? The clock is stopped just before midnight and the session goes on, sometimes for several hours, sometimes even for several days, under the fiction that stopping the clock is stopping time.[10]

Harris argues that a restriction on the number of *ekklesiai* would have been in conflict with common sense and would have to be violated in an emergency. He is absolutely right, but this is precisely what has always happened in all states in all periods. Thus, I have no difficulty in believing both that the Athenians had a rule limiting the number of *ekklesiai* per prytany and that, occasionally, they broke the rule and held an extra meeting. Whether this exceptional extra meeting was warranted by some exemption clause in the law regulating the number of *ekklesiai* (the Texas/Montana model) or was held unconstitutionally (the stopping-the-clock model) we do not know, since we have no indisputable evidence that such a meeting was ever held. But

---

[9] Constitution of Texas (1876) Art. III Sect. 5; Constitution of Montana (1972) Art. V Sect. 6.

[10] On the Montana legislators' practice of stopping the clock on the last day of a session *cf.* J. J. Lopach, ed., *We the People of Montana* (Missoula 1983) 69. The device is used in many other states, *e.g.* in Texas, regularly for a few hours only but sometimes for longer periods; and in Britain, committees of the House of Commons may stop the clock for several days.

the Athenians may well have convened such sessions of the *ekklesia* on more than one occasion in the course of the period *ca* 355–322. We simply do not know.

Harris's other reason for accepting the traditional definition of *ekklesia synkletos* is that it is endorsed by some scholiasts and lexicographers (364–66). He grants me that several of the lexicographical notes are muddled and betray ignorance of Athenian institutions. Furthermore, of the three lexicographical notes quoted by me (*AE* 73) and reproduced by Harris (364) only two (Σ *ad* Dem. 18.73 and 24.20) define *ekklesia synkletos* as an extra meeting held in an emergency.[11] The third note, by Harpocration, is ambiguous and defines *ekklesia synkletos* as an emergency meeting only: τῶν ἐκκλησιῶν αἱ μὲν ἐξ ἔθους καὶ κατὰ μῆνα ἐγίνοντο· εἰ δέ τι ἐξαίφνης κατεπείξειεν ὥστε γενέσθαι ἐκκλησίαν, αὕτη ἐκαλεῖτο σύγκλητος ἐκκλησία· Δημοσθένης ἐν τῷ κατ' Αἰσχίνου. Harpocration is undoubtedly the most reliable of the three, and he is even good enough to identify his source, Dem. 19.123: ἐφοβοῦντο δὴ μὴ σύγκλητος ἐκκλησία γένοιτ' ἐξαίφνης. This passage does support the view that *ekklesia synkletos* was an emergency meeting, but contains no explicit information about whether or not it was an additional meeting. Thus, it is cautiously and correctly reproduced by Harpocration; Harris notes, "even though the authors of the scholia and lexica in this case do not name any sources, it does appear that they must have had some" (365). But Harpocration *does* mention his source, and the two scholia may be based only on the same source. The difference is that, like many modern historians, they tend to infer that an emergency meeting must be an extra meeting.

It is probably worth while to elaborate the point that the learned Harpocration cites Dem. 19.123 as his source. This is an indication (but admittedly no proof) that he could find no better source to quote. The reason may well be that the lexicographers were as badly informed about the exact meaning of *ekklesia synkletos* as we are today. Admittedly they had access to hundreds of speeches now lost. Nevertheless they may have found no better source to rely on for the meaning of *ekklesia synkletos* than Dem. 19.123. This is not at all surprising. There

---

[11] It may be useful to adduce a fourth late account of the *ekklesia synkletos*, Liban. *Decl.* 32.18: γέμει δὲ (τὸ βαλάντιον) πλείονα κἂκ τῆς ἐκκλησίας τρίτον διδούσης ἑκάστου μηνός, ἵνα τοὺς συγκλήτους ἀφῶ. Here the *ekklesiai synkletoi* are obviously extra meetings, and we learn that citizens were paid for attending an *ekklesia synkletos*. But in the following lines we are told that the Pnyx was locked with a key kept by the *epistates*; that higher rates were paid if important matters were debated; and that first-comers were paid twice, first when they arrived before others and again, with all the others, when they left the *ekklesia* after the session. This account does not inspire confidence but may well have inspired the scholiasts.

are numerous parallels, *e.g.* the lexicographers' attempt to explain what a *lexiarchikon grammateion* was.[12]

Having discussed the evidence that supports the traditional definition of *ekklesia synkletos*, Harris proceeds to the negative part of his argument. My definition was based on a number of passages which he now submits to a penetrating scrutiny, arguing that my interpretation of each is wrong or at best not cogent. The passages are Dem. 19.154, Aeschin. 2.61, Arist. *Ath.Pol.* 43.3–6, Aeschin. 2.72, *IG* II[2] 212.57ff, some sources relating to the number of *ekklesiai* held in Elaphebolion 346, and finally the Hellenistic decrees in which the term *ekklesia synkletos* is actually attested.

On one count I plead guilty. I misinterpreted Aeschin. 2.61, προυφαιρῶν τὰς ἐκκλησίας. The correct interpretation was pointed out to me by David Lewis,[13] and is now stated independently by Harris (368). I add that in my latest treatment of the problem, published in 1984, I omitted Aeschin. 2.61 from the account; as to the other sources I am still inclined to uphold my original interpretation.

(1) Dem. 19.154. Referring to the period after 25 Elaph. 346 Demosthenes states: ἐπειδὴ γὰρ ἐκκλησία μὲν οὐκέτ' ἦν ὑπόλοιπος οὐδεμία διὰ τὸ προκατακεχρῆσθαι ... γράφω ψήφισμα βουλεύων, τὴν βουλὴν ποιήσαντος τοῦ δήμου κυρίαν. ... My interpretation of this passage was, and remains, that Demosthenes' emphatic expression must comprise both regular and extraordinary meetings (*AE* 36)—which Harris does not deny, but he believes that Demosthenes attempts to take in his audience and that "the possibility of summoning an extra meeting of the assembly ... is cunningly passed over in silence" (367). I agree with Harris that Demosthenes often tries to mislead his audience, and I am willing to accept his interpretation of the passage if he can demonstrate from other sources that an *ekklesia synkletos* was an extra meeting. As the passage stands, Dem. 19.154 points in my favour and has to be explained away in order to uphold the traditional interpretation of *ekklesia synkletos*.

(2) In the *Ath.Pol.*, extra meetings are mentioned neither at 43.3–6 (the detailed description of the four meetings held in each prytany) nor at 62.2 (briefly listing the rates for ecclesiastic pay).[14] The second

---

[12] Photius and *Suda s.v.*; cf. D. Whitehead, *The Demes of Attica* (Princeton 1986) 35 with n.130.

[13] "M. H. Hansen on the Athenian *Ecclesia*," unpublished paper read in September 1984 at the Norman Baynes Annual Meeting of UK Ancient Historians (cf. *AV* 29 with n.105).

[14] Harris (374 n.33) finds it unlikely that *ekklesiastikon* was paid at *ekklesiai synkletoi*. But if I am right in maintaining that an *ekklesia kyria* could be held as an *ekkle-*

passage is of little consequence for our problem; the first, on the other hand, carries some weight. Harris (368f) and I (*AE* 203f) agree that *argumenta e silentio* based on the *Ath.Pol.* are of no value if other sources point to the existence of institutions or procedures that Aristotle omits from his account. But again my point is that there *is* no reliable source indicating that an *ekklesia synkletos* was an extra meeting. Therefore, until new evidence points the other way, I am inclined to accept the information given by Aristotle as it stands: the Athenians held four *ekklesiai* in a prytany, neither more nor less. How they were summoned (as ordinary *ekklesiai* or as *ekklesiai synkletoi*) is another matter passed over in silence by Aristotle.

(3) In his speech on the embassy (2.72) Aeschines tells the jurors that, because of their fear and the general confusion, the Athenians had to convene more ἐκκλησίαι σύγκλητοι than ἐκκλησίαι τεταγμέναι ἐκ τῶν νόμων. In my first article I pointed out that the reference must be to the spring of 346, in particular to prytany VIII running from early Elaphebolion to mid-Mounichion.[15] This is accepted by Harris (371, 373). Again, we both believe that Aeschines is probably telling the truth and that this piece of information is to be taken seriously and literally. We also agree, essentially, that ἐκκλησίαι τεταγμέναι ἐκ τῶν νόμων—i.e., arranged for by law—must be 'regular' or 'ordinary' meetings.[16] But on the meaning of *ekklesia synkletos* our roads part. On my interpretation Aeschines' statement implies that three out of four *ekklesiai* held in prytany VIII were *synkletoi*, i.e. summoned in a special way and not just held as ordinary meetings (*AE* 57f). Harris, by contrast, takes the passage to mean that "things were so bad in early 346 that, in addition to the four ordinary meetings, at least five ἐκκλησίαι σύγκλητοι were called every prytany for purposes of discussing urgent business" (371). Now, according to Harris, Aeschines (in 2 and 3) and Demosthenes (in 18 and 19) discuss only four meetings held in prytany

---

sia synkletos, (cf. 46 infra) there can be little doubt that the Athenians were paid the usual rate, i.e., in the age of Aristotle, nine obols for an *ekklesia kyria synkletos* and one drachma for other *ekklesiai synkletoi*.

[15] *AE* 44–46, 64. We must keep in mind, however, that the period described by Aeschines may cover not only prytany VIII, but also prytany VII; cf. Harris 371.

[16] Harris 370. His distinction between ἐκκλησίαι τεταγμέναι and προγεγραμμέναι misrepresents my ideas: on my interpretation, Aeschines' phrase ἐκκλησίαι τεταγμέναι ἐκ τῶν νόμων is synonymous with ἐκκλησία ἐκ τοῦ νόμου (*Hesperia* Suppl. 17 [1978] 4 lines 86–88; cf. *AE* 63) and is an antonym of ἐκκλησία κατὰ ψήφισμα (sources listed and discussed at *AE* 40, 49, 68, 76, 81). Since I take an ἐκκλησία κατὰ ψήφισμα to be an ἐκκλησία σύγκλητος, I have no difficulty in explaining Aeschines' use of the opposed terms ἐκκλησία σύγκλητος versus ἐκκλησία τεταγμένη ἐκ τῶν νόμων.

VIII, *i.e.* the assemblies held on Elaph. 16, 18, 19, and 25.[17] Of these assemblies the meeting held on Elaph. 16 in the precinct of Dionysus after the Dionysia was undoubtedly an ordinary meeting. And so were probably, according to Harris, the meetings convened on Elaph. 18 and 19.[18] We have no information about the meeting held on Elaph. 25. Thus we have evidence of three, perhaps four, ordinary meetings as against one *ekklesia synkletos*, or none at all. Harris proceeds, "We cannot rule out the possibility that Aeschines and Demosthenes did not report all meetings of Assembly which took place during prytany viii of the archonship of Themistokles. After all, they were only interested in discussing the Peace of Philocrates and may well have left out of their speeches any references to other meetings of the Assemby which met during prytany VIII simply because these meetings did not discuss business which was relevant to this treaty" (373). True enough. It is unlikely, but not inconceivable, that an *ekklesia* was held between Elaph. 19 and 25 in which the envoys were (re-)elected.[19] And it is just possible that yet another *ekklesia* was held that has left no trace in our sources (*cf. AE* 49, 58). But Harris asks us to believe that no less than five meetings are passed over in silence in all four speeches delivered by Aeschines and Demosthenes in 343 and 330. Moreover, he asks us to believe that at least four of these unknown meetings were *ekklesiai synkletoi, i.e.*, according to his view, extra emergency meetings. This is simply impossible. If Harris is right about *ekklesiai synkletoi* being extra meetings, held in addition to the four ordinary meetings, the inference must be that, at 2.72, Aeschines is lying about the number of *ekklesiai synkletoi* held in prytany VIII during Elaph. 347/6.

(4) If, on the other hand, Aeschines at 2.72 is right that, in connection with the peace negotiations, the Athenians convened more *ekklesiai synkletoi* than ordinary meetings, it follows that most of the sessions described by Aeschines and Demosthenes must have been *ekklesiai synkletoi*. Now, the *ekklesia* held after the Dionysia, on Elaph. 16, was probably an ordinary meeting. Accordingly, at least one and probably all of the *ekklesiai* held on Elaph. 8, 18, and 19 must have been *ekklesiai synkletoi*. These meetings, however, were *not* summoned at

---

[17] On the meeting of Elaph. 8 see 44 *infra*. The evidence for the meetings held on Elaph. 16 (?), 18, 19, and 25 is listed and discussed at *AE* 47f and 70f.

[18] These two were not summoned at short notice, but before the Dionysia in accordance with the decree proposed and carried by Demosthenes (Aeschin. 2.61; *cf. AE* 40). Harris (371 and esp. 375) rejects my view that *ekklesiai* summoned by decree of the *demos* and *boule* were *ekklesiai synkletoi*. Thus, according to Harris, the sessions held on Elaph. 18 and 19 were ordinary *ekklesiai*, not *ekklesiai synkletoi*.

[19] *AE* 52, 57, and esp. the addendum at 68, where the problem is discussed in the light of what we know from other sources about the appointment of envoys.

short notice but many days in advance in accordance with decrees proposed and carried by Demosthenes. The inference is that an *ekklesia synkletos* was not only a session called overnight; it could also be a session summoned by decree, as against a session summoned by the *prytaneis* on their own initiative. Furthermore, we must not forget that of the five unquestionable examples of *ekklesiai synkletoi*, all attested in Hellenistic decrees, three were convened στρατηγῶν παραγγειλάντων (*IG* II² 911, *SEG* 24.134, *I.Délos* 1507.39f), while the other two were summoned κατὰ τὸ ψήφισμα ὃ ὁ δεῖνα εἶπεν (*IG* II² 838, 945). This is a strong indication that an *ekklesia synkletos* could be called in two different ways, and that one way was to pass a decree for this purpose.

(5) Now, the *ekklesia* held on Elaph. 18 is not only described in Aeschin. 1-3 and in Dem. 18-19; it is also referred to in a decree honouring the Bosporan princes, *IG* II² 212.53-57: περὶ δὲ τῶν χρημάτων τῶν [ὀφει]λ[ο]μένων τοῖς παισὶ τοῖς Λεύκωνος ὅπ[ως ἂ]ν ἀπολάβωσιν, χρηματίσαι τοὺς προέδ[ρος οἳ] ἂν λάχωσι προεδρεύειν ἐν τῶι δήμωι [τῆι ὀγ]δόηι ἐπὶ δέκα πρῶτον μετὰ τὰ ἱερά.... This provision shows, on my interpretation, that on Elaph. 18 the peace and alliance with Philip was not debated until the Athenians had dealt with the sacred business (three items, according to *Ath.Pol.* 43.6) and the debt to the Bosporan princes.

According to Harris, "there is only one problem with this last argument, but it is a fatal one: τὰ ἱερά does not refer to a discussion of the τρία ... ἱερῶν mentioned at *Ath.Pol.* 43.6, but to the sacrifices which were performed at the beginning of every meeting of the assembly. In the inscription no reference is made to *a discussion* of sacred matters, but to *the* sacred matters. It is important to note the presence of the article in the phrase μετὰ τὰ ἱερά and its absence in the phrase τρία ... ἱερῶν" (370). Harris's sharp distinction, however, between ἱερά with the article (referring to sacrifices before the *ekklesia*) and without it (referring to sacred matters on the agenda) breaks down in the face of *IG* II² 74.7-9, εἶναι δὲ αὐ[τῶι πρόσοδον πρὸς] τὴν βολὴν κ[αὶ τὸν δῆμον πρώτωι μ]εθ' ἱερά. Harris' interpretation of μετὰ τὰ ἱερά is also contradicted by the frequent usage of cities in Hellenistic kingdoms, μετὰ τὰ ἱερὰ καὶ τὰ βασιλικά (*i.e.*, post legationes epistolasque a regibus missas).²⁰ The analogy with τὰ βασιλικά strongly indicates that τὰ ἱερά refers to sacred business, not to sacrifices. Moreover, the business given priority by the phrase πρῶτον μετὰ τὰ ἱερά must, on Harris's

---

²⁰ An example is *Syll.*³ 333.21-24 (Samos, after 306 B.C.), εἶναι δ' αὐτῶι καὶ ἔφοδον ἐπὶ τὴν βουλὴν καὶ τὸν δῆμον, ἄν του δέηται, πρώτωι μετὰ τὰ ἱερὰ καὶ τὰ βασιλικά.

interpretation, follow immediately after the sacrifices; but we know from Aeschines 1.23 that the sacrifices were followed not by the first item on the agenda but by the *procheirotonia*, and the debate on the first item on the agenda was opened only after the *procheirotonia* with the herald's proclamation: τίς ἀγορεύειν βούλεται; (*cf. AE* 123f). For these reasons I still prefer the traditional view that πρῶτον μετὰ τὰ ἱερά means immediately after the (three items of) sacred business had been completed.[21] The consequence, as I pointed out in 1977 (*cf. AE* 43), is that the debate on the peace treaty was only the fifth item on the agenda for the meeting held on Elaph. 18. On the other hand, I can well imagine that the first four items on the agenda may have been transacted in only a few minutes.[22] Again, as indicated above, Harris has not disproved my view that this meeting was an *ekklesia synkletos*. Thus, the preferable view seems still to be that an *ekklesia synkletos* was one of the meetings described by Aristotle at *Ath.Pol.* 43.3–6, which, however, was summoned in a special way and not by the *prytaneis* on their own initiative in accordance with the *nomoi*.

(6) The examination of Aeschin. 2.72 naturally entails closer scrutiny of the *ekklesiai* held in Elaphebolion 346. Harris and I disagree about two important problems: (a) Were the *ekklesiai* of Elaph. 18 and 19 two separate meetings or rather a double meeting to be reckoned as only one of the four sessions convened (συνάγειν) by the *prytaneis* (Arist. *Ath.Pol.* 43.3)? (b) Did the Athenians convene an *ekklesia* on Elaph. 8, the day for the *proagon* and a festival day for Asclepius?

Re (a): I find this question very difficult. In 1977 I suspended judgement and left both possibilities open (*AE* 51); in the addenda of 1983 (*AE* 71) I preferred to see them as a double meeting, reckoned as one by virtue of a single summons and a single agenda. Harris has no doubt (371f): "it is simply unacceptable to count the two meetings on 18 and 19 Elaph. as one meeting. Reading from the decree of Demosthenes which sets the dates for the meetings, Aeschines (2.61) refers quite plainly to two meetings (δύο ἐκκλησίας). Cf. Aeschin. 2.60, 65, 67; Dem. 19.13." Harris seems to have overlooked Aeschin. 2.53, ἐκκλησίαν ἐπὶ δύο ἡμέρας.[23] Next, *pace* Harris, there can be no doubt that Demosthenes' decree (Aeschin. 2.61) by which the *prytaneis* were instructed to summon the people, covered both sessions.[24] Third, a

---

[21] *Cf. e.g.* Tod II 104 (on lines 33–38); Rhodes (*supra* n.3) 529; A. S. Henry, *Honours and Privileges in Athenian Decrees* (Hildesheim 1983) 197.

[22] For the speedy transaction of business *cf. AE* 128f, 216f.

[23] For discussion of Demosthenes' decree referred to in Aeschin. 2.53, 61, 109f, and 3.68 see the addendum in *AE* 64–67.

[24] Harris (371) takes my expression that the agenda was the same for both meetings

double meeting (or two consecutive meetings) seems to have been a statutory requirement for the conclusion of peace and probably of other important treaties as well.[25] Fourth, given the ambiguous nature of the problem, we must consider the possibility that a double session or two sessions on consecutive days was the Athenians' way of 'stopping the clock' (*cf. supra* 37). Harris presents an oversimplified version of the evidence.

Re (b). On the other hand, Harris wants to eliminate the meeting that, according to Aeschin. 3.67f, was held on Elaph. 8. He believes (372f) that Aeschines attempts to mislead the jurors by telling them about an *ekklesia* that in fact never took place. This is a strikingly novel interpretation. Furthermore, if Harris is right in his view that there was no meeting of the *ekklesia* on Elaph. 8 of 347/6, but two on Elaph. 18 and 19, he ends with a total of four attested *ekklesiai* held in prytany VIII (Elaph. 16, 18, 19, 25) and, as he himself admits, has removed a possible objection to my hypothesis that there was a limit to the number of meetings that could be called in one prytany.

Harris's interpretation of Aeschin. 3.67f, however, should not be accepted for the following reasons. According to Harris "we need to note that Aeschines does not say whether or not this proposal was passed and nothing in the text allows us to give a definite answer to this question" (372). This is not true; in the following section (Aeschin. 3.68) we are told that Demosthenes *succeeded* in having *yet another* decree passed: ἐνταῦθ᾽ ἕτερον νικᾷ ψήφισμα Δημοσθένης. The inference is that Demosthenes proposed *and carried both* decrees.[26] We must of course consider the possibility that Aeschines is simply lying; but if he is, he is lying both about the proposal and about its passage by the people. Next, it is unlikely that Aeschines should lie about a decree proposed and carried by Demosthenes. One could probably always lie about what was said during an *ekklesia* and about who said it. For in all probability no exact minutes were kept and the audience's memory, undoubtedly vague after sixteen years, was the only possible check. But to allege that non-existent decrees had been proposed and carried

---

(*AE* 51) to mean that the agenda on Elaph. 18 must have comprised exactly the same items as the agenda on Elaph. 19. This is of course not true and has never been my view. What I meant, and still mean, is that both sessions were warranted by one and the same decree and that this decree prescribed business to be transacted on both days.

[25] Aeschin. 2.60 (τὸ τῶν συμμάχων δόγμα); *IG* I³ 71.33–36; II² 21.9–11; Thuc. 1.44.1, 3.36.4–6. Two *ekklesiai* on consecutive days are attested for the year 302/1, prytany VIII 27 and 28 (*IG* II² 500, 501; *cf. Hesperia* 9 [1940] 341f). *Cf. AE* 51.

[26] *Cf.* Aeschin. 2.62f, discussing two decrees proposed and carried by Philocrates and connected with the phrase νικᾷ γὰρ ἕτερον ψήφισμα Φιλοκράτης.

is a different matter, for decrees were recorded and kept in the Metroon.²⁷ Similarly, it would be hard to lie about a session of the *ekklesia* that never took place. Harris points out, correctly, that this meeting is mentioned only in Aeschin. 3, delivered in 330, and not in Aeschin. 2, delivered in 343; but the same applies to other pieces of information, not to be doubted for that reason alone.²⁸ I cannot of course preclude the possibility that Aeschines is simply deceiving the jurors about the *ekklesia* allegedly held on Elaph. 8. But I prefer the traditional view: that an *ekklesia* was in fact held on this (festival) day in accordance with a decree proposed and carried by Demosthenes. Thus it was, on my interpretation, an *ekklesia synkletos*: it was festival day and was warranted by a decree of the *demos* (or of the *boule*) and not just summoned by the *prytaneis* on their own initiative.

(7) Holding meetings on festival days is a crucial problem only briefly touched on by Harris in his discussion (373) of the fourth century and almost brushed aside in his section (375) on the Hellenistic period.²⁹ The problem, however, deserves serious consideration. According to Mikalson (followed by both Harris and me) the Athenians did their utmost to avoid *ekklesiai* on festival days. Thus the few cases of *ekklesiai* attested on annual or monthly festival days must have

---

²⁷ *Cf.* Aeschines' revealing comment on a decree passed in the following *ekklesia* (3.75): ὅτι δ' ἀληθῆ λέγω, ἀνάγνωθί μοι, τίς ἦν ὁ ταῦτα γράψας, καὶ τίς ὁ ταῦτα ἐπιψηφίσας. ΨΗΦΙΣΜΑ. καλόν, ὦ ἄνδρες Ἀθηναῖοι, καλὸν ἡ τῶν δημοσίων γραμμάτων φυλακή· ἀκίνητον γάρ ἐστι, καὶ οὐ συμμεταπίπτει τοῖς αὐτομολοῦσιν ἐν τῇ πολιτείᾳ, ἀλλ' ἀπέδωκε τῷ δήμῳ, ὁπόταν βούληται, συνιδεῖν τοὺς πάλαι μὲν πονηρούς. . . .

²⁸ Harris (372 with n.28) claims to have detected five other false charges made by Aeschines in 330 but not in 343. None of them is straightforward. Two can be dealt with fairly briefly. The story of the exclusion of Chersobleptes (3.73–75) is, according to Harris, refuted by Aeschin. 2.83–86, where evidence is produced "that Chersobleptes did indeed have a person in Athens who could have acted as his *synedros*, namely Critobulus of Lampsacus. . . ." Now, at 3.74 Aeschines claims that Chersobleptes had no *synedros* in Athens, which was probably true, since, at 2.83, Aeschines tells the jurors that Critobulus of Lampsacus *claimed* that he had been sent by Chersobleptes, *i.e.* he was *not* a *synedros* and an ackowledged member of the *synedrion* in Athens. There is no contradiction. Aeschines, of course, prefers to tell the jurors what suits him best in both cases, but that is different. Next, it is true that the charge against Demosthenes for having bribed his way onto the council in 347/6 is mentioned by Aeschines in 330 (3.62) and not in 343. But we must not forget that Meidias, in 347, attacked Demosthenes in the *dokimasia*, and Demosthenes admits (21.111) that Meidias' charges against him proved to be dangerous. Thus there is no reason to believe that Aeschines, in 330, invented the charge that Demosthenes had used bribery to become a councillor. Since Harris announces a forthcoming study on these problems, I will take this point no further until I have seen his arguments.

²⁹ "Hansen assumes that these meetings must have been ἐκκλησίαι σύγκλητοι because they were summoned on festival days. I see nothing which compels us to accept such an assumption and to rule out *a priori* the possibility that these could have been ordinary meetings of the assembly, whether the term ordinary is used in the traditional sense or in the sense which Hansen prefers" (375).

been emergency meetings,[30] and accordingly, on Harris's own definition, *ekklesiai synkletoi*, i.e., extra meetings called at short notice, and not ordinary meetings as described by Aristotle (*Ath.Pol.* 43.3-6). Some of the (few) meetings, however, that *were* held on festival days are explicitly labelled ἐκκλησία κυρία, and the inference seems to be that the Athenians could hold an ἐκκλησία κυρία σύγκλητος. This applies not only to several Hellenistic decrees,[31] but also to one fourth-century decree, *IG* II² 359. The preamble of this decree was restored by Meritt to give [Elaph.] 8=pryt. [VII] 30. The restoration has been questioned both by Mikalson and by Harris, but for no good reason. No matter how the month is restored, there can be no doubt that this decree was passed on the eighth of the month, a festival day in all twelve months (*cf. AE* 88f). So even if we reject the perfect equation [Elaph.] 8=pryt. [VII] 30, we must still admit that this *ekklesia* was held on a festival day and thus was an *ekklesia synkletos*. But in line 7 we learn that the meeting was an *ekklesia kyria*: i.e., the meeting must have been an ἐκκλησία κυρία σύγκλητος. Thus the attestation of *ekklesiai kyriai* held on festival days seems to disprove Harris's clearcut distinction between *ekklesiai synkletoi* (always extra meetings held in an emergency) and ordinary *ekklesiai* (four per prytany, of which one was the *ekklesia kyria*).

(8) The term βουλὴ σύγκλητος is attested in three Hellenistic inscriptions: *SEG* 21.440, *IG* II² 897, and 954. The formula used is the same in all three: βουλὴ ἐν βουλευτηρίωι σύνκλητος στρατηγῶν παραγγειλάντων καὶ ἀπὸ βουλῆς ἐκκλησία κυρία ἐν τῶι θεάτρωι.[32] On my interpretation σύγκλητος goes with both βουλή and ἐκκλησία, and as a parallel I adduced (*AE* 76) the assembly held in 339 after Philip's capture of Elateia (Dem. 18.168ff): the Athenians had, overnight, to summon first the *boule* for an early meeting and then the *ekklesia* for an emergency meeting. Harris admits (375) that the assembly held in 339 was probably an *ekklesia synkletos*, but (to avoid the attestation of ἐκκλησία κυρία σύγκλητος) he prefers a different interpretation of the Hellenistic decrees (375):

---

[30] J. D. Mikalson, *The Sacred and Civil Calendar of the Athenian Year* (Princeton 1975) 189f. Furthermore, if we follow Harris in assuming that meetings summoned on festival days were probably ordinary meetings but that meetings held on festival days were extremely rare and were held only because the Athenians could not postpone the meeting until the festival was over, we will have to admit that both ordinary *ekklesiai* and *ekklesiai synkletoi* could be held as emergency meetings, and Harris's sharp distinction between the two types of meeting tends to break down anyway.

[31] *Cf. AE* 78 nos. 13-17 and Mikalson (*supra* n.30) 72, 128 144, 146.

[32] The formula ἐκκλησία κυρία appears in *SEG* 21.440 and *IG* II² 897; in 954 we find ἐκκλησία ἀρ[χαιρεσίαι.

one could argue that the meetings of the Assembly referred to in these inscriptions had already been scheduled by the *prytaneis* several days earlier and that the *prytaneis* had posted the agenda for each of these meetings well in advance. At the last moment, however, a new concern arose, one which the generals wished to be dealt with immediately, but to be placed on the agenda for this meeting it needed to be approved first by the Council. To clear this hurdle, an emergency meeting of the Council was called at the request of the generals. At this meeting of the Council the new item was introduced, passed and placed on the agenda of the previously scheduled meeting of the Assembly, which was then convened immediately afterwards. This explanation certainly makes more sense than Hansen's....

It does not, however, for the following reasons. First, I note that the reconstructions suggested by Harris and by myself both presuppose that, in the Hellenistic period, the *boule* and the *ekklesia* were run more or less according to the same rules as in the fourth century.[33] Thus the *boule* probably met every day, except on holidays. Let us now examine one of the inscriptions according to which a *boule synkletos* was followed by an *ekklesia*, e.g. IG II² 897. This decree was passed on Moun. 11, which was an ordinary 'weekday', as were also Moun. 9 and 10.[34] Let us assume, following Harris, that the *ekklesia* had been summoned already on e.g. Moun. 5, but that a new concern suddenly arose that needed to be placed before the people immediately and, accordingly, discussed first in the *boule*. If the emergency occurred more than twenty hours before the *ekklesia* to be held on Moun. 11, the *strategoi* would not have had to summon a *boule synkletos*. They could simply have raised the matter in the ordinary meeting of the *boule* held the day before the *ekklesia*. And even if the urgent business had been reported to the *strategoi* so late that the ordinary meeting held on Moun. 10 was finished, the *strategoi* would not have had to summon

---

[33] This assumption is difficult to test, *inter alia* because in the Hellenistic period the epigraphical sources cannot be supplemented with literary sources explaining the institutions in greater detail. We must bear in mind that the system was changed in at least one respect: when the number of tribes was raised from ten to twelve, the number of *ekklesiai* convened in a prytany was reduced from four to three, thus giving a total of 36 *ekklesiai* per year instead of 40. In one case, 303/2 pryt. XII, decrees passed in all three *ekklesiai* have survived: IG II² 498 with p.661, passed on the 8th day of the prytany in an *ekklesia kyria*; 493+518 and 494, both passed on the 23rd day of the prytany in an *ekklesia kyria*; and 495, 496+507, and 497, all passed on the 31st of the prytany in an *ekklesia*. I should like to thank Christian Habicht for drawing my attention to these decrees. I find it worth noting that the *ekklesiai* held on the 8th and the 23rd were both *ekklesiai kyriai*, i.e., there were two *ekklesiai kyriai* in the same prytany.

[34] *Cf.* Mikalson (*supra* n. 30) 141f.

an extra meeting of the *boule*, for the council would in any case have to convene before the *ekklesia* required for selecting *proedroi* by lot (*cf. AE* 135). The only anomaly would then have been to have the urgent business debated during the early session in connection with the allotment of the *proedroi*. On my interpretation, however, an emergency meeting of the *ekklesia* presupposed an emergency meeting of the *boule*, since the *boule* would normally not meet before sunrise, except on assembly days when the allotment of *proedroi* had to be completed before the *ekklesia* began early in the morning. Thus an emergency occurring on Moun. 8–10 and resulting in an *ekklesia* held on Moun. 11 would necessitate a *boule synkletos* held on Moun. 11 before the *ekklesia*. *IG* II² 897 and *SEG* 21.440 were both passed in an *ekklesia kyria*, and I still find most likely the assumption that these sessions of the assembly were *ekklesiai kyriai synkletoi*. We must bear in mind, however, that the reconstructions advanced by Harris and by myself only apply if the rules affecting sessions of *boule* and *ekklesia* were basically the same as in the fourth century, and this is admittedly a far-reaching assumption.

(9) Finally a word about the contents of the decrees passed in *ekklesiai synkletoi* in the Hellenistic period. For the sake of argument I grant Harris that the examination should be restricted to those decrees in which the phrase ἐκκλησία σύνκλητος is actually attested; thus I leave out decrees passed on festival days, on one of the first four days in the prytany, and during meetings introduced by a *boule synkletos*.[35] Now, five decrees are attested as passed during an *ekklesia synkletos*, but in two cases (*IG* II² 911 and *SEG* 24.134) only the preamble is preserved. So we are left with three decrees, all honorific. I found it remarkable (*AE* 79) that such decisions were regularly on the agenda of an *ekklesia synkletos*, and I concluded that an *ekklesia synkletos* cannot have been a session reserved for some urgent matter. Harris objects that "the honorary decrees *IG* II² 838 and 945 were not just passed for some minor *proxenoi* from small towns in Thrace. They were for close friends of Ptolemy III and Eumenes II. These men merited special treatment and what could be more flattering than to call an entire meeting of the assembly just to confer honours on them?" (376). I suspect that Harris makes too much of these honorific decrees and note his further comment: "One might ask, didn't the Athenians have better things to do at the meetings in this period? The unfortunate answer to this question is 'probably not.'" More important, Harris offers no discussion of the third honorific decree passed during an *ek-*

---

[35] *I.e.* the decrees listed at *AE* 75–78 nos. 5–17.

klesia synkletos, I.Délos 1507.37–54: this is a mere ratification by the Athenian *ekklesia* of some honours conferred by the Delian cleruchs on some of their own officials![36] Furthermore, *IG* II² 911 was passed in an *ekklesia synkletos* held in the summer of 168. In this case only the prescript survives, but we have a second decree passed during the same session.[37] The decree is honorific, bestowing a crown on a certain Calliphanes, who had served in the Roman army and reported their victory to Athens. As Meritt suggests, the *ekklesia synkletos* may in fact have been occasioned by the Roman victory at Pydna. The honorary decree for Calliphanes, however, is probouleumatic, and the probouleumatic formula includes the standard phrase that the business in question be transacted εἰς τὴν ἐπιοῦσαν ἐκκλησίαν (line 29). This indicates that the matter was not urgent but rather was to be taken up in the next assembly—which now happened to be an *ekklesia synkletos*—and thus that this type of meeting was not reserved for urgent matters.

To sum up. I still hold that my view of *ekklesia synkletos* and the restricted number of meetings is supported by Arist. *Ath.Pol.* 43.3–6, and, much more important, by Dem. 19.154 and Aeschin. 2.72; that my position is considerably strengthened by the fact that *ekklesiai kyriai* were sometimes held on festival days; and that additional support is provided by the Hellenistic decrees in which the phrase *ekklesia synkletos* occurs. Demosthenes *is* right: by Moun. 3 the Athenians had used up all the *ekklesiai* to be held in pryt. VIII. Aristotle's information can be accepted as it stands: the *prytaneis* convened four meetings of the *ekklesia* in a prytany, neither more nor less. Demosthenes and Aeschines do *not* mislead the jurors by suppressing information, in all four speeches, about numerous sessions of the *ekklesia*. They report the meetings actually held but disagree of course fundamentally—and lie—about what was said during these meetings. On the other hand, Aeschines is probably right about the Athenians having held more *ekklesiai synkletoi* than ordinary *ekklesiai* during pryt. VIII 347/6 (2.72), and he has not invented a meeting that never took place, *i.e.*, the meeting held on Elaph. 8 (3.67f). If *ekklesia synkletos* denotes an urgent meeting (as opposed to ordinary meetings called at several days' notice) it follows that the extremely infrequent *ekklesiai* held on festival days must have been *ekklesiai synkletoi*, and we have to accept

---

[36] Quoted and discussed in the addendum *AE* 81.

[37] Moretti, *I.stor.ellen.* 35 (=B. D. Meritt, *Hesperia* 3 [1934] 18–21). In this inscription the session is described as an ἐκκλησία ἐν Πειραιεῖ only, not as an ἐκκλησία σύγκλητος, which proves that the term *synkletos* was optional. I should like to thank Christian Habicht for drawing my attention to this inscription.

that the Athenians sometimes held an *ekklesia kyria synkletos*. At least one—and probably several more—of the *ekklesiai synkletoi* convened in the Hellenistic period was *not* reserved for some urgent matter but included the transaction of routine business.

What can be placed in the other scale? An *a priori* argument of no value (*supra* 37). The unproved assumption that Demosthenes and Aeschines repeatedly misinformed the jurors about the number and dates of *ekklesiai* held in Elaph. 346. And two scholia, both at variance with the best lexicographical note we have (Harpocration's explanation of *ekklesia synkletos*, referring to Dem. 19.123). For me it has been reassuring to see that Harris's well argued and clearly structured attack on my interpretation has led no further than taking away one of my testimonies, *viz.* Aeschin. 2.61, which I misinterpreted in my first article. Thus I am inclined to maintain my view: from the 350's on there was a limit on the number of *ekklesiai* to be held in a prytany,[38] and an *ekklesia synkletos* was not an extra meeting, but one of the stipulated meetings summoned in a special way, often at short notice, to deal with urgent matters in addition to the regular business to be transacted.[39]

THE INSTITUTE FOR ADVANCED STUDY, PRINCETON
January, 1987

---

[38] In passing (373f) Harris disputes my suggestion that in the fifth century the Athenians called only one obligatory meeting of the *ekklesia* in a prytany, the *ekklesia kyria*. Harris refers only to Hansen and Mitchel (*supra* n.2). The full discussion of this point appears in J. Christensen and M. H. Hansen, "What is *Syllogos* at Thukydides 2.22.1?" *ClMed* 34 (1983) 15-29.

[39] I should like to thank Christian Habicht for reading a draft of this paper and for making several valuable suggestions on Hellenistic decrees (cited above). Let me add, however, that he has not endorsed my views on *ekklesia synkletos* and the number of meetings, and for the present suspends judgement.

ADDENDA

177: For a collection and discussion of (*ekklesiai*) *synkletoi* in the Greek world cf. F. Ghinati, 'Richerche sulle *synkletoi* di Graecia,' *PP* 15 (1960) 354-73. On the Athenian *ekklesiai synkletoi* Ghinati offers the traditional interpretation, i.e. »riunioni straordinarie dell' Assemblea« as against *ekklesia kyria* »la prima (*sic!*) di ogni pritania« and *ekklesiai nomimoi (sic!)* »le altre tre della pritania« (355-58).

179: As a further illustration of this point I will adduce an example that is peculiar to representative democracies, but illustrates the same problem: if restrictions imposed on indirect democracies become too narrow (which often happens) the rules have to be disregarded or circumvented: in the West German constituent state Schleswig-Holstein the parliament (*Landtag*) is elected for a quadrennial period. During this term it cannot be dissolved and no extraordinary election can be held. After an election the *Landtag* elects a prime minister (*Ministerpräsident*) who then forms his government. To be elected *Ministerpräsident* a candidate must win a majority in the *Landtag*. But the constitution does not prescribe any procedure in the case of a tie. After the election in 1987, due to a political scandal, no candidate could win a majority in the *Landtag* and consequently no government could be formed. Then the *Landtag* resolved, unconstitutionally, to have an extraordinary election in May 1988.

180: As a noun *synkletos* means »council« (cf. e.g. Arist. *Pol.* 1275b8) and is the regular term for the Roman senate (cf. e.g. Polyb. 21.1.3). Sometimes, however, *synkletos* is used about a general assembly and may, in this sense, denote an extraordinary session cf. *SIG* 675.12 and Polyb. 29.24.6 with Walbank's comment: »The Achaeans had a council and a primary assembly which met at four annual *synodoi* right down to 146. From the time the Romans appeared on the scene, towards the end of the third century, certain delicate issues were removed from the competence of the regular *synodoi* and reserved for discussion and decision at a specially convened *syncletos* with a single item on the agenda; such *syncletoi* would normally consist of the council and assembly;« *A Historical Commentary on Polybios* III (Oxford 1979) 414. It is presumably this meaning of *synkletos* which, erroneously in my opinion, some lexicographers and scholiasts have applied to the Athenian *ekklesiai synkletoi*.

180: The scholion on Dem. 18.73 is late and has no authority, cf. M.R. Dilts, 'Palaeologian scholia on the Orations of Demosthenes,' *ClMed* 36 (1985) 257-59. The source is probably the scholion on Dem. 19.123 (referred to in *Ath. Eccl.* 73 note 2) which I will quote instead: ὅτι τρεῖς

ADDENDA

ἐκκλησίαι τοῦ μηνὸς γίνονται ὡρισμέναι· ἡ δὲ σύγκλητος οὐκ ὡρισμένη (263a, Dilts) σύγκλητος ἐκκλησία ἡ γινομένη διά τι ἐξαίφνης κατεπεῖγον (263b, Dilts). The term ὡρισμένη is also used in schol. Ar. *Ach.* 19; Schol. Dem. 24.20; *Suda* s. v. ἐκκλησία κυρία. The phrase εἰ δέ τι ἐξαίφνης κατεπείξειεν is found in Harp., *Suda* and *Etym. Magn.* s.v. σύγκλητος (ἐκκλησία). I should like to thank Edward Harris for drawing my attention to the correct understanding of the relation between the two scholia (Dem. 18.73 & 19.123).

184: For an updated survey of all attestations of *ekklesia* or *boule synkletos* in Hellenistic decrees cf. S.V. Tracy, '*EKKLESIA SYNKLETOS*: A Note,' *ZPE* 75 (1988) 186-88.

188: In *I. Délos* 1507.39-40 (cf. *Ath. Eccl.* 81) Tracy (*supra ad* 184) suggests [κυρι]α instead of [μετ]α which is indeed impossible. If Tracy's restoration is correct we have one (more) attestation of an *ekklesia kyria synkletos*.

WHAT IS *SYLLOGOS* AT THUKYDIDES 2.22.1?

BY

JOHNNY CHRISTENSEN AND MOGENS HERMAN HANSEN

When the Peloponnesian army invaded Attika in 431 many Athenians wanted to defend the countryside and risk an open battle outside the walls. Perikles, however, prevented any rash decision and his cunning methods are described by Thukydides in the following words: πιστεύων δὲ ὀρθῶς γιγνώσκειν περὶ τοῦ μὴ ἐπεξιέναι, ἐκκλησίαν τε οὐκ ἐποίει αὐτῶν οὐδὲ ξύλλογον οὐδένα, τοῦ μὴ ὀργῇ τι μᾶλλον ἢ γνώμῃ ξυνελθόντας ἐξαμαρτεῖν, τήν τε πόλιν ἐφύλασσε καὶ δι' ἡσυχίας μάλιστα ὅσον ἐδύνατο εἶχεν. (2.22.1) This passage raises at least three questions[1] concerning the Athenian political institutions: (a) what does οὐκ ἐποίει mean? (b) How did Perikles prevent the summoning of an ἐκκλησία? (c) What is a ξύλλογος?

The first question has been discussed especially by K.J. Dover,[2] who notes that 'the coordination of ἐκκλησίαν τε οὐκ ἐποίει with τήν τε πόλιν ἐφύλασσε is abnormal if it is antithetical in character .... but normal if the point is 'to the Assembly he did this, and to the city that', investing οὐκ ἐποίει with a positive character, despite its negative form.' Dover persuasively suggests the interpretation: 'he was opposed to the convening of any assembly or meeting'.

The next question to ask is of course: how did Perikles oppose the summoning of any *ekklesia* or *syllogos?* Perikles was a member of the board of generals, and several sources show that the *Strategoi* were empowered to have an *ekklesia* summoned.[3] The procedure was that the *strategoi* applied to the *boule* and asked it to summon the *ekklesia*. So οὐκ ἐποίει ἐκκλησίαν probably means (1) that Perikles prevailed on his colleagues in the board of generals to take no initiative towards the *boule;* (2) that Perikles persuaded the council not to use its prerogative to summon an *ekklesia* on its own authority. (We return to this question on page 20).

So far we have only discussed the meaning of οὐκ ἐποίει in relation to the *ekklesia*. What does it mean in relation to the *syllogoi*? Or rather what does *syllogos* mean? Apart from the passage under discussion ξύλλογος occurs nine times in Thukydides and denotes: (A) The people's assembly in Athens (2.59.3), in Sparta (1.67.3), in Korinth (5.30.5), in Syracuse (6.41.5) and in Kamarina (6.75.4). (B) A meeting of the people summoned by a (foreign) general who addresses the assembly in Torone (4.114.3) and in Skione (4.120.3). (C) A staff-meeting summoned by a king of Sparta (2.12.1). (D) Informal gatherings of citizens in Mytilene (3.27.3). These four different uses of *syllogos* may illuminate the meaning of the word in 2.22.1.

According to Gomme (ii 76) 'ξύλλογος here clearly means 'informal meeting of citizens' (Latin *contio*), as at 3.27.3'. Commentators before Gomme seem to ignore the problem raised by *syllogos,* and after Gomme historians usually repeat his note[5] although it is, on reflection, self-contradictory.

At 3.27.3 Thukydides describes informal and spontaneous gatherings of citizens discussing the situation in Mytilene and criticizing the authorities. There is no summons, no presidency and no formal address. A *contio,* on the other hand, is only informal in so far as the citizens are not organized into centuries or tribes and not empowered to make decisions. Apart from that, a *contio* is a formal meeting of the people, summoned by the authorities, presided over by a magistrate and formally addressed by one or more speakers.[6]

So we must now ask whether ξύλλογος in Th. 2.22.1 denotes (a) a spontaneous informal gathering (as at 3.27.3) or (b) a *contio*-like type of meeting of the people or (c) some other kind of assembly.

Re (a): It is most unlikely that Perikles abrogated the 'freedom of assembly' and prohibited spontaneous gatherings of citizens in the agora or elsewhere.[7] Furthermore οὐκ ἐποίει suggests that *syllogos*, like *ekklesia,* was a formal meeting summoned and presided over by officials (cf. supra page 17).

Re (b): Neither the literary nor the epigraphical sources support the belief that the Athenians, in addition to the *ekklesiai,* summoned the people to *contio*-like meetings in which they listened to speeches but made no decisions. The closest parallel is Th.4.114.3 and 120.3 where Brasidas convenes respectively the Toronians and the Skionians and delivers a speech to explain the situation. In both cases, however, the meeting is presided over by a foreigner and not by the authorities. Furthermore, Thukydides states that Perikles avoided the calling of a *syllogos* in order to prevent the Athenians from making a rash decision about attacking the Peloponnesian forces in Attika. So *syllogos*, like *ekklesia*, is presumably a decision-making assembly of some kind and not a *contio*.

Re (c): Since *syllogos* is neither an informal meeting of citizens nor a *contio*-like meeting the conclusion seems to be that it denotes some other kind of assembly, but which? First, we must make a choice between two possibilities: either Thukydides has a specific type of assembly in mind and *syllogos* may even be a technical term for this type of meeting, or ξύλλογον οὐδένα is used comprehensively about political assemblies and denotes several different types. We have already listed occurrences of *syllogos* in Thukydides and can now go on to discuss the use of the word in other sources:

Syllogos may mean 'a meeting' without further specification.[8] In other passages the reference is to private gatherings either for social or for political purposes e.g. a private party[9] or a spontaneous gathering in the agora or elsewhere of citizens or soldiers complaining of the situation.[10] Mostly, however, *syllogos* denotes a public assembly, sometimes occasioned by a festival[11] but more frequently summoned by the officials for political purposes.[12] In sources dealing with institutions outside Attika *syllogos* may denote an assembly of the people[13] or of the army.[14] Furthermore *syllogos* is used about councils and similar assemblies e.g. about the Amphictyonic Council,[15] about the nocturnal council in Plato's *Laws*[16] or about a staff meeting attended by the officers.[17] In sources relating to Athens *syllogos* may refer to the people's assembly, the council of five hundred, the people's court and in one case to the assembly of *demotai* in one of the demes.[18]

On the basis of the various uses of *syllogos* in Thukydides and in other sources we can now attempt to determine the meaning of ξύλλογον οὐδένα in Th.2.22.1. First, we must examine the possibility that *syllogos* is used synonymously with *ekklesia*. In support of this interpretation we can adduce Th. 2.59-60. In 59.3 Thukydides reports that Perikles ξύλλογον ποιήσας (ἔτι δὲ ἐστρατήγει) ἐβούλετο θαρσῦναι ... and in 60.1 Perikles opens his speech by saying ἐκκλησίαν ... ξυνήγαγον. On the other hand, it is most unlikely that *ekklesia* and *syllogos* in 2.22.1 are perfect synonyms, since a simple pleonasm is not in the manner of Thukydides. But it is still possible that *syllogos* denotes some special form of *ekklesia*. In the fourth century we have evidence of three different types of *ekklesia:* ἐκκλησία, ἐκκλησία κυρία and ἐκκλησία σύγκλητος. The ἐκκλησία σύγκλητος is not attested before 346[19] but the term ἐκκλησία κυρία occurs already in fifth-century inscriptions. Now[20] the system of four obligatory meetings of the *ekklesia* every prytany, one ἐκκλησία κυρία and three other ἐκκλησίαι, was probably not introduced until the middle of the fourth century,[21] and, in the fifth century, the Athenians may have held only one obligatory *ekklesia* every prytany, i.e. the ἐκκλησία κυρία, whereas other *ekklesiai* were summoned by the *prytaneis* and the *boule* as occasion required. In Th. 2.22.1 we may then take ἐκκλησίαν to be a reference to the obligatory ἐκκλησία κυρία, and ξύλλογον οὐδένα to be a reference to other meetings of the people's assembly. This explains how Perikles could easily avoid the summoning of a *syllogos,* but would it not be unconstitutional not to convene the ἐκκλησία κυρία? No, not in our opinion, since οὐκ ἐποίει does not necessarily imply *suspension* of an *ekklesia* but only *delay.* We know that the ἐκκλησία κυρία could be held on any day in a prytany,[22] and so the interval between two obligatory *ekklesiai* varied from a few days to more than two months. Now, the Peloponnesians invaded Attika late in May 431 (Th. 2.19.1 with Gomme's note) and left Attika again when they had consumed their provisions (Th. 2.23.3). The duration of the invasion is not stated, but at 2.57.2 Thukydides reports that the invasion of 430 was the longest and lasted 40 days. So the invasion of 431 must have lasted about one month, or at least less than one prytany, and Perikles may, quite constitutionally, have prevented the summoning of any *ekklesia* during this month simply by not taking any initiative himself and by persuading the council not to summon the ἐκκλησία κυρία until late in the (next) prytany and not to use their powers to summon other meetings (σύλλογοι).

On any interpretation of *syllogos* this is in our opinion the best interpretation of ἐκκλησίαν οὐκ ἐποίει: there was only one obligatory *ekklesia* in a prytany and it could be delayed constitutionally until after the Peloponnesians had left Attika.[23] Whether or not *syllogos* refers to the optional meetings is a different question and here we have to admit that the distinction suggested above between *ekklesia* (obligatory meeting) and *syllogos* (optional meeting) does not quite square with Th. 2.59-60 where both terms (*ekklesia* and *syllogos*) are used about the same meeting. The obstacle is not insurmountable but we must envisage the possibility that *syllogos* in 2.22.1 refers to other meetings than meetings of the people's assembly.

It is most unlikely that Perikles suspended meetings of the council of five hundred or meetings of the council of the Areopagos or sessions of the people's court. In 2.21.3 it is stated that especially the Acharnians were angry with Perikles. We know from Pl. *La.* 187e2 that *syllogos* may denote a meeting of the *demotai* in a deme. It is just possible that ξύλλογον οὐδένα in 2.22.1 refers to, or includes, meetings in the various deme-assemblies, but such a measure would certainly have been unconstitutional (or warranted only by martial law). The *nomothetai* were not introduced until after 403, and so we have exhausted the various political assemblies mentioned in modern accounts of the Athenian political institutions. It is apparent, however, from Pl. *Grg.* 452e that the Athenians applied the term σύλλογος to other types of public meeting than the *ekklesia,* the *boule* and the *dikasteria:* τὸ πείθειν ἔγωγ' οἷόν τ' εἶναι τοῖς λόγοις καὶ ἐν δικαστηρίῳ δικαστὰς καὶ ἐν βουλευτηρίῳ βουλευτὰς καὶ ἐν ἐκκλησίᾳ ἐκκλησιαστὰς καὶ ἐν ἄλλῳ συλλόγῳ παντί, ὅστις ἂν πολιτικὸς σύλλογος γίγνηται. In this passage we are faced with the same problem as in Th. 2.22.1: to which kind of meeting does *syllogos* refer? Now, there is one type of assembly which has been unfairly treated by historians but is extremely relevant in this case, *viz.* a meeting or review of the armed forces. Such meetings are frequently called *syllogoi* and a discussion of them is best introduced by quoting another passage from Plato, *viz. R.* 492b: ὅταν, εἶπον, συγκαθεζόμενοι ἀθρόοι πολλοὶ εἰς ἐκκλησίαν ἢ εἰς δικαστήρια ἢ θέατρα ἢ στρατόπεδα ἤ τινα ἄλλον κοινὸν πλήθους σύλλογον σὺν πολλῷ θορύβῳ τὰ μὲν ψέγωσι τῶν λεγομένων ἢ πραττομένων, τὰ δὲ ἐπαινῶσιν, ὑπερβαλλόντως ἑκάτερα, καὶ ἐκβοῶντες καὶ κροτοῦντες, πρὸς δ' αὐτοῖς αἵ τε πέτραι καὶ ὁ τόπος ἐν ᾧ ἂν ὦσιν ἐπηχοῦντες διπλάσιον θόρυβον παρέχωσι τοῦ ψόγου καὶ ἐπαίνου.

In this passage we have a description of gatherings where young people will be bewildered because of the unseemly manner in which approval or disapproval of proposals and actions is expressed. Various types of formal public meetings, κοινοὶ σύλλογοι: The Assembly, the Popular Courts, the Theatres, are mentioned, together with στρατόπεδα. The context seems to indicate that all the particular occasions are assemblies where certain things are discussed and decided. They are, presumably, typical examples of Democracy at work. 'Theatres' we take to refer to the dramatic festivals in their character of public events presided over by officials and ending up with the judges of the agon awarding prizes, and after the Dionysia, with an *ekklesia* held in the theatre to discuss the manner in which the festival has been conducted.[24]

Now, why mention *stratopeda*? It is certainly not a reference to camp life or life in the field in general.[25] Apparently Plato thinks that meetings of military personnel at military locations constitute an important type of public *syllogos*. In *Lg*. 943b8 Plato describes *syllogoi* of the various armed forces deciding formally on matters of military justice and conferring military rewards. In *Lg*. 755e4 *syllogoi* of the whole army or parts of it elect officers. So these are functions one could imagine army meetings to perform under some constitutions. Thus, in Plato's usage, πολιτικός or κοινὸς σύλλογος covers the Assembly, the Council (*Grg*. 452e), the Popular Courts, certain proceedings related to the theatre, *and* certain army meetings.

To get an idea of how army meetings worked in general it is natural to turn to Xenophon's *Anabasis*. Even though the army of the Ten Thousand is a case apart it still seems as if the system of debate, communication, and decisionmaking embodied in various types of meeting is not something new and amazing to Xenophon. He seems to take it for granted that something of the kind takes place in the army when organized and in operation.[27] The procedures can be described in outline as something like the following: the leader(s) call meetings ranging from meetings of the High Command (*strategoi*) to a general assembly of the army, with meetings of company commanders as one of the intermediate types.[28] Sometimes a meeting in session is extended to include lower echelons or specially interested parties. The types seem to make up a system of flexible extending of participation.[29] It seems, also, that meetings of local groups or units are called on local initiative, in critical periods, where resolutions may be passed and forwarded to the High Command. Sometimes such initiative is taken up by the High Command and legitimized by calling a general assembly.[30] Meetings may have more technical purposes, inspection of arms, drill, etc., but certainly a soldier will expect briefing and consultation on operational matters to take place at various levels of organization and sometimes at a general assembly.

Elections of officers take place at a general assembly when necessary.[31] The terminology describing debate, voting, passing of decrees is that of a civilian assembly.[32] An assembly of soldiers is most often referred to by forms of the verb συλλέγειν or, once, the noun σύλλογος,[33] whereas staff meetings are usually referred to by forms of συγκαλεῖν. The strict technical term for a general assembly, as opposed to a local or officers' meeting, seems to be ἐκκλησία.[34]

The picture of an army trained so to say in the procedure of meetings is confirmed by examples other than the *Anabasis*. Cypriot mercenaries under Konon, probably in 395, fearing to be cheated of their pay, gather in *ekklesia* and elect their own *strategos*. He negotiates with Konon and is on his way with Konon to consult with the assembly (τὸ πλῆθος τὸ τῶν στρατιωτῶν), when tumult breaks out, etc.[35] In 418 the Spartans and their allies, under King Agis, are ready to join in battle with the Argives, in Argive territory. Suddenly Agis agrees to a truce and withdraws, after a meeting with two Argives, one of whom was a *strategos*, set up on the private initiative of the two Argives. Both armies are amazed at the decision. The army as a whole (τὸ πλῆθος) should have been consulted. The Spartan army is legally obligated to follow Agis, but when he returns to Sparta he barely avoids a harsh sentence. The Argive general apparently acted quite illegally and is courtmartialled by the army outside Argos and almost stoned to death.[36] In 410 the Syracusan High Command in the Aegean is deposed following a democratic coup in Syracuse. The soldiers are summoned to a general meeting where Hermokrates reports on the situation and asks the soldiers to elect interim generals. They refuse and enjoin the incumbent generals to function until a new High Command arrives.[37] When the Athenian armed forces on Samos in 411 at a number of *ekklesiai* recall Alkibiades and elect *strategoi*,[38] they are following the same procedure: the High Command is no longer effective, and it falls to the army assembly to elect a new one.

Returning to Athens proper we want to draw attention to a crucial passage in Isokrates, 7.82, complaining that Athenians will not attend reviews (ἐξετάσεις) if they are not paid for it.[39] This indicates that reviews were held fairly regularly, even in peacetime, and that they, like other political meetings, were an occasion for *misthos* to be paid out to the citizens. Reviews[40] may have been called for the purpose of mustering personnel,[41] inspection of arms and equipment[42], parade or drill under arms.[43]

We know of several parade grounds.[44] The *Suda* tells us that ἐξοπλίσεις took place at the Lykeion before expeditions.[45] Reviews will have concerned either smaller units, *taxeis* or the cavalry,[46] or the army as a whole.[47] It would seem that a review could have turned into an assembly, and that this would be expected if the occasion of calling the troops in question was some kind of emergency. The order would then be given to ground or pile arms, whereupon the soldiers gathered round the leaders.[48] Aristotle tells the story of how Peisistratos disarmed the people of Athens. He held a˙ review (under arms, ἐξοπλισία) and then began to hold an assembly (ἐκκλησιάζειν). He then tricked the people some distance away, from where they had piled arms apparently, and his agents then removed the arms.[49] The same trick is ascribed to Hippias by Thukydides[50] and used by the Thirty to disarm the army except the Three Thousand.[51] In 411 the 'moderate' hoplites in the Piraeus meet in the Theatre of Mounichia,[52] ground arms and hold an *ekklesia*. They adopt a motion and march to another military assembly point, the Anakeion, and ground arms. Having been somewhat conciliated by representatives of the Four Hundred they agree to convene an *ekklesia* 'on concord'.[53]

To corroborate the point that military bodies did sometimes have proper political functions we want finally to refer to two things. First, the courts dealing with military offences consisted of citizens that had participated in the campaign in question, and were presided over by the *strategoi*.[54] Second, we have rather full epigraphical evidence that garrisons in the Athenian forts of Panakton, Eleusis, Phyle *etc.* passed regular honorary decrees for various officials.[55] The cavalry is also represented by a few inscriptions.[56] This evidence is from the late 4th and the 3rd century, but one inscription referring to 430/29 indicates that the recommendation of the soldiers at Poteideia is to be a condition for ratifying friendly relations between Athens and the King of Macedon.[57]

We have argued that there did exist in Athens meetings of military bodies and that such meetings did debate and sometimes decide matters of some significance. Furthermore, we have argued that such meetings could be referred to by σύλλογος, with κοινός or a similar adjective added or understood, this being a general term for public, formal meetings. The technical terms for the kind of meeting relevant to our discussion were probably ἐξέτασις, review, often under arms and implying parade and drill, ἐξοπλισία and σύνταξις. An ἐξέτασις could be turned into an occasion for information and debate, presumably called an ἐκκλησία (τῶν στρατιωτῶν). Syllogos, then, in Th. 2.22.1, would be understood by contemporaries, we suggest, to refer to a military meeting, first, because this was the only important type of public meeting it could reasonably refer to under the circumstances, and, second, because such an interpretation could have been reinforced by the military associations of the term: its use as denoting the act of gathering or mobilizing an army, and as denoting formal meetings of soldiers in a military context.

Aeneas Tacticus tells us[58] that the first thing to do for a commander in a city threatened by enemy invasion is to occupy certain strategic positions outside the city and then to summon an assembly of the soldiers or the citizens, explain the situation, and brief them on planned operations. In a situation like the one in 431 the Athenians might reasonably have expected the generals to call a meeting of the army, in some form. Such a meeting would have ended with strategy being explained, commands issued, and operation procedures being set up. There would have been an opportunity for debate. Perikles made sure that no such meeting was called. His purpose was to avoid the rise of a pressure of opinion[59] by quelling the public posing of questions and voicing of discontent relative to the measures envisaged by the High Command.[60]

NOTES

[1] References in this article, herafter cited by by author's name and page number, are to: P.A. Brunt *Spartan Policy and Strategy in the Archidamian War, Phoenix* 19 (1965) 255-80. K.J. Dover ΔΕΚΑΤΟΣ ΑΥΤΟΣ, *JHS* 80 (1960) 61-77. Ch. W. Fornara *The Athenian Board of Generals from 501 to 404, Historia* Einzelschriften 16 (1971). A.W. Gomme *A Historical Commentary on Thucydides* II (Oxford 1956). M.H. Hansen *How Often Did the Ecclesia Meet?, GRBS* 18 (1977) 43-70. Idem 'Εκκλησία σύγκλητος in Hellenistic Athens, *GRBS* 20 (1979) 150-56. Idem *Atimistraffen i Athen i Klassisk Tid* (Odense 1973). C. Hignett *A History of the Athenian Constitution* (Oxford 1952). A.H.M. Jones *Athenian Democracy* (Oxford 1957). D. Kagan *The Outbreak of the Peloponnesian War* (Ithaca 1969). U. Kahrstedt *Untersuchungen zur Magistratur in Athen* (Stuttgart 1936). W.A. McDonald *The Political Meeting Places of the Greeks* (Baltimore 1943). L. Moretti *Iscrizioni storiche ellenistiche* (Firenze 1967). G.B. Nussbaum *The Ten Thousand* (Leyden 1967). A. W. Pickard-Cambridge *The Dramatic Festivals of Athens* (2nd ed. Oxford 1968). W.K. Pritchett *The Greek State at War* II (Berkeley 1974). P.J. Rhodes *The Athenian Boule* (Oxford 1972). G.E.M. de Ste Croix *The Constitution of the Five Thousand, Historia* 5 (1956) 1-23. H.D. Westlake *Individuals in Thucydides* (Cambridge 1968).

[2] Dover 75, followed by Kagan 56, Westlake 32-33 and Brunt 265 n. 37 (with reservation).

[3] For the prerogative of the *strategoi* to convene an assembly see Th. 2.59.3 (discussed *infra*) and Plu. *Phoc.* 15.1. For the *boule* and the *prytaneis* as intermediaries between the *strategoi* and the *ekklesia* see Th.4.118.14; *IG* II² 897, 911, 954; *SEG* XXI.440, XXIV.134; restored at *IG* I² 98.20 (not at *IG* I³ 93). For *ekklesiai* convened by orders of the *boule* (and not by the *prytaneis* on their own initiative) see *Hell.Oxy.* 6.2; X. *HG* 6.5.33; *Hesperia* 7 (1938) 476-79 no. 31. The Hellenistic decrees are discussed in Hansen (1979) 151-52. Cf. Kahrstedt 268; Hignett 246; Gomme 167; Dover 75; Rhodes 44.

[4] It is now generally believed that Perikles had no special powers and no precedence over his colleagues. So he must have acted in concert with the nine other *strategoi*. Cf. Hignett 247; Jones 126; Dover 62, 72, 75; Brunt 265 n. 37; Westlake 33; Fornara 11-19; Kagan 56.

[5] Without any discussion of the problem ξύλλογον οὐδένα is translated by 'meeting' (Dover 75; Jones 127) or 'informal meeting' (Hignett 246) or 'informal gathering' (Kagan 55).

[6] Th. 3.27.3: ὁ Σάλαιθος καὶ αὐτὸς οὐ προσδεχόμενος ἔτι τὰς ναῦς ὁπλίζει τὸν δῆμον πρότερον ψιλὸν ὄντα ὡς ἐπεξιὼν τοῖς Ἀθηναίοις. οἱ δὲ ἐπειδὴ ἔλαβον ὅπλα, οὔτε ἠκροῶντο ἔτι τῶν ἀρχόντων, κατὰ ξυλλόγους τε γιγνόμενοι ἢ τὸν σῖτον ἐκέλευον τοὺς δυνατοὺς φέρειν ἐς τὸ φανερὸν καὶ διανέμειν ἅπασιν, ἢ αὐτοὶ ξυγχωρήσαντες πρὸς Ἀθηναίους ἔφασαν παραδώσειν τὴν πόλιν. γνόντες δὲ οἱ ἐν τοῖς πράγμασιν οὔτ' ἀποκωλύειν δυνατοὶ ὄντες, ... Gomme obviously refers to the civil *contio* held in Rome (which, incidentally, is the only form of *contio* mentioned in *OCD*). Later in this article we suggest that a more obvious parallel would be the military *contio* held outside Rome. Cf infra.

[7] Cf. however Aen.Tact. 10.4: τάς τε ἑορτὰς κατὰ πόλιν ἄγειν, συλλόγους τε ἰδίους μηδαμοῦ μήτε ἡμέρας μήτε νυκτὸς γίγνεσθαι, τοὺς δὲ ἀναγκαίους ἢ ἐν πρυτανείῳ ἢ ἐν βουλῇ ἢ ἐν ἄλλῳ φανερῷ τόπῳ. μήτε θύεσθαι μάντιν ἰδίᾳ ἄνευ τοῦ ἄρχοντος. μηδὲ δειπνεῖν κατὰ συσσιτίαν ἀλλ' ἐν ταῖς αὐτῶν οἰκίαις ἑκάστους, ἔξω γάμου καὶ

περιδείπνου, καὶ ταῦτα προαπαγγείλαντας τοῖς ἄρχουσιν. So we cannot preclude the possibility that Perikles interfered with the 'freedom of assembly'.

[8] Isoc. 12.9.
[9] Isoc. 7.48; 15.136, 147.
[10] X. An. 5.7.2; D. 19.122; Aen.Tact. 10.4 (quoted supra n. 7); SIG 526.15. Same use of σύλλογος as at Th. 3.27.3.
[11] Lys. 33.2.
[12] κοινὸς σύλλογος: Hyp. 1.18; Pl. R. 492b; Lg. 764a, 871a, 935b; Arist. Pr. 952b14. πολιτικὸς σύλλογος: Pl. Grg. 452e; Arist. Rh.Al. 1445a40. δημόσιος σύλλογος: Pl. Phdr. 261a.
[13] σύλλογος refers to the people's assembly in Sparta (Isoc. 6.106), in Achaia and Arkadia (Hyp. 1.18), in Priene (SIG 278, 282), in Knossos (Michel 439) and in the ideal polis described in Plato's Laws 764a, 765a, 871a, 935b).
[14] Hdt. 8.24.2; 8.83.1; X. An. 5.6.22; Oec. 4.6 (ἐξέτασις); Cyr. 6.2.11 (= ἐξέτασις); Pl. Lg. 755e, 943b; E. IA 514, 1545. Cf. infra page 21.
[15] Aeschin. 3.126. Cf. M&L 32 (joint meeting of citizens from Halicarnassus and Salmakis).
[16] Pl. Lg. 908a, 909a, 951d-e, 961a-b, 962c, 968a.
[17] Hdt. 7.8.1; 7.74.2. Cf. also X. HG 4.1.39.
[18] σύλλογος refers to the ekklesia and the boule Isoc. 4.157, (cf. D. 19.70 and Din. 2.16). σύλλογος is mentioned side by side with δικαστήριον and refers inter alia to the ekklesia and the boule Pl. Hp.Ma. 304d; Phdr. 261a). σύλλογος is mentioned side by side with ἐκκλησία and refers to the boule and/or the dikasteria (Pl. Grg. 456b). In Pl. Grg. 455b σύλλογος probably refers to the ekklesia, and in Pl. La. 187a the reference is to a deme assembly. – It is worth noting that admission to the ekklesia was checked by a committee of the boule called συλλογεῖς τοῦ δήμου (IG II² 1749. 75-76; Poll. 8.104). Cf. also Lex.Seg. 327.23.
[19] Aeschin. 2.72; D. 19.122-23. Cf. Hansen (1977) 46-49.
[20] IG I³ 41.37; 49.10.
[21] Cf. Hansen (1977) 68-70.
[22] Cf. M. H. Hansen When Did the Athenian Ecclesia Meet?, GRBS 23 (1982) 337-338. We have no information concerning the fifth century and we admit that the argument is based on an extrapolation of fourth-century sources back into the fifth century.
[23] It is worth noting that Perikles' avoidance of summoning an ekklesia was imitated by Theramenes in the very last months of the Peloponnesian War: Lys. 12.71: καὶ τὸ τελευταῖον, ὦ ἄνδρες δικασταί, οὐ πρότερον εἴασε τὴν ἐκκλησίαν γενέσθαι, ἕως ὁ λεγόμενος ὑπ' ἐκείνων καιρὸς ἐπιμελῶς ὑπ' αὐτοῦ ἐτηρήθη, ... Lysias does not say that Theramenes overstepped his powers by not convening the assembly and, considering his intention to blacken Theramenes' reputation, the inference is that Theramenes acted constitutionally.
[24] On the ekklesia after the Dionysia cf. Pickard-Cambridge 68ff. On the awarding of prizes id. 95ff. Plato reverts to the problems facing the judges in Lg. 659a and 700c-701b. – The theatre of Dionysos is not a regular meeting-place of the ekklesia before c. 300, cf. McDonald 47-51 & 56-61. An implied reference to the ekklesia examining the ephebes, cf. Arist. Ath. 42.4, would be anachronistic.
[25] στρατόπεδον is registered in dictionaries and indices as having simply two meanings: 1) camp, 2) army. This is not satisfactory. LSJ correctly lists as a meaning of the cognate

verb στρατοπεδεύω/-ομαι 'to take up a position'. In view of the word's perspicuous derivation we would say that its denotational potential covers (a) any stationary location that is connected with an organized operational army or navy (unit), and, by a well known semantic transformation: (b) such an army or navy unit itself. (a) may be a camp or navy base in the ordinary sense of the word, fortified or not, permanent or not, or it may be quarters or a cantonment (cf. *LSJ* s.v. καταστρατοπεδεύω); a defensive position as at Thermopylai (Hdt. 7.208; X. *HG* 7.5.8); the position of the army before offensive action (cf. the use of the verb in X. *HG* 2.4.30); a position in general (cf. Th. 5.64.5; 65; 66.1); in X. *Eq.Mag.* 7.10 it should perhaps be rendered 'theatre of operations'. It could, in *R.* 492b, be the parade ground, where an army (unit) would conduct the meetings in question. We will not, however, venture to decide whether the denotation here is the army or the place where it meets. The total meaning of the passage would not be affected anyway, the reference being to the army as deliberating, not resting or fighting.

[26] Cf. Nussbaum, esp. section 4 pp. 48ff.
[27] By way of contrast, Kyros, in *Cyr.* 2.2.18-3.1, has to argue at some length with his officers and peers in order to convince them of the usefulness of calling a general assembly of the soldiers to discuss the principles for the sharing of booty. Of some 30 military meetings mentioned in the work, only 3 are general assemblies proper. The word ἐκκλησία (cf. *infra* n. 30) is not used.
[28] General assemblies: e.g. *An.* 1.3.2; 1.4.11; 5.1.2; 5.4.19; 6.1.25; 6.2.4; 6.6.11; 7.6.7. Meetings of the High Command: e.g. 1.4.8; 2.1.2; 3.3.3; 4.8.9-14. Meetings of High Command and company commanders (*lochagoi*): e.g. 1.7.1; 3.5.7; 6.5.12.
[29] Cf. e.g. 1.4.11; 2.2.3; 4.4.21; 5.6.1-14; 6.1.3. A famous example is afforded by what happens after Kunaxa, on Xenophon's initiative (3.1-2): Xenophon calls the company commanders of his 'division' (3.1.15); this results in a meeting, presided over by the senior company commander, of the remnants of the army High Command and the company commanders. A new HC is elected and in 3.2.1ff a general assembly is called to discuss the present situation and future strategy. Several proposals are put forward and carried. – Cf. also 6.1.18-32 on the election of a Commander in Chief (*autokrator*).
[30] In X. *An.* 5.6.37-7.4 there is a discussion in the High Command whether to put a certain proposal to the army. Xen. uses the word συλλέξαντες (sc. τὴν στρατιάν). Another general advises not to call a general assembly (ἐκκλησιάζειν), but to discuss matters with the company commanders singly. The soldiers get wind of the affair and local *syllogoi* take place. Xen. then decides to have the matter out in the open, not to permit the soldiers to hold meetings on their own (συλλεγῆναι αὐτομάτους), but rather to call a general assembly (συλλέξαι ἀγοράν; for an interesting parallel cf. Arr. *An.* 5.25.29). In 6.4.10-11, at a time when the army has split up, the soldiers, mainly on the initiative of two company commanders, hold a meeting and pass a resolution in formal terms against dividing the army and confirming the authority of the incumbent High Command. Then Xenophon makes a speech. The unity of the army is reestablished, the *strategoi* take over the meeting. – The events in Th. 3.27.3 may be a parallel to the above examples, esp. X. *An.* 5.6. The Mytilenean people, once incorporated into the hoplite army, adopt the procedure of conducting local meetings. These are apparently coordinated and a resolution passed and presented to the government, who legitimize the army's proposal and enters into negotiations with the Athenians.
[31] Cf. again 6.1.18ff. The army elects delegates to negotiate with the Sinopeans (5.6.14). In

5.7.35 the general assembly decides that judicial examinations of the High Command shall be carried out with the company commanders as jurors, cf. *infra* n. 54. In 6.2.9-12 the Achaeans and Arkadians secede and hold a separate 'divisional' assembly where ten *strategoi* are elected. Cf. Paus. 9.15.2.

[32] Cf. e.g. 3.2.9 and 31ff; 5.1.4ff; 7.3.14.
[33] σύλλογος is used 5.6.22, forms of συλλέγειν e.g. 1.4.13; 3.1.39; cf. also note 30. Other verbs are συνάγειν, συνελθεῖν.
[34] ἐκκλησία is used at 1.3.2; 1.4.11; ἐκκλησιάζειν at 5.6.37.
[35] *Hell.Oxy.* 20 (15).
[36] Th. 5.59-60; 60.1: οὐ μετὰ τῶν πλεόνων, of Agis; οὐ τοῦ πλήθους κελεύσαντος, of the two Argives; 60.5: ἄνευ τοῦ πλήθους, of the same. The Argive court martial, 60.6. On proceedings against Agis, 63. – A Spartan who does use the consulting procedure is Kallikratidas, X. *HG* 1.6.4-5.
[37] X. *HG.* 1.1.27-31; is *synedrion,* 31, a term for the general assembly of soldiers? The context seems to point that way.
[38] Th. 8.81.1-82.3. The *ekklesiai* (8.81.-1-2 and 82.3) elect *strategoi,* they do not set up a full scale 'government-in-exile'. Note the expression πλῆθος τῶν στρατιωτῶν in 81.1.
[39] Isoc. 7.82: τῶν δὲ περὶ τὸν πόλεμον οὕτω κατημελήκαμεν, ὥστ' οὐδ' εἰς ἐξετάσεις ἰέναι τολμῶμεν ἢν μὴ λαμβάνωμεν ἀργύριον. Cf. also D. 13.4.
[40] The references in the following notes seem to indicate that the general term for review was ἐξέτασις; inspection and/or drill under arms (ἐν ὅπλοις) had the specific term ἐξοπλισία (*vel sim.*); drill (in formation) is sometimes σύνταξις; mustering or roll call is specifically ἀριθμός, possibly, in Plu. *Phoc.* 10, κατάλογος; parades for display may have been ἐπιδείξεις (or ἀπο- if the text in *Suda* 801 is sound). On *exetasis* in general cf. also Poll. 1.176 s.v. and *IG* II² 500; *IG* XII 5.647; Moretti 18 (cf. *SEG* XIV. 64).
[41] Cf. X. *Oec.* 4.6; Arist. *Pol.* 1322a35ff; Th. 7.33.6 and 35.1; Timaeus Sophista (ed. Ruhnken) 109 s.v. ἐξετασμός; *Lex.Seg.* 277.10; cf. also X. *An.* 1.7.10; 5.3.3; 7.1.7.
[42] Cf. X. *Oec.* 4.6 and 9.15; X. *HG* 2.3.20.
[43] Cf. Arist. *Pol.* 1322a35ff; *Suda* 801; metaphorically in D. 18.320; cf. also X. *Cyr.* 2.4.1; Plb. 10.24.
[44] The technical term may have been δρόμος, cf. X. *Cyr.* 2.3.22, and, possibly, X. *HG* 2.4.27. As parade grounds or at least assembly points are mentioned: in Athens the Akademeia (X. *HG* 6.5.49; *Eq.Mag.* 3.1 and 14); the Agora (X. *HG* 2.3.20; Arist. *Ath.* 38.1; cf. X. *HG* 2.4.23); the Anakeion (And. 1.45, the cavalry; Th. 8.93, the hoplites; Polyaen. 1.21.2); the Lykeion (Ar. *Pax* 355; *Suda* 801; *Lex.Seg.* 277.10; X. *Eq.Mag.* 3.1 and 6, the cavalry; X. *HG* 1.1.33; 2.4.27); the Odeion (X. *HG* 2.4.10; 2.4.24); the Theseion (Arist. *Ath.* 15.4, cf., however, Polyaen. 1.21.2; And. 1.45). In the Piraeus area: the Dionysos Theatre, 'in Mounichia' or 'in the Piraeus' (Th. 8.93.1; X. *HG.* 2.4.32); the Hippodamian Agora (And. 1.45; X. *HG* 2.4.11); the Hippodrome: we believe that the references in X. *Eq.Mag.* 3.1, 10, 14 are to one locality, the Hippodrome in Phaleron, that was on the Halipedon plain, referred to in X. *HG* 2.4.30, cf. *Lex.Seg.* 208.17-20; cf. also *IG* II² 1303.
[45] *Suda* 801 (= Schol. Ar. *Pax* 353): Λύκειον: γυμνάσιον Ἀθήνησιν, ὅπου πρὸ τοῦ πολέμου ἐδόκει γυμνάζεσθαι, πρὸ γὰρ τῶν ἐξόδων ἐξοπλίσεις τινὲς ἐγίνοντο ἐν τῷ Λυκείῳ, διὰ τὸ παρακεῖσθαι τῇ πόλει, καὶ ἀποδείξεις τῶν μᾶλλον πολεμικῶν ἀνδρῶν. Cf. *Lex.Seg.* 277.10; Ar. *Pax* 353.

[46] Cf. e.g. X. *Oec.* 9.15; *Eq.Mag.* 3.1ff; Th. 7.35.1.
[47] Cf. e.g. Th. 6.45 and 7.33.6; X. *An.* 1.7.10.
[48] The procedure, and its use by a skillful leader, is described in X. *An.* 7.1.21-35.
[49] Arist. *Ath.* 15.4.
[50] Th. 6.58.1-2.
[51] X. *HG* 2.3.20; The Thirty hold an *exetasis* of the Three Thousand in the Agora, of the rest of the armed citizens in various places; then on the order to pile arms, the soldiers apparently adjourn somewhere and while they are away, their arms are collected by the Spartans and other agents of the Thirty. The expression ἐπὶ τὰ ὅπλα need not, perhaps, be corrected, if we take it to mean: '(go) to(where) your arms (are usually piled)', sc. either to fetch them or to deposit them. Cf. X. *An.* 3.1.30. – A somewhat similar ruse, perpetrated by the Thirty, and involving a misuse of the *exetasis,* is described in X. *HG* 2.4.8, where the Thirty call an *exetasis* in Eleusis, ostensibly to hold a simple muster (possibly without arms) and ascertain the need for further defensive forces. After a bogus enrolment procedure, the Eleusinians leaving one by one through a postern are arrested and brought to Athens. The Three Thousand are forced to condemn them to death by open ballot. Cf. also the behaviour of the returning Megarian oligarchs in Th. 4.74.3.
[52] Th. 8.93.
[53] We take the subject of ξυνεχώρησαν ... ἐκκλησίαν ποιῆσαι (8.93.3) to be the hoplites. And in 94.1 we can see no reason to delete τῶν πολλῶν ὁπλιτῶν.
[54] In Athens military offences were heard by a jury composed of soldiers (Lys. 14.5) and presided over by the strategoi (Lys. 15.1-4). In the *Laws* Plato states that hoplites were brought before a jury of hoplites, and knights before a jury of knights (*Lg.* 943a-b). It is apparent from Lys. 14.7 and 15 that the γραφὴ ἀστρατείας in question was heard by the hoplites, and so we can safely assume that Plato, in this case, has based his ideal constitution on Athenian institution. Cf. Hansen (1973) 85.
[55] Some of the less mutilated decrees are: *IG* II^2 1270, 1272, 1281, 1299, 1302 (note the expression τῷ κοινῷ τῶν στρατευομένων ἐπὶ Σουνίου), 1303 (the garrisons of Eleusis, Panakton and the cavalry), 1304. Dedicatory inscriptions: 2968, 2969, 2973, 2977, 2978. Cf. Moretti numbers 2, 22 (cf. *SEG* III.122), 25, 32 (cf. *SEG* 15.113). The decrees are couched in terms quite similar to those of decrees of the council or the people.
[56] E.g. *IG* II^2 1264, Moretti 16 (cf. *SEG* XXI.525).
[57] *IG* I^3 61.1 ἐὰν Ηοι στρατι[ōται Ηοι] ἐμ Ποτιδ[ά]αι ἐπαινōσι (lines 27-28).
[58] Aen. Tact. 9.1: ἂν δὲ θρασύνεσθαί τι ἐπιχειρῶσιν οἱ ἐπιόντες πρός σε, τάδε ποιητέον. πρῶτον μὲν χρὴ σώμασι τόπους τινὰς τῆς οἰκείας χώρας καταλαβεῖν, ἔπειτα ἐκκλησιάσαντα τοὺς αὑτοῦ στρατιώτας ἢ πολίτας ἄλλα τε προειπεῖν αὐτοῖς, ὡς ὑπαρχούσης τινὸς αὐτοῖς πράξεως εἰς τοὺς πολεμίους, καὶ ὅταν νυκτὸς σημάνῃ τῷ σάλπιγγι, ἑτοίμους εἶναι τοὺς ἐν τῇ ἡλικίᾳ, ἀναλαβόντας τὰ ὅπλα καὶ ἀθροισθέντας εἰς χωρίον ῥητὸν ἕπεσθαι τῷ ἡγουμένῳ.
[59] An example of the army in assembly exerting pressure on the High Command is the part played by the Achaean army in Euripides' *Iphigenia in Aulis.* It is in fact termed Ἀχαιῶν σύλλογος στρατεύματος twice in the play, 515 and 1545, cf. also 825. Euripides seems to be the only one among archaic and classical poets who uses the word, so apparently it is not 'poetic'. In *Heracl.* 335 Demophon says he will summon the citizens' army to resistance, σύλλογον ποιήσομαι. There are three examples of its denoting some kind of

deliberating council or assembly (*Hel.* 878, *Or.* 730, and *Telephos fr.* 149.12 Austin) and one occurrence in an idiom, 'pull oneself together', *HF* 626.

[60] Considering the fact that army meetings are often called *ekklesiai* we cannot preclude an alternative interpretation of Th. 2.59-60. If ξύλλογος is used in a more technical and ἐκκλησία in a less technical sense, the meaning is that Perikles summons a meeting of the army (ξύλλογον ποιήσας 2.59.3) but opens his speech by calling the army meeting an *ekklesia* (ἐκκλησίαν τούτου ἕνεκα ξυνήγαγον 2.60.1).

ADDENDA

195: The meaning of *ekklesia* and *syllogos* at Thuc. 2.22.1 has recently been discussed by Edmund F. Bloedow, »Pericles' Powers in the Counterstrategy of 431,« *Historia* 36 (1987) 9-27. Bloedow (12-13) follows us (196-197) against Gomme (II 76) in believing that *syllogos* must denote a formal meeting of some kind. Gomme's »»informal meeting of citizens« (Latin *contio*), as at 3.27.3« makes no sense in this context. Furthermore, Bloedow (12) agrees with us (198) that *ekklesia* and *syllogos* must refer to different types of meeting. And we also agree that *syllogoi* in all probability were general meetings of all Athenians, and not just staff-meetings or meetings of the *boule* or a *dikasterion*. But then our roads part. Bloedow believes (1) that *ekklesia* denotes regular and *syllogos* extraordinary meetings of the assembly (15, 17), (b) that Perikles' refusal to convene *ekklesia* and *syllogoi* must in the circumstances be regarded as unconstitutional in the strict sense (17).

Bloedow's article is based on two (in our opinion) erroneous assumptions: (1) that Tkoukydides took special interest in and was meticulously accurate about constitutional details, and (2) that he tended to use technical constitutional terms. We think that regular readers of Thoukydides will agree with us that Thoukydides took little interest in constitutional mechanisms, that he often did not care to spell out constitutional refinements and that, in many cases, he (deliberately) avoided technical constitutional terms, cf. e.g. Andrewes' notes in the *Commentary* on 8.67-72 *et passim*.

In the light of these general observations we have the following objections against Bloedow's interpretation.

Re (a). *Syllogos* is not a technical term for an extraordinary meeting of the assembly. Neither in Thoukydides nor in any other source does *syllogos* bear that meaning. On the contrary, it is obvious from all sources that *syllogos* is a vague general term which, according to the context, may denote any type of public meeting, including *ekklesiai*. In Thuc. 2.59-60.1 both *syllogos* and *ekklesia* occur only five lines apart describing *one and the same meeting* of the assembly. Thus we find it unlikely that, at 2.22.1, Thoukydides used both words as technical terms denoting *different* types of assembly. If Perikles' policy concerned the assembly only to the exclusion of other institutions, ἐκκλησίαν οὐκ ἐποίει αὐτῶν would have sufficed. As we understand the passage, Thoukydides juxtaposes a technical term, i.e. *ekklesia* denoting the assembly and a general term, i.e. *syllogos* denoting various types of public meeting, perhaps including extraordinary meetings of the assembly (cf. *supra* page 193), but principally referring to army meetings as described in our article. The point in using *syllogos* instead of a technical term like *ekklesia synkletos* or *exetasis*

ADDENDA

(as Bloedow would have expected, cf. 15-16) *vel sim.* is that Thoukydides (who took little interest in constitutional details) after having specified the most important type of public meeting, i.e. the *ekklesia*, subsumed other types of meeting under the general term *syllogos*. We still believe that the most important type of public meeting referred to was army meetings, an important category of public meetings neglected by most historians. On Thoukydides' impatience with constitutional detail cf. e.g. Andrewes, *Commentary*, Book VIII p. 168.

Re (b). Beloch's view of Perikles as »*Oberstratege*« i.e. commander-in-chief with special powers is, in our opinion, disposed of by Dover and Fornara (*supra* page 204 note 1). We cannot follow Bloedow's attempt (25, 27) to revive the view that δέκατος αὐτός is a technical term designating some kind of specific status conferred on Perikles by the assembly.

Re (c). Bloedow does not discuss but simply takes it for granted that the people were convened to regular assemblies several times in a prytany. But the frequency of regular assemblies in the age of Perikles is a moot point on which we have no specific information in our sources and can easily be misled by applying a fourth-century analogy. We suggest that, in the fifth century, there may have been only one obligatory session of the people in a prytany, i.e. the *ekklesia kyria*. On this hypothesis, there is no basis for assuming that Perikles resorted to unconstitutional measures in order to avoid meetings of all Athenians during the Spartan occupation of Attica. The method used by Perikles (cf. *supra* page 198) was presumably to prevail on his colleagues in the board of generals and then again to persuade the council and/or the *prytaneis* not to convene an assembly until after the Peloponnesian army had left Attica.

DEMOS, EKKLESIA, AND *DIKASTERION.*
A REPLY TO MARTIN OSTWALD
AND JOSIAH OBER.

BY
MOGENS HERMAN HANSEN

I

In several publications[1] I have argued that the term *demos*, when it denotes an institution and not the Athenian state or the Athenian democracy, invariably refers to the *ekklesia* and never to the *dikasteria*. My thesis has been disputed by several historians,[2] often without discussion of the problem. Recently, however, Martin Ostwald has addressed the problem and presented a detailed criticism of my views. In his impressive monograph *From Popular Sovereignty to the Sovereignty of the Law*[3] he defends the traditional view as follows: »It is true that δῆμος refers in the fourth century almost exclusively to the *ekklesia* and in only three instances to the *dikasteria* (p. 131), but Hansen's argument is weakened or invalidated in that by his own showing (p. 130) δῆμος refers to the *ekklesia* in only about half of the six hundred instances, and then only in phrases such as ἐν τῷ δήμῳ, in conjunction with expressions signifying an election or a vote, or to contrast the βουλή with the Assembly. Since δῆμος is a more comprehensive term than either ἐκκλησία or δικαστήριον, including, as Hansen points out, the Athenian democracy and the Athenian state (p. 130), as well as the common people as distinct from the upper and middle classes (p. 139-141), this result is not surprising: βουλή, ἐκκλησία and δικαστήρια are all organs of the Athenian δῆμος, so that one would expect δῆμος, when used in a loose political sense, to be applied only to the most representative of these three and less in connection with such smaller bodies as βουλή and δικαστήριον. In

---

[1] '*Demos, Ecclesia* and *Dicasterion* in Classical Athens', *Ath. Eccl.* (1983) 139-58, with addenda 159-60; *The Athenian Assembly in the Age of Demosthenes* (Oxford 1987) 96-97, 102-07.
[2] Cf. e. g. P. J. Rhodes, *A Commentary on the Aristotelian Athenaion Politeia* (Oxford 1981) 318, 545; R. K. Sinclair, *Democracy and Participation in Athens* (Cambridge 1987) 70-71, 79, 103, 106, 211; K. W. Welwei, *Die griechische Polis* (Stuttgart 1983) 204.
[3] Berkeley (1986).

other words, the result that δῆμος is more frequently associated with the assembly and only rarely with the law courts does not mean that δικαστήρια were not regarded as representative of the people as a whole« (34-35, note 131).

I have several objections to this note. (1) since — as all historians admit — *demos* has more than one meaning, that it refers to the *ekklesia* in only half of the six hundred instances is no argument against my thesis. (2) Ostwald's contention that *demos* refers to the *ekklesia* only in the phrases he specifies is contradicted by numerous sources, cf. e. g. Dem. 3.31; Aeschin. 3.25; Din. 1.31 and the text of the eisangeltic law: ῥήτωρ ὢν μὴ λέγῃ τὰ ἄριστα τῷ δήμῳ χρήματα λαμβάνων (Hyp. 3.8) etc. (3) The statement that *demos* in three instances refers to the *dikasteria* is not an entirely accurate report of the evidence I presented. In my article (p. 143) I listed three passages in which *demos* is connected with the *dikasteria*: Aeschin. 1.141; Hyp. 1.29 and Din. 3.19. Now, in Aeschines and in Dinarchos *demos* is used in a social sense (the common people) and not in an institutional sense (the people's assembly), and in the Hypereides papyrus [τοῦ δήμ]ου is restored. Thus, strictly speaking, there is no occurrence whatsoever of *demos* in an institutional sense referring to the *dikasteria*. (4) That »the *dikasteria* were representative of the people as a whole« is precisely what I have been arguing for more than a decade,[4] but I have also pointed out that the idea of representation implies distinction and not identity.[5] (5) It is somewhat misleading to describe the *ekklesia* as »the most representative« of the three organs (*ekklesia, boule, dikasteria*). The *ekklesia* is not *representative of* the *demos*. It *is* the *demos*, cf. e. g. the enactment formula of all the fourth century *psephismata*: ἔδοξε (τῇ βουλῇ) καὶ τῷ δήμῳ.

In a letter of 6 August 1987 Martin Ostwald made a few comments on my points 1-3 above as well as a long and important answer to point 4: »Your fourth point (4) is one on which, I think, you and I have been at cross-purposes. I completely agree that »the *dikasteria* were representative of the people as a whole« and that »the idea of representation implies distinction and not identity.« This is true when one thinks of the *dikasteria* as an institution: there can be no doubt whatever that they were always institutionally distinct from *boule, ekklesia*, archons, ναυκραροι, etc. But it is also true that this kind of »institutional thinking« was not as central to

---

[4] *The Sovereignty of the People's Court in Athens in the Fourth Century B.C.* (Odense 1974) 21; *Ath. Eccl.* 159-60.
[5] *The Athenian Ecclesia* 159; *The Athenian Assembly* 104.

the Athenian constitution (especially in the sixth and fifth centuries) as it is for us. As Peter Rhodes put it to me, to speak of *dikasteria* as »a unified body of government« (as you do) is wishing the modern way of looking at things on the Athenian. What I contend is that, however great the institutional difference between *ekklesia* and *heliaia* was, the personnel constituting these two organs of government remained (initially) identical and with the development of dikastic panels one can start to speak metaphorically of a *dikasterion* as »representing« the people as a whole — not in its capacity as *ekklesia* but in its capacity as *heliaia*. ... «

Ostwald's comment shows that we do in fact agree on the difference between *demos* (= *ekklesia*) and *dikasteria* as institutions, but that we disagree on how much institutions mattered to the Athenians and determined their understanding of their own constitution. What I dispute is principally the statement »this kind of »institutional thinking« was not as central to the Athenian constitution (especially in the sixth and fifth centuries) as it is for us.« In the following article (in this volume, pp. 107 ff.) I will argue that Athenian democracy was centered on institutions much more than modern democracies and that it is anachronistic — but increasingly common — to minimize the importance of the political institutions in classical Athens. It follows that the distinction, sometimes amounting to an opposition, between *demos* (= *ekklesia*) and *dikasteria* was an essential aspect of Athenian democracy and not to be brushed aside as a terminological detail.

II

Still more recently a completely different treatment of the same problem has been advanced by Josiah Ober in his review article on *The Athenian Assembly in the Age of Demosthenes, CP* 84 (1989). Like Ostwald Ober will maintain the traditional link between *demos* and *dikasterion*, but to achieve this end he rejects the idea of representation altogether, and suggests instead a novel interpretation of the interrelationship between *demos, ekklesia* and *dikasterion*. Like Ostwald he accepts my thesis: *demos* (people, state) ≠ *demos* (assembly)[6] as well as my further thesis: *demos* (*ekklesia*) ≠ *dikasteria*. But he objects to my general explanation of the relation between *demos, ekklesia* and *dikasteria* and to my view of representation, i. e. that a *dikasterion* acted on behalf of the *demos* (*hyper tou demou*

---

[6] In *The Athenian Assembly* 107 there is a deplorable printing error. In line 9 read: »But the step from the supreme *demos* [to the supreme *demos*] in the *ekklesia* is conspicuously absent from all our fourth-century sources.« The words in brackets dropped out.

= the state, Din. 1.84 etc). Ober attempts instead to establish a connection between *demos* (people, state) and *dikasteria* in the following way: »I would suggest, as an alternative, the concept of »synecdoche,« a figure of speech in which a part symbolically stands for and refers to a whole, or *vice versa*. Each of the various institutional »parts« of the citizen body (*ekklesia, dikasteria, nomothetai, boule*) could stand for and referred to the whole citizen body. Orators could speak of jurors as having made decisions in Assembly because both a jury and an Assembly were parts of the whole. the words *demos* and *Athenaioi* (whose primary meanings were the whole of the citizen body) could be used respectively to refer to the »part« of the citizen body which attended a given Assembly or sat in a given jury.«

In Ober's synecdoche I object to the words *vice versa*. It is true that the different organs of government could stand for the whole citizen body, cf. the address ὦ ἄνδρες 'Αθηναῖοι used in ecclesiastic, bouleutic and forensic speeches (references in *AE* 147-48). But it is misleading to say that the Assembly was »a part« of the whole. Of course, if we count heads, or rather hands, Ober is right. Of the ca. 30,000 adult male citizens only some 6,000 could attend a session of the *ekklesia*, cf. *The Athenian Assembly* 17-19. As an ideological construct, however, the assembly was conceived as *the whole* of the people, and not just a part. The *demos* (= the *ekklesia*) is regularly described as *all* Athenians, and the fiction is sometimes carried so far that an author may refer to a decision made by 30,000 Athenians (Hdt. 5.97.2; Pl. *Axiochos* 369A). Admittedly, sometimes the *ekklesia* is described as a part only (cf. the passages listed in *The Athenian Assembly* note 40), but then the intention is regularly to cast doubt on the session in question and to suggest manipulation or fraud, cf. Lys. 12.75; Aeschin. 2.125-26. By contrast, a *dikasterion* is often described as a part of the whole and without any pejorative connotation (Dem. 21.2; 25.27, 43, 98; Aeschin. 3.28; Hyp. 3.24 etc). Thus, *demos* = *ekklesia* is, ideologically, the institutional equivalent of *demos* in the sense »the whole of the people«, and the attempt to bring the Assembly closer to the *dikasteria* by viewing it as »a part« of the people (as a *dikasterion* certainly was) is, in my opinion, misguided. As to the last part of the synecdoche, Ober is right about *Athenaioi*, cf. above, but wrong about *demos*. Pace Ober, *demos* could *not* »be used ... to refer to the »part« of the citizen body which ... sat on a given jury.« Furthermore, although there are instances where *demos* changes its meaning from »the Athenian state« at the beginning of a paragraph to »the people's assembly« later on in the same passage,[7] there is no similar instance of *demos* sliding from meaning »the whole people« to »the popular courts«.

Ober offers his synecdoche theory in place of the notions of manifestation/embodiment (the *demos* in assembly) and of representation (the *dikasteria* which I advocated (and here in agreement with Ostwald, Rhodes and others). Ober's criticism of the view that the *dikasteria* represent the *demos* runs as follows: »H. points out (pp. 102-04) that the concepts of »delegation of powers« and »committee« are problematic for analyzing Athenian government; but we should recognize that »representation«, »embodiment« and »manifestation« may be equally troublesome. Representation, in a constitutional sense, implies delegation of authority and/or formal appointment or election. Since H. argues that the authority of the lawcourts was not delegated and since the Athenian juror was not appointed or elected to represent a larger constituency, representation does not seem the ideal way to conceptualize the relationship between lawcourts and Demos.« Thus, according to Ober, I run into a contradiction when I reject the idea of delegation but am prepared to accept the idea of representation. But Ober forgets that the view I reject is that the powers of the *dikasteria* were delegated *from the assembly*, i. e. from the *demos* in its institutional sense. What I hold is that the powers of the *dikasteria* were felt, in some sense, to be delegated from the Athenian *demos* = the Athenian state, cf. e. g. Din. 1.84, where it is stated that the jurors act on behalf of the *demos*, or Aeschin. 3.8, where we learn that all Athenian citizens have entrusted the *polis* and the *politeia* to the jurors. The Athenian *dikasteria* acted on behalf of the Athenian people and, in a loose sense, their powers were derived from the Athenian *demos*, but they did not represent the assembly, nor is there any indication that the powers of the *dikasteria* were derived from the powers of the *ekklesia*. Thus, there is no contradiction, and I will end this note by restating the views I advanced in my 1977 article: in the strictly institutional sense the term δῆμος denotes the ἐκκλησία and means »the people in assembly« (cf. *AE* I 142-43 with notes 13-18); in its broader sense it means »the whole people« = all Athenians (141 with note 8) = the Athenian state (142 with note 12); in its constitutional sense it is used synonymously with δημοκρατία and means »democracy« (142 with note 10), and in its social sense — mostly avoided by the democrats themselves but frequently invoked by their critics — it means »the common people« and has

---

[7] Dem. 59.88-90.

almost invariably a pejorative meaning (142 with note 9, 150-53). There is no support for the view that the *dikasteria* were a manifestation of the *demos* either in its institutional sense (a *dikasterion* = a committee of the *ekklesia*) or in its broader sense (*dikasteria* = the whole of the people), but the *dikasteria* were, in a loose sense, felt to be representative of the *demos* (= the whole people, the state) and furthermore, the critics (but not the advocates) of Athenian democracy held that the *dikasteria* were controlled by the *demos* in the social sense, i. e. by the poor.

THE ATHENIAN *HELIAIA* FROM SOLON TO ARISTOTLE

BY

MOGENS HERMAN HANSEN

Like the council af the Areopagos, the ἡλιαία[1] is known primarily from classical sources relating to the classical period but nevertheless extrapolated and used in accounts of archaic history or in discussions of the origins of Athenian democracy. The relevant literature is extensive, but scattered and inadequate. The ἡλιαία is mentioned in numerous commentaries, monographs and manuals,[2] but usually only a couple of lines or at most a few pages have been devoted to this enigmatic institution. In this article I intend to collect the sources and to discuss them at greater length than previously done. My account is organized in two parts. First I discuss the ἡλιαία in the classical period, where we have some contemporary sources in addition to some late notes in scholia and lexica commenting on passages in classical authors. Next, I discuss the origins of the ἡλιαία by extrapolating the evidence derived from the sources dealing with the classical period, and by adducing the few late classical sources explicitly dealing with the archaic period. By way of introduction I shall state my conclusions briefly.

In the classical period the *Heliaia* was the largest (roofed) courtroom in Athens with accommodation for juries numbering several thousand *dikastai*. Accordingly, I question the traditional identification of the *Heliaia* with the rectangular (unroofed) enclosure at the southwest corner of the Agora, which is too small for juries manned by more than 1,500 *dikastai*. As an institution, the *heliaia* was simply the unambiguous old designation for the people's court or any section of the people's court, and it was not, specifically, the section presided over by the *thesmothetai*. Furthermore, the *heliaia* did not have to meet in the *Heliaia*. The sessions might take place in any of the buildings used as lawcourts, e.g. in the

Parábyston, or in the Odeion *etc*. The *heliaia* was probably instituted by Solon, and, if we trust the information given in Aristotle's *Politics* and in the *Ath. Pol.*, it was from the very beginning a court manned by jurors selected annually by lot. There is no evidence supporting the view that the *heliaia* was, originally, a meeting of the people's assembly in its judicial capacity. Admittedly, our sources may be rejected as unreliable, but in that case we must suspend judgement and confess our ignorance of what the *heliaia* was in the archaic period.

I. THE ARISTOTELIAN *HELIAIA*

In the age of the orators (ca. 420-320) the word ἡλιαία refers to (a) an institution or (b) a building. In sense (a) *heliaia* denotes either the people's court in general or, specifically, a section of the people's court. In sense (b) *Heliaia* refers to a courtroom described in later sources as the largest court in Athens. Furthermore, if we group the sources according to sense (a) and (b) a curious pattern emerges: in laws and decrees (preserved on stone or inserted as documents in the forensic speeches) sense (a) is predominant, and there is no unquestionable example of sense (b).[3] Conversely, in the literary sources ἡλιαία seems invariably to be attested in sense (b) and no indisputable occurrence of sense (a) is preserved.[4] Accordingly, I will organize my account of the ἡλιαία in the classical period in two parts and discuss the *heliaia* first as an institution and second as a building.

A. The heliaia

The accepted view about *heliaia* as an institution is succinctly expressed by D.M. MacDowell in his article in *OCD*. He states that *heliaia*, in the classical period, 'was sometimes used to mean the whole body of jurors, and ἡλιαστής was a word for 'juror', synonymous with δικαστής. But more often *heliaia* was used as the name of one particular court, the court of the *thesmothetai*.' I agree with the first half of this description, but the identification of the *heliaia*, in its specific sense, with the court of the *thesmothetai*[5] needs some modification. By way of introduction, I shall quote the relevant sources:[6]

1. *IG* I[3] 40.70-76: Ἀρχέστρατο[ς] εἶπε· τὰ μὲν ἄλλα καθάπερ Ἀντικλὲς· τὰς δὲ εὐθύνας Χαλκιδεῦσι κατὰ σφῶν αὐτῶν ἔναι ἐν Χαλκίδι καθάπερ

Ἀθένεσιν Ἀθεναίοις πλὲν φυγἒς καὶ θανάτο καὶ ἀτιμίας· περὶ δὲ τούτον ἔφεσιν ἔναι Ἀθέναζε ἐς τὲν ἐλιαίαν τὲν τὸν θεσμοθετὸν κατὰ τὸ φσέφισμα τὸ δέμο.

2. *M&L* 45.5-7: ἐσα[γέτω ὁ βουλόμενος αὐτίκα μάλα εἰς τ]ὴν ἠλιαίαν τὴν τῶ[ν θεσμοθετῶν τοὺς ἠδικηκότας· ο]ἱ δὲ θεσμοθέ[τ]αι πέ[νθ ἡμερῶν δό]ντων [δίκας τοῖς φήν]ασι ἕκαστον.

3. *IG* I³ 71.13-14: [ἐσαγογέον δὲ hο λα]χὸν κα[ὶ h]ο πολέμαρ[χος ἀνακρινάντον τὰς δίκας ἐν τ]ε̄ι ἐλιαίαι [καθάπερ τὰς δίκας τὰς ἄλ]λας τὀ[ν ἐ]λιαστὀν·⁷

4. Lys. 10.16: ΝΟΜΟΣ δεδέσθαι δ' ἐν τῇ ποδοκάκκῃ ἡμέρας πέντε τὸν πόδα, ἐὰν [μὴ] προστιμήσῃ ἡ ἡλιαία.

5. D. 24.105: ΝΟΜΟΙ ὅ τι ἄν τις ἀπολέσῃ, ἐὰν μὲν αὐτὸ λάβῃ, τὴν διπλασίαν καταδικάζειν, ἐὰν δὲ μή, τὴν διπλασίαν πρὸς τοῖς ἐπαιτίοις. δεδέσθαι δ' ἐν τῇ ποδοκάκκῃ τὸν πόδα πένθ' ἡμέρας καὶ νύκτας ἴσας, ἐὰν προστιμήσῃ ἡ ἡλιαία. προστιμᾶσθαι δὲ τὸν βουλόμενον, ὅταν περὶ τοῦ τιμήματος ᾖ. – ἐὰν δέ τις ἀπαχθῇ, τῶν γονέων κακώσεως ἑαλωκὼς ἢ ἀστρατείας ἢ προειρημένον αὐτῷ τῶν νόμων εἴργεσθαι, εἰσιὼν ὅποι μὴ χρή, δησάντων αὐτὸν οἱ ἕνδεκα καὶ εἰσαγόντων εἰς τὴν ἡλιαίαν, κατηγορείτω δὲ ὁ βουλόμενος οἷς ἔξεστιν. ἐὰν δ ἁλῷ, τιμάτω ἡ ἡλιαία ὅ τι χρὴ παθεῖν αὐτὸν ἢ ἀποτεῖσαι. ἐὰν δ ἀργυρίου τιμηθῇ, δεδέσθω τέως ἂν ἐκτείσῃ.

6. D. 23.28: ΝΟΜΟΣ τοὺς δ' ἀνδροφόνους ἐξεῖναι ἀποκτείνειν ἐν τῇ ἡμεδαπῇ καὶ ἀπάγειν, ὡς ἐν τῷ <α> ἄξονι ἀγορεύει, λυμαίνεσθαι δὲ μή, μηδὲ ἀποινᾶν, ἢ διπλοῦν ὀφείλειν ὅσον ἂν καταβλάψῃ. εἰσφέρειν δὲ τοὺς ἄρχοντας, ὧν ἕκαστοι δικασταί εἰσι, τῷ βουλομένῳ. τὴν δ' ἡλιαίαν διαγιγνώσκειν.

7. D. 43.75: ΝΟΜΟΣ ὁ ἄρχων ἐπιμελείσθω τῶν ὀρφανῶν καὶ τῶν ἐπικλήρων καὶ τῶν οἴκων τῶν ἐξερημουμένων καὶ τῶν γυναικῶν, ὅσαι μένουσιν ἐν τοῖς οἴκοις τῶν ἀνδρῶν τῶν τεθνηκότων φάσκουσαι κυεῖν. τούτων ἐπιμελείσθω καὶ μὴ ἐάτω ὑβρίζειν μηδένα περὶ τούτους. ἐὰν δέ τις ὑβρίζῃ ἢ ποιῇ τι παράνομον, κύριος ἔστω ἐπιβάλλειν κατὰ τὸ τέλος. ἐὰν δὲ μείζονος ζημίας δοκῇ ἄξιος εἶναι, προσκαλεσάμενος πρόπεμπτα καὶ τίμημα ἐπιγραψάμενος, ὅ τι ἂν δοκῇ αὐτῷ, εἰσαγέτω εἰς τὴν ἡλιαίαν. ἐὰν δ' ἁλῷ, τιμάτω ἡ ἡλιαία περὶ τοῦ ἁλόντος, ὅ τι χρὴ αὐτὸν παθεῖν ἢ ἀποτεῖσαι.

8. D. 21.47: ΝΟΜΟΣ ἐάν τις ὑβρίζῃ εἴς τινα .... γραφέσθω πρὸς τοὺς

θεσμοθέτας ὁ βουλόμενος Ἀθηναίων οἷς ἔξεστιν, οἱ δὲ θεσμοθέται εἰσαγοντων εἰς τὴν ἡλιαίαν τριάκοντα ἡμερῶν ἀφ' ἧς ἂν γραφῇ, ἐὰν μή τι δημόσιον κωλύῃ, εἰ δὲ μή, ὅταν ᾖ πρῶτον οἷόν τε. ὅτου δ' ἂν καταγνῷ ἡ ἡλιαία, τιμάτω περὶ αὐτοῦ παραχρῆμα, ὅτου ἂν δοκῇ ἄξιος εἶναι παθεῖν ἢ ἀποτεῖσαι ...

9. D. 46.26: ΝΟΜΟΣ ἐάν τις συνιστῆται, ἢ συνδεκάζῃ τὴν ἡλιαίαν ἢ τῶν δικαστηρίων τι τῶν Ἀθήνησιν ἢ τὴν βουλὴν ἐπὶ δωροδοκίᾳ χρήματα διδοὺς ἢ δεχόμενος, ἢ ἑταιρείαν συνιστῇ ἐπὶ καταλύσει τοῦ δήμου, ἢ συνήγορος ὢν λαμβάνῃ χρήματα ἐπὶ ταῖς δίκαις ταῖς ἰδίαις ἢ δημοσίαις, τούτων εἶναι τὰς γραφὰς πρὸς τοὺς θεσμοθέτας.

10. D. 24.63: ΝΟΜΟΣ Τιμοκράτης εἶπεν· ὁπόσοι Ἀθηναίων κατ' εἰσαγγελίαν ἐκ τῆς βουλῆς ἢ νῦν εἰσιν ἐν τῷ δεσμωτηρίῳ ἢ τὸ λοιπὸν κατατεθῶσι, καὶ μὴ παραδοθῇ ἡ κατάγνωσις αὐτῶν τοῖς θεσμοθέταις ὑπὸ τοῦ γραμματέως τοῦ κατὰ πρυτανείαν κατὰ τὸν εἰσαγγελτικὸν νόμον, δεδόχθαι τοῖς νομοθέταις εἰσάγειν τοὺς ἕνδεκα εἰς τὸ δικαστήριον τριάκονθ' ἡμερῶν ἀφ' ἧς ἂν παραλάβωσιν, ἐὰν μή τι δημοσίᾳ κωλύῃ, ἐὰν δὲ μή, ὅταν πρῶτον οἷόν τ' ᾖ. κατηγορεῖν δ' Ἀθηναίων τὸν βουλόμενον οἷς ἔξεστιν. ἐὰν δὲ ἁλῷ, τιμάτω ἡ ἡλιαία περὶ αὐτοῦ ὅ τι ἂν δοκῇ ἄξιος εἶναι παθεῖν ἢ ἀποτεῖσαι. ἐὰν δ' ἀργυρίου τιμηθῇ, δεδέσθω τέως ἂν ἐκτείσῃ ὅ τι ἂν αὐτοῦ καταγνωσθῇ.

11. *Hesperia* 49 (1980) 263-64.28: φαίνεν δὲ τὸμ βολομένο[ν Ἀθηναίων, καὶ ὁ βασι]λεὺς εἰσαγέτω εἰς τὴν ἡλιαίαν κα[...32: ἐ]ὰν δὲ μείζονος δοκῆι ζημίας ἄξιος εἶναι, εἰσάγε[ιν τούτος εἰς τὴν ἡλιαί]αν προσκαλεσάμενος κατὰ τὸν νόμον· ἐ[πιθέσθω δὲ ἡ] ἡλιαία ὅτι ἂν δοκῆι ἄξιος εἶναι παθεῖν ἢ ἀποτεῖσ[αι ...] 49: ... ἐὰν κατ]αγνῶι ἡ ἡλιαία ποιεῖν τι παρὰ τὰ γ[εγραμμένα ...

12. *Hesperia Suppl*. 17 (1978) 2-4.101-04: ε]ἰσαγαγεῖν δὲ καὶ τοὺς θεσμοθέτας τὴν δοκιμασίαν τῆς δ[ωρ]εᾶς αὐτῶι εἰς τ<ὴ>ν ἡλιαίαν ἐπειδὰν αἱ ἡμέραι αἱ ἐκ τοῦ νόμ[ου] διεξέλθωσιν·

13. D. 23.97: διόπερ καταρᾶται καθ' ἑκάστην ἐκκλησίαν ὁ κῆρυξ, οὐκ εἴ τινες ἐξηπατήθησαν, ἀλλ' εἴ τις ἐξαπατᾷ λέγων ἢ βουλὴν ἢ δῆμον ἢ τὴν ἡλιαίαν.[8]

Of these sources the curse proclaimed by the herald in the assembly (no. 13) is an unquestionable example of *heliaia* referring to the people's court in general = the system of *dikasteria*, and in the law D. 46.26 (no. 9) *heliaia* probably has the same meaning (cf. *infra* page 31), but the other sources show that *heliaia,* in its more specific sense, may denote *any* section of the people's court no matter who the presiding magistrate was and no matter which kind of action the dikasts were hearing.

In the νόμος κλοπῆς (*supra* nos. 4 & 5) it is stated that the *heliaia,* passing sentence upon a thief, may impose an additional penalty of 'five days and five nights in the pillory'. Commenting on this law Demosthenes says that this additional penalty applies *inter alia* to thieves put on trial by a *dike klopes,* i.e. a private action: εἰ δέ τις ἰδίαν δίκην κλοπῆς ἁλοίη, ὑπάρχειν μὲν αὐτῷ διπλάσιον ἀποτεῖσαι τὸ τιμηθέν, προστιμῆσαι δ' ἐξεῖναι τῷ δικαστηρίῳ πρὸς τῷ ἀργυρίῳ δεσμὸν τῷ κλέπτῃ, πένθ' ἡμέρας καὶ νύκτας ἴσας ... καὶ τούτων ὀλίγῳ πρότερον ἠκούσατε τῶν νόμων (D. 24.114). The implication is that *dikai klopes* were heard by a section of the *heliaia,* and so *heliaia,* when meaning a section of the people's court, may refer not only to sections of 501, 1001 or 1501 jurors hearing public actions, but also to the small sections of 201 or 401 jurors selected by lot to hear ordinary private actions.

Similarly, the preserved laws indicate that any magistrate with ἡγεμονία δικαστηρίου was entitled to preside over the *heliaia.* Admittedly, the *thesmothetai* are mentioned more frequently than other *archai,*[9] but the phrase ἡ ἡλιαία ἡ τῶν θεσμοθετῶν, which occurs in the inscriptions *supra* nos 1 & 2, is a sufficient indication that *heliaia* without this addition had no specific connection with the *thesmothetai;*[10] and this is confirmed by the other preserved laws. We know that the *heliaia* could be presided over by the *archon* (D. 43.75, *supra* no.7), the *basileus* (*Hesp.* 49 (1980) *supra* no. 11), the eleven (D. 24.105, 63, *supra* nos. 5 & 10), the *epimeletai ton Mysterion* (*Hesp.* 49 (1980) *supra* no. 11) and in the law quoted in D. 23.28 (*supra* no. 6) it is prescribed that *any* magistrate with ἡγεμονία δικαστηρίου may preside over the *heliaia.*[11] Later in this article (page 21) I shall argue that the *Heliaia* building probably was reserved for the *thesmothetai,* but the laws show that *heliaia* as an institution was either the people's court in general or *any* section of the people's court.

The comprehensive meaning 'people's court' is also confirmed by all the derivatives of the noun ἡλιαία. The oath taken by all the 6,000 jurors is called ὁ ἡλιαστικὸς ὅρκος,[12] and similarly the adjective ἡλιαστικός can be used about dicastic pay in general.[13] The task performed by the jurors is described both with the verb ἡλιάζεσθαι[14] and with the noun ἡλίασις;[15]

and the noun ἡλιαστής is used synonymously with δικαστής,[16] just as ἡλιαία is synonymous with δικαστήριον.[17] If there is any difference between the two words, it must be stylistic or chronological rather than semantic.

In the texts of all the preserved forensic speeches the word ἡλιαία occurs only twice,[18] and in both cases the reference is to the building rather than to the institution. The people's court is usually called δικαστήριον/δικαστήρια or referred to simply by using the second person plural in addresses to the jurors. On the other hand, in laws, decrees, oaths and official proclamations ἡλιαία seems to be as common a word as δικαστήριον and is used as a regular official designation of the people's court, in fact the only unambiguous designation, since the word *dikasterion* might be applied also to the Areopagos and to the other special homicide courts.[19] Admittedly, many of the laws and proclamations quoted above are part of the Solonian law code as revised in 403-399, and these laws may well preserve archaic terminology. It was like the Athenians to stick to the archaic usage and leave a law untouched whenever possible.[20] But it would be wrong to infer that *heliaia* was used in old laws only and replaced by *dikasterion* in the fourth century. εἰσάγειν εἰς τὴν ἡλιαίαν and τιμάτω ἡ ἡλιαία are phrases found in Timokrates' law about *eisangelia* (*supra* no. 10) and in the law about the Eleusinian mysteries (*supra* no. 11), both passed in the middle of the fourth century, and even in an honorary decree of the third century we find εἰσάγειν εἰς τὴν ἡλιαίαν (*supra* no. 12). The conclusion seems to be that *heliaia*, when referring to an institution, is an old word surviving in the conservative official language rather than in regular prose, including forensic speeches. It is significant that the legal term *heliaia*, when a law is paraphrased, is replaced with the common word *dikasterion:* the law about theft is quoted by Demosthenes in 24.105 (*supra* no. 5), but when he paraphrases the law in 24.114 the provision ἐὰν προστιμήσῃ ἡ ἡλιαία is transformed into προστιμῆσαι δ᾽ ἐξεῖναι τῷ δικαστηρίῳ. Similarly, ἐάν τις ὀφείλων τῷ δημοσίῳ ἡλιάζηται found in the law about petitions quoted in D. 24.50 becomes ἐάν τις ... ὀφείλων τῷ δημοσίῳ ... δικάζῃ when paraphrased by Demosthenes in 24.123.[21]

Summing up, in the official language (laws, decrees, proclamations, curses *etc.*) *heliaia* is the unambiguous technical term denoting either the people's court as such or any section of it, and *heliaia* is used synonymously with *dikasterion* (or *dikasteria*). In the literary sources (forensic speeches included) the term is avoided (apart from quotations) and replaced by the term *dikasterion*. On the other hand, the noun *heliastes* occurs several times in Aristophanes' comedies and was probably used in ordinary speech more frequently than *heliaia*, from which it was derived.

B. *The Heliaia*
As pointed out already by the lexicographers the word ἡλιαία denotes sometimes an institution and sometimes a building. In the *Lex. Seg.* 189.20-21, for example, we find the following note on the words ἡλιαία καὶ ἡλιάζεσθαι. δικαστήριον ἀνδρῶν χιλίων καὶ ὁ τόπος, ἐν ᾧ οὗτοι δικάζουσιν.[22] I shall now turn to those passages where *Heliaia* denotes a building, and again I will quote the principal sources:
Ar. *Eq.* 894-98: Αλ. καὶ πρότερον ἐπεβούλευσέ σοι. τὸν καυλὸν οἶσθ' ἐκεῖνον / τοῦ σιλφίου τὸν ἄξιον γενόμενον; Δη. οἶδα μέντοι. / Αλ. ἐπίτηδες οὗτος αὐτὸν ἔσπευδ' ἄξιον γενέσθαι, / ἵν' ἐσθίοιτ' ὠνούμενοι, κἄπειτ' ἐν ἡλιαίᾳ / βδέοντες ἀλλήλους ἀποκτείνειαν οἱ δικασταί.
Antipho 6.21: ἔλεξε μὲν γὰρ Φιλοκράτης οὑτοσὶ ἀναβὰς εἰς τὴν ἡλιαίαν τὴν τῶν θεσμοθετῶν, τῇ ἡμέρᾳ ᾗ ὁ παῖς ἐξεφέρετο, ὅτι ἀδελφὸν αὐτοῦ ἀποκτείναιμι ἐγὼ ἐν τῷ χορῷ, φάρμακον ἀναγκάσας πιεῖν. ἐπειδὴ δὲ οὗτος ταῦτα ἔλεγεν, ἀναβὰς ἐγὼ εἰς τὸ δικαστήριον τοῖς αὐτοῖς δικασταῖς ἔλεξα ὅτι .... (ἡλιαίαν Taylor: ἡλιακήν codd.)
D. 47.12: ἡ μὲν γὰρ δίαιτα ἐν τῇ ἡλιαίᾳ ἦν· οἱ γὰρ τὴν Οἰνῇδα καὶ τὴν Ἐρεχθῇδα διαιτῶντες ἐνταῦθα κάθηνται·
Arist. *Ath. Pol.* 68.1: τὰ δὲ δημόσι]α τῶν [δικ]αστηρίων ἐστὶ φ[α' ....]σο .. [..]ασιν· ὅταν δὲ δέ[ῃ τὰς .... γραφ]ὰς εἰς ἃ εἰ]σαγαγεῖν, συν[έρχεται β' δικαστή]ρια εἰ[ς] τὴν ἡλιαίαν τα. [............] κνα .. εἰς φ' καὶ ἃ τρία [δικαστήρια.[23]

In Demosthenes and Aristotle *Heliaia* is used exclusively in the local sense; in Aristophanes and Antiphon the local sense is predominant, but possibly the author has the institution in mind as well. Here, I fully agree with R.E. Wycherley's judicious comment that 'the word *Heliaia*, like agora, probably meant primarily the assembly, secondarily the place; as with such words as *synedrion*, *dikasterion*, *boule*, the meanings are closely bound up together; often both are present and are not to be separated.'²⁴ The distinction, however, between the two senses must not be obliterated. It is important to emphasize that ἡλιαία, when referring to an institution, has a much broader meaning than when it denotes a building. It would be wrong to suppose that, in the classical period, the *heliaia* had to meet in the *Heliaia*. As pointed out above (on page 13) *heliaia* may denote any section of the people's court, and so the *heliaia* must have held its sessions in all the various buildings used as lawcourts. We need not be surprised if a new source should turn up, telling us that an action was heard by the *heliaia* in the Parabyston. Such an information would only be the corollary of what we know from Demosthenes 47.12 that the *diaitetai* from two of the *phylai* met in the *Heliaia*.

In addition to the classical sources quoted above we have quite a number of Hellenistic and Byzantine notes about the *Heliaia* beginning with Pausanias and Pollux and ending with late Byzantine scholia which cannot be dated precisely. Apart from simple paraphrases of the *Ath. Pol.*²⁵ these notes constantly repeat two rather precise pieces of information: first that the *Heliaia* was unroofed and the *heliastai* exposed to the sun, and second that the *Heliaia* was the largest court in Athens. Since the modern attempts to locate the *Heliaia* are based on these notes, I shall organize my account in the following three parts (a) Was the *Heliaia* an unroofed enclosure? (b)Do we know anything about its size? (c) Is it possible to identify the *Heliaia* with any of the buildings excavated in the Agora in recent years?

(a) Was the *Heliaia* roofed or unroofed? According to many scholia and lexicographical notes the *Heliaia* was unroofed and the *heliastai* exposed to the sun. But the basis of this information is exclusively the belief that ἡλιαία is derived from ἥλιος, and this etymology is in all probability wrong.²⁶ Furthermore, in all the notes the wording is either identical or very similar. The notes are interdependent sources and can in fact be treated as one single note repeated nine times with minor variations.

Schol. Ar. *Av.* 109: οὕτως δὲ ἐκλήθη (ἡ ἡλιαία), διὰ τὸ ἐν ὑπαίθρῳ εἶναι τόπῳ καὶ ὑπὸ τοῦ ἡλίου βάλλεσθαι.

Suda s.v. ἡλιαστής (215): οὕτω δὲ ἐκλήθη (ἡ ἡλιαία), διὰ τὸ ἐν ὑπαίθρῳ εἶναι τόπῳ καὶ ὑπὸ τοῦ ἡλίου βάλλεσθαι. Ἀριστοφάνης.

Schol. Ar. V. 88: ... τῆς ἡλιαίας, ὅπερ οὕτω καλεῖται διὰ τὸ ἐν ὑπαιθρίῳ εἶναι καὶ ἡλίῳ βάλλεσθαι.
Schol. Ar. Nu. 862: ἡλιαία δὲ, ... διὰ τὸ ὑπαίθριον εἶναι καὶ τῷ ἡλίῳ βάλλεσθαι.
Lex. Seg. 310.32-34: ἡλιαία δὲ ἐκλήθη ἤτοι .... ἢ διὰ τὸ ὕπαιθρον εἶναι τὸν τόπον καὶ ἡλιοῦσθαι.
EM. s.v. ἡλιαία: εἰς τὸ ὕπαιθρον προκαθημένων τῶν δικαστῶν· ἢ παρὰ τὸ ὑπαίθριον· καὶ προϋποτίθεται ἥλιον εἶναι· παρὰ τὸ ἡλιοῦσθαι τοὺς ἐκεῖ ἀθροιζομένους.
Schol. Ar. Eq. 255: ἡλιαία δὲ καλεῖται, διὰ τὸ ὑπαίθριον αὐτὸ εἶναι καὶ ὑπὸ τῷ ἡλίῳ καθέζεσθαι τοὺς συνελθόντας δικαστάς.
Schol. Luc. Tim. 51: δικαστήριον Ἀθήνησιν ἡ ἡλιαία, εἰς ὕπαιθρον προκαθημένων τῶν δικαστῶν, παρ᾽ ὃ καὶ ἡλιαία ἐκαλεῖτο. παρὰ τὸ ἡλιοῦσθαι τοὺς ἐκεῖ ἀθροιζομένους.
Schol. D. 24.21: ἡλιαία δὲ ἐκλήθη ὁ τόπος ... τινὲς δὲ λέγουσιν ἐκ τοῦ ὕπαιθρον εἶναι τὸν τόπον καὶ τὸν ἥλιον ἐκεῖ ἔνδον προσβάλλειν.
Schol. Ar. V. 772: τὸ δ᾽ ἡλιάσῃ (μήποτε δὲ ψιλῶς προενεκτέον) παρὰ τὴν ἡλιαίαν, πρὸς ἥλιον δικάσειν. ἅμα δὲ παίζει παρὰ τὴν τοῦ ἡλίου ὀνομασίαν. ψυχρῶς δὲ πέπαιχε, φησὶν ὁ Δίδυμος, πρὸς τοὔνομα. ἐπειδὴ γὰρ εἴλη λέγεται ἡ τοῦ ἡλίου αὐγή, Ἡλιαία δὲ τὸ δικαστήριον, παίζων ἔφησε πρὸς τὸ φιλόδικον ὅτι ἐπειδὰν ἀνάσχῃ ὁ ἥλιος, ἡλιάζειν ἐνέσται σοι. οὕτως δὲ οἱ Ἀττικοὶ διὰ τοῦ ι εἴλην λέγουσιν. οὕτως Δίδυμος. δικάσεις, φησί, πρὸς τὸν ἥλιον καθήμενος. ἔπαιξε δὲ παρὰ τὴν ἡλιαίαν, τὸ μέγιστον δικαστήριον, ὃ ταύτης τῆς ὀνομασίας ἔτυχε διὰ τὸ ἐν ὑπαίθρῳ αὐτὸ ἀναπεπταμένον βάλλεσθαι τῷ ἡλίῳ.

The most detailed and informative of these notes is the scholion on Ar. V. 772 referring to Didymos. In this passage Aristophanes makes a pun on ἡλιάζεσθαι/ἥλιος, and there can be little doubt that it is Aristophanes' joke and Didymos'[27] learned comment on it which has given rise to the mistaken etymology repeated in all the notes. Aristophanes' verses run as follows: καὶ ταῦτα μὲν νῦν εὐλόγως, ἢν ἐξέχῃ / εἴλη κατ᾽ ὄρθρον, ἡλιάσει πρὸς ἥλιον· / ἐὰν δὲ νείφῃ, πρὸς τὸ πῦρ καθήμενος· / ὕοντος εἴσει· κἂν ἔχῃ μεσημβρινός,/οὐδείς σ᾽ ἀποκλείσει θεσμοθέτης τῇ κιγκλίδι./ (Ar. V. 771-75). We are in the second half of the play. By his victory in the epirrhematic agon Bdelykleon has forced his father to stay at home instead of serving as a juror in the *dikasteria*. He now attempts to entertain his father by arranging mock trials in which Philokleon can sit in judgement in his own house and pass sentence upon the members of the household, the animals included. One of the advantages is that Philokleon may decide for himself whether he prefers to hear a case outside or indoors according to whether it is sunshine or rain. From this we can of course infer that an ordinary *dikastes* did not have any choice, but the passage makes sense both if the *Heliaia* was roofed and if it was unroofed. If it was roofed, the *dikastai* had no possibility of hearing a case in the sun, and if it was unroofed, they had to perform their duty even when exposed to snow or rain. Obviously there is a play on the words ἡλιάζεσθαι and ἥλιος, but it would be hazardous to follow the scholiasts in taking this pun as evidence that the *heliastai* were exposed to the sun.[28] On the contrary, the point may well be that the home-made court offers the possibility of *heliasis* in the sun and not (as usual) in the shade.

So the lexicographical tradition is based on an overinterpretation and probably even a misinterpretation of Ar. *V.* 771-75 and there is in fact another passage in Aristophanes, which points to the conclusion that the *Heliaia* was a roofed building, *viz. Eq.* 894-98 (quoted above on page 15). The sausage-monger alleges that the tanner once on purpose brought about a price-reduction on *silphion* (which has a peculiar effect on the digestion). The ulterior motive was to induce the Athenians to eat too much *silphion* so that they would suffocate each other by excessive farting when they were sitting densely packed in the *Heliaia*. Obviously, the sinister plan would be thwarted if the *Heliaia* was unroofed, whereas one can easily imagine the disatrous effect if the *Heliaia* was a roofed building and not only a walled enclosure. On balance, the scanty evidence favours the view that the *Heliaia* was roofed, like at least some other[29] and perhaps all other courtrooms used by the people's court.

(b) In several lexicographical notes we learn that the *Heliaia* was τὸ μέγιστον δικαστήριον Ἀθήνησιν,[30] and in the *Ath. Pol.* 68.1 (quoted above on page 15) it is stated that the *Heliaia* was the courtroom used for public actions to be heard by more than 501 *dikastai*.[31] The passage is admittedly badly damaged, but if we trust the plausible restorations printed above, we learn that trials involving 1,000 jurors (= two *dikas-*

teria) were brought to the *Heliaia*, and then we hear about trials involving 1,500 jurors (= three *dikasteria*). Now, 68.1 is an appendix to the long and detailed description in 63-67 of the manning of the *dikasteria* hearing ordinary private actions. Aristotle chooses, *exempli gratia*, to describe the sortition which takes place on a court day reserved for actions heard by 401 jurors,[32] but it seems safe to assume that the same procedure was applied on court days set aside for private actions heard by 201 jurors or for ordinary public actions heard by 501 jurors.[33] So the Athenian jury system in the late fourth century B.C. can be summarized thus: on an ordinary court day set off for private or public actions involving panels of either 201 or 401 or 501 jurors, several trials were heard simultaneously in a series of courtrooms all located within an enclosure with ten entrances where the jurors of the day were first selected by lot and then divided into subgroups, each subgroup forming a *dikasterion* to be assigned to one of the courtrooms. But occasionally a major public action had to be brought before a jury manned with more than 500 jurors. In this case either 1,001 or 1,501 or even more jurors were selected by lot to form one *dikasterion* and the case was heard in the *Heliaia* building. It is reasonable to assume that, on such a court day, only one *dikasterion* was formed,[34] and accordingly only one case could be tried, since a full day from sunrise to sunset had to be set aside for the hearing of a public action.[35]

In addition to Aristotle's general information we know about six trials actually heard by more than 500 jurors,[36] and one more trial where the *ekklesia* by decree had requested a large jury. As far as this evidence goes, only two types of public action were heard by large juries, i.e. *graphe paranomon* and *eisangelia*, including the related procedure *apophasis*.[37]

In the speech *On the Mysteries* Andokides alleges that his father's *graphe paranomon* against Speusippos in 415 was heard by 6,000 *dikastai*.[38] The *graphe paranomon* brought by Androtion, Glauketes and Melanopos against Euktemon in 353 involved 1,000 *dikastai*,[39] and Phanostratos' indictment of Aristogeiton's decree in *ca*. 331 was probably brought before a jury manned with 1,500 *dikastai*.[40] According to Philochoros, *eisangeliai* were heard by either 1,000 or 1,500 jurors.[41] His information is confirmed by some sources: Plutarch states that Perikles was tried by 1,500 *dikastai*;[42] but we also have evidence of larger juries: The trial of the *strategoi* and *taxiarchoi* in 404 would have been heard by 2,000 jurors if it had been handled constitutionally,[43] and in the period 336-24 the speaker of Deinarchos I had Pistias put on trial by an *eisangelia* which was heard by no less than 2,500 dikastai.[44] Finally, the *apophasis* presented by the Areopagos in the Harpalos affair resulted in ten trials, each heard by 1,500 jurors.[45]

Comparing Arist. *Ath. Pol.* 68.1 with Philochoros *Fr.* 199 we can infer that large juries usually numbered either 1,000 or 1,500 *dikastai* but it is important to notice that, in the forensic speeches, we hear about juries composed of more than 1,500 jurors. First, the 6,000 jurors hearing the *graphe paranomon* in 415, second, the 2,000 jurors prescribed by decree in 404, and third, the 2,500 jurors hearing the *eisangelia* against Pistias.

Andokides' information about 6,000 jurors is undoubtedly a rhetorical exaggeration to underpin the massive support given to his father, but it is a pardonable one and not difficult to explain. I suggest that the doors were thrown open to all 6,000 jurors and that the Athenians in this particular case returned to the old system (cf. *infra* page 36), used regularly before the introduction of dikastic pay in the middle of the fifth century: to admit all jurors who volunteered without applying any restriction. If, for example, 40% or 60% of the 6,000 turned up, the trial of Speusippos must have been heard by either 2,400 or 3,600 jurors. So the true statement that the *graphe paranomon* was heard by the panel of jurors without any restricted admission is twisted by Andokides into the exaggerated statement that the case was tried by all the 6,000 jurors serving on the panel. Exactly the same form of exaggeration is used in descriptions of decrees passed by the people in the *Ekklesia*. If it favours his view, a speaker or an author may state that a decree was passed by *all* Athenians,[46] or he may even say that it was passed by 30.000 Athenians,[47] although the maximum attendance on the Pnyx was ca. 6,000 in the fifth century, and ca. 6,500-8,000 in most of the fourth century.[48] So, taking the rhetorical exaggeration into account, I suggest that the *graphe paranomon* in 415 was certainly not heard by 6,000 jurors, but undoubtedly by more than 2,000 jurors, and even perhaps more than 3,000.[49] On the other hand, Deinarchos' information in the speech *Against Demosthenes* seems to me to be reliable, and I can see no reason to reject the information that the *eisangelia* against Pistias was brought before a jury composed of five *dikasteria* of 500 *dikastai* each.

Let us return to the *Ath. Pol.* 68.1. Aristotle states that cases involving 1,000 jurors were tried in the *Heliaia* and that some cases were brought before a jury composed of 1,500 *dikastai*. He does not explicitly say that the 1,500 jurors met in the *Heliaia*, and trials involving more than 1,500 jurors are left unmentioned. So we are left with a choice between three possible interpretations: (a) Only cases involving 1,000 jurors were heard in the *Heliaia*, and public actions involving 1,500 (or more) *dikastai* were heard elsewhere. (b) All cases involving 1,000 or 1,500 *dikastai* were heard in the *Heliaia*, and it is insignificant that Aristotle mentions the *Heliaia* only in connection with the 1,000 *dikastai*. Larger juries were not in use any longer or assembled elsewhere. (c) All cases involving more than 500 jurors were tried in the *Heliaia* and it is accidental that Aristotle omits from his account (as does Philochoros) the occasional use of juries larger than 1,500.

Of these three possibilities I prefer (c), and I think that both (a) and (b) can be eliminated. *Re* (a): Harpokration (followed by other lexicographers)[50] paraphrases Aristotle's account in 68.1 by saying that either 1,000 or 1,500 jurors were summoned to the *Heliaia*, and he had access to the full and undamaged text of the passage.[51] *Re* (b): the *eisangelia* against Pistias, heard by 2,500 jurors, is contemporary with the *Ath. Pol.*, and so we can reject the possibility that juries numbering more than 1,500 *dikastai* had been abolished when the *Ath. Pol.* was composed. There are innumerable major and minor omissions in the *Ath. Pol.* It is almost to be expected that the occasional use of more than 1,500 *dikastai* is simply passed over in silence. Furthermore, it is not plausible to assume that the *Heliaia* could accommodate only 1,500 *dikastai* so that larger juries had to meet elsewhere. Many lexicographers state that the *Heliaia* was the largest of the Athenian courts[52] and I am inclined to accept this piece of information as reliable. But if juries numbering more than 1,500 *dikastai* had to meet elsewhere we must reject the lexicographers.

Summing up, (c) seems to be the most plausible solution, and if so, the *Heliaia* must have been a court with accommodation for a minimum of 2,500 jurors. Furthermore, a connection is established between the *thesmothetai* and the *Heliaia* building. As I pointed out above (on page 19) large juries were presumably appointed only in *graphai paranomon* and in *eisangeliai* (including the *apophasis*). These types of public action were presided over by the *thesmothetai*,[53] and if the *Heliaia* was used exclusively in cases heard by large juries, ἡ ἡλιαία ἡ τῶν θεσμοθετῶν would be a proper description of this courtroom.

(c) We can now calculate the minimum size of the *Heliaia* and discuss the possible identification of the *Heliaia* with one of the buildings excavated in the Agora. We know that the jurors were seated during the trial, probably on narrow wooden benches.[54] Next, the minimum space required for a human being attending a large meeting seems to be 0.4 m², a figure comprising the space filled by rows of benches and the space between the rows.[55] So a hall or an enclosure with seats for 2,500 jurors must have had a floor space of 1,000 m² *min*. But in addition to seating facilities for the jurors, the courtroom must have had some extra space for the platforms (βήματα), the water clock (κλεψύδρα), the chests containing the jurors' tickets (πινάκια), and facilities for the president (ἡγεμὼν δικαστηρίου), the secretary reading out documents, all the other officials and the witnesses *etc*. Probably, some 50 m² are sufficient for all these persons and their equipment, and so we arrive at a minimum floorage of 1,050 m². On the other hand, 1,050 m² may have been sufficient. If I am right in my interpretation of And. 1.17, nothing prevents us from assuming that only some 2,500 of the 6,000 jurors turned up and were admitted when the *graphe paranomon* against Speusippos was heard.

There is a building in the Agora which many scholars believe to be the *Heliaia*.[56] At the southwest corner of the Agora a large rectangular structure has been found. It was erected some time in the period 480-60,[57] and in its original form it was a walled enclosure with interior measurements of 26.50 × 31.00 meters yielding an area of about 821 m². In the third quarter of the fourth century a series of rooms was inserted in the west side of the building and the remaining free space amounted to some 661 m².[58]

Although no dicastic equipment has been found in the area, this enclosure is tentatively, and often confidently, identified with the *Heliaia*. But I am highly sceptical of the identification, primarily because the seating capacity is insufficient. If we deduct a bare minimum of 21 m² for all

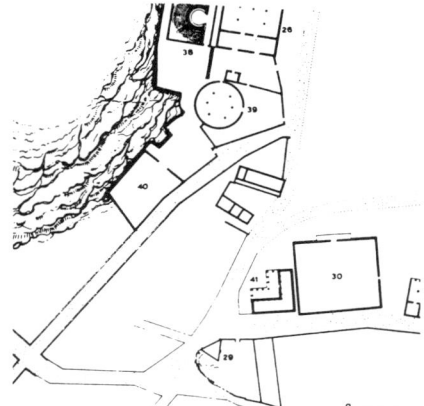
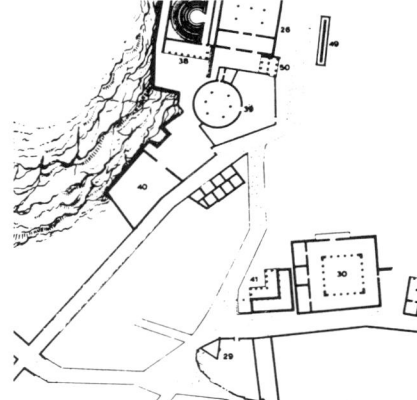

The south-west corner of the Agora at the end of the 5th c. B.C. (I Travlos 1967).

The south-west corner of the Agora around the end of the 4th. c. B.B. (I Travlos 1967).

other facilities, the floorage left for the jurors amounts to 800 m² in the fifth century down to the third quarter of the fourth century, and after the reconstruction only 640 m² are left. Even when the *Ath. Pol.* was composed (in the 320's) the enclosure may have been large enough to contain 1,500 jurors (requiring 600 m² *min.*). It is just possible, but unlikely, that the building could accommodate 2,000 jurors in 404, and it is certainly impossible to find room for 2,500 seated jurors hearing the *eisangelia* against Pistias in the period 336-24.

If, as suggested above, all cases involving more than 500 jurors were tried in the *Heliaia*, we must give up the identification of the *Heliaia* with the rectangular structure in the southwest corner of the Agora, and it can be upheld only if one is prepared to accept one of the following two modifications of the view that the large juries were convened in the *Heliaia*.

Even after the reduction of the floor space in the third quarter of the fourth century the enclosure had seating capacity for 1,500 jurors. Aristotle and Philochoros indicate that most large juries were composed of either 1,000 or 1,500 *dikastai*. When exceptionally a major public action had to be tried by 2,000 or 2,500 *dikastai*, we may assume that the jurors had to listen to the debate standing. In that case the space required for each juror is reduced from 0.4 to 0.25 m². *min.*[59] The 2,500 jurors hearing the *eisangelia* against Pistias would require an auditorium of no more than 625 m². If the case was tried after the reconstruction, when the enclosure was yielding an open space of 661 m², some 36 m² would be left for all other facilities, which is just possible. On the other hand, if the *eisangelia* antedated the reconstruction, there can be no doubt that the rectangular building could accommodate 2,500 standing jurors. So space is not an insurmountable problem, but what about time? One whole day was set off for the hearing of a public action, and if both parties made full use of their speaking time, the trial might run for ca. nine and a half hours.[60] Is it possible for a large crowd, densely packed in a small enclosure to remain standing for one whole day? It is not unprecedented that a mass meeting attended by a standing crowd may run for four or five hours, but I have my doubts about sessions lasting more than nine hours,[61] and so I am inclined to reject the idea of a standing audience when the jurors selected by lot numbered more than 1,500.

Alternatively, it may be held that juries of 1,000 or 1,500 *dikastai* met in the *Heliaia*, whereas the session took place elsewhere if the number of jurors exceeded 1,500. On this assumption the first question to be asked is of course: where did the very large juries meet? Even with our restricted knowledge of the administrative centres in ancient Athens there is one possible answer to this question: In Perikles' Odeion. We know that this building was sometimes used as a law-court in the fifth and in the fourth century.[62] Both the actual remains and the literary sources show that the Odeion could easily accommodate all the 6,000 jurors. According to the excavators' reconstruction the exterior dimensions of the Odeion are approximately 62.40 m × 68.60 m yielding an area of 4.280 m²,[63] and we know from the literary sources that the *proagon* before the Lenaia and the Greater Dionysia took place in the Odeion and that the *proagon* was attended by a large crowd.[64] My principal objection to this assumption is that it does not square with the tradition that the *Heliaia* was the largest of the law courts. It vould be strange to describe the *Heliaia* as τὸ μέγιστον δικαστήριον Ἀθήνησιν, if the Odeion was used whenever a jury of more than 1,500 *dikastai* was convened. On the other hand, it is not impossible: the statement that the *Heliaia* was the largest court may well be taken to mean that it was the largest building used solely or primarily for this purpose, whereas we know that the Odeion was used only occasionally as a law court and normally served other purposes.

THE ATHENIAN *HELIAIA*   25

So far as size is concerned, the identification of the rectangular enclosure with the *Heliaia* is unlikely but not impossible. I have, however, two more objections against the identification: first, the rectangular enclosure was probably unroofed,[65] whereas the *Heliaia* was roofed, if we trust Aristophanes (cf. *supra* page 18). Second, the rectangular enclosure at the southwest corner of the Agora is smaller than other buildings excavated in the north-eastern part of the Agora and convincingly described as law-courts. Beneath the north half of the Stoa of Attalos are the foundations of a series of public buildings most of which have been identified as law-courts. The identification is based primarily on a large concentration, in this area, of finds of dicastic equipment, *viz.* bronze *symbola* and bronze *psephoi*.[66]

Many problems remain to be solved but at the present stage of inquiry the foundations are reconstructed thus: the largest of the buildings in the old block is (A) 'measuring about 22 × 41 m internally with an area of about 900 square meters'.[67] It dates from the period around 400 B.C. and was in use down to the Lycurgan period when the whole area was cleared to make room for a huge square peristyle (never finished) with a total area of more than 3,000 m² and an open court covering 1,500 m².

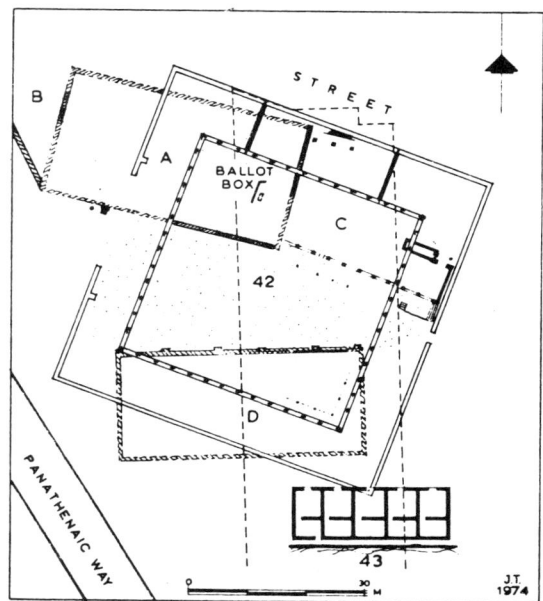

Early Buildings beneath the Stoa of Attalos

Now, if we accept that these buildings were law-courts, and that the *Heliaia* was the largest law-court in Athens, the implication is that both building (A) and the square peristyle have a better claim to be the *Heliaia* than the rectangular enclosure at the southeast corner of the Agora, covering only some 820 m². On the other hand, 'a better claim' does not mean that I intend to locate the *Heliaia* in the northeast corner of the Agora. Building (A) was destroyed in the fourth century B.C. to make room for the square peristyle which, in turn, was demolished in the second century B.C. to make room for the Stoa of Attalos. But Pausanias tells us that the *Heliaia* could still be seen in in the second century A.D.[68] On the assumption that the *Heliaia* (from the archaic to the Roman imperial period) was either the same building or rather, when reconstructed, at least a building located in the same area, Pausanis' information amounts to a rejection of an identification of the *Heliaia* with any of the buildings beneath the Stoa of Attalos.

It is usually assumed that the *Heliaia* was located in the Agora. But we have no evidence. Ar. V. 1108-09 gives the impression that the courtrooms were spread over the city and not concentrated in the Agora.[69] We know that some of the buildings used by the people's court were in the Agora,[70] but we have no source stating that the *Heliaia* was one of these. The only information we have about the location of the *Heliaia* amounts to some notes in lexica and scholia stating that the ἀγορὰ κερκώπων was close to the *Heliaia*.[71] The Kerkopes were ape-like dwarfs connected by legend with Herakles but, metaphorically, κέρκωψ may be used about knaves and rascals,[72] and, according to Eustathios, the ἀγορὰ κερκώπων was the market of the rascals where stolen goods were disposed of. Now, we have no idea whatsoever of where in Athens the ἀγορὰ κερκώπων was to be found, and moreover, the ironical juxtaposition of the *Heliaia* and the 'market of rascals' sounds suspicious. I fear that the source of the lexicographers' notes may be no more than a joke in a comedy or a sardonic remark in some forensic speech.[73]

In conclusion, I question the traditional identification of the *Heliaia*, firstly because the rectangular enclosure at the southwest corner of the Agora is too small to be the *Heliaia;* secondly because it was unroofed whereas the *Heliaia* was presumably roofed; and thirdly because it is smaller than other buildings in the Agora convincingly identified as law-courts, whereas the *Heliaia* was reputed to be the largest court in Athens. The implication is that the *Heliaia* has not yet been found. It was presumably a roofed building with a floorage of more than one thousand square metres. If it was in the Agora, we must look for it on the east side, either to the north or to the south of the Stoa of Attalos.[74] But it is far from certain that the *Heliaia* was situated in the Agora, and here we must leave the question.

II. THE SOLONIAN *HELIAIA*.

I now turn to the history of the *heliaia* and ask: when was the *heliaia* instituted? what kind of institution was the old *heliaia?* and how far back into archaic history can the word *heliaia* be traced? These are difficult questions since we have very few sources antedating the Peloponnesian War. The first datable occurrence of the word *heliaia* is τὴν ἡλιαίαν τὴν τῶν θεσμοθετῶν in Archestratos' rider to the decree about Chalkis of 446/5 (cf. *supra* page 10 no. 1). We must turn to the laws quoted by the orators some of which may be archaic; but since the laws quoted in forensic speeches were taken from the revised law-code of 403-399, how can we know that the word *heliaia* was used in the original version of the law?

One of the laws often held to be from the archaic period and perhaps even Solonian is the section af the homicide law quoted by Demosthenes in 23.28 (cf. *supra* page 11 no. 6).[75] Here δικαστής is used in the same sense as δικάζειν in the original Drankonian *axon* and, once more, opposed to διαγιγνώσκειν.[76] So the section quoted may be an early revision of Drakon's homicide law. On the other hand, ἡλιαία is obviously not a court of appeal but a court of first instance, which, according to the traditional view of the Solonian ἔφεσις εἰς τὸ δικαστήριον, points to a much later date.[77]

The preserved section of the νόμος κλοπῆς provides us with a much better clue to the problem. The section is quoted both in Lys. 10.16 and in D. 24.105 (cf. *supra* page 11 nos. 4 & 5). In Lysias the speaker discusses a whole series of archaic laws described as τοὺς νόμους τοὺς Σόλωνος τοὺς παλαιούς.[78] The speech was delivered in 384/3[79] and, after Ruschenbusch's careful investigations of Solon's laws,[80] there can be little doubt that οἱ παλαιοὶ νόμοι (in opposition to the revised version of the code) are the original Solonian *axones*. The Lysias passage shows that the word ἡλιαία was used by Solon in his law code, and the phrases ἐὰν προστιμήσῃ ἡ ἡλιαία (Lys. and Dem.) and προστιμᾶσθαι δὲ τὸν βουλόμενον (Dem.) are incompatible with a verdict passed by a single judge and strongly suggest some form of jury system.

So far we are on safe ground. The next step in the argument is more debatable. There was in fourth-century Athens a strong tradition that the people's court was introduced by Solon.[81] If we combine this tradition with the belief that the word *heliaia* occurred on the Solonian *axones* (demonstrably in the νόμος κλοπῆς and probably in many other *nomoi* as well) the implication is that Solon instituted the *heliaia* = the people's court. The tradition about the origin of the *dikasteria* can of course be questioned but it seems to be accepted by most scholars.[82]

Conversely, the fourth-century tradition is almost universally rejected when we ask which kind of institution the *heliaia* was. According to Aristotle's *Politics,* and probably the *Ath. Pol.* as well, the *heliaia* comprised a plurality of law courts manned with sworn jurors. But most contemporary historians prefer to believe that the *heliaia* was the *ekklesia* in its judicial capacity. Again the accepted opinion is judiciously stated by MacDowell: 'it is now generally assumed that Solon's lawcourt was simply the assembly of Athenian citizens, the *Ekklesia;* for some reason not known to us it was conventional to call the assembly *Eliaia* instead of *Ekklesia* when the purpose of its meeting was judicial.'[83]

This view of the *heliaia* is based, first, on a debatable etymology and interpretation of the word *heliaia;* second, on an interpretation (which in my opinion is a misinterpretation) of Arist. *Ath. Pol.* 9.1-2; third, on a questionable set of *a priori* assumptions about the development of Athenian institutions. Finally, two sources which may support the identification of the *heliaia* with the *ekklesia* are never adduced. I shall discuss the foundation of the accepted opinion and at the same time state my own view, which is in fact a dilemma: if we trust the sources, the *heliaia* was a new body of government and not a judicial session of the *ekklesia*.[84] On the other hand, if we reject the unanimous fourth-century tradition about Solon as a reflection of the political controversy over the *patrios politeia,* we must suspend judgement.

The main argument adduced in support of the identification of the

Solonian *heliaia* with the people's assembly is the etymology of the word *heliaia*. The Attic form ἡλιαία is derived form the Doric ἁλιαία/ἁλία.[85] Now, *haliaia/halia* mean 'assembly' and in many Doric city states these two words are used as technical terms for the people's assembly.[86] The inference is that the Attic *heliaia* has the same meaning as the Doric *haliaia* and must denote a meeting of the entire people. This line of argument is open to several objections.

First, the etymology is not straightforward. Both ἁλία and ἁλιαία are dirived from ἁλής, the etymology of which is ἁ-Fἰ-νής.[87] The long α in ἁλής is the result of a contraction, but this α is retained in Ionic/Attic and is never changed to an η. Accordingly Herodotos has ἁλίη and not ἡλίη.[88] So ἡλιαία cannot, phonologically, be derived from ἁλιαία, and we must admit either that the etymology is wrong or, preferably, that ἡλιαία is a Doric loan-word transformed into a hyper-Attic form. The second possibility is, of course, adopted by all scholars supporting the identification of the *heliaia* with the people's assembly.

Second, the view that *heliaia* must denote a meeting of the entire people is based on a too narrow interpretation of the words *halia/haliaia*. The meaning of *halia/haliaia* is indeed 'assembly' and the words usually denote the people's assembly, but the words *halia/haliaia* do not *mean* 'popular assembly', and they may sometimes refer to other forms of assembly. One example is a decision made by the Delphic *phratria* the Labyadai, ἐν τῇ ἁλίᾳ.[89] Here *halia* applies to a meeting of a section of the people. Consequently, even accepting that *heliaia* is derived from *haliaia/halia* and has the same meaning, we need not infer that *heliaia* must denote a meeting of the entire people (all citizens above 18) rather than a major section of the people (a thousand or perhaps even several thousand sworn citizens above thirty selected by lot for one year). In my opinion the word ἡλιαία may apply equally well to the entire people or to a major section, and so the argument from etymology carries no weight.

If we assume, with most historians, for the sake of argument, that the *heliaia* was a meeting of the entire people, there is a problem in the terminological distinction between political and judicial meetings. A rigid distinction is usually drawn between judicial and political meetings, while it is maintained that the *institution* is the same in both cases, *viz.* the people's assembly. It is of course possible, but not very likely, that Solon invented a new name for a familiar institution because it was invested with new powers. It is much simpler to assume that the new name was invented because it was a new institution. Furthermore, if we accept that *heliaia* was no more than the technical term for the people's assembly when sitting in judgement, we would expect the term to survive in those cases where the assembly, in the classical period, was transformed into a jury hearing major political actions. And Rhodes does in fact suggest that 'the last active occurrence of the old sense of the word [*heliaia*] is its restoration in Clinias' tribute decree,' passed some 15 years after Ephialtes' reforms.[90] But, even accepting the restoration, there is no evidence whatsoever that *heliaia* here denotes the assembly and not a *dikasterion*. On the contrary, we know that a judicial session of the assembly later in the fifth century was called *ekklesia* (and not *heliaia*.).[91] Nothing prevents us from assuming that this is the traditional terminology and that a judicial meeting of the assembly was called *ekklesia* also in the sixth century B.C.

There are, however, two sources which may support an identification of the Solonian *heliaia* with the people's assembly. But to the best of my knowledge they have never been adduced by any of the adherents of the identification. As I mentioned previously on page 27, the only preserved *nomos* mentioning the *heliaia* which can safely be assigned to the Solonian *axones* is the law about theft quoted in Lys. 10.16 and D. 24.105 (cf. *supra* page 11 nos 4 & 5). The final clause quoted by Demosthenes is that the additional penalty of five days and nights in the pillory is to be proposed by *ho boulomenos*. Who is *ho boulomenos*? According to Lipsius,[92] the meaning of the phrase προστιμᾶσθαι δὲ τὸν βουλόμενον is that any of the *heliasts* is entitled to propose that the additional penalty be applied in this case. Now, this provision points to ekklesiastic procedure and is unique in a law dealing with the *dikasteria*. One of the major differences between the *ekklesia* and the *dikasteria* is that the *ekklesiastai* were entitled not only to vote but also to speak and to make proposals, whereas the only task performed by the *dikastai* was to vote. In the *ekklesia*, where an open debate takes place, *ho boulomenos* denotes any citizen attending the meeting,[93] whereas, in the *dikasterion*, there is only one *ho boulomenos*, viz. the prosecutor.[94] The debate is restricted to the parties in the case, and the jurors are supposed to remain impassive and to listen. The only way in which the *dikastai* may interfere with the debate is θόρυβος, which was probably tolerated although it was against the rules of procedure.

Now, a Solonian law about theft providing for a proposal to be moved from the floor is in conformity with the usual form of debate in the *ekklesia,* and does not square with what we know about procedure in the *dikasteria.* This is, in my opinion, the only argument which lends some support to the view that the *heliaia* was the people's assembly, But, on reflexion, I find even this argument invalid: *ho boulomenos* in the law about theft is probably no more than a standard reference to the prosecutor, and not to anyone present who so wishes = *hoi heliastai,* and this can be demonstrated by a comparison with the law about *apagoge* quoted by Demosthenes immediately after the law about theft. The procedure in an *apagoge* is that the offender is first arrested, then imprisoned, and then brought before the *heliaia* to be prosecuted by ὁ βουλόμενος οἷς ἔξεστιν. But here *ho boulomenos* is certainly the man who arrested the offender, and not any Athenian citizen who takes it upon himself to prosecute the imprisoned offender. We have numerous sources showing that prosecution in an *apagoge* was an obligation incumbent on ὁ ἀπαγαγών.[95] Similarly, in the νόμος κλοπῆς, *ho boulomenos* is not 'anyone who so wishes' i.e. one of the *heliastai,* but the prosecutor. This is the interpretation offered by e.g. Weil and Harrison,[96] and it is in my opinion to be preferred to Lipsius' reconstruction of the procedure. But then the law no longer supports the identification of the *heliaia* with the people's assembly.

The other source is the law quoted in D. 46.26 (*supra* page 12 no. 9) where, apparently, a *distinction* is made between *heliaia* and *dikasteria:* ἐάν τις συνιστῆται, ἢ συνδεκάζῃ τὴν ἡλιαίαν ἢ τῶν δικαστηρίων τι τῶν 'Ἀθήνησιν ἢ τὴν βουλήν ... If τῶν δικαστηρίων τι is interpreted as a reference to the people's court, *heliaia* may be taken to denote the people's assembly in its judicial capacity, so that the law testifies to the traditional tripartition of the bodies of government: *demos, boule* and *dikasteria.*[97] But this interpretation presupposes that the law is archaic and dates before Ephialtes' reforms. According to Arist. *Ath. Pol.* 27.5, however, the first occurrence of any attempt to bribe the jurors was the trial of Anytos in 409. Similarly, the phrase ἑταιρείαν συνιστῇ ἐπὶ καταλύσει τοῦ δήμου (later in the law) indicates that the law was passed only after the oligarchic revolution in 411 and is contemporaneous with the *nomos eisangeltikos*. So the law quoted in D. 46.26 must be fairly recent, and I agree with Gernet who suggests in the Budé edition of the speech (193 note 2) that the *nomos* quoted was probably passed in connection with the revision of the law code in the last decade of the fifth century. But in this case *heliaia* must be a reference to the people's court and τῶν δικαστηρίων τι is a general reference to all courts, i.e. the people's court and other courts such as the homicide courts (cf. *supra* note 19).[98]

So there is no support for the identification of the *heliaia* with the people's assembly, and a serious objection against the view is that it is contradicted by an important passage in Aristotle's *Politics* and by the account of Solon's reforms in the *Ath. Pol.* I begin with the passage from the *Politics*, 1273b35-74a5: Σόλωνα δ' ἔνιοι μὲν οἴονται νομοθέτην γενέσθαι σπουδαῖον· ὀλιγαρχίαν τε γὰρ καταλῦσαι λίαν ἄκρατον οὖσαν, καὶ δουλεύοντα τὸν δῆμον παῦσαι, καὶ δημοκρατίαν καταστῆσαι τὴν πάτριον, μείξαντα καλῶς τὴν πολιτείαν· εἶναι γὰρ τὴν μὲν ἐν Ἀρείῳ πάγῳ βουλὴν ὀλιγαρχικόν, τὸ δὲ τὰς ἀρχὰς αἱρετὰς ἀριστοκρατικόν, τὰ δὲ δικαστήρια δημοτικόν. ἔοικε δὲ Σόλων ἐκεῖνα μὲν ὑπάρχοντα πρότερον οὐ καταλῦσαι, τήν τε βουλὴν καὶ τὴν τῶν ἀρχῶν αἵρεσιν, τὸν δὲ δῆμον καταστῆσαι, τὰ δικαστήρια ποιήσας ἐκ πάντων. διὸ καὶ μέμφονταί τινες αὐτῷ· λῦσαι γὰρ θάτερα, κύριον ποιήσαντα τὸ δικαστήριον πάντων, κληρωτὸν ὄν. In this passage it is explicitly stated that the Solonian *dikasteria* were manned by jurors selected by lot. Historians who believe that the Solonian *heliaia* was a session of the whole people sometimes attempt to 'exonerate' Aristotle and discredit the information by maintaining that this view is held, not by Aristotle, but by some other authors who are even criticized by Aristotle, so that Aristotle's own view may indeed have been that the *heliaia* was originally identical with the people's assembly. (*cf.* e.g. Rhodes [1979] 104) A closer analysis of the passage lends no support to this interpretation. On the contrary. Aristotle opens his account of Solon by paraphrasing some other authors who *praise* Solon for having created the ancestral democracy by mixing the Areopagos, election of magistrates and the popular courts. The paraphrase stops at 1273b41,[99] and in the ἔοικε δέ clause Aristotle objects that Solon did not interfere with the Areopagos and election of magistrates, but was responsible only for the creation of democracy by reforming the judiciary. Then he proceeds to quote some other authors who *criticize* Solon for diminishing the powers of the Areopagos and the elected magistrates by giving sovereignty to the people's court which was manned by jurors selected by lot. Admittedly, Aristotle does not say explicitly to what degree he accepts the view of the second group of authors, but the entire passage allows us to draw two conclusions: (a) in 1274a3 the reference to *dikasteria* in the plural is part of Aristotle's own view, and (b) in the same line Aristotle states that the courts were manned, not by the entire people, but by jurors *selected from the entire people* (ἐκ πάντων), and since sortition, in this case, is the only conceivable form of selection he must agree with Solon's critics that the jurors were selected by lot. So Aristotle holds that there was a plurality of *dikasteria* manned with jurors, and the view that the *heliaia* was a judicial session of the assembly can only be maintained if we reject the information given by Aristotle (1273b41-74a3) and by the authors referred to, both those who praise Solon (1273b35-41) and those who criticize his reform (1274a3ff).

An inspection of *Ath. Pol.* 7-9 leads to the same conclusion. The relevant passages are 7.3 and 9.1-2: τοῖς δὲ τὸ θητικὸν τελοῦσιν ἐκκλησίας καὶ δικαστηρίων μετέδωκε μόνον (Σόλων) (7.3). δοκεῖ δὲ τῆς Σόλωνος πολιτείας τρία ταῦτ᾽ εἶναι τὰ δημοτικώτατα· ... τρίτον δέ, <ᾧ> μάλιστά φασιν ἰσχυκέναι τὸ πλῆθος, ἡ εἰς τὸ δικαστήριον ἔφεσις· κύριος γὰρ ὢν ὁ δῆμος τῆς ψήφου κύριος γίγνεται τῆς πολιτείας. ... καὶ πάντα βραβεύειν καὶ τὰ κοινὰ καὶ τὰ ἴδια τὸ δικαστήριον (9.1-2).

Is this account of Solon's reforms compatible with the information given in the *Politics,* or conversely with the modern historians' belief that the *heliaia* was originally a session of the whole people? The only way of answering this question is to study the use of the word *dikasterion.* In the singular, *dikasterion* possibly, perhaps even plausibly, denotes an undivided *heliaia* to be identified with the people's assembly. But *dikasteria* in the plural must be a reference to a system of courts and the identification with the assembly must be abandoned.

Some scholars, most recently Rhodes, contrast *dikasteria* in *Pol.* 1273b-74a with ἔφεσις εἰς τὸ δικαστήριον in *Ath. Pol.* 9.1-2.[100] They hold that the singular in *Ath. Pol.* may be a reliable transmission of a genuine tradition about the undivided *heliaia,* whereas the plural *dikasteria* in Arist. *Pol.* 1273b is an anachronism reflecting only the fourth-century debate about the ancestral constitution and Solon's introduction of the Athenian democracy. But against this preference of the *Ath. Pol.* over the *Politics* it must be objected that the plural *dikasteria* occurs not only in *Pol.* 1273b, but also in *Ath. Pol.* 7.3. And so, if we treat the description of the Solonian reforms in the *Ath. Pol.* as a whole, we have to make a choice between two interpretations. (a) *Dikasterion* in 9.1-2 represents the author's correct view of an undivided *heliaia,* whereas *dikasteria* in 7.3 is an inconsistency, or perhaps an inadvertent extrapolation of contemporary terminology back into the archaic period. (b) The author is consistent in his description of the Solonian reforms; *dikasterion* in 9.1 has the same meaning as *dikasteria* in 7.3 and refers to the system of *dikasteria*. Now, an examination of the fourth century terminology leaves little doubt that (b) is the preferable view. In general references to the people's court in classical texts the plural τὰ δικαστήρια is the common form,[101] but sometimes the institution is referred to in the singular. One example is the recently discovered silver coinage law, *Hesperia* 43 (1974) 24-27: οἱ [ἄ]ρχοντες ... ἐσαγόντων ἐς τὸ δικαστήριον. οἱ δὲ θε[σ-μ]οθ[έται π]αρεχόντων αὐτοῖς ἐπικληροῦντες δικα[στήριον ... Another example is Arist. *Pol.* 1282a34-36: οὐ γὰρ ὁ δικαστὴς οὐδ' ὁ βουλευτὴς οὐδ' ὁ ἐκκλησιαστὴς ἄρχων ἐστίν, ἀλλὰ τὸ δικαστήριον καὶ ἡ βουλὴ καὶ ὁ δῆμος.[102] There is nothing surprising about this use of the generic article denoting the system of *dikasteria,* and so the singular τὸ δικαστήριον in *Ath. Pol.* 9.1 has no specific historical significance. It denotes the system of *dikasteria* and is consistent with the use of the plural in 7.3 and in *Pol.* 1273b-74a. In conclusion, the account of Solon's reforms in the *Ath. Pol.* testifies to a distinction between the people's assembly and the people's court and to a plurality of *dikasteria* as early as the sixth century B.C.

Historians who identify the *heliaia* with the people's assembly reject the information given in Aristotle's *Politics* and in the *Ath. Pol.* about a plurality of law-courts manned by jurors appointed by lot. The reason adduced is an argument *a priori.* According to these historians it is an anachronism to assume the existence in the early sixth century of a plurality of *dikasteria* manned by citizens drawn by lot from a panel of 6,000 jurors, which was chosen annually from those who volunteered for service.[103]

It would of course be anachronistic to extrapolate the classical system of law courts back into the sixth century. But it is not Aristotle who is guilty of the anachronism, but the modern historians who impute to Aristotle much more than he says. Aristotle never says that the Solonian panel of jurors numbered 6,000. There may have been a panel composed of, say, 1,000 or 2,000 jurors. We do not know. The magic figure 6,000 is not attested until the introduction of ostracism and the construction of Pnyx I around 500 or perhaps even later.[104] In the *Politics*, Aristotle refers to sortition, but he does not say that there was a *daily* sortition of jurors. On the contrary, we know from Aristophanes that a daily sortition was not introduced until the fourth century.[105] Consequently, the sortition referred to in *Pol.* 1273b-74a must be the annual sortition of jurors serving on the panel, and so the anachronism disappears. Many scholars are now inclined to accept a Solonian council of four hundred and sortition of minor magistrates, and, accepting sortition as an archaic procedure, they can have no objection against an annual sortition of jurors. They must be bound by an argument *a fortiori*. On the other hand, I admit that even an annual sortition of jurors for the panel may be rejected as an anachronism by scholars who maintain that sortition was a purely democratic procedure and that a council of four hundred, sortition of minor magistrates, and sortition of a panel of jurors in the sixth century is a fantasy created by fourth-century political propaganda.

Furthermore, we do not know when the number of *dikastai* hearing a case was fixed to, say, 201, 401, or 501 *etc*. But it seems reasonable to suppose that the limitation on the number of jurors hearing a case was necessitated by the introduction of dikastic pay, and accordingly introduced in the middle of the fifth century at the same time as the *dikastikon*.[106] Before this reform, a case may have been heard by all those jurors who cared to turn up on a particular day.

Finally, many historians reject the possibility of 'a plurality of law courts as early as the time of Solon' and prefer the idea of a single undivided *heliaia*, which was not split up into *dikasteria* until the reforms of Ephialtes in 462.[107] In the previous section of this article I hope to have demonstrated that the occurrence of the singular *dikasterion* in the *Ath.*

Pol. cannot be adduced as evidence of an undivided Solonian *heliaia*, and I shall now discuss the possibility of a plurality of jury courts in the sixth century B.C.

First, what does a plurality of jury courts mean? It is an ambiguous phrase which allows of several interpretations, *viz.* (a) successive sessions of one jury presided over by different magistrates and hearing different types of action; (b) simultaneous sessions of several juries presided over by different magistrates; (c) several different court buildings (or places) to be used either simultaneously or one at a time according to the type of action to be heard.

On the reasonable assumption that Solon allowed the magistrate who received a case to preside over the *dikasterion* which heard the case, there is nothing anachronistic about a plurality of *dikasteria* in sense (a), and it is easy to suggest *exempli gratia* a reconstruction which leaves room for a plurality of law-courts in sense (b) but avoids the anachronisms involved in extrapolating the late fifth century dikastic system back into the Solonian period. On any court day all the *heliastai* who so wished turned up and served as jurors. Presumably, the panel of *heliastai* present might hear several cases in the course of one day. Sometimes the same magistrate presided over the *heliaia* in all the cases, and different magistrates had different court days assigned to them. Sometimes the presidency might have changed during the day, and it cannot be precluded that the *heliaia* very early, perhaps even from the beginning, might split up into two sections, so that two different (boards of) magistrates might have their cases heard simultaneously. In this case the *heliastai* were presumably divided into two sections of equal strenght. Probably no limitations were put on the number of *heliastai* hearing a case until the introduction of dikastic pay in the middle of the fifth century. And, in any case, the *heliastai* were not split up into ten annual sections each assigned to an individual magistrate until after the introduction of the ten *phylai* by Kleisthenes.

On the other hand, I believe that we can safely reject a plurality of law-courts in sense (c). In the classical period, as stated above on page 10. *heliaia* denoted either the people's court or a courtroom. It is reasonable to assume that the name of the institution was assigned to a specific locality because, originally, all sessions of the *heliaia* took place in the

Heliaia. But this view is not incompatible with a plurality of law courts in sense (b). We have no idea whether the first *Heliaia* was a building or a fenced area. In the classical period it was a large building probably with accommodation for at least 2,500 jurors, and nothing prevents us from assuming that, in the sixth century, two cases may have been heard simultaneously in the *Heliaia* by two different sections of *heliastai*.

I have now discussed and, I hope, disposed of the *a priori* arguments adduced against the information we have from Aristotle's *Politics* and the *Ath. Pol.* I shall now in turn adduce some *a priori* arguments against the identification of the *heliaia* with the people's assembly.

Let us assume, for the sake of argument, that the *heliaia* created by Solon was a meeting of the entire people. In this case every petty dispute referred by a magistrate to the *dikasterion* would lead to a hearing of the case by the entire people. Now, accepting with Ruschenbusch and others[108] that *ephesis* means 'reference' (and not appeal), the result would be an incredibly high number of sessions of the people, and the identification of the *heliaia* with the assembly is simply ruled out. But even accepting the traditional interpretation of *ephesis* i.e. that it means 'appeal against a magistrate's decision',[109] it is most unlikely that all major and minor appeal cases had to be heard by the entire people. The Athenians were undoubtedly less litigious before the introduction of radical democracy in the second half of the fifth century; but if the assembly in addition to the political meetings had to hear all appeal cases, the result must have been a very high number of sessions.[110] Rhodes, however, following Hignett and others, suggests that the number of ordinary meetings was raised from ten to forty only towards the end of the fifth century.[111] The figures ten and forty are both questionable,[112] but I find the general view of the development of the *ekklesia* plausible, and it is incompatible with the theory that the *heliaia* was not separated form the *ekklesia* until after Ephialtes. There is much to be said for Ruschenbusch's interpretation of *ephesis,* and so the identification of the *heliaia* with the assembly is impossible, and even on the traditional interpretation of *ephesis,* the identification is most unlikely.

Second, the traditional Anglo-American reconstruction of how political trials were heard in Archaic Athens leads to a peculiar view of the development of the Athenian administration of justice. It is generally believed that the author of the *Ath. Pol.* is right when he ascribes to Solon a law about *eisangeliai* heard by the Areopagos, and that the Areopagos did in fact hear all *eisangeliai* down to 462.[113] Next, the accepted opinion is that the essence of Ephialtes' reform was to deprive the Areopagos of its right to hear *eisangeliai,* and to transfer most of the judicial powers from the *heliaia* = the people's assembly to the new *dikasteria* = a plurality of law-courts manned with jurors selected by lot. Now, let us assume that Ephialtes created the *dikasteria* and took away from the Areopagos the right to hear *eisangeliai.* We know that *eisangeliai* after Ephialtes and down to the middle of the fourth century were sometimes heard by the people's assembly and sometimes referred to a *dikasterion.*[114] So we are asked to believe that Ephialtes took away from the people's assembly (= the undivided *heliaia*) all its traditional jurisdiction, but by the same reform invested the assembly with new judicial powers which the people had never had before. It is of course possible, but not very likely. I prefer to believe that the people had a very old right to hear at least some political trials, and that this right was maintained first when Solon created the *heliaia* and again when the *eisangelia* was introduced, presumably by Kleisthenes. So the *eisangelia* heard by the assembly was not a novelty introduced by Ephialtes, but a traditional form of administration of justice. And this view is in conformity with our scanty sources: Aristotle states in the *Ath. Pol.* 25.2 that Ephialtes deprived the Areopagos of its powers and gave some of them to the *boule,* some to the *demos* and some to the *dikasteria:* ἔπειτα τῆς βουλῆς ... περιείλετο τὰ ἐπίθετα ... καὶ τὰ μὲν τοῖς πεντακοσίοις τὰ δὲ τῷ δήμῳ καὶ τοῖς δικαστηρίοις ἀπέδωκεν. A literal interpretation of this passage shows that the people's court was different from the people's assembly and that it was divided into a plurality of courts before Ephialtes.

Summing up, there is no foundation for the modern view the *heliaia* was the people's assembly sitting in judgement. On the contrary, this view is contradicted by the information we obtain from Arist. *Pol.* and from the *Ath. Pol.* But one crucial question remains: is this information reliable? In our fourth-century sources at least seven judicial and constitutional reforms are ascribed to Solon: (1) *nomothesia* by *nomothetai,*[115] (2) the distinction between *nomoi* and *psephismata,*[116] (3) the γραφὴ νόμον μὴ ἐπιτήδειον θεῖναι,[117] (4) *eisangelia* to the Areopagos for κατάλυσις τοῦ δήμου,[118] (5) a council of four hundred,[119] (6) the ἔφεσις εἰς τὸ δικαστήριον, probably implying the creation of the *heliaia*,[120] (7) every citizen's right to prosecute on behalf of the injured person.[121] Of these seven reforms at least 1-4 are undoubtedly anachronisms, reforms called Solonian because Solon in the fourth century was glorified as the creator of Athenian democracy. But 5 is sometimes and 6-7 are often accepted as genuine Solonian reforms. The rejection of 1-4 or 1-5, however, throws suspicion on 6-7 and there is a case for rejecting all the reforms as anachronisms.[122] I shall reserve a discussion of this crucial problem for a future article and state my conclusion as a dilemma: if we trust our sources (Arist. *Pol.* and the *Ath.Pol.*) the Solonian *heliaia* was a new institution and not the people's assembly in its judicial capacity. The *heliastai* were selected annually by lot from among citizens above thirty who then had to take a solemn oath (ὁ ἡλιαστικὸς ὅρκος), whereas the *ekklesia* was open to all citizens above eighteen without the swearing of any oath. On the other hand, if we reject these sources, the rest is silence.[123]

NOTES

[1] The fifth-century inscriptions (cf. *infra* page 10 nos. 1-3) show that ἡλιαία has no H = [h] *Cf.* L. Threatte *The Grammer of Attic Inscriptions I. Phonology* (Berlin 1980) 500. So the correct form is *Eliaia*, but, for convenience, I retain the traditional *Heliaia*.

[2] The following works will be cited by author's name alone: K. J. Beloch *Griechische Geschichte* I (Strassburg 1912) 365. R.J. Bonner and G. Smith *The Administration of Justice from Homer to Aristotle* I (Chicago 1930) 151-62. G. Busolt *Griechische Geschichte* II (Gotha 1895) 283-87. G. Busolt and H. Swoboda *Griechische Staatskunde* II (München 1926) 850, 1151, 1155. J. Day and M. Chambers *Aristotle's History of Athenian Democracy* (Amsterdam 1967) 87, 183-84. G. Gilbert *Griechische Staatsalterthümer* I (Leipzig 1893) 153-55. G. Grote *A History of Greece* III (London 1847) 170. M.H. Hansen *Demos, Ecclesia and Dicasterion in Classical Athens*, *GRBS* 19 (1978) 141-43 A.R.W. Harrison *The Law of Athens* II (Oxford 1971) 3, 44, 72, 239. C. Hignett *A History of the Athenian Constitution* (Oxford 1952) 97, 216-18. H. Hommel *Heliaia* (Leipzig 1927) 74. F. Jacoby *FGrHist* IIIb (*Suppl.*1954) I 164-67, II 146-53. J.H. Lipsius *Das attische Recht und Rechtsverfahren* I-III (Leipzig 1905-15) 27-30, 168-69. D.M. MacDowell *Heliaia*, *OCD* (Oxford 1970) 493. D.M. MacDowell *Aristophanes' Wasps* (Oxford 1971) 273-75. D.M. MacDowell *The Law in Classical Athens* (London 1978) 29-33. P.J. Rhodes *The Athenian Boule* (Oxford 1972) 168-69. P.J. Rhodes *Eisangelia at*

Athens, JHS 99 (1979) 104. E. Ruschenbusch ῾Ηλιαία. *Die Tradition über das solonische Volksgericht, Historia* 14 (1965) 381-84. E. Ruschenbusch *Untersuchungen zur Geschichte des athenischen Strafrechts* (Köln 1968) 78-82. S.B. Smith, *The Establishment of the Public Courts at Athens, TAPhA* 56 (1925) 106-19. Th. Thalheim, ῾Ηλιαία, *RE* VII (1912) 2852. H.A. Thompson and R.E. Wycherley *The Athenian Agora XIV. The Agora of Athens* (Princeton 1972) 63-65. H.T. Wade-Gery *Essays in Greek History* (Oxford 1958) 173-74, 195-97. R.E. Wycherley *The Athenian Agora III. Literary and Epigraphical Testimonia* (Princeton 1957) 145-46. R.E. Wycherley *The Stones of Athens* (Princeton 1978) 35, 53-54.

[3] The documents are quoted *infra* on pages 10-12. In all cases the reference is to the institution. The only problematical source is no. 3 *IG* I³ 71.13-14, cf. note 7.

[4] The literary sources are quoted *infra* on page 15. In addition to the preserved references to the *Heliaia* (all in sense b) we know from Harp. s.v. ἡλιαία that Lysias in his (lost) speech *Against Glaukon* mentioned the *heliaia* frequently: Λυσίας ἐν μὲν τῷ πρὸς Γλαύκωνα τὴν ἡλιαίαν πολλάκις ὀνομάζει, ἐν δὲ τῷ κατὰ Φιλωνίδου, εἰ γνήσιος, τῷ ἡλιάζεσθαι ἐχρήσατο. Here, of course, we do not know whether ἡλιαία was used in sense (a) or (b).

[5] The same view is expressed by e.g. Busolt/Swoboda (1151), Bonner and Smith (156) and Hignett (216).

[6] In addition to the inscriptions where ἡλιαία can be read on the stone, the word has been restored in the following cases: *IG* I³ 21.33-34 as restored by J.H. Oliver cf. *SEG* X.14.35-36: h[οι δ' ἄρχοντες δικαστὰς καθιστάντον, κατὰ φυλὰς] νέμαντες καὶ κλερόσαντε[ς αὐτὸς ἐν τῆι ἐλιαίαι ...] *IG* I³ 105.40 as restored by H.T. Wade-Gery in *ABSA* 33 (1932-33) 121: ['Αθεναίον] μεδὲ hενί: μέ[τε] βολει μέτε ἐ[λιαίαι. *IG* I³ 34.37-39 as restored by Hill and Meritt cf. *SEG* X.31: [hō δ' ἄν] καταγνοῖ h[ε βολέ, μὲ τιμᾶν αὐτ]ōι κυρία ἔστο [ἀλλ' ἐσ]φερέτο ἐς τ[ὲν ἐλιαίαν εὐθύ]ς. *IG* I³ 71.49: δίκ]ας [ἐσαγόντον ἄνευ τές ἐλιαίας καὶ τ]ὸν ἄλλον δικαστερίον ... *Hesperia* 10 (1941) 67 no. 31.32 as restored by J.H. Oliver [καὶ κατὰ τὰς στ]ήλα[ς] τε[ι]μάτω αὐτῷ ἡ [ἡλιαία, ἐὰν ἁλῷ] τ[ί χρὴ παθεῖν ἢ ἀπο]τεῖσ[αι (first century B.C.). *IG* I² 412.4-5 as restored by M.H. Hansen *infra* page 119: προστιμάτω δὲ [αὐτῶι ἡ ἡλιαία ὅτου ἄ]ν δ[οκε]ῖ ἄξιος εἶναι ἀπ[οτεῖσαι ...

[7] If we accept the restoration of the end of line 13, the meaning must be that a person selected by lot and the *polemarchos* shall perform the *anakrisis* in the *Heliaia*. Since the *anakrisis* was carried out by the magistrate unassisted by the jurors, ἐν τῇ ἡλιαίᾳ must refer to the building and not to the institution, cf. D. 47.12 quoted *infra* on page 15. But not a single letter of the phrase ἀνακρινάντων τὰς δίκας is left, and the restoration is so arbitrary that it cannot be adduced as an occurrence of *Heliaia* in sense (b).

[8] Admittedly, this source is not a document inserted in a speech and read out to the jurors by the secretary. It is part of Demosthenes' argumentation, but at the same time it is a direct quotation of the curse which in D. 19.70 is called a *nomos*. So the passage must be classified as a document testifying to official language, and not to the language used by the orators.

[9] Nos. 1, 2, 10, 12. Cf. furthermore Ar. *V.* 891 (ἡλιαστής) and 935 (ὁ θεσμοθέτης)

[10] Cf. e.g. Lipsius 169 and Wycherley (1957) 145.

[11] For the phrase τοὺς ἄρχοντας ὧν ἕκαστοι δικασταί εἰσι cf. D. 43.71: τὰς δὲ δίκας εἶναι περὶ τούτων πρὸς τοὺς ἄρχοντας, ὧν ἕκαστοι δικασταί εἰσι.

¹² D. 24.21: τοὺς δὲ νομοθέτας εἶναι ἐκ τῶν ὀμωμοκότων τὸν ἡλιαστικὸν ὅρκον. Hyp. 3.40: ὑπαναγνῶναι ... τὸν ὅρκον τὸν ἡλιαστικόν. Cf. Harp. s.v. Ἀρδηττος; Suda s.v. ἡλιαστής (215); Schol. D. 24.21. D. 24.148-50: ὁ τῶν ἡλιαστῶν ὅρκος.
¹³ Ar. Nu. 863: ὂν πρῶτον ὀβολὸν ἔλαβον ἡλιαστικόν. Cf. Ar. V. 195.
¹⁴ D. 24.50: ΝΟΜΟΣ ... ἔνδειξιν εἶναι αὐτοῦ, καθάπερ ἐάν τις ὀφείλων τῷ δημοσίῳ ἡλιάζηται; Ar. V. 772 ἡλιάσει πρὸς ἥλιον; Ar. Lys. 380: ἀλλ' οὐκέθ' ἡλιάζει. cf. Ar. Eq. 798. and Lys. Fr. 246 (= Harp. s.v. ἡλιαία καὶ ἡλίασις).
¹⁵ D. 24.150: ΟΡΚΟΣ ΗΛΙΑΣΤΩΝ ... οὐδὲ δῶρα δέξομαι τῆς ἡλιάσεως ἕνεκεν οὔτ' αὐτός ...
¹⁶ Ar. Eq. 255: ὦ γέροντες ἡλιασταί; V. 88: φιληλιαστής ἐστιν ὡς οὐδεὶς ἀνήρ; V. 206: ἡλιαστὴς ὀροφίας; V. 891: εἴ τις θύρασιν ἡλιαστής, εἰσίτω· V. 1341: ποῦ 'στιν <ἡμῖν>- ἡλιαστής; Fr. 210: ὁ δ' ἡλιαστὴς εἷρπε πρὸς τὴν κιγκλίδα.
¹⁷ In Hesperia Suppl. 17 (supra no. 11) εἰσαγαγεῖν δὲ καὶ τοὺς θεσμοθέτας τὴν δοκιμασίαν εἰς τὴν ἡλιαίαν is the equivalent of the much more common: τοὺς δὲ θεσμοθέτας εἰσαγαγεῖν τὴν δοκιμασίαν εἰς τὸ δικαστήριον (IG II² 682.96-98 etc.).
¹⁸ In Antipho 6.21 and D. 47.12 (quoted infra page 15). All the other occurrences of heliaia and its derivatives are in documents inserted in forensic speeches or quoted by the speaker. On Lys. Fr. 66 (= Harp. s.v. ἡλιαία καὶ ἡλίασις) cf. supra n. 4.
¹⁹ Cf. M.H. Hansen The Prosecution of Homicide in Athens: A Reply, GRBS 22 (1981) 16 with note 10.
²⁰ Cf. the examples discussed by Lysias in 10.15-21. In the republication of Drakon's law on homicide the provision καὶ οἱ πρότερον κτείναντες ἐν τῷδε τῷ θεσμῷ ἐνεχέσθων is retained (IG I³ 104.19-20 = D. 43.57) although it has no longer any meaning, Similarly, in Solon's law on adoption and wills, the provision ὅσοι μὴ ἐπεποίηντο ... ὅτε Σόλων εἰσῄει εἰς τὴν ἀρχήν, ... is left unchanged in the revised law code of 403-399 (D. 46.14; 44.68). And in Patrokleides' decree of 405 an exemption clause (And. 1.78) seems to be a verbatim repetition of a similar clause in Solon's amnesty law (Plu. Sol. 19.4).
²¹ Furthermore, ἐν τῷ τῶν θεσμοθετῶν δικαστηρίῳ (And. 1.28) is probably Andokides' paraphrase of ἡ ἡλιαία ἡ τῶν θεσμοθετῶν found in the documents (supra nos. 1 & 2).
²² Cf. also Lex. Seg. 310.28; Phot. s.v. ἡλιαία; Suda s.v. ἡλιαία καὶ ἡλιάζεσθαι (218); Schol. D. 24.21.
²³ Quoted from the Teubner edition by H. Oppermann who, cautiously, follows Hommel. It is of no consequence for my argument whether or not the Ath. Pol. is by Aristotle and I take no position on the question.
²⁴ Wycherley (1957) 145.
²⁵ Harp. s.v. ἡλιαία καὶ ἡλίασις: ἡλιαία μέν ἐστι τὸ μέγιστον δικαστήριον τῶν Ἀθήνησιν, ἐν ᾧ τὰ δημόσια τῶν πραγμάτων ἐκρίνετο, χιλίων δικαστῶν ἢ χιλίων καὶ πεντακοσίων συνιόντων. συνῄεσαν δὲ οἱ μὲν χίλιοι ἐκ δυοῖν δικαστηρίων, οἱ δὲ χίλιοι πεντακόσιοι ἐκ τριῶν. Suda s.v. ἡλιαία καὶ ἡλίασις (219): ἡλιαία μέν ἐστι τὸ μέγιστον δικαστήριον Ἀθήνησιν, ἐν ᾧ τὰ δημόσια τῶν πραγμάτων ἐκρίνετο, χιλίων δικαστῶν ἢ χιλίων καὶ πεντακοσίων συνιόντων. συνίασι δὲ οἱ μὲν χίλιοι ἐκ δυοῖν δικαστηρίων, οἱ δὲ χίλιοι πεντακόσιοι ἐκ τριῶν. Lex. Seg. 262.10-13: ἡλιαία μέγα δικαστήριον Ἀθήνησιν, ἐν ᾧ τὰ μέγιστα τῶν δημοσίων πραγμάτων ἐκρίνετο. ἦν δὲ χιλίων πεντακοσίων καὶ ἑνός. συνῄεσαν δὲ οἱ μὲν χίλιοι πεντακόσιοι ἐκ τριῶν φυλῶν. Lex Patm. in D. 23.28: Ἡλιαία: τὸ μέγα δικαστήριον, ἐν ᾧ τὰ μέγιστα τῶν δημοσίων πραγμάτων ἐκρίνετο. ἦν δέ ποτε μὲν χιλίων ἀνδρῶν καὶ πεντακοσίων καὶ ἑνός· ἦσαν

δὲ οἱ χίλιοι καὶ πεντακόσιοι ἐκ τριῶν δικαστηρίων, οἱ δὲ χίλιοι ἀπὸ δύο δικαστηρίων. Poll. 8.123: ἡ ἡλιαία πεντακοσίων· εἰ δὲ χιλίων δέοι δικαστῶν συνίστατο δύο δικαστήρια, εἰ δὲ πεντακοσίων καὶ χιλίων, τρία. *EM.* s.v. ἡλιαία (427.35) ἡλιαία δέ ἐστι τὸ μέγα δικαστήριον Ἀθηναίων, ἐν ᾧ τὰ δημόσια τῶν πραγμάτων ἐκρίνετο. Schol. D. 24.9: ἐν τοῖς μεγάλοις καὶ ἐσπουδασμένοις πράγμασι συνήρχοντο ἐκ β΄ δικαστηρίων, πληροῦντες ἀριθμὸν χιλίων καὶ ἑνός. Phot. s.v. ἡλιαία: τόπος Ἀθήνησιν, εἰς ὃν συνάγεται δύο δικαστήρια ὅταν χίλιοι δικάζωσιν. *Lex. Seg.* 189.20-21: ἡλιαία καὶ ἡλιάζεσθαι: δικαστήριον ἀνδρῶν χιλίων καὶ ὁ τόπος ἐν ᾧ οὗτοι δικάζουσιν. *Lex. Seg.* 310.29-30: ἡλιαία, καλεῖται δὲ μέγα δικαστήριον καὶ οἱ χίλιοι δικασταί. - Harp. = *Suda* (219); *Lex. Seg.* = *Lex. Patm;* The note in *Lex. Seg.* is closer to Harp. than the note in *Lex. Patm.* All four notes are (via some intermediary source) dependent on Arist. *Ath. Pol.* 68.1. The other notes reproduce only small parts of the information given in *Ath. Pol.*
26 For the etymology cf. *infra* page 29 with note 87. *Cf.* futhermore A. Boegehold, *Philokleon's Court, Hesperia* 36 (1967) 119 with note 33.
27 Didymos' comments on the word *Heliaia* are referred to again in Harp. s.v. ὁ κάτωθεν νόμος.
28 Many scholars do in fact believe that the *Heliaia* was unroofed: cf. Busolt-Swoboda 1155; Thompsom and Wycherley 63; Wycherley (1957) 145; (1978) 59;
29 In Antipho 5.10-11 the speaker objects that the hearing of a homicide trial by the people's court leads to an infringement of the rule that the family of the deceased is not allowed to be ὁμωρόφιος with the person accused of the homicide. Moreover, the Stoa Poikile and the Odeion were roofed buildings used as lawcourts.
30 Harp. s.v. ἡλιαία καὶ ἡλίασις; *Suda* s.v. ἡλιασταί (214) and ἡλιαία (219); Schol. Ar. *Eq.* 255; Schol. Ar. *V.* 88, 772. Other lexicographers state only that the *Heliaia* was τὸ μέγα δικαστήριον: *Lex. Patm.* in D. 23.28; *Lex. Seg.* 262.10-13, 310.29; *Suda* s.v. ἡλιαία (217); *EM* s.v. ἡλιαία (427.36); Schol. D. 24.21 Schol. Ar. *Eq.* 898; Schol. Ar. *Av.* 109. But some of these notes go on to say that the most important cases (τὰ μέγιστα) were heard in the *Heliaia: Lex. Patm.; Lex. Seg.* 262.10-13, 310.29.
31 On the basis of the notes referred to in note 30, Lipsius suggests the following restoration in *Ath. Pol.* 68.1: ὅταν δὲ δέ[ῃ τὰς μεγίστας γραφ]ὰς εἰσαγαγεῖν, συν[έρχεται β΄ δικαστή]ρια εἰς τὴν ἡλιαίαν, and Hommel suggests: τα[ῖς δὲ μεγίσταις συνι]κν[εῖται] εἰς φ΄ καὶ ἃ τρία [δικαστήρια. But against both these restorations it must be objected that some cases were heard by more than 1,500 jurors cf. page 20. So μέγιστον is probably not based on any single word in the *Ath. Pol.* but is either an inference from what Aristotle says or a piece of information based on some other source.
32 Cf. Hommel 72, 77, 79-83.
33 *Ath. Pol.* 67.1 & 3.
34 Cf. Hommel 74. - There is only one source indicating that the *Heliaia* was used simultaneously with the other courts, *viz.* Schol. D. 24.123 (ed. Dindorf 781.13ff.) which, on this question, deserves little attention if any at all.
35 *Ath. Pol.* 67.3; X. *HG* 1.7.23; Aeschines 3.197.
36 I leave out the enigmatic 700 jurors in a homicide trial described by Isokrates in 18.54 and the 1,000 jurors in *IG* I³71.16:hoι δὲ [....]θέτα[ι δικαστέριον] νέον κα[θ]ιστάντον χ[ιλίος δικαστάς. The passage is almost entirely restored and even accepting the restorations we do not learn much about Athenian law since the inscription deals with the federal administration of justice.

³⁷ Cf. M.H. Hansen *Eisangelia* (Odense 1975) 10 with note 14.
³⁸ And. 1.17: καὶ ἠγωνίσατο ἐν ἑξακισχιλίοις Ἀθηναίων, καὶ μετέλαβε δικαστῶν τοσούτων οὐδὲ διακοσίας ψήφους ὁ Σπεύσιππος. Cf. M.H. Hansen *The Sovereignty of the People's Court in Athens in the Fourth Century B.C. and the Public Action against Unconstitutional Proposals* (Odense 1974) Cat. No. 1.
³⁹ D. 24.9: δικαστηρίοιν δυοῖν εἰς ἕνα καὶ χιλίους ἐψηφισμένων. Cf. Hansen (*supra* n.38) Cat. No. 13.
⁴⁰ D. 25.28: γνώσει δικαστηρίων τριῶν (γνώσει Weil: γνώσεσι codd.) Cf. Hansen (*supra* n.38) Cat. No. 29 and M.H. Hansen *Apagoge, Endeixis and Ephegesis* (Odense 1976) 147.
⁴¹ *FGrHist* (328) Fr. 199: ἔστι δ᾽ ὅτε ... τοὺς συκοφαντουμένους εἰσήγγελλον, ὡς μὲν Φιλόχορος, χιλίων καθεζομένων, ὡς δὲ Δημήτριος ὁ Φαληρεύς, χιλίων πεντακοσίων. Poll. 8.53. Cf. D. 21.223.
⁴² Plu. *Per*. 32.4: κρίνεσθαι δὲ τὴν δίκην ἔγραψεν ἐν δικασταῖς χιλίοις καὶ πεντακοσίοις, ... Cf. Hansen (*supra* n.37) Cat. No. 6.
⁴³ Lys. 13.35: ὁ δὲ δῆμος ‘ἐν δικαστηρίῳ ἐν δισχιλίοις’ ἐψήφιστο. Cf. Hansen (*supra* n. 37) Cat. No. 67.
⁴⁴ Din. 1.52: καὶ πονηρὸν καὶ προδότην ὄντ᾽ εἰσαγγείλας καὶ ἐξελέγξας ἐν πεντακοσίοις καὶ δισχιλίοις τῶν πολιτῶν... Cf. Hansen (*supra* n. 37) Cat. No. 117.
⁴⁵ Din. 1.107: καὶ πεντακόσιοι καὶ χίλιοι ὄντες τὴν ἁπάσης τῆς πόλεως σωτηρίαν ἐν ταῖς χερσὶν ἔχετε.
⁴⁶ Lys. 13.32, 86; D. 21.180, 194; D. 24.48; Aeschin. 2.13; 3.224; Din. 1.4.
⁴⁷ Hdt. 5.97.2; Pl. *Ax*. 369a. Cf. Pl. *Smp*. 175e.
⁴⁸ Cf. M.H. Hansen, *How Many Athenians Attended the Ecclesia?*, *GRBS* 17 (1976) 131.
⁴⁹ It is apparent from *Ath. Pol*. 66.1 that at least four and presumably even more juries were appointed on an ordinary court day reserved for private actions heard by 401 jurors. So a minimum of 4 × 400 = 1,600 were selected by lot and, estimating the jurors who were rejected at 500-1,500, we arrive at a total of 2-3,000 volunteering for service in the 320's. I have little doubt that the number of *dikastai* volunteering for service in the late fifth century was either the same or greater. My reasons are partly demographic (to be stated elsewhere) and partly that the three obols paid out as *dikastikon* were of greater value in the late fifth century than in the late fourth century. – Leogoras' trial of Speusippos was probably heard before the expeditionary force left Athens for Sicily.
⁵⁰ Harp. s.v. ἡλιαία καὶ ἡλίασις; *Suda* s.v. ἡλιαία καὶ ἡλίασις (219); *Lex. Seg*. 262.10-13; *Lex. Patm*. in D. 23.28; Poll. 8.123; *EM*. 427.35, all quoted *supra* note 25.
⁵¹ Some lexicographers, however, mention only 1,000 *dikastai*: Schol. D. 24.9; Phot. s.v. ἡλιαία; *Lex. Seg*. 189.20-21, 310.28ff. (qouted *supra* n. 25). But these notes are short and preserve only a minimal selection of the information given in the *Ath. Pol*. So an argument from silence based on these notes carries no weight.
⁵² References in note 30.
⁵³ *Graphe paranomon*: Arist. *Ath. Pol*. 59.2; D. 26.8; Hyp. 3.6; Poll. 8.87. *Eisangelia*: Arist. *Ath. Pol*. 59.2; D. 24.63. *Apophasis*: Arist. *Ath. Pol*. 59.2 (καταχειροτονία) cf. Hansen (*supra* n. 37) 44.
⁵⁴ Ar. *V*. 89-90. Cf. A. Boegehold, *Aristotle's ATHENAION POLITEIA 65.2: The Official Token*, *Hesperia* 29 (1960) 400-01.
⁵⁵ The Danish Building Regulations of 1972 (6.6.1 sec. 6) prescribe a maximum of two persons *per* square meter, but this figure is fixed with a view to the fire hazard. An

architect constructing lecture halls and a consultant architect designing sports centres have informed me that o.4 m² is sufficient space for a person attending a large open-air meeting if the audience is seated on narrow benches or on cushions. I have checked this information in Switzerland where political mass meetings are still being convened annually in some of the smaller cantons. So in Obwalden the people's assembly (Landsgemeinde) is usually attended by some 3,000 citizens. Most of them are standing, but two sets of narrow benches are constructed for those who want to be seated. Each set of benches covers an area of 80 m² and accommodates 200 citizens, cf. Hansen (*supra* n. 48) 131, and R. Stillwell *Corinth II The Theatre* (Princeton 1952) 31-32 with note 20.

[56] Cf. e.g. Thompson and Wycherley 62-65 and Wycherley (1978) 35, 54. The identification was advanced by Thompson in *Hesperia* 23 (1954) 33-39.

[57] In conversation (Princeton Jan. 1981) Homer Thompson stated his reasons for believing that both Pnyx I, the *Heliaia*, the Old *Bouleuterion* and the *Stoa Basileios* were constructed in the second quarter of the fifth century, probably around 460. I am convinced and looking forward to seeing the argumentation in print. Cf. Thompson's review of Wycherley (1978) in *Archaeology* (1978) 63.

[58] Cf. Thompson and Wycherley 62.

[59] Again I refer to the Swiss Landsgemeinden (*supra* n. 55). In Sarnen, Obwalden the Landsgemeindeplatz covers an area of about 1,000 m² and it accommodates without difficulty 3,500 citizens, most of whom are standing whereas a few hundred are seated.

[60] Arist. *Ath. Pol.* 67.4.

[61] Cf. W. Stauffacher *Die Versammlungsdemokratie in Kanton Glarus* (Zürich 1962) 284-85. Cf. however for occasional longer meetings: H. Ryffel *Die schweizerischen Landsgemeinden* (Zürich 1903) 109. Cf. futhermore M.H. Hansen, *The Duration of a Meeting of the Athenian Ecclesia*, *CPh* 74 (1979) 48-49.

[62] Ar. *V.* 1109; D. 59.52.

[63] J. Travlos *Pictorial Dictionary of Ancient Athens* (New York 1971) 387.

[64] Pl. *Smp.* 194a. Cf. A.W. Pickard-Cambridge *The Dramatic Festivals of Athens* 2nd ed. (Oxford 1968) 67.

[65] Thompson and Wycherley 62, 64.

[66] Thompson and Wycherley 56-61.

[67] Thompson and Wycherley 57.

[68] Paus. 1.28.8: ἔστι δὲ Ἀθηναίοις καὶ ἄλλα δικαστήρια ... τὸ δὲ μέγιστον καὶ ἐς ὃ πλεῖστοι συνίασιν, ἡλιαίαν καλοῦσιν.

[69] Ar. *V.* 1108-09: οἱ μὲν ἡμῶν οὗπερ ἄρχων, οἱ δὲ παρὰ τοὺς ἕνδεκα,/ οἱ δ' ἐν Ὠιδείῳ δικάζουσ', οἱ δὲ πρὸς τοῖς τειχίοις,

[70] Antipho 5.10; Lys. 19.55; Pl. *Tht.* 173c-d; – Ar. *Ec.* 681 is too problematical to be adduced as evidence of law courts in the Agora.

[71] Eust. 1430.36-38: ἣν δέ φασι καὶ ἀγορὰ Κερκώπων Ἀθήνησι πλησίον Ἡλιαίας, ἔνθα τὰ κλοπιμαῖα ἐπωλοῦντο, τοιοῦτοι γὰρ καὶ οἱ κέρκωπες περιάδονται; Eust. 1669.59-60: ὁμοίως δὲ καὶ οἱ Κέρκωπες, ἀφ' ὧν καὶ ἀγορὰ καλουμένη κερκώπων Ἀθήνησιν ἐν Ἡλιαίᾳ ... Hsch. s.v. ἀγορὰ Κερκώπων (705): τόπος πλησίον Ἡλιαίας. Cf. D.L. 9.114.

[72] Aeschines 2.40.

[73] MacDowell (1971) 273-74 identifies the *Heliaia* with the *Metiocheion* by comparing *Lex. Seg.* 310.29-30 (quoted *supra* n. 25) with Hsch. s.v. Μητίχου τέμενος (1290): εἴη ἂν τὸ

THE ATHENIAN *HELIAIA* 45

Μητιχεῖον δικαστήριον μέγα, ἐν ᾧ προσεκληρώθησαν <χίλιοι> δικασταί. The evidence is too weak to allow of any conclusion and, as regards location, it does not help, since we have no idea of where the *Metiocheion* was, cf. Wycherley (1957) 148.

[74] *Cf.* Travlos (*supra* n. 63) Fig 5 and page 520 (cf. however Fig. 722 and page 578).
[75] The law is accepted as Solonian by Ruschenbusch and printed as Fr. 16 in his *SOLONOS NOMOI, Historia* Einzelschriften 9 (1966) 74 (cf. 59).
[76] *IG* I³ 104.11-13. *Cf.* R.S. Stroud *Drakon's Law on Homicide* (Berkeley and Los Angeles 1968) 42-45.
[77] On ἔφεσις *cf. infra* page 37.
[78] Lys. 10.15-21.
[79] Lys. 10.4.
[80] *Supra* n. 75.
[81] In Arist. *Pol.* 1273b35-1274a5 the institution of the people's court is ascribed to Solon both by Aristotle and by the authors mentioned by Aristotle, comprising some who praise Solon and others who criticize his reforms. In the *Ath. Pol.* 9.1 Solon is credited only with the introduction of the ἔφεσις εἰς τὸ δικαστήριον, and not directly with the institution of the δικαστήριον itself. But in an earlier chapter (3.5) the author states that the magistrates had the exclusive right to sit in judgement, and so the implication is that Solon made the ἔφεσις possible by creating the δικαστήριον.
[82] Gilbert 153; Lipsius 27-28; Beloch 365; Smith 110-11; Hignett 97; Harrison 239; MacDowell (1978) 29-30; *cf.* also V. Ehrenberg *The Greek State* (London 1969) 72; W.G. Forrest *The Emergence of Greek Democracy* (London 1966) 170. Other scholars suggest that the *heliaia* was older than Solon and was only reformed by him: Busolt and Swoboda 1151; Bonner and Smith 158; Day and Chambers 87.
[83] MacDowell (1978) 30. This view was first put forward by Grote (Vol.3, Part 2.170 n.1): 'I imagine the term Ἡλιαία in the time of Solon to have been used in its original meaning – the public assembly, perhaps with a connotation of employment in judicial proceeding'. Grote's view seems now to be universally accepted, at least among Anglo-American scholars: Smith 111; Bonner and Smith 153-57; Wade-Gery 173-74; Hignett 97; Day and Chambers 87, 183; Ehrenberg (*supra* n. 82) 72; Harrison 3, 72; Rhodes (1972) 168; (1979) 104.
[84] My view is in fact a modified restatement of the older German view. Cf. Gilbert 153; Busolt 287; Beloch 365; Lipsius 30; Busolt and Swoboda 1151; V. Ehrenberg *From Solon to Socrates* (London 1968) 67.
[85] Bonner and Smith 157 n.5 (note by C.D. Buck); Wade-Gery 173-74; Hignett 97.
[86] O. Schulthess, *Halia, RE* VII (1912) 2232-41; M. Wörrle *Untersuchungen zur Verfassungsgeschichte von Argos im 5. Jahrhundert vor Christus* (Erlangen-Nürnberg 1964) 32ff.
[87] P. Chantraine *Dictionnaire étymologique de la langue grecque* (Paris 1968) s.v. ἁλής with further references. The etymology ἁλιαία/ἁλίζεσθαι is suggested already in some of the lexica: *Lex. Patm.* in D. 23.28; *EM* s.v. ἡλιαία (427.34-35); Schol. D. 24.21 *Lex. Seg.* 310.32-33.
[88] Hdt. 1.125.2; 5.29.2; 5.79.2; 7.134.2.
[89] *SIG*² 438.21, 41, 191.
[90] Rhodes (1972) 169.
[91] X. *HG.* 1.7.7, 8, 9, 11, 31.

⁹² Lipsius 255: 'Dagegen machte sich eine Abstimmung über einen aus der Mitte der Richter gestellten Antrag jedenfalls dann erforderlich, wenn auf eine Zusatzstrafe erkannt werden sollte,'... (with reference to the law D. 24.105).
⁹³ Aeschines 3.2; cf. *IG* II² 337.20-23.
⁹⁴ *Hesperia* 43 (1974) 158.34; *Hesperia* 49 (1980) 263.28, 41 *etc*. The term ὁ βουλόμενος applies also to a *synegoros* assisting either the prosecutor (Hyp. 2 Fr. 3) or the defendant (Hyp. 3.11). Cf. M.H. Hansen, *Initiative and Decision. Reflections on the Separation of Powers in Fourth-Century Athens, GRBS* 22 (1981) n. 54. It is worth noting, however, that, in And. 1.23 and 26, ὁ βουλόμενος must denote any person present in the court, i.e. the prosecutors, the witnessess *and the jurors*. Furthermore, we learn from Antipho 6.21 (quoted *supra* page 15) that even outsiders were sometimes allowed to address the court.
⁹⁵ D. 22.26. Cf. Hansen (*supra* n. 40) 10 with further references in note 3.
⁹⁶ H. Weil *Les plaidoyers politiques de Démosthène* II (Paris 1886) 119: 'προστιμᾶσθαι, au moyen, ne se dit pas des juges, mais des parties. Il faut donc entendre τὸν βουλόμενον ni d'un des juges, ni de tous les Athéniens, mais des demandeurs.' Cf. Harrison 166-67. Cf. Hansen 132-33.
⁹⁸ In addition to the sources discussed we have two late and unreliable sources which support the identification of the *heliaia* with the *ekklesia*: D.L. 1.66: εἶτα δὲ ἑαυτῷ τραύματα ποιήσας (Πεισίστρατος), παρελθὼν ἐφ' ἡλιαίαν ἐβόα φάμενος πεπονθέναι ταῦτα ὑπὸ τῶν ἐχθρῶν. *Lex. Seg.* 310.31-32: ἡλιαία ... ἐκαλεῖτο δὲ καὶ μεγάλη ἐκκλησία.
⁹⁹ Cf. W.L. Newman *The Politics of Aristotle* II (Oxford 1897) 374.
¹⁰⁰ Bonner and Smith 153; Rhodes (1979) 104.
¹⁰¹ Ar. *V.* 595; X. *Ath.* 1.18; D. 24.99; 25.20; 57.56; Arist. *Ath. Pol.* 25.2; 41.2 *etc.*
¹⁰² Cf. κύριον ποιήσαντα τὸ δικαστήριον πάντων in Arist. *Pol.* 1274a4-5 (quoted *supra* page 32).
¹⁰³ Smith 106-19; Bonner and Smith 152ff; Hignett 216; Day and Chambers 87; Rhodes (1979) 104.
¹⁰⁴ For the connection between 6,000 citizens and the size of Pnyx I cf. M.H. Hansen, *How Many Athenians Attended the Ecclesia?, GRBS* 17 (1976) 132. For a late date of Pnyx I cf. *supra* n. 57.
¹⁰⁵ Cf. Lipsius 138-39.
¹⁰⁶ For a discussion of when the *dikastikon* was instituted *cf.* Wade-Gery 235-38; Hignett 342-43 and J.J. Buchanan *Theorika* (New York 1962) 14-17. The question: when was the *dikastikon* introduced? is of course connected with the question: was the original *heliaia* identical with the *ekklesia*? We know that the *ekklesiastikon* was introduced in the fourth century. Historians who hold that the *heliaia* was originally the people's assembly must infer that the *dikastikon* was introduced only after the *heliaia* had been split up into *dikasteria*. Wade-Gery believes that a plurality of courts existed before Ephialtes (196) and he holds consistently that the *dikastikon* may have existed before Ephialtes' reform (235). Hignett, on the other hand, who connects the reform of the *heliaia* with Ephialtes (217), dates the introduction of the *dikastikon* to the 450's (342-43). I suggest that a plurality of *dikasteria* existed already in the sixth century, and so it makes no difference to me whether the *dikastikon* was introduced in 460's or in the 450's.
¹⁰⁷ Most recently Rhodes (1979) 104.

[108] In addition to the works mentioned *supra* n. 2 cf. E. Ruschenbusch, Ἔφεσις. *Ein Beitrag zur griechischen Rechtsterminologie, ZRG* 78 (1961) 386-90.
[109] The traditional view of *ephesis* is sponsored by e.g. Wade-Gery 173-74; Rhodes (1972) 200; MacDowell (1978) 30-33.
[110] Cf. Hansen 143.
[111] Rhodes (1972) 213, 227.
[112] There is no evidence supporting 10 meetings, and the number of meetings was not fixed to forty until the middle of the fourth century. *Cf.* M.H. Hansen, *How Often Did the Ecclesia Meet?, GRBS* 18 (1977) 68-70.
[113] Cf. Rhodes (1979) 103-06.
[114] Cf. Hansen (*supra* n. 37) 37 with notes 2-3. In note 2 I admit that none of the eleven trials heard by the *ekklesia* is explicitly called an *eisangelia* in our sources. Nevertheless I accept the traditional view that these trials were, technically, *eisangeliai*.
[115] D. 20.93-94.
[116] Hyp. 5.22.
[117] D. 24.212-14.
[118] Arist. *Ath. Pol.* 8.4 Cf. Rhodes (1979) and M.H. Hansen, *Eisangelia in Athens. A Reply, JHS* 100 (1980) 90-91.
[119] Arist. *Ath. Pol.* 8.4, 21.3; Plu. *Sol.* 19.1; Hdt. 5.72.2 as interpreted e.g. by Rhodes (1972) 208. – To these usually discussed sources must be added. D. 24.148 proving that Demosthenes believed in a Solonian council which can only be the Council of Four Hundred. Cf. And. 1.111; D.20.90; Isoc 15.313.
[120] Arist. *Ath. Pol.* 9.1; Plu. *Sol.* 18.3. Cf. page 37.
[121] Arist. *Ath. Pol.* 9.1; Plu. *Sol.* 18.6; Isoc. 20.2.
[122] For the possibility, before Solon, of a public action raised by ὁ βουλόμενος cf. Hansen (*supra* n. 40) 115.
[123] I should like to thank first, Professor Alan Boegehold who in October 1980 guided me through the Agora and showed me the physical remains of the *dikasteria*. Second, Professor Martin Ostwald who at the *APA* annual meeting in New Orleans in December 1980 read a paper about the origin of the *dikasteria* and admirably argued in favour of the view I attack in part II of this article. Third, Professor Homer Thompson who kindly explained to me his reasons for redating many of the important public buildings in the Agora. Finally I should like to express my gratitude to the *Danish Research Council for the Humanities* for defraying the costs of my visit to Athens in October 1980 and my visit to New Orleans in December 1980.

ADDENDA

237: My interpretation of the Solonian *heliaia* has been questioned by M. Ostwald in *From Popular Sovereignty to the Sovereignty of the Law* (Berkeley 1986). In his first chapter (9-12, cf. also 28-40, 67-76) Ostwald offers a profound analysis of the evidence for the Solonian *heliaia* and in note 29 on pages 10-11 he sets out to refute my view of the *heliaia*. Ostwald's own position is that the *heliaia* was a new institution created by Solon, not just a judicial session of the *ekklesia*. It was a popular court manned by all citizens who had taken the heliastic oath; but it was exclusively a court of appeal. By *ephesis* a litigant who was dissatisfied with an archon's verdict could appeal to the *heliaia* for a new trial. Ostwald's refutation is subsumed under three headings: (1) a linguistic observation on the term *heliaia*, (2) an interpretation of the crucial passages in Arist. *Pol.* and *Ath. Pol.* about the origin of the Solonian *heliaia* and (3) some remarks on *a priori* assumptions.

(1) Ostwald agrees with me (*supra* pages 238-39) that the conventional view of the *heliaia* (a judicial session of the assembly) is based on a debatable etymology. He notes, however, »the fact that the noun [*heliaia*] is never found in the plural« and argues that if the *heliaia* from the very beginning had been subdivided into panels, we should expect to find some instances of the plural.

(2) Ostwald and I agree that the *heliaia* was a new institution created by Solon (*supra* pages 238 & 249), and not just a judicial session of the *ekklesia*, as e.g. P.J. Rhodes and many others believe. But we disagree on the question of how the *heliaia* was manned. Ostwald believes that the *heliaia* was undivided and manned by all citizens who had taken the heliastic oath. He disputes my view that, both in *Pol.* and in *Ath. Pol.* Aristotle credits Solon with having established a plurality of law courts manned with jurors selected by lot. (a) At *Pol.* 1273a3 »τὰ δικαστήρια ποιήσας ἐκ πάντων does not necessarily imply selection from the entire people (so Hansen 33), but may equally well mean »composed of the entire people.«« (b) At *Pol.* 1273a3 »κληρωτὸν ὄν is clearly a part of the fourth-century censure of Solon and not part of Aristotle's own views of the Solonian constitution.« (c) There is no reason for the plurals δικαστήρια at *Ath. Pol.* 7.3 and 25.2 to be taken literally, especially since they come from a fourth-century author who uses singular and plural indifferently.

(3) Ostwald and I have different views about which *a priori* assumptions to accept. Ostwald can accept sortition in the age of Solon, but not fully developed dicastic panels. »Moreover, *ephesis* is not likely to have been so common in the sixth century that several panels had to be created in order to cope with all cases.« (4) In addition to the explicit criticism of my views Ostwald offers a novel interpretation of *IG* I^3 105: the *boule*

ADDENDA

referred to in the original version is the Areopagos and it is only in the republication that the reference is to the council of five hundred (38-39). Furthermore, at line 36 and 40 the phrase ἄνευ τō δέμο τō 'Αθηναίον πλεθύοντος refers to the *heliaia* which then is a session of the entire people, but not of the assembly which is referred to at line 35 and again at lines 54-55 (ἐκκλεσίαι) (33-34).

I am not persuaded by Ostwald's criticism of my views and take this opportunity to state my reply:

Re 1. There are very few attestations of the term *heliaia* (cf. *supra* pages 220-22) and they all occur in laws and decrees or in contexts where the singular is to be expected. Furthermore, the absence of *heliaia* in the plural is worth noting no matter whether the term denotes a popular tribunal manned by all citizens (Ostwald's view) or a plurality of law courts manned by panels of jurors (as I suggested). On Ostwald's interpretation we should expect to find the plural *heliaia* used about a number of sessions of the popular tribunal, just as the plural ἐκκλεσίαι is used about a number of sessions of the people's assembly. The missing plural may (on both theories) be due to lack of evidence, and cannot be adduced in a debate about which of the two interpretations to prefer.

Re 2. The phrase ἐκ πάντων or ἐξ ἀπάντων occurs 32 times in Arist. *Pol.* (19 times alone in the section 1300a2-1301a16) and invariably denotes a *selection* from all. The presumption is that Aristotle when he wrote *Pol.* believed that the Solonian *heliaia* was manned, not by all citizens, but by citizens selected from all Athenians, cf. Newman's *Commentary* IV 272 *ad* 38. Of the two possible forms of selection - election or sortition - he had probably sortition in mind since there is no evidence that jurors were elected. Furthermore, at *Pol.* 1273b41-1274a3, Aristotle is evidently stating his own view, cf. Newman's *Commentary* I 374. Thus, at 1274a3, ἐκ πάντων shows that Aristotle shared the view expressed 1274a5: that the *dikasterion* was κληρωτόν. Finally, at *Ath. Pol.* 7.3 and 25.2 the plural δικαστήρια does suggest that the author, i.e. Aristotle and/or his pupil, was thinking of panels of jurors. Whether the fourth-century author was right or wrong about the Solonian *heliaia* is a different question, on which I am inclined to suspend judgement, cf. *infra*.

Re 3. I never suggested that Solon introduced dicastic panels in their fully developed form. My view is that, *if* sortition of jurors goes back to Solon, the reference is probably to the annual sortition of a panel whose members took the heliastic oath, cf. *supra* page 245. Next, whether the Solonian *heliaia* could be subdivided into panels depends on what type of court the *heliaia* was. Ostwald believes that it was exclusively a court of appeal, as is indicated by Arist. *Ath. Pol.* 9.1, where we learn about ἡ

ADDENDA

εἰς τὸ δικαστήριον ἔφεσις. But, apart from Plutarch, who quotes the *Ath. Pol.*, there is no other evidence that the *heliaia* was a court of appeal, and the scanty contemporary sources indicate that it was a court of first instance. The laws quoted at Dem. 23.28 and 24.105 are commonly accepted as genuine Solonian laws included among the laws recorded on the *axones*. Ostwald shares this view and finds (10 note 27) that Solon's use of the term *heliaia* is guaranteed by the quotation in Lys. 10.16 and Dem. 24.105. But the laws quoted at Dem. 23.28 and 24.105 refer to the *heliaia* as a court of first instance, not as a court of appeal. Consequently, the *heliaia* must have met frequently, and frequent meetings of the *heliaia* are difficult to combine with the view that it was a popular court manned by all citizens. The view of the undivided *heliaia* attended by all citizens is closely linked with the view that the *heliaia* was summoned only infrequently in cases of *ephesis*. The evidence that the *heliaia* was (also?) a court of first instance points to the view that, from the very beginning, it could be subdivided into panels of jurors.

Re 4. The idea that the *boule* originally referred to the Areopagos is not *per se* implausible, but, in my opinion, it is ruled out by lines 46-48 where we find the obligatory items on the agenda of the council of five hundred and the assembly, as well as regulations concerning financial administration. In both cases the reference must be to the council of five hundred, not to the council of the Areopagos. Furthermore, I cannot believe that δῆμος πληθύων refers to one institution in line 35, namely to the *ekklesia*, but to a different institution in lines 36 and 40, namely to the *heliaia*. In line 35 the reference is to the *ekklesia*, as Ostwald admits. Then, in lines 36 and 40, the reference must also be to the assembly. Next, *pace* Ostwald pages 32-33 note 221, the reference to the *ekklesia* in lines 53-54 should cause no problem. In numerous other sources the assembly is referred to indiscriminately as ὁ δῆμος or ἡ ἐκκλησία; in this inscription the reference is to the δῆμος πληθύων and to the ἐκκλησία.

In conclusion, if we trust our sources, the Solonian *heliaia* was both a court of first instance (Dem. 23.28 & 24.105) and a court of appeal (Arist. *Ath. Pol.* 9.1). It was not a judicial session of the whole people (for which cf. ἄνευ τō δέμο τō 'Αθεναίον πλεθύοντος at *IG* I^3 105.36 and 40) but was manned by jurors (probably the core of the heliastic oath goes back to the institution of the *heliaia*) who had been selected from all (ἐκ πάντων Arist. *Pol.* 1274a3), by an annual (?) sortition (κληρωτόν, 1273a5 taken together with ἐκ πάντων at 1274a3). Sometimes a case was heard by all jurors (extrapolation from Andoc. 1.17, cf. *supra* page 230) but sometimes the *heliaia* was divided into panels (δικαστήρια Arist. *Ath. Pol.* 7.3 and 25.2, combined with the *a priori* assumption that a court of

ADDENDA

first instance must have met too frequently to have been composed of all citizens).

On the other hand, there is much to be said for the view that the information obtained from Arist. *Pol.* and *Ath. Pol.* cannot be trusted, because it reflects the contemporary debate over the ancestral constitution and because the knowledge about the sixth-century constitution rested principally on oral tradition. In that case it is virtually impossible to reconstruct the Solonian *heliaia* and we will have to suspend judgement on its nature and composition, cf. *supra* page 249.

237: In the law quoted at Dem. 23.28 ὡς ἐν τῷ <α'> ἄξονι ἀγορεύει is probably a reference to Drakon's *axones*, and not to Solon's, cf. R.S. Stroud, *The Axones and Kyrbeis of Drakon and Solon* (Berkeley 1979) 11. Furthermore, the emendment that follows is probably a revision of Drakon's homicide law necessitated by Solon's introduction of the *heliaia*. — The fact that the law refers to the *heliaia* as a court of first instance is — after all — not incompatible with Aristotle's statement that Solon instituted ἡ εἰς τὸ δικαστήριον ἔφεσις.

239: In a building inscription from Tegea (Michel no. 585.24, 27) *haliastai* probably denotes a board of officials (*RE* VII [1912] 2244 s.v. ἁλιασταί), and in any case not the assembly.

242: Ostwald and I agree that the law quoted at Dem. 46.26 cannot be adduced in support of the identification of the *heliaia* with the *ekklesia* (in its judicial capacity) as against the *dikasteria*. According to Ostwald (11 note 29) *heliaia* refers to the people's court whereas *dikasterion* refers to any tribunal (other than the people's court), including, for example, the Areopagos. I believe that the law refers to the *heliaia* and to all courts i.e. the people's court and other courts such as the homicide courts. The juxtaposition of a specific and a comprehensive term is very common in Greek, cf. e.g. the juxtaposition, at Arist. *Ath. Pol.* 63.3 of ὀφείλοντες and ἄτιμοι (= ὀφείλοντες and other ἄτιμοι).

243: Another observation indicates that, at *Ath. Pol.* 9.1, Aristotle is thinking of the jury courts and not of a judicial session of the assembly. He states that the common people become masters of the constitution when they become masters of the *psephos*. But voting with *psephoi* was a characteristic of the jury courts, whereas the *ekklesia* regularly voted by show of hands even when transformed into a law court. Thus, the form of voting points to dicastic rather than ecclesiastic procedure. This argument

ADDENDA

is a valid objection to the traditional view: that the *heliaia* was a session of the *ekklesia*, but not to Ostwald's view. His new popular court manned by all citizens may well have voted with pebbles and not by show of hands, cf. my review of Rhodes' *Commentary* in *CP* 80 (1985) 58.

244: For a discussion of the term δικαστήριον cf. my forthcoming study: 'The Political Powers of the Athenian Dikasteria,' in *The Greek City and its Institutions* (Oxford 1990).

248: For all the constitutional reforms ascribed to Solon cf. my study 'Solonian Democracy in Fourth-Century Athens,' *ClMed* 40 (1989).

ON THE IMPORTANCE OF INSTITUTIONS IN AN ANALYSIS OF ATHENIAN DEMOCRACY

BY

MOGENS HERMAN HANSEN

In recent years some students of Greek history in general and Athenian democracy in particular have advocated a shift of the focus of interest from institutions to extra-institutional forces such as political groups, public opinion and social structure. Basically it has been a sound development which has opened up new perspectives. But a corollary has sometimes been a tendency to minimize the importance of political institutions. As an example I will quote a passage by R. W. Connor whose seminal and very influential study *The New Politicians of Fifth-Century Athens* appeared in 1971. In his introductory chapter (4-5) Connor writes: »The organization of civic machinery, the ways of selecting archons and generals, the relations between assembly and council, all the apparatus which we somewhat misleadingly called the »constitution« of Athens cannot be neglected, ... but, as historians have come increasingly to recognize in recent years, the formal structure of the state is but the sceleton of her politics. The nerves, the tendons, the musculature of the body political is to be found in the organization of forces and often of interest groups within it. It is this structure, rather than the bare bones of the »constitution«, which gives vitality to a city and makes her history come alive.«

What »historians have come increasingly to realize« is, in fact, a new trend in political science whereby the concept of »state« has been replaced by the broader concept of »political system«,[1] and the study of institutions and constitutions has been toned down in favour of investigations of political behaviour in general. In Jean Blondel's well known reader *Comparative Government*, for example, the first contribution surveys previous treatments of the topic and states that »these books are limited primarily to political morphology or what might also be called political anatomy. They describe

---

[1] Cf. e.g. D. Easton, *The Political System* (New York 1953); R.A. Dahl, *Modern Political Analysis* (3rd ed. Yale 1976) 1-11 and *passim*.

various political institutions generally without attempting to compare them; what comparison *is* made is limited exclusively to the identifications of differences between types or systems, such as federal versus unitary system, or parliamentary versus presidential system ... «.[2] Here, as well as in numerous other modern studies of politics and political systems, the traditional study of political institutions is criticized for being »limited primarily to political morphology or what might also be called political anatomy.« The implication is that a preferable analysis of political systems investigates »political syntax« or, in medical terms, »political physiology«.[3] The imagery is both significant and well chosen. And the criticism of earlier forms of »*Staatskunde*« is pertinent when applied to modern societies in which »the organization of civic machinery,« to quote Connor, matters less and less compared with the increasingly important and influential network of informal groups and political organizations that exist alongside the bodies of government. The problem is whether the recent trend in the study of of contemporary political systems is suitable in an analysis of the Greek *polis*.

Let me adopt the imagery used by many students of political science and elaborate the comparison between politics and language. Some languages have a simple morphology but a complex syntax. English is an obvious example. Other languages and, in many cases earlier forms of modern languages have a much more elaborate morphology which, on the other hand, is balanced by a less complex syntax. My point is that a simple morphology goes with a complex syntax and *vice versa*. Ancient Greek is a language that combines a very complicated morphology with a much simpler and less rigid syntax, and in a Greek grammar to pass over morphology and to focus on syntax would result in a very strange description of the language. If we leave aside the analogy from language and return to the study of politics we observe that some societies have a very complicated system of organs of government whereas others have hardly any official political institutions at all. The Greek *poleis* in general and democratic Athens in particular were notorious for their abundance of political institutions. A society at the other end of the spectre was the medieval republic of Iceland, in which there was one single official: the *lögsögumadr* (»the speaker of the laws« elected for a

---

[2] R. C. Macridis, 'A Survey of the Field of Comparative Government', *Comparative Government* ed. J. Blondel (London 1969) 4-5.
[3] Cf. e. g. G. A. Almond & G. B. Powell, 'The Political System,' in Blondel (*supra* n. 2) 10: »In all societies the role of formal governmental institutions is shaped and limited by informal groups, political attitudes, and a multitude of interpersonal relationships.«

period of three years) who chaired the annual meeting of the *Althing* and here recited from memory all laws concerning the *Althing* as well as a third of the law code.[4]

In this study I will not treat the Greek *polis* generally but concentrate on Athens and state an observation which, in my opinion, all students of Athenian history must discuss and on which they must commit themselves: never before or since in world history has such an elaborate network of political institutions been created and developed in order to run a very small and fairly simple society. Every year the Athenians convened 40 *ekklesiai* and a session was regularly attended by 6,000 citizens; several times a year laws were passed by boards of *nomothetai* numbering at least 500, and probably 1,000 or more; the council of five hundred met on all weekdays, i.e. on ca 250 days out of 354; on some 150-200 court days thousands of jurors were appointed by lot from a panel of 6,000 citizens aged 30 or more; every year some 700 magistrates (*archai*) were elected or selected by lot; most were organized in boards of 10; some boards met only rarely but many were active regularly and some even daily; envoys elected by the assembly and sent on a mission to other cities were counted by the score and must, in some years, have exceeded a hundred. To sum up, a majority of the Athenian citizens were frequently, some even regularly, involved in the running of the democratic institutions. In this respect there is an important difference between ancient direct and modern representative democracy. For ninety-nine per cent of the citizens in a contemporary democracy institutionalized political participation is restricted to voting once every second year or so; and alongside the nation's political institutions there is a complicated network of semi-private and private institutions which tend to absorb the citizens' time and interest more than the political institutions. Also, public opinion is formed by the media and not any longer in the parliaments. Thus the focus of interest tends to shift from political institutions to the network of private or semi-private organizations that dominate and control society: the party organizations, the unions, the corporations, the media and all the various kinds of organization which, in a political context, we tend to call pressure groups. By contrast, ancient Athens had no guilds or trade companies (as at least the medieval cities had), no unions, no media, and no political parties that can reasonably be compared to modern parties. As a corollary to the thesis stated above I will add the following observation: the

---

[4] Cf. J. Jóhannesson, *Islands Historie i Mellomalderen* (Oslo 1969) 40-42.

extremely complicated and developed system of political institutions in ancient Athens becomes even more conspicuous when it is contrasted with the absence of social and economic organizations of any importance. We have evidence of private and semi-private religious organizations and of small informal groups of political leaders, for which cf. *infra*. But apart from that the sources give no information about important social organizations alongside the political institutions.

Not only was political life thoroughly institutionalized; the sources show that the Athenians tended to understand their own »political system« in terms of institutions. Let me adduce some examples: (a) the second part of the Aristotelian *Athenaion Politeia* (42-68) is one long unbroken description of institutions and nothing else. (b) A typical Athenian law was conceived and drafted with institutions in mind, cf. the law of 375/4 on silver coinage which — in addition to the *nomothetai*, the *boule* and the *dikasteria* — refers to seven different boards of magistrates and is almost exclusively connected with all the various types of public procedure that might arise out of having one *dokimastes* sitting in the Agora and another in the Peiraeus.[5] (c) Forensic speeches in public actions bristle with references to and discussions of public institutions and procedures. One example is the opening of Aeschines' speech *Against Ktesiphon* (1-8) in which an alleged crisis of the democratic constitution is traced back to irregular ekklesiastic procedure and the necessity of dikastic control. Admittedly, Thucydides, Xenophon and other historians take little interest in social and constitutional history and prefer to describe international relations and military campaigns. But when the historians describe policy-making and reflect on constitutional matters, these parts of their account are typically presented in the form of speeches delivered in an assembly. Even here the institutional aspect is conspicuous, and extra-institutional forces appear mostly in descriptions of revolutions and civil war, cf. e.g. Thucydides' description of the oligarchic revolution in 411.

The historians' use of assembly speeches leads to another observation that illustrates the importance of institutions for a proper understanding of Athenian democracy. In fourth-century Athens political influence was inseparably bound up with eloquence, and it is significant that *rhetor* was the most common term for what we in contemporary democracies tend to call politicians.[6] Greek rhetoric was almost exclusively official and political,

---

[5] Cf. *Hesperia* 43 (1974) 157-88.
[6] Cf. M. H. Hansen, 'The Athenian »Politicians« 403-322 B.C.', *GRBS* 24 (1983) 39-42.

and hardly existed in the private sphere.⁷ Furthermore, the audiences for which the speeches were intended and held were the ordinary political assemblies, principally the popular assembly and the popular courts. Similarly, the subdivision of rhetoric into genres followed institutional lines: one type of oratory was the *genos symbouleutikon*. A synonymous term is *genos demegorikon*, i.e. the speech delivered in the people's assembly.⁸ Another type was the *genos dikanikon*, i.e. speeches delivered in a court, in Athens typically the people's court. Of the third genre, the *genos epideiktikon*, the best known type is the *epitaphios logos* which again was occasioned by a public institutionalized event: the annual burial of citizens killed in war in the past year. The importance of the institutional network for the structure of rhetoric is apparent from the very few exceptions we have: when an author composed a political pamphlet meant for reading or private delivery, he imitated the institutional setting and pretended that it was a speech delivered before the people's assembly or the people's court.⁹

My concern with political institutions has sometimes been taken to imply a denial or at least a minimization of the elitist aspect of Athenian democracy.¹⁰ But I have always argued, most recently in *The Athenian Assembly* 56-65, that political influence in classical Athens tended to be concentrated in the hands of a small elite. My point is that the elite exercized its power *through* the political institutions, not independently of or in opposition to the institutions (*ibidem* 85-86). If power and political influence had been based principally on extra-institutional factors, such as family ties, friendship, local influence and wealth, then rhetoric would have played a much smaller role than it obviously did. The issues would often have been decided informally in private negotiations among the members of the elite. But the most important talent required of a political leader in classical Athens seems to have been eloquence.¹¹ The leaders had to per-

---

⁷ For the political and institutional aspects of Greek Rhetoric cf. e. g. Pl. *Phdr*. 261 A-C; Arist. *Rhet*. 1356a25-27; *Rhet. ad Alex*. 1421b7-11. In all three passages rhetoric is, in principle, treated generally; nevertheless, for all practical purposes, the scope of rhetoric is narrowed down to the political sphere and to speeches delivered in an institutionalized setting.

⁸ Arist. *Rhet*. 1354b23; *Rhet. ad Alex*. 1421b7; Pl.*Grg* 502 C-D. *Phdr*. 261.

⁹ Cf. Isoc. 7 (*Areopagiticus*), 8 (*On the Peace*) and 14 (*Plataicus*) which all take the form of a *demegoria* and 15 (*Antidosis*) which takes the form on a *dikanikos logos*. Similarly Thrasymachos fr 1 and Lys. 34 are probably political pamphlets written in the form of a *demegoria*.

¹⁰ E. g. by J. Ober, 'The Nature of Athenian Democracy,' review article in *CP* 84 (1989).

¹¹ Cf. Thucydides' portrait of Perikles at 2.65: it is Perikles' capability of persuading the

suade the ordinary citizens who attended the *ekklesia*, the *boule*, and the *dikasteria*, not just once every second year when leaders had to be elected, but every day whenever decisions were to be made by a political assembly, and the conspicuous absence of organized political groups, apart from small groups of leaders, made persuasion and thus rhetoric much more important than it is in any modern society. The crucial importance of political and forensic eloquence in fourth-century Athens is inextricably bound up with democracy[12] and the importance of assemblies in which the speeches were delivered.

The importance of political institutions in classical Athens can be seen in a broader perspective. In the Greek *polis* political life was separated from social life by being the prerogative of the *politai*. In the social sphere citizens mingled with metics and often even with slaves; and some social activities were open to women as well as to men. In the Agora, for example, people of all kinds worked side by side, Athenians and foreigners, masters and slaves, men and women (at least some).[13] In the building accounts of the late fifth century a citizen, a metic and a slave were paid the same fee for a day's work.[14] In the theatre members of all groups were found in the audience[15]. Metics were sometimes admitted to *hetaireiai* and invited to *symposia*.[16] But in the political assemblies the citizens isolated themselves, and all other groups were excluded. Political life was reserved for citizens and exercized when they met publicly.[17] Admittedly, in the Agora even metics and slaves could stand before the *eponymoi* and read the agenda for the next session of the *ekklesia*. But to attend an *ekklesia* or to be a juror was a mark of honour

---

Athenians (65.8-9) that leads to the famous dictum (2.65.10) that Athens was a democracy by name, but in reality power was in the hands of its leader.

[12] The close connection between democracy and forensic rhetoric is emphasized by Antiphon in his speech for the defence, fr. 3 (Gernet). The connection between democracy and political eloquence is pointed out by Thucydides in the Melian dialogue: the point in having a dialogue instead of the usual set of speeches is, according to Thuc. 5.85, that dialogue fits an (oligarchic) council whereas a set of speeches is appropriate in a (democratic) assembly.

[13] For metics cf. V. Ehrenberg, *The People of Aristophanes* (Oxford 1951) 150-54. For women cf. D. M. Shaps, *Economic Rights of Women in Ancient Greece* (Edinburgh 1979) 61-63.

[14] *IG* I² 374, cf. M. M. Austin & P. Vidal-Naquet, *Economic and Social History of Ancient Greece* (London 1977) no. 73.

[15] A. W. Pickard-Cambridge, *The Dramatic Festivals of Athens* (2nd ed. Oxford 1968) 263-65.

[16] Cf. O. Aurenche, *Les Groupes d'Alcibiade, de Léogoras et de Teucros* (Paris 1974) 197, 213-14, 224, 226, 228.

[17] Cf. M. H. Hansen, *Was Athens a Democracy?* in *Hist. Filos. Skr. Dan. Vid. Selsk.* 59 (1989) 17-21. For a seminal and profound discussion of these problems cf. O. Murray, 'Cities of Reason,' *European Journal of Sociology* 28 (1987) 324-46.

that distinguished even a poor citizen from a rich metic. The isolationism of the citizens in the political sphere was bound up with the institutions from which women, foreigners and slaves were banned, and the isolationism underlines the importance of the political institutions.

These observations illustrate, I hope, one of the major differences between a Greek *polis* and a modern political system. In the European nation state political institutions have never mattered as much as they did in an ancient Greek *polis*. And in this century they tend to matter less and less. Accordingly, political science has moved away from the study of »political morphology«, that is of political institutions, and has focused instead on extra-institutional forces in political decision-making. But by extrapolation to apply the modern analysis of political systems to the ancient Greek *polis* may be misleading and is, in any case, dangerous. I much appreciate the new studies of political groups, social structure and public opinion. I am myself responsible for some studies in this line, but they must not lead to a minimization of the importance of the political institutions.

GRAPHE PARANOMON AGAINST *PSEPHISMATA* NOT YET PASSED BY THE *EKKLESIA**

BY
MOGENS HERMAN HANSEN

A *graphe paranomon* could be brought against any *rhetor* who moved a *psephisma* in the *ekklesia*, and the action entailed a reconsideration before a *dikasterion* of the issue already debated in the *ekklesia*. The indictment might be brought either before[1] or after[2] the passing of the decree by the people, and the hearing by the *dikastai* would cause the *psephisma* to be either upheld[3] or quashed.[4] Thus, we have four variants of the public action against unconstitutional proposals. (a) A decree is appealed against prior to being passed by the people and is quashed by the court.[5] (b) A decree is appealed against after being passed by the people and is quashed by the court.[6] (c) A decree is appealed against prior to being passed by the people and is upheld by the court.[7] (d) A decree is appealed against after being passed by the people and is upheld by the court.[8]

In (a), (b) and (d) the verdict pronounced by the jurors was undoubtedly the end of the matter. In (a) and (b) the motion put to the people or the decision made by the people was stopped for ever, and in (d) the *psephisma*

---

* This is a much extended version of a view which I stated only briefly in my *The Sovereignty of the People's Court in Athens in the Fourth Century B. C. and the Public Action against Unconstitional Proposals* (Odense 1974) 51-52. It is occasioned by the criticism of my view raised, in particular, by J.-M. Hannick in his *Note sur la* graphè paranomôn, *AC* 50 (1981) 393-97. I appreciate Hannick's objections, but I am not persuaded and will here present a more detailed and thoroughly argued version of my view.
[1] X. *H.G.* I.vii.12-14: Euryptolemos objects to Kallixenos' proposal before it has been put to vote.
[2] D. xxii.5, 9-10: Euktemon brings his *graphe paranomon* against Androtion's honorary decree for the *boule* after the *epistates ton proedron* has put the motion to the vote and after the people have voted by a show of hands.
[3] D. xxiv.14, cf. below.
[4] Aeschin. iii.8, 197; [D.] lix.91; [Plut.] *Mor.* 835f-36a.
[5] No example is attested.
[6] Cf. Hansen (above, n. 1); Cat. nos. 4, 15, 16, 18, 38.
[7] Cat. nos. 13, 30.
[8] Cat. nos. 5, 17, 27.

passed by the people must have taken effect as soon as the jurors, by acquitting the *rhetor*, had approved of the decree he had proposed and carried.[9] But what happened if the court upheld a proposal that had been stopped by a *graphe paranomon* before being passed by the people in assembly? Most historians would undoubtedly assume, *a priori*, that the proposal would once more be turned over to the *ekklesia*, where the people, after a renewed debate, would take the vote on whether to pass or reject what the *dikastai* had now declared to be constitutional (but perhaps not expedient).[10] This *a priori* assumption, however, is not borne out by the two attested cases, i. e. Aeschines' *graphe paranomon* against Ktesiphon in 330, and (more important) the *graphe paranomon* brought in 353 against Euktemon by Androtion, Glauketes and Melanopos. In both cases there is no indication that the acquittal was followed by a renewed debate in the *ekklesia*. On the contrary, the debate before the *dikasterion* seems to have been final. The inference must be that in a *graphe paranomon* brought against a proposal or a *probouleuma* the jurors decided not only whether the motion was constitutional but also whether it was expedient. By acquitting the proposer the *dikastai* also ratified the decree so that it could take effect immediately after the trial, as in those cases where the *graphe paranomon* had been brought against a *psephisma* already passed by the people. Since the implications are far-reaching, both the *graphai paranomon* in question deserve a closer scrutiny.

In early spring 336 Ktesiphon proposed that Demosthenes be crowned with a golden crown for his efforts to have the trenches and walls repaired and that the crown be awarded in the theatre at the Greater Dionysia. The decree was immediately indicted by Aeschines as unconstitutional, but for reasons unknown to us the trial was postponed for six years, and Aeschines' *graphe paranomon* was not brought before a *dikasterion* until August 330.[11]

---

[9] In two cases (Cat. nos. 17, 27) we are told only that the defendant was acquitted (Aeschin. ii.14; iii.62; [Plut.] *Mor*. 849a); but in both cases the decree was probably never implemented. In the third case (Cat. no. 5), however, a published copy of the decree has been found (*Hesperia* 40 [1971] 280-301 no. 7) which shows that the *rhetor* attacked was acquitted and the decree put into effect.

[10] Cf. Platner, *Der Process und die Klagen bei den Attikern* (Darmstadt 1824-25) II 54, 56 followed by E. Gerner, s. v. *Paranomon Graphe*, *RE* 18 (1949) 1288-89.

[11] In Thargelion 337 Demosthenes proposed and carried a decree about the repair of the walls and the trenches, and in Skirophorion he himself became a member of the committee of *teichopoioi* (Aeschin. iii.27). The walls and trenches were repaired in the following year (Aeschin. iii.23) when Demosthenes was both a member of the Theoric Board (Aeschin. iii.24) and *teichopoios* (Aeschin. iii.27, 31). Then Ktesiphon moved a *psephisma* that

Aeschines appeared for the prosecution with his speech *Against Ktesiphon*, whereas Demosthenes acted as *synegoros* for Ktesiphon and delivered the speech *On the Crown*. In both speeches Ktesiphon's proposal is usually called a *psephisma*,[12] but occasionally Demosthenes uses the more specific term *probouleuma*,[13] and similarly Aeschines sometimes refers to the decree as a *gnome*, i. e. a proposal.[14] Thus, Ktesiphon must have been a member of the council, and his honorary decree must have been passed by the *boule* but stopped by Aeschines' *graphe paranomon* before it had been ratified by the people in the *ekklesia*. Now, we know from the Aristokrates speech that *probouleumata* (including *probouleumata* that had been stopped by a *graphe paranomon*) would lapse after a year.[15] Accordingly, we would expect the trial held in 330 to be a demonstration only: if Aeschines won the case Ktesiphon could not be punished, and even if he lost the case Demosthenes could no longer be crowned. Nevertheless both Aeschines and Demosthenes seem to take it for granted that conviction will entail that Ktesiphon will be punished and his proposal quashed,[16] whereas acquittal will result in the crowning of Demosthenes.[17] There is no indication that Ktesiphon has reopened the issue by moving his proposal for a second time. The *psephisma* attacked seems to be the *probouleuma* of 336. Nevertheless the whole trial is conducted on the asumption that the verdict passed by the

---

Demosthenes be crowned for his efforts to have the trenches repaired (Aeschin iii.236). The proposal included a provision that the crown be proclaimed in the theatre during the Dionysia (held in Elaphebolion 336) (Aeschin. iii.49). But Ktesiphon's proposal was indicted by Aeschines as unconstitutional before the death of Philip in June 336 (Aeschin iii.219) and undoubtedly before the Dionysia in Elaphebolion (April), since Demosthenes was never crowned. For reasons we do not know the trial was postponed for six years. In Aeschines' account of Demosthenes' political career the most recent events mentioned are the trial of Leocrates (Aeschin. iii.252), which took place in 330, and the embassy sent to Kleopatra on the death of Alexander of Epirus (Aeschin. iii.242) in the spring of 330. On the other hand, the *terminus ante quem* is the Pythia (Aeschin. iii.254) to be celebrated in August 330. Both D.H. (*Amm.* 12) and Plut. (*Dem.* 24.2) date the trial of Ktesiphon in the archonship of Aristophon (330/29). The conclusion is that the indictment was brought in the early spring of 336, but the trial postponed until July or early August 330.

[12] Aeschin. iii.9, 12, 24 etc. D. xviii.56, 59, 83 etc.

[13] D. xviii.9, 53, 118-19.

[14] Aeschin. iii.8, 213, 230, cf. the probouleumatic formula: γνώμην δὲ ξυμβάλλεσθαι τῆς βουλῆς κτλ.

[15] D. xxiii.92-93.

[16] The trial is a ἀγὼν τιμητός (Aeschin. iii.210), and Demosthenes indicates (xviii.13-16) that Aeschines has proposed, or will propose, a fine of such an amount that Ktesiphon will become indebted to the state and, consequently, *atimos*.

[17] Cf. Aeschin. iii. 53, 147, 152, 153, 156, 160, 167, 176, 188, 210, 231, 232, 236, 244, 254, 259.

jurors will have consequences for the persons involved. Thus, it is important to note that both speakers take it for granted that the verdict passed by the jurors will be the end of the matter and that Demosthenes will be crowned if Ktesiphon is acquitted. There is no indication that the *probouleuma*, if declared constitutional by the court, must be sent back to the *ekklesia* for ratification. On the contrary, Aeschines assumes that the jurors have the power not only to acquit Ktesiphon but also to crown Demosthenes: ἐν τοῖς αὐτοῖς δικαστηρίοις τοὺς μὲν τὰς τῶν δώρων γραφὰς ἁλισκομένους ἀτιμοῦτε, ὃν δ' αὐτοὶ μισθοῦ πολιτευόμενον σύνιστε, στεφανώσετε; (232). A warning, however, must be appended to my reconstruction of Aeschines' *graphe paranomon* against Ktesiphon. First, we know that Ktesiphon was acquitted, but we have no information that Demosthenes was crowned. Second, several commentators have assumed that after the trial the bill was promptly passed, first in the *boule* and then in the *ekklesia*, so that Demosthenes could eventually receive his golden crown at the Greater Dionysia of 329.[18] This reconstruction is pure fantasy and does not accord with the two speeches as well as mine but, given our ignorance of what happened after the trial, it cannot be disproved. Third, the presumption is that Ktesiphon's *probouleuma* lapsed after a year. Thus we are faced with a dilemma: either both speeches were delivered (or published) on the assumption that the *probouleuma* had *not* lapsed, or we are ignorant of some measure by which the case had been reopened before the hearing of it in 330. On either view it would be dangerous to take at face value what we are told by Demosthenes and Aeschines in their speeches. Both speakers indicate that the jurors' acquittal of Ktesiphon will entail the crowning of Demosthenes. But an indication is far from being a proof, especially when made by an Attic orator in a forensic speech. It is of course reassuring to note that Demosthenes and Aeschines seem to agree on this count, but caution is nevertheless to be recommended.

The second attested case of a proposal upheld by the jurors in a *graphe paranomon* is the indictment of Euktemon by Androtion, Glauketes and Melanopos described by Demosthenes in the opening of the Timokrates speech. The background for the trial is as follows. In the assembly Aristophon proposes and carries a *psephisma* that a commission of inquiry be appointed and that all citizens give information about holders of sacred or public money in private hands. At a later date Euktemon lays information to the commission that two named trierarchs are holding public money

---

[18] Cf. e. g. W. W. Goodwin, *Demosthenes On the Crown* (Cambridge 1904) 273; H. Wankel, *Demosthenes: Rede für Ktesiphon über den Kranz* (Heidelberg 1976) I 41.

worth nine and a half talents. He approaches the *boule* and a *probouleuma* is passed. In the following *ekklesia* this *probouleuma* is passed in the *procheirotonia*. Euktemon then addresses the people and, in spite of protests raised by Androtion, Glauketes and Melanopos, moves a proposal that the money be collected from the trierarchs, who in turn shall have recourse to those who possess the money. Androtion, Glauketes and Malanopos immediately indict Euktemon's *psephisma* as unconstitutional, but in the ensuing *graphe paranomon* a *dikasterion* manned with 1001 jurors upholds the *psephisma*.[19] The verdict puts an end to the matter, and no further steps are taken until the first *ekklesia* of the following year, where Epikrates proposes and carries a *psephisma* that *nomothetai* be appointed on the following day; and here Timokrates succeeds in proposing and carrying a *nomos* about the collection of public debts.[20]

This is one of the best surviving descriptions of ecclesiastic procedure and certainly deserves a very close scrutiny. First, it is important to note that Euktemon approaches the *boule* and that a *probouleuma* is passed (προσῆλθε τῇ βουλῇ, προβούλευμ' ἐγράφη). Euktemon is probably not a *bouleutes*,[21] and consequently not the proposer of the *probouleuma* presented to the people in the subsequent *ekklesia*. Thus, Euktemon's proposal, indicted by the *graphe paranomon*, must be different from the *probouleuma* on which a *procheirotonia* is taken at the opening of the session. Second, the aorist προυχειροτόνησεν strongly indicates that in the *procheirotonia* the people voted not against but for the *probouleuma*.[22] Third, as I have argued in a previous study, the *procheirotonia* was probably a vote by which a *probouleuma* was passed if the show of hands was unanimous in its support but postponed for a debate later in the sesssion if only one hand was raised against it.[23] Now, since the *procheirotonia* described in the Timokrates speech, although favourable, was nevertheless followed by a debate, the *probouleuma* cannot have been a proposal drawn up in every detail and ratified by the people. It must have been an open *probouleuma*

---

[19] D. xxiv.11-14, cf. Hansen (above, n. 1) Cat. no 13; P. J. Rhodes, *The Athenian Boule* (Oxford 1972) 158.
[20] D. xxiv.14, 19, 26 ff.
[21] Cf., however, Aeschin iii.220 and D. xxv.42. Thus we cannot rule out the possibility that Euktemon was a member of the *boule* and, possibly, the man who moved the *probouleuma*.
[22] D. xxiv.11. Cf. the simplex χειροτονεῖν which in the present tense means »to vote by a show of hands«; but in the aorist the meaning is invariably »to pass by a show of hands«, cf. Lys. xii.76; Aeschin. ii.13, 27; D. xviii.248, 285-88; xix.121; xxi.171, 179; xxii.20, 62; xxxix.19; liii.5; Hyp. ii.13.
[23] Cf. M. H. Hansen, *The Athenian Ecclesia* (Copenhagen 1983) 127-28.

ordering a debate. But what then was the purpose of this *procheirotonia*? It is worth remembering that there was no clearcut distinction between specific *probouleumata* (to be ratified) and open *probouleumata* (to be debated). An open *probouleuma* might incorporate a positive proposal, the passing of which would necessarily result in a debate.[24] An obvious example of this is Apollodorus' *probouleuma* described in the opening of the Neaira speech.[25] On the analogy of this case the *procheirotonia* in the Timokrates speech should be interpreted as follows: the *probouleuma* occasioned by Euktemon's denunciation to the commission of inquiry may have prescribed that any citizen in possession of public money pay back immediately what he has and that any citizen who knows about public money in private possession immediately inform the people of what he knows. Moreover, the *probouleuma* may have prescribed the procedure to be followed and the penalties to be imposed on defaulters. In the *procheirotonia* this *probouleuma* was passed by the people (unanimously), whereupon Euktemon in the ensuing debate revealed to the people what he had already told the commission about the trierarchs.

During the debate Euktemon moved a proposal (ἔδωκε γνώμην Εὐκτήμων) which Androtion and his companions indicted as unconstitutional (γράφονται τὸ ψήφισμα). In his account of the episode Demosthenes passes immediately from Euktemon's proposal to the indictment brought against it, without mentioning any vote by which it had been passed by the people.[26] In 1974 I inferred, *e silentio*, that no vote was ever taken and that, consequently, the bringing of the *graphe paranomon* must have stopped the debate in the *ekklesia* before the decree had been passed.[27] My argument from silence, however, has been questioned. J.-M. Hannick objects that the term *psephisma* is enough to disprove my reconstruction of the case: »au § 14 d'ailleurs, l'orateur est plus catégorique: ce que les ambassadeurs ont attaqué, c'est un véritable décret (γράφονται τὸ ψήφισμα); et l'on retrouve le même terme au § 101 du discours (τὸ ψήφισμα τὸ Εὐκτήμονος).«[28] But Hannick's line of argument is disproved by several sources which show that ψήφισμα is a term applied not only to decrees actually passed by the people but also to proposals moved from the floor (but never put to vote) and to

---

[24] Cf. Hansen (above, n. 24) 126.
[25] D. lix.3-5, cf. Hansen (above, n. 24) 126-27.
[26] D. xxiv.13.
[27] Hansen (above, n. 1) 51.
[28] Hannick (above, n. 1) 396.

probouleumata (including *probouleumata* that were never passed).²⁹ Thus, ψήφισμα means both 'act' and 'bill'. And in D. xxiv.14 it is impossible to see whether or not Euktemon's *psephisma* was passed. Similarly, in xxiv.101, τὸ ψήφισμα τὸ Εὐκτήμονος does not necessarily imply ratification by the people. The passing of the decree would be implied only if Demosthenes, instead of τὸ ψήφισμα τὸ Εὐκτήμονος, had used the phrase τὸ ψήφισμα τὸ ὑμέτερον³⁰ *vel sim.* In xxiv.117, however, we do find the phrase τὸ ὑμέτερον δόγμα in a reference to the *ekklesia* in which Euktemon moved his proposal: What Demosthenes has in mind must be a decision made by the people, but probably not a decision on Euktemon's proposal. A study af the term *dogma* reveals that it often denotes a decision made by a non-Athenian body of government,³¹ and sometimes denotes, vaguely, a decision made by the Athenian state or some Athenian body of government.³² However, although the term is rather common and is attested both in litterary and in epigraphical sources, it is never once used about a *psephisma tou demou*. Thus, in xxiv.117, δόγμα may be a reference to the decision made by the people in the *procheirotonia*, which occasioned the *psephisma* moved by Euktemon, but it is most unlikely that it is a reference to the *psephisma* itself. On the contrary, Demosthenes' choice of the idiom τὸ ὑμέτερον δόγμα instead of the straightforward τὸ ὑμέτερον ψήφισμα indicates that Euktemon's *psephisma* was never passed by the people in assembly.

With this in mind I return to the passage xxiv.9-14 and to the argument from silence based on this passage. Admittedly, most passages in Attic speeches are ill-suited for arguments from silence, since an orator will report only those facts which favour his case, and tend to omit intermediary procedures which would interest (only) the constitutional historian. But the purpose of the passage D. xxiv.9-14 is precisely to list as many stages of

---

²⁹ For ψήφισμα denoting a προβούλευμα, cf. D. xxiii.90, 92, etc. and the passages quoted above, n. 13. Ψήφισμα is used about a proposal in Aeschin ii,64-68.
³⁰ In D. xxiii.70 τὸ ψήφισμα τὸ τούτου, sc. Ἀριστοκράτους is used about a *probouleuma*; for the idiom τὸ ψήφισμα τὸ ὑμέτερον referring to a decree passed by the people, cf D. xliv.38.
³¹ Τὸ τῶν συμμάχων δόγμα: *IG* II² 96.24; 97.14-15; 103.10-11; 112.13; 123.11-12; D. xix.15, 144; Aeschin. ii.60-61; iii. 69-71; cf. X. *HG* V.ii.37; V.iv.37; VII.iii.11. Τὸ τῶν Ἀμφικτυόνων δόγμα: D. v.19; xviii.153; xix.61, 63-64; Aeschin. iii.116, 124-27. Decision made by a klerouchy: D. xii.16. Decision made by an army: X. *An.* VI.vi.8, 27. Various other types of decision made by foreign states: X. *HG* VI.v.2, 5; VII.3.1; D. xvii.26; xviii.140 Aeschin ii.32. Cf. also D. xxv.16, 62.
³² Δόγμα in a rather vague sense applied to a decision made by the Athenians: X. *HG* VI.2.2 κατὰ δόγμα τῆς πόλεως; And. iv.6; Lys. vi.43; Aeschin. iii.42. The term refers once to a decision of the jurors (D. xxvi.13) and twice to a decision made by the *boule* (D. li.22; X. *HG* VI.v.33.

the procedures as possible. A kind of enumeration is obviously intended, and since the passing of Euktemon's proposal by the people would have strengthened the case argued by Demosthenes, its omission from the account is significant. The whole character of the passage was aptly described by Wilamowitz in another context: »Die Absicht des Redners ist ausschließlich darauf gerichtet, den Eindruck der peinlichsten Genauigkeit zu erwecken, daher verweilt er bei jeder Station, die ein Antrag zu passiren hat, nicht weil auf sie in diesem Falle etwas besonderes ankäme, sondern zum Beweise, daß keine überschlagen ist.«[33] If Wilamowitz' observation is correct, as I believe it is, the argument from silence has force. If the proposal had been put to the vote and passed by the people, Demosthenes would have reported it by inserting, e. g., ὑμεῖς ἐψηφίσασθε or ὑμῖν ἔδοξε between ἔδωκε γνώμην Εὐκτήμων and γράφονται τὸ ψήφισμα. And this observation is strengthened by the juxtaposition of *boule*, *demos* and *dikasterion* in § 9: τοῦ δὲ πράγματος οὐκέτ' ὄντος ἀμφισβητησίμου, ἀλλὰ πρῶτον μὲν τῆς βουλῆς κατεγνωκυίας, εἶτα τοῦ δήμου μίαν ἡμέραν ὅλην ἐπὶ τούτοις αὐτοῖς ἀναλώσαντος, πρὸς δὲ τούτοις δικαστηρίοιν δυοῖν εἰς ἕνα καὶ χιλίους ἐψηφισμένων, ἐνούσης δ' οὐδεμιᾶς ἔτ' ἀποστροφῆς τοῦ μὴ τὰ χρήματα ἔχειν ὑμᾶς, Τιμοκράτης ... ὑπερεῖδεν ... κτλ. Here Demosthenes emphasizes the decisions made by both the *boule* and the *dikasterion*, but about the *ekklesia* he can say only that the *demos* spent an entire session debating the matter. There is no indication that the debate resulted in a decision. Later on in the same section Demosthenes refers, more vaguely, to τὰ γνωσθένθ' ὑπὸ τῆς βουλῆς καὶ τοῦ δήμου καὶ τοῦ δικαστηρίου. A comparison with the following account (in 11-14) indicates that the reference is to the council's provisional decree (προβούλευμα in 11), to the people's vote on the *probouleuma* (προυχειρτόνησεν ὁ δῆμος in 11) and to Euktemon's acquittal in the *graphe paranomon* (ἀπέφυγεν in 14).

But if the people did not vote on Euktemon's *psephisma* before the *graphe paranomon*, they may have had an opportunity to reconsider the matter in a session held after Euktemon had been acquitted by the court. Again, an argument from silence indicates that the hearing before the *dikastai* was the end of the matter. In section 9 Demosthenes enumerates the authorities which treated Euktemon's denunciation of the trierarchs: the *boule*, the *demos* and the *dikasterion*. Then he goes on: ἐνούσης δ' οὐδεμιᾶς ἔτ' ἀποστροφῆς .... There is no indication that the case was submitted to the *ekklesia* for a forth and final treatment. Similarly in 14, having told the

---

[33] U. von Wilamowitz-Moellendorff, *Aristoteles und Athen* (Berlin 1893) II 255.

jurors that Euktemon was acquitted in the *graphe paranomon*, the speaker continues: ἐνταῦθα τί προσῆκεν; τὰ μὲν χρήματα ἔχειν τὴν πόλιν κτλ. The impression conveyed is that the case was closed with the *graphe paranomon* and only reopened when Timokrates proposed his law a month later.

Summing up. Demosthenes' description of the *graphe paranomon* brought against Euktemon indicates that the *psephisma* moved by Euktemon was stopped in the *ekklesia* before the vote was taken, and never sent back to the *ekklesia* after the court had acquitted Euktemon.

The sources we have for *graphe paranomon* against proposals (D.xxiv) and *probouleumata* (Aeschin iii & D. xviii) indicate that a motion acquitted by the court was not only declared constitutional; by the jurors' vote it was also ratified and could take effect without further consideration. It follows that the jurors hearing a *graphe paranomon* must have been concerned not only with legal but also with political problems. And this view is abundantly attested in all preserved speeches and fragments of speeches delivered in a *graphe paranomon*: The speakers debate not only whether a *psephisma* is constitutional but also whether it is expedient. The discussion of the political aspects of a case usually fills the larger part of a speech,[34] and they are often singled out as the most important.[35] Some historians, especially legal historians, take the view that these arguments are irrelevant from a legal point of view and that the tendency to use the *graphe paranomon* as a field for political battle was undoubtedly very effective but essentially a misuse of the legal system.[36] In my opinion this is a misrepresentation of the political aspects of the Athenian administration of justice. In contemporary Europe we expect the courts to be independent and separate institutions

---

[34] D. xxii: Androtion's decree is unconstitutional (5-34) and inexpedient (35-78). D. xxiii: Aristokrates' decree is unconstitutional (22-99) and inexpedient (100-214). Aeschin iii: Ktesiphon's decree is unconstitutional (9-48) and inexpedient (49-200). The political aspects of the *graphe paranomon* are also mentioned side by side with the legal aspects in Lycurg. fr. 57, Conomis.

[35] In the speech *Against Androtion* Demosthenes is so much carried away by the political arguments that he never returns to the unconstitutionality of the *psephisma*, not even in the *epilogos*. In the speech *Against Aristokrates* the political arguments are emphasized in the opening of the speech (xxiii.7) and in 101 we learn that, though the decree is certainly unconstitutional, it is to an even higher degree harmful to the interests of the Athenian people. In his speech *Against Ktesiphon* Aeschines stated that in his opinion the political arguments carry more weight than the legal (iii.49).

[36] Cf. e. g. J. N. Madvig, *Eine Bemerkung über die Gränze der Competenz des Volkes und der Gerichte bei den Athenaiern* in *Kleine Philologische Schriften* (Leipzig 1875) 378-90; H. J. Wolff, »Normenkontrolle« *und Gesetzesbegriff in der attischen Demokratie* (Heidelberg 1970) 13-14; D. M. MacDowell, *The Law in Classical Athens* (London 1978) 52.

which ought to do their best to keep out of politics. The Athenian courts, on the other hand, were an integrated part of the political system, and to use the courts for policy-making was certainly not an abuse of the system. Thus, in a *graphe paranomon*, the jurors were obliged to rescind a *psephisma* not only if it was unconstitutional in form or content but also if it was inexpedient; and a citizenship decree, for example, could be quashed on the sole ground that the honorand was unworthy of the privilege granted him by the people.[37] Thus the political arguments advanced in *graphai paranomon* are not only important but also relevant; and since the jurors in all kinds of *graphe paranomon* were used to discussions of the political aspects of the case, it is no wonder that when a proposal had been indicted they could be entrusted with taking a position not only on the constitutionality of the *psephisma* but also on its expediency and merits from a political point of view.

What arguments can be adduced against my reconstruction? To the best of my knowledge no passage in any other source counterbalances or weakens my interpretation of the *graphai paranomon* brought against the proposals moved by Euktemon and Ktesiphon: The only argument that can be thrown into the other scale is the *a priori* assumption mentioned above: that it is unbelievable that the Athenians would have allowed the *dikasteria* to arrogate powers belonging to the *ekklesia* and to take an active part in the political decision-making process by passing or rejecting a *psephisma* instead of simply deciding whether it was *paranomon*. Thus a proposal or a *probouleuma* declared constitutional by the *dikastai* must have been sent back to the *ekklesia* to be passed (or rejected) by the sovereign people.

The problem about this line of argument is that, in fourth-century Athens, the *ekklesia* was no longer sovereign[38] and that, from 403/2 on, an important part of political decision-making was indisputably entrusted to the jurors, i. e. the passing of all *nomoi* (permanent general rules).[39] I trust that no historian will any longer deny that legislation in the true sense of the word had been transferred from the *demos* in assembly to the *nomothetai*. But the *nomothetai* were appointed from the panel of 6,000 jurors.[40] Thus, given that the Athenians had entrusted the passing of *nomoi* to sections of

---

[37] D. lix.89-91; cf. Aeschin. iii.50.
[38] Cf. M. H. Hansen, *The Athenian Assembly* (Oxford 1987) 94-107.
[39] Cf. D. M. MacDowell, *Taw-making at Athens in the Fourth Century B. C.*, *JHS* 95 (1975) 63.
[40] Cf. M. H. Hansen, *Athenian* Nomothesia, *GRBS* 26 (1985) 363-65.

jurors acting as *nomothetai*, there can be no *a priori* obstacle to the view that they may have entrusted the passing of a *psephisma* to another section of the jurors acting as *dikastai* in a *graphe paranomon*. All speeches delivered in a *graphe paranomon* show that the issue at stake was not only the legal problem of whether the *psephisma* was constitutional but also the political problem of whether it was expedient. Furthermore, when the *dikastai* acquitted the proposer of a *psephisma* already passed by the people, his decree took effect automatically. I have no problem in believing that the Athenians followed the same procedure when the *dikastai* had heard and upheld a proposal indicted by a *graphe paranomon*. The sources we have do not allow us to state a final answer but, on the evidence we have, I hold that the interpretation of Aeschin. iii and D. xxiv outlined above is the most likely reconstruction of the procedure, and constitutes yet another piece of the jig-saw puzzle which shows the increased importance of the *dikasteria* in fourth-century Athens.

TWO NOTES ON DEMOSTHENES' SYMBOULEUTIC SPEECHES

BY
MOGENS HERMAN HANSEN

I. WERE DEMOSTHENES' SYMBOULEUTIC SPEECHES DELIVERED IN SUPPORT OF PROPOSALS?

In the reconstruction of Demosthenes' political activities a major problem is whether or not his published symbouleutic speeches were delivered in support of proposals to be voted on after the debate. In my opinion, the *First Philippic* is the only speech to be connected with a bill. In all the other *demegoriai*, Demosthenes analyses and advises without moving proposals. Probably, we have preserved all Demosthenes' published *demegoriai*,[1] and if the published speeches do report what Demosthenes actually told the people,[2] the inference is that he stated in writing only his general views on Athenian and Macedonian policy, whereas he regularly left unpublished all the speeches he delivered in support of his numerous proposals. This view can be substantiated by a review of the preserved speeches:

Although the speech *On the Symmories*, delivered in 354/3, includes detailed provisions for a reform of the liturgic system (16-23) and although there is a vague reference to a vote to be taken (14 ψηφίζεσθαι), I believe that Schäfer is right in maintaining that 'wir haben dagegen keine Spur davon dass er seinen Organisationsplan förmlich als Gesetzesantrag eingebracht habe.' (I, 468-69).[3] The speech was, apparently, well received (D. 15.6) but led to nothing.

In the Speech *On the Syntaxis* (353/2) Demosthenes explicitly states (§§ 13-14) that he has come forward only to advise the people and not to move a proposal. Similarly, in the speech *For the Megalopolitans* (352/1) there is no trace whatsoever of an appended proposal.

The *First Philippic,* however, is different from the other speeches. Demosthenes proposes the mobilization of (a) an expeditionary force of 50 triremes held in readiness in Athens, (b) a permanent force of 2,000 men foot and 500 men horse, of which a quarter are to be Athenian citizens. The force shall operate in the Thracian sea supported by 10 triremes. Demosthenes appends a budget for the permanent force, and a detailed scheme for how it can be financed is read out to the people at the end of § 29.[4] The proposal was probably voted down by the people,[5] but that Demosthenes in this case moves a proposal and not only advises the people is apparent from the following four observations: (a) the proposal is very detailed and fills the whole central part of the speech (13-29), (b) it is once described as a bill handed in writing (ταῦτ' ἐστὶν ἃ ἐγὼ γέγραφα, 33), (c) Demosthenes expects his proposal to be put to the vote (ἐπειδὰν δ' ἐπιχειροτονῆτε τὰς γνώμας, ἂν ὑμῖν ἀρέσκῃ, χειροτονήσετε ..., 30). (d) a document (now lost) was inserted in the speech and read out to the people (29).[6]

The *First Philippic* is exceptional. In his speech *For the Liberty of the Rhodians* (351/0) Demosthenes only exhorts the Athenians to assist the exiled Rhodian democrats (28) and he has no proposal to make about any definite course of action. The three *Olynthiacs* are also general political speeches, delivered in the autumn of 349/8. In *Ol.* I Demosthenes supports the idea of an auxiliary force to be sent to Olynthos but he does not venture to move any proposal on how to provide the necessary money for the campaign (σὺ γράφεις ταῦτ' εἶναι στρατιωτικά; μὰ Δί' οὐκ ἔγωγε, 19). Similarly in *Ol.* II there is only one single section (11) in which he suggests (without referring to any proposal) that an auxiliary force be sent to Olynthos and an embassy to the Thessalians. *Ol.* III may have been delivered in support of a proposal to appoint *nomothetai,* not to pass any new law but to abrogate some of the laws in force. The central section (10-13) is rather explicit, but it is probably significant that Demosthenes washes his hands and exhorts the political leaders who proposed and carried these *nomoi* to take it upon themselves to abrogate them. The explanation may of course be that Demosthenes proposes the *psephisma tou demou* by which *nomothetai* are appointed and *ho boulomenos* is invited to propose the abrogation of the inexpedient laws, viz. the laws on the Theoric Fund. We know from the speech *Against*

Timokrates that the *psephisma* appointing *nomothetai* and the *nomos* to be voted on by the *nomothetai* were proposed by different persons (viz. Epikrates, 27, and Timokrates, 39-40, 71). A similar division of labour may apply to the *Third Olynthiac*. On the other hand, the optative ἕλοισθε in the *epilogos* (36) is the only, very vague, indication of a decision to be made, and my impression is that Demosthenes outlines a definite course of action but will not assume the responsibility for a proposal.

On the Peace (346/5) is undoubtedly a general speech and has no reference to any proposed *psephisma*. The *Second Philippic* is more problematical. It was delivered in a debate attended by foreign envoys (28), probably the Macedonian embassy to Athens in 344/3 headed by Python of Byzantion. No definite line of action is on the agenda, only a reply to the embassy. The crucial passage is 28: περὶ μὲν δὴ τῶν ἡμῖν πρακτέων καθ' ὑμᾶς αὐτοὺς ὕστερον βουλεύσεθε, ἂν σωφρονῆτε· ἃ δὲ νῦν ἀποκρινάμενοι τὰ δέοντ' ἂν εἴητ' ἐψηφισμένοι, ταῦτ' ἤδη λέξω. <ΑΠΟΚΡΙΣΙΣ>. ἢν μὲν οὖν δίκαιον ... κτλ. If we follow Abbé d'Olivet and some editors (e.g. Butcher in *OCT*) in inserting ΑΠΟΚΡΙΣΙΣ the inference is that Demosthenes' speech comments on an explicit reply to the envoys. But the emendation is questionable, and I prefer to follow the MSS, in which case Demosthenes restricts himself to warning the Athenians against Philip without suggesting any specific reply to be voted on.

In the speech On the *Chersonese* (342/1) Demosthenes predicts that he will probably be criticized for addressing the *ekklesia* without assuming the responsibility for his advice by proposing a *psephisma* (68, 73). The *Third Philippic* (342/1) is an analysis of the present political situation and its background. Only in the concluding sections does Demosthenes suggest a course of action, but even here he speaks generally about armament (70), embassies (71, 73) and financial support to the troops in the Chersonese. So the two phrases: ἐγὼ νὴ Δί' ἐρῶ, καὶ γράψω δέ, ὥστ' ἂν βούλησθε χειροτονήσετε (70) and: ἐγὼ μὲν δὴ ταῦτα λέγω, ταῦτα γράφω (76) are probably no more than a statement of his intention in near future to move *psephismata* concerning these questions. Finally, the *Fourth Philippic* (342/1?) contains only one specific proposal, that an embassy be sent to the King of Persia (33). It is certainly not coined as a *psephisma,* but stated as a general idea to be taken up by others or by Demosthenes himself later on.

II. DEMOSTHENES' PUBLICATION OF HIS SYMBOULEUTIC SPEECHES

It is often stated, but never substantiated, that Demosthenes virtually initiated the custom of publishing speeches delivered in the assembly,[8] and it is often implied but never discussed, that all genuine Demosthenic *demegoriai,* published in his lifetime and known to the ancient critics, are still preserved.[9] An examination of the evidence supports this view and allows us to ask some very interesting questions: Why were *demegoriai* hardly ever published? and why did Demosthenes publish precisely those speeches which we can still read today? In this note I will give a survey of the evidence and leave a detailed discussion of the implications to a future study.

Of all the 150 preserved speeches by Attic orators, a maximum of 19 are *demegoriai* delivered in the Athenian *ecclesia*: Lysias 28 and 34, Andokides 2 and 3, Demosthenes 1-10 and 13-17.[10] Now, if we take *demegoria* to mean a symbouleutic speech actually heard by the people, the number is reduced to 16. Lys. 28 is not a symbouleutic speech, but a speech for the prosecution delivered in an *eisangelia* heard by the people.[11] Lysias 34 is probably a pamphlet never delivered (cf. *infra* page 64), and Andokides 2 is a petition and not an ordinary symbouleutic speech. In the *Corpus Demosthenicum,* 7 is probably, and 17 is possibly, a speech by Hegesippos, erroneously ascribed to Demosthenes.[12] So concentrating on proper *demegoriai,* we have one by Andokides, two ascribed to Hegesippos, and thirteen by Demosthenes.[13] But, as usual, the preservation of texts is haphazard, and the listing of preserved speeches must be supplemented with the exciting but laborious hunt for fragments and titles of lost speeches.

I will first discuss fragments of Demosthenic speeches. In addition to the preserved speeches, we have fragments and titles of six forensic speeches and one epideictic speech.[14] Some of the lost court room speeches may have been genuine, we don't know. On the other hand, a list of Demosthenes' lost *demegoriai* comprises only three items, all questionable: (a) a speech ὑπὲρ τῶν ῥητόρων, allegedly delivered in 335 in reply to Alexander's request for the extradition of 8 or 10 Athenian political leaders, including Demosthenes. (b) A speech περὶ τοῦ μὴ ἐκδοῦναι Ἅρπαλον, allegedly delivered in support of Demosthenes' proposal that Harpalos be arrested and his money confiscated. (c) A speech for Diphilos called: Διφίλῳ δημηγορικός αἰτοῦντι δωρεάς. None of the three can be accepted as a genuine Demosthenic *demegoria*, once published but now lost.

Re (a). The principal authority is *Suda* s.v. ἅμα. δοτική. Δημοσθένης ἐπὶ τοῦ εὐθέως καὶ παραχρῆμα ἔταξε, καὶ ἐν τῷ ὑπὲρ τῶν ῥητόρων λόγῳ εἰπών· οὐ γὰρ ὁ θάνατος τοῖς εὖ φρονοῦσιν οἰκτρός· τοῦτο γὰρ ἅμα τῷ γενέσθαι πάντων κατέγνωσται (1458, Adler = Sauppe fr. 12). To this reference is added Diod. 17.15.3: Δημοσθένους δὲ λόγον πεφροντισμένον διελθόντος, and Livius 9.18: *id quod ex monumentis orationum patet*. There may have been a published speech, but was it by Demosthenes? All critics have pointed out, correctly in my opinion, that the silence of Dionysios is crucial.[15] If a genuine Demosthenic speech on this subject had existed, Dionysios would have mentioned it, if not in his *Demosthenes*, then in his *Letter to Ammaios*. Some scholars assume that a genuine *demegoria* has been erroneously ascribed to Demosthenes (e.g. Blass III. 1 p. 61). Judging from the fragments assigned to this speech, I prefer to follow Sauppe in believing that the speech was a later rhetorical composition and not a genuine *demegoria*.

Re (b) Our only source for the speech on the extradition of Harpalos is Dion. *Dem*. 57: εἰ μέντοι τινὲς ἐν τοῖς ψευδεπιγράφοις εἰσὶ λόγοις ἀηδεῖς καὶ φορτικαὶ καὶ ἄγροικοι κατασκευαί, ὡς ἐν τοῖς κατ' Ἀριστογείτονος β' καὶ ἐν τῇ ἀπολογίᾳ τῶν δώρων καὶ ἐν τῷ ‹περὶ τοῦ› μὴ ἐκδοῦναι Ἅρπαλον καὶ ἐν τῷ κατὰ Νεαίρας καὶ ἐν τῷ περὶ τῶν πρὸς Ἀλέξανδρον συνθηκῶν ἐν ἄλλοις τε συχνοῖς, οὓς ὁ Δημοσθένης οὐκ ἔγραψεν, ἐν ἑτέρᾳ δηλοῦταί μοι πραγματείᾳ τὰ περὶ Δημοσθένη. The title is identical with the speech referred to in *Din*. 11: ὑπὲρ τοῦ μὴ ἐκδοῦναι Ἅρπαλον Ἀλεξάνδρῳ· "οὐκ ἄξιον ἄρα θαυμάζειν." οὐδ' οὗτος ὁ λόγος ἐμφαίνει τὸν Δεινάρχου χαρακτῆρα· εἰ γὰρ κἂν μηδὲν ἄλλο, τὸ γ' οὖν ἠλίθιον καὶ σοφιστικὸν εὕροι τις ἂν ἐν αὐτῷ πολύ, τὸ πλεῖστον ἀπέχον τῶν Δεινάρχου χαρακτήρων (660 = Sauppe fr. XL). Both references are probably to the same speech which, according to

Dionysios, was neither by Demosthenes, nor by Deinarchos. Both the notorious occasion and the description in Dion. *Din.* 11 suggest a rhetorical composition.

Re (c). The speech for Diphilos is discussed by Dionysios in his essay on Deinarchos and is recorded among the ψευδεπίγραφοι δημόσιοι. The incipit is διὰ τὸ μὴ ῥᾴδιον εἶναι and Dionysios brings the following comment: τοῦτον ἐπείσθην ὑπὸ Δημοσθένους γεγράφθαι τὸν λόγον, ὅτι τὰς δωρεὰς ἔγραψεν αὐτῷ Δημοσθένης, ὡς Δείναρχος ἐν τῷ κατὰ Δημοσθένους λόγῳ δεδήλωκε, καὶ ὅτι ἐπὶ τέλει τοῦ λόγου ὁ Δίφιλος Δημοσθένην παρακαλεῖ συνήγορον. ἀπίθανον δὲ οἶμαι εἶναι τὰς μὲν τιμὰς οὕτω γράφειν εὐνοοῦντα τῷ Διφίλῳ τὸν Δημοσθένην, λόγον δὲ παρὰ Δεινάρχου λαβόντα περιιδεῖν. (659 = Sauppe fr. XXXVI). Arguing from the occasion and the persons involved Dionysios prefers to ascribe the speech to Demosthenes, but he does not mention it among the *demegoriai* in his letter to Ammaios,[16] and Blass notes (III. 1 page 56 note 1) that the accumulation of short syllables in the opening words makes the ascription unlikely. Since Diphilos was probably not prominent enough to be an obvious choice for a late rhetorical exercise, the lost speech may well have been a genuine *demegoria*, published in the 4th century but wrongly ascribed by some to Demosthenes and by others to Deinarchos.

Apart from these three lost speeches, ancient and medieval authors bring some 60 apothegms ascribed to Demosthenes but not to be found in any of the preserved speeches.[17] Some may have been taken from lost forensic speeches, others however seem to come from *demegoriai,* especially some of those transmitted by Agatharkides and Lucilius Rufus.[18] But of these several have been ascribed to the speech ὑπερ τῶν ῥητόρων, discussed above,[19] others are aphorisms and sayings, all anecdotal and, if genuine, reported by historians and rhetoricians and not fragments of published speeches.[20]

According to the *Lives of the Ten Orators* ascribed to Plutarch, the *Corpus Demosthenicum* comprised 65 genuine speeches.[21] As transmitted to us, the corpus consists of 61 speeches. Admittedly it includes some speeches already questioned in Antiquity. But (like their modern colleagues) the ancient critics never agreed on which speeches were spurious. So any count of allegedly genuine speeches would undoubtedly include some speeches questioned by others. So some of the spurious speeches in the surviving corpus are undoubtedly included among the 65 'genuine' speeches reported by Pseudo-Plutarch. The conclusion seems to be that only 5-10 speeches, regarded by some but not by all as genuine works by Demosthenes, have been lost, and they were probably all court room speeches. There is no reason to suppose that Demosthenes published other *demegoriai* than those transmitted to us. The corpus of 65 speeches may have comprised the three spurious *demegoriai* discussed above.

Finally, a few words must be said about the collection of *prooimia* transmitted in the *Corpus Demosthenicum*. This very interesting part of the corpus has never attracted the attention it deserves, and here I will restrict myself to reporting the view of Blass, Rupprecht and Focke, as modified by Clavaud.[22] (a) The 55 (or 56) short pieces are all, as they purport to be, introductions to *demegoriai*. (b) They are all by Demosthenes. (c) According to Blass, they are exercises composed in advance in order to have a suitable *prooimion* ready for any possible occasion.[23] (d) According to Clavaud, they are written introductions to speeches actually delivered by Demosthenes in the *ekklesia*. Some of them may have been reused, revised or unrevised. Five are indeed almost identical with *prooimia* of published *demegoriai*.[24] Here Clavaud takes the separately published *prooimia* to be the final versions, more polished than the *prooimia* of the published speeches. (e) The *prooimia* were not published by Demosthenes, but left among his papers and published posthumously, perhaps by Demochares.[25] If Clavaud's interpretation is on the right lines, it follows that Demosthenes never published the central parts and the *epilogoi* of all the *demegoriai* for which the *prooimia* were composed. According to Clavaud, a written introduction may often have been followed by an improvised and not elaborately prepared speech.[26] So the posthumous publication of the *prooimia* strengthens the view that we have preserved all the full-size *demegoriai* published by Demosthenes.

Titles and fragments of lost speeches by other orators point to the same conclusion: that remarkably few *demegoriai* published in classical Athens have been lost during late Antiquity and the Middle Ages.

Three of Antiphon's lost speeches may have been delivered before the Athenian *ekklesia*, viz., περὶ τοῦ Λιμναίων φόρου (Fr. IX, Sauppe), περὶ τοῦ Λινδίων φόρου (Fr. X, Sauppe) and περὶ τοῦ Σαμοθρακῶν φόρου (Fr. XVI, Sauppe). – All three speeches were probably written by Antiphon for envoys from these three *poleis,* and the issue was probably the same in all three cases: protests stated by allies against the Athenian assessment of the *phoros.* Although the speeches may have been delivered in the *ekklesia,* they are not symbouleutic speeches, but rather forensic speeches concerning the Naval Confederacy.

From Andokides' hand we have preserved two *demegoriai:* The second speech *On His Return* and the third speech *On the Peace,* cf. *supra* page 60. But in the lexica there are two references to a lost symbouleutic speech which may have been a *demegoria* delivered in the Athenian *ekklesia,* cf. Fr. II, Sauppe. Nothing more can be learned from the two short notes, both quoting Ἀνδοκίδης Συμβουλευτικῷ as their source for a word (*Lex. Seg.* 94.21; Phot. s.v. ναυκρατίαν).

Of all the 138 speeches ascribed to Lysias only two are *demegoriai,* i.e. Ὑπὲρ Νικίου (Fr. 191-93, Sauppe, = D.H. *Lysias* 483) and Περὶ τοῦ μὴ καταλῦσαι τὴν πάτριον πολιτείαν Ἀθήνησι (Lys. 34 = D.H. *Lysias* 525-33). The first is allegedly a speech held by Nikias in the *ekklesia* in Syracuse after the Athenian defeat in 413. According to Dionysios, it is not by Lysias, and, in any case, it was a fiction, a literary composition written several years after Nikias' death and never delivered in an *ekklesia.* The speech on the ancestral constitution is Lysias' famous attack on Phormisios' proposal that full citizen rights be restricted to Athenians who own landed property. A long part of the speech is quoted by Dionysios in his essay on Lysias. Dionysios reports that it was written for a distinguished political leader (526). If so, this speech is our only known example of a *demegoria* written by a logographer for a client. Neither among the preserved speeches nor among the fragments and titles of lost speeches is there any other reliable evidence for a logographic *demegoria* (On Din. fr. XXXVI, Sauppe, cf. *supra* page 62). Furthermore, we cannot even be sure that Lysias did write the speech for an Athenian citizen who delivered it in the *ekklesia.* Dionysios expresses his doubt as to whether it was ever delivered: εἰ μὲν οὖν ἐρρήθη τότε ἄδηλον (526). So the speech may well have been a pamphlet or an essay written in the manner of a *demegoria,* which was quite usual, cf. *infra* page 67.

Among Hypereides' works Blass (III, 2 19) records no less than seven symbouleutic speehes (nos. 8-14), but several items on his list are questionable. No. 10 is called Πλαταικός (Plut. *Mor.* 350 B) and to judge from the title this speech was delivered by Hypereides as an ambassador (cf. Blass nos. 1-7) and not as a *rhetor* addressing the *ekklesia*. The only evidence for nos. 11 and 12 is the following note in Ps. Plut. *Vitae X Oratorum* 848E: καὶ περὶ τῶν στρατηγῶν ὧν ᾔτει (Alexander) παρ' Ἀθηναίων ἀντεῖπε (Hypereides) καὶ περὶ τῶν τριηρῶν (= Fr. 190 & 194, Sauppe). The reference is undoubtedly to symbouleutic speeches delivered in the *ecclesia,* but there is no evidence that the source was a published version of the speeches. It may as well have been a work of history, a biography of Hypereides or some forensic speech now lost. The same observation applies to Blass no. 13: Ὑπὲρ Χάρητος περὶ τοῦ ἐπὶ Ταινάρῳ ξενικοῦ for which the only source is (again) Ps. Plut. *Vitae X Oratorum* 848 E: συνεβούλευσε δὲ καὶ τὸ ἐπὶ Ταινάρῳ ξενικὸν μὴ διαλῦσαι, οὗ Χάρης ἡγεῖτο, εὐνόως πρὸς τὸν στρατηγὸν διακείμενος (= Fr. 225, Sauppe). Finally I believe that Blass is right in bracketing no. 14, Ὑπὲρ Ἁρπάλου (= Fr. 49, Sauppe) as a forgery: εἰ δὲ μὴ ψευδὴς ὁ Ὑπερείδου λόγος ὑπὲρ Ἁρπάλου, ... (Poll. 10.159). So we are left with nos. 8 and 9 as genuine symbouleutic speeches published by Hypereides: No. 8 is referred to three times by Harpocration: Ὑπερείδης ἐν τῷ περὶ τοῦ Πολύευκτον στρατηγεῖν (= Fr. 182-84, Sauppe). In the *ekklesia* Hypereides was probably supporting a proposal that Polyeuktos be appointed commander-in-chief of an armed force. No. 9 deals with the colony sent to the Adriatic in 325, and is referred to twice by Harpocration: Ὑπερείδης ἐν τῷ περὶ τῆς φυλακῆς τῶν Τυρρήνων (= Fr. 195-96, Sauppe). I follow Böckh (*Seeurkunden* 459-61) in assuming that the speech was symbouleutic and delivered before the people.

Most of Deinarchos' lost speeches are obviously forensic to be delivered before a *dikasterion* in a public or in a private action. But Dionysios' list of titles includes one unquestionable *demegoria*, and some other titles of lost speeches are problematical and deserve discussion. The *demegoria* is the speech for Diphilos (D.H. *Din.* 658 = Fr. XXXVI, Sauppe, Fr. XLI, Conomis) discussed above page 62. Titles of speeches that may have been *demegoriai* are (a) Τυρρηνικός (Sauppe and Conomis fr. XII) which, however, was rather a speech made by a trierarch in a public action heard by the jurors and related to the colony to be sent to the Adriatic in 325 (Cf. Böckh, *Seeurkunden* 459). (b) Ὑπὲρ τοῦ μὴ ἐκδοῦναι Ἅρπαλον Ἀλεξάνδρῳ (Fr. XL, Sauppe, Fr. XLV, Conomis), according to Dionysios not by Deinarchos and, if we follow Blass III.2 301-02, perhaps to be identified with the same title of a lost speech in the *Corpus Demosthenicum*, cf. *supra* 61. (c) Δηλιακός (Fr. XLI. Sauppe, Fr. XLVI, Conomis) on which Blass (III.2 302) has the following comment: Scheint gar keine Rede gewesen zu sein, sondern die Schrift eines älteren, aus Delos gebürtigen Deinarchos.

Minor orators can be treated under one heading: in numerous cases Aristotle (in the *Rhetoric*) or Plutarch or some other late author brings a quotation from a *demegoria* and, on the basis of such quotations, Sauppe has often included the speaker in his edition of the fragments of the Attic Orators. This is fair enough, but must not entail the misleading assumption that the fragment(s) come(s) from a published version of the speech(es). What is quoted is often some famous saying which was probably transmitted indirectly and not taken from a published speech. One example may suffice: In *Rhet*. 1411a5-6 Aristotle says: ὥσπερ ... ἔφη ... Λεπτίνης περὶ Λακεδαιμονίων, οὐκ ἂν περιιδεῖν τὴν Ἑλλάδα ἑτερόφθαλμον γενομένην, cf. Sauppe XXXIX page 250. This quotation, ascribed to different orators on different occasions, may be anecdotal, and in any case there is no reason to assume that Aristotle studied an edition of Leptines' speech. The same observation applies to famous sayings ascribed to Kydias (Sauppe LVI page 318 = Arist. *Rhet*. 1384b32-35), Demokrates (Sauppe LIX page 320 fr. 2 = Plut. *Mor*. 803 D) and Polycharmos (Sauppe LXXII page 344 = Plut. *Mor*. 726 A). In other cases, however, there can be no doubt that the source of a quotation is a published work, but then the speech quoted or referred to is forensic and not symbouleutic, cf. Polyxenos (Sauppe LXXI page 344 = Greg. Cor. ad Hermog. 7 p. 1272, Walz). One exception is a fragment of Philinos, quoted by Harpokration s.v. θεωρικά and referred to in the following way: Φιλῖνος δὲ ἐν τῇ πρὸς Σοφοκλέους καὶ Εὐριπίδου εἰκόνας περὶ Εὐβούλου λέγων φησίν ... κτλ.[27] The lost speech is sometimes taken to be a *demegoria*,[28] but if it is to be connected with Lykourgos' law about the tragic poets (PsPlut. *Vitae X Oratorum* 841 F, cf. Sauppe 319a29ff), it may as well have been a speech delivered before the *nomothetai* (cf. for a possible parallel Theodektes fr. i, Sauppe XXXII page 247a), or a speech delivered before a *dikasterion* in a *graphe nomon me epitedeion theinai, vel sim.* We must confess our ignorance and cannot take the fragment of Philinos to be sufficient evidence for a published *demegoria.*

The symbouleutic speech, as a genre, was used not only for *demegoriai* actually delivered in the *ekklesia,* but also for essays dealing with political problems. The most famous examples are Isokrates' speeches *Areopagitikos* (7), *On the Peace* (8) and *Plataikos* (14); but in the fragments of the orators other examples can be found: According to the *Suda,* (s.v. Θρασύμαχος Adler 462) the writings of Thrasymachos the sophist included some symbouleutic speeches, and fragments of two are preserved: the most important is the long fragment on the ancestral constitution (Diels/Kranz 85 fr. 1 = Sauppe fr. 2) in which the speaker addresses the Athenian people. Since Thrasymachos was a citizen of Chalkedon it is most unlikely that he ever attended the Athenian *ekklesia,* and the whole character of the fragment indicates that the treatise was rather a pamphlet or an essay cast in the form of a *demegoria.* The much shorter fragment of the speech *For the People of Larisa* is more difficult to classify. Thrasymachos may have held the speech in Athens as an ambassador (as Gorgias did in 427) or written the speech for the ambassadors, but he may also have published an exercise, a possibility suggested by Sauppe (162): Legatis Larisaeorum Thrasymachus orationem vel re vera scripsit vel quasi scribenda esset composuit, ut exemplum discipulis exstaret. The third example is Isokrates' son, Aphareus, who in the *Vitae X Oratorum* (839 C) is described as the author of forensic and symbouleutic speeches: συνέγραψε μὲν λόγους, οὐ πολλοὺς δέ, δικανικούς τε καὶ συμβουλευτικούς. Aphareus may have been politically active and he may have delivered his speeches before the jurors and the people. But though recorded as a trierarch, he is never mentioned as a political leader. He is furthermore the author of numerous tragedies, and, following Blass (II. 72), I suspect that his *demegoriai* were essays, in the manner of his father, and not speeches to be held before the people.

The examination of fragments and titles of speeches of Attic orators shows that, of lost *demegoriai,* we have evidence of only one by Andokides, two by Hypereides, and one ascribed by some to Demosthenes by others to Deinarchos. To these four may perhaps be added one by Philinos and one of the two other *demegoriai,* erroneously ascribed to

Demosthenes, *viz.*, the speech ὑπὲρ τῶν ῥητόρων, which may have been a genuine speech by some other *rhetor*, but probably was a rhetorical exercise. A total of four to six lost *demegoriai* is remarkably small, especially when compared with the number of lost forensic speeches: of Hypereides 5 court room speeches are preserved, but we have titles and/or fragments of 53 lost forensic speeches. For other *rhetores* the figures are: Lysias 30 (128), Isaios 12 (44), Lykourgos 1 (14), Deinarchos 3 (90). The bracketed figures of lost forensic speeches are based on Sauppe and on Blass. For all orators the number of lost forensic speeches is many times greater than the number of preserved speeches. By analogy we must conclude that, if it had been customary to publish *demegoriai*, many more would have been known to us, perhaps not directly by the preservation of the full text, but at least indirectly through quotations and references to numerous *demegoriai,* once published but now lost.

It is often stated that Demosthenes initiated the custom to publish *demegoriai*. It seems more correct to say that Demosthenes was exceptional in publishing several of the speeches he delivered in the assembly. Moreover, considering Demosthenes' unmatched fame in Antiquity, it is almost certain that if he had published more *demegoriai* than those transmitted to us, the ancient critics would have preserved at least the titles and some quotations from these speeches. The silence of our sources is significant and gives rise to at least three important questions: (a) why did Demosthenes publish his *demegoriai*? (b) Why (as already Dionysios noted)[29] are all his published *demegoria* earlier than the final war against Philip in 340-38? (c) Why did he never publish any of his numerous *demegoriai* delivered in support of a decree which he proposed and carried in the *ekklesia*?[30] These questions will be discussed in a future study on Demosthenes' symbouleutic speeches.[31]

NOTES

[1] Discussed and substantiated in the following note pages 60-68.

[2] For a discussion of this important problem cf. Ch. D. Adams *Are the Political "Speeches" of Demosthenes to be Regarded as Political Pamphlets?*, *TAPA* 43 (1912) 5-22, and M. Lavency, *Aspects de la logographie judiciaire attique* (Louvain 1964) 189-94 with further references.

[3] A Schäfer *Demosthenes und seine Zeit* I-III (2nd ed. Leipzig 1885-87). Note, moreover, that Demosthenes' scheme is in the nature of a general and permanent rule. It takes the

form of a *nomos* and not of a *psephisma,* and the competent body of government is accordingly the *nomothetai* and not the *ekklesia.* Demosthenes may have proposed to appoint *nomothetai.* It would have been unconstitutional to ask the people to vote on his scheme. cf. M. H. Hansen, *Did the Athenian Ecclesia Legislate after 403/2?, GRBS* 20 (1979) 27-53.

4 D. 4.13-15: introduction to the proposal, 16-18: the force of 50 triremes, 19-22: the permanent force, 23-27: the purpose of the force, 28-29: the cost of the force with a πόρου ἀπόδειξις read out to the people at the end of 29.

5 Cf. G.L. Cawkwell, *Philip of Macedon* (London 1978) 81.

6 It is worth noting that D 4 is the only *demegoria* containing documents to be read out to the people (πόρου ἀπόδειξις in 29, and ἐπιστολῆς ἀνάγνωσις in 37). In the *Second Philippic* 28 ἀπόκρισις has been inserted by some modern editors (cf. *infra*), and in the *Third Philippic* 46 ἐκ τοῦ γραμματείου ἀναγιγνώσκει is preserved only in some MSS and deleted by most editors, correctly in my opinion.

7 cf. G. L. Cawkwell, *Demosthenes' Policy after the Peace of Philocrates, CQ* 13 (1963) 123-27.

8 Cf. e.g. G. Kennedy *The Art of Persuasion in Greece* (London 1963) 205-06; H. Ll. Hudson-Williams *Political Speeches in Athens, CQ* 1 (1951) 73.

9 Cf. e.g. the survey of preserved and lost speeches in F. Blass *Die attische Beredsamkeit* III. 1 (3rd ed. Leipzig 1893) 54-60.

10 Demosthenes 12 is in fact a letter from Philip to the Athenians, and Demosthenes 11, the reply to Philip's letter, is probably not a real *demegoria,* but a speech inserted in a historical treatise, according to Didymos by Anaximenes of Lampsakos (Didymos, In Demosthenem Col. 11,10).

11 Cf. M. H. Hansen *Eisangelia* (Odense 1975) Cat. No. 73.

12 On Demosthenes 7, cf. Harp. s.v. Ἡγήσιππος; D. 7 hypoth 3; Phot. *Bibl.* 491a. On Demosthenes 17, cf. D. 17 Schol. 195.6-7, Dilts. The authorship is discussed by Blass (*supra* n. 9) III. 2 135ff, 146.

13 Cf. D. F. McCabe, *The Prose-Rythm of Demosthenes* (New York 1981). The authenticity of Dem. 13 is still disputed.

14 The six forensic speeches are: (1) Ἀπολογία δώρων, rejected by Dionysios. Fr. IV, Sauppe; No. 30, Blass. Cf. D. H. *Dem.* 57. (2) Κατὰ Δημάδου. Fr. II, Sauppe: omitted by Blass, cf. III. 1 60-61 with note 3. Cf. *Lex. Seg.* 335.27. (3) Πρὸς Κριτίαν περὶ τοῦ ἐνεπισκήμματος, accepted by Kallimachos, rejected by Dionysios. Fr. VI, Sauppe; No. 57, Blass. Cf. Harp. s.v. ἐνεπίσκημμα. (4) Κατὰ Μέδοντος. Fr. VII, Sauppe; No. 64, Blass. Cf. Harp. s.v. δεκατεύειν; Poll. 8.53. (5) Πρὸς Πολύευκτον παραγραφή. Fr. X, Sauppe; No. 45, Blass. Cf. *Lex. Seg.* 90.28. (6) Ὑπὲρ Σατύρου τῇ ἐπιτροπῇ πρὸς Χαρίδημον, by Kallimachos assigned to Deinarchos. Fr. XII, Sauppe; omitted by Blass, cf. III.1 60. Cf. Phot *Bibl.* 491b29. - The epideictic speech is: Παυσανίου ἐγκώμιον, rejected by Dionysios. Fr. IX, Sauppe; No. 67, Blass. Cf. D. H. *Dem.* 44.

15 Sauppe 252b34ff; Schäfer (*Supra* n. 3) III. 141-42 note 2; Blass (*supra* n. 9) III. 1 62. Furthermore, in Diodoros, πεφροντισμένος does not mean 'published', and Livius does not mention Demosthenes, nor does he refer explicitly to Alexander's request in 335.

16 It is worth noting, however, that Dionysios explicitly states that he will mention only the most famous of Demosthenes' speeches: ἀλλὰ καὶ τοὺς ἄλλους αὐτοῦ λόγους τοὺς μάλιστ' εὐδοκιμοῦντας ἐπιδείξω, τούς τε δημηγορικοὺς καὶ τοὺς δικανικούς (D. H. *Amm.* 10).

[17] Fr. XIII, 1-64, Sauppe.
[18] Nos. 2-3 (Agatharkides), 46-54 & 64 (Lucilius Rufus).
[19] Cf. Sauppe 253a16-22 & Fr. XIII, 2-3.
[20] Cf. Phot. Bibl. 495a12: φέρονται δὲ αὐτοῦ ἀποφθέγματα πλεῖστα καὶ γνωμολογίαι, ἅπερ αὐτὸς μὲν ἑκάστοτε πρὸς τὴν ἀνακύπτουσαν χρείαν ἁρμοττόμενος ἔλεγεν, οἱ δὲ ἀκούοντες μνήμῃ τε καὶ γραφῇ διεσώσαντο (= Fr. XIII, 1, Sauppe).
[21] Ps.Plut. Vitae X Oratorum 847 E: φέρονται δ᾽ αὐτοῦ λόγοι γνήσιοι ἑξήκοντα πέντε.
[22] Blass (supra n. 9) III. 1 322-28; A. Rupprecht Die demosthenische Prooimiensammlung, Philologus 82 (1928) 365-432; F. Focke Demosthenesstudien (Stuttgart 1929); R. Clavaud, ed. Démosthène, Prologues (Paris 1974), Collection Budé.
[23] Blass (supra n. 9) III. 1 327.
[24] Clavaud (supra n. 22) 44-50. The five prooimia identical with published speeches are: Prooem. 1.1 = D. 4.1; Prooem. 3 = D. 1.1; Prooem. 6 (7) = D. 14.1-2; Prooem. 7 (8) = D. 16.1-3; Prooem. 26 (27) = D. 15.1-2.
[25] Clavaud (supra n. 22) 49.
[26] Clavaud (supra n. 22) 46-48.
[27] The text is corrupted and at least one word is missing. In Harpokration it is unparalleled to have ἐν τῇ ... without a booknumber or a noun added, e.g. Φιλόχορος ἐν τῇ δ᾽ or Λυκοῦργος ἐν τῇ πρὸς Δημάδην ἀπολογίᾳ. Furthermore, ἐν τῇ ...δημηγορίᾳ never occurs in Harpokration, and the noun to be restored is rather ἀπολογίᾳ, εἰσαγγελίᾳ, ἀντιγραφῇ vel sim.
[28] e.g. by Adams (supra n. 2) 8.
[29] D. H. Amm. 12.
[30] A very interesting answer to these questions is suggested by Plato in Phdr. 257-58: successful political leaders have their ambitions satisfied by the passing and publication of all the decrees they move in the ekklesia, and do not have to resort to the (rather suspect) publication of speeches. If applied to Demosthenes this view leads to the following interpretation: In the years 341-38, when the Athenians passed almost all the decrees he proposed, the psephismata published in his name were a sufficient recognition of his policy, whereas, in the years 355-41, when the Athenians often rejected his proposals and refused to follow his advice, the publication of his demegoriai was the only way to make his policy known in a lasting form.
[31] I would like to thank G. L. Cawkwell and Johnny Christensen for reading and commenting on this article. Furthermore, I would like to thank the Institute for Advanced Study in Princeton for appointing me a visiting member for spring 1983, the Commission for Educational Exchange between Denmark and the United States for appointing me a Fulbrigth scholar for the same period, and the Danish Research Council for the Humanities for supporting me with a grant-in-aid.

ADDENDA

291: In *P. Oxy.* 3360, a fragmentary list of titles and incipits of Hypereides' speeches, the first entry is ἀλλ]ὰ πάντα μὲν ἴσως -[πρὸς Π]λαταιεῖς ὑπὲρ ὁρίων The theme of the speech was probably, in connection with the refounding of Plataiai, to come to an agreement about where to draw the border between Plataiai and Athens. Thus, a speech delivered by Hypereides in Plataiai as envoy send by the Athenians is not the only possibility; the speech may have been delivered as a forensic speech in connection with some kind of international arbitration between Athens and Plataiai; or it may have been delivered in the Athenian assembly in reply to a speech made by envoys from Plataiai, in which case it is the third (possible) example of a published *demegoria* by Hypereides.

INDEX OF SOURCES

AELIANUS
Varia Historia
5.12   40 bis

AENEAS TACTICUS
6f   134
9.1   208
10.4   204, 205

AESCHINES
Against Timarchus
1.2   60
1.23   98, 145, 185
1.26   14, 164
1.28   7, 15
1.28ff   8
1.30   7
1.33f   161, 162, 178
1.34   7, 15, 59, 161,
1.34f   8
1.64   27, 47
1.71   47bis
1.80   59, 72
1.81   28, 34, 39, 59, 60, 104
1.81ff   115
1.84   58
1.86   43, 103
1.97   80
1.109ff   56, 60
1.109   72
1.112   16
1.113   10
1.120   14, 30, 60
1.132ff   64
1.141   214
1.166   42
1.186   7, 8, 15
1.188   7, 16, 97
1.195   14

On the False Embassy
2   10
2.12   53, 63bis, 104
2.13   62, 253, 275
2.13f   62
2.14   42, 53, 272
2.15   37
2.16   49, 117
2.17   41bis, 117
2.18   34, 42, 56, 62bis,
2.19   42
2.20   49
2.21   52
2.27   49, 275
2.30   50bis
2.32   277
2.40   254
2.42   53
2.46   41
2.47   40, 62, 98
2.52   37
2.53f   41
2.53   185
2.55   42
2.60   185, 186
2.60f   277
2.61   41, 181, 183, 185, 192,
2.62f   186
2.64   14
2.64ff   139, 158, 159, 162, 277
2.65   185
2.67   185
2.71   20
2.72   171, 181, 182, 183, 191, 205,
2.73   52
2.74   7
2.78   52
2.79   34, 40
2.80   161
2.82   35
2.83   35, 102, 187
2.83ff   187
2.85   35, 102
2.90ff   64
2.94f   35
2.94   39
2.109f   185
2.110   161
2.124   21
2.125f   216
2.126   49
2.133   58
2.140   40, 59
2.149   39 bis, 62
2.161   7
2.169f   115
2.179   39, 62
2.184   4, 6, 15, 46, 56, 63bis,
2.233   13

Against Ctesiphon
3.2   7, 15, 256
3.4   7, 161, 178
3.7   6, 21

3.8	14, 34, 217, 271, 273,	3.143	59
3.9	53, 273	3.146	6, 18
3.9ff	279	3.147	273
3.12	53, 103, 273	3.148	15
3.16	7	3.152	273
3.23	272	3.153	273
3.24	43, 272, 273	3.154	161
3.25	46, 47, 117, 214	3.155	53
3.27	42, 272	3.156	273
3.28	216	3.159	56, 97, 116
3.31	7, 15, 16, 31, 272	3.160	273
3.34	53	3.161	43
3.38ff	169	3.167	273
3.42	277	33.176	273
3.49	53, 273, 279	3.187	38
3.49ff	279	3.188	273
3.50	280	3.194	38, 51, 123
3.51f	51	3.195	38, 48, 49
3.52	42	3.196	21
3.53	53, 273	3.197	252, 271
3.54	62, 123	3.199f	8
3.55	7, 15	3.203	15
3.62	53, 70, 187, 272	3.203f	7, 16
3.66f	42	3.209	80
3.67f	186, 191	3.210	273bis
3.68	185	3.213	273
3.69ff	277	3.214	14, 16, 31
3.73	15, 30, 31	3.219	273
3.73ff	187	3.220	13, 275
3.74	62, 163	3.223	34
3.75	187	3.223f	42
3.76	161	3.224	41, 130, 146, 253
3.78	14	3.226	14
3.83	37	3.227	35
3.85	42 bis	3.230	273
3.92f	41	3.231	273
3.95ff	41	3.232	273
3.97	43	3.233	14
		3.235f	14
3.101	53	3.236f	53
3.113	43	3.236	273bis,
3.115	35, 49, 55	3.242	30, 53, 97, 273
3.116	277	3.244	273
3.118	47	3.252	14, 53, 273
3.124ff	277	3.254	273bis
3.125	14, 97, 121	3.256	43 bis
3.126	205	3.259	273
3.130	35, 115		
3.134	15	**ANAXANDRIDES**	
3.138	48, 49	*Fragments*	
3.139	30, 38bis, 53, 58	41.18	51
3.142ff	42		

ANDOCIDES
On the Mysteries
1.8	35
1.10	35
1.17	253, 260
1.28	251
1.33	51
1.45	207ter
1.78	251
1.83	14
1.83f	59
1.87	148
1.94	55
1.95	45
1.111	257
1.121f	51
1.133	34
1.150	36, 49, 51

On his Return
2	286
2.1	3

On the Peace
3.41	35

Against Alcibiades
4.6	277
4.27	15

Fragments
2	290

ANDROTION
Fragments
18	34
30	62, 102, 111

ANTIPHON
On the Murder of Herodes
5.10f	252
5.10	254

On the Choregos
6.21	225, 251
6.24	14

Fragments
ix	289
x	290
xvi	290
3Gernet	268

ARISTOPHANES
Acharnians
20	145
21ff	145
24	150
42	150, 161
43f	145
44	145
45	98

Birds
463	10

Ecclesiazusae
84ff	159
128f	145, 146
130	98
131	10
243f	130
244ff	6
281	152
282ff	148, 150, 159
283f	133
283	152
290ff	147
291	133
292	152
296f	139, 147
300f	147
302	159
308	152
312	149
352ff	149
372ff	159
378f	146
380f	148, 149
380	152
389	149
390f	133
392	152
431ff	148, 159
681	254
740f	133
825	47

Knights
255	251
575	161
702ff	161
798	251
894ff	225
1227	10

Clouds
863   251

Peace
252   207
347   10
395   207
1310   163

Plutus
174f   57
329ff   150

Thesmophoriazusae
376   133
658   135

Wasps
89f   253
195   251
206   251
595   256
771ff   227, 228
772   251
891   250, 251
935   250
1108f   236, 254
1109   254

Fragments
210   251

ARISTOTLE
Athenaion Politeia
3.5   255
4.2   7
7.3   243, 244, 258, 259, 260
8.4   257
9.1f   238, 243, 244
9.1   255, 257, 259, 260
15.4   207, 208
21.3   257
21.4   86
24.3   28
25.2   248, 256, 258, 259, 260
27.5   241
28.2f   17
38.1   207
38.4   58
40.2   38 bis, 48, 49
41.2   167, 256
41.3   34, 47, 148, 152, 153,
42.4   205
43.3   28, 167, 168, 170, 185,
43.3ff   71, 172, 177, 181, 185, 191
43.4   99
43.4ff   174
43.5   10, 27, 28
43.6   99bis, 184
44.1ff   83
54.5   97
59.2   253ter
62.2   26, 99
62.3   77
66.1   253
67.1ff   252
67.3   252
67.4   254
68.1   225, 228, 230, 231, 252bis

Politics
1255a8   9
1273b35ff   242, 243, 255
1273b41   242
1273bff   244
1273b41ff   243, 259
1274a3   243, 258, 260
1274a4f   256
1275b8   193
1292a9   161
1298b23ff   149
1300a2ff   259
1305a7ff   18
1309a21   161
1322a35ff   207bis

Problems
916b36   6
952b14   205

Rhetoric
1354b23   267
1356a25ff   267
1361a35   161
1364a19ff   51, 53
1364a21ff   53
1374b25f   10, 51
1374b25   55
1380b10   45
1380b10ff   50
1384b15   47
1384b32   53, 292
1386a14   44

1388b18	6	3.10ff	97, 284
1406b27	35	3.22	7
1411a4f	53	3.29ff	14
1411a5f	292	3.31	214
1411a6	51	3.36	285
1411a6ff	51, 115		
1411b6f	53		
1418b10	51		

Rhet. ad Alex.
1421b7	267
1421b7ff	267
1445a40	205

ARISTOGEITON
Fragments
i	42
iii	36, 44, 60

ARRIAN
Anabasis
1.10.3	40
2.15.2ff	42
3.6.2	39, 44
5.25.29	206

Fragments
9.13	40

ATHENAEUS
Deipnosophistae
171E	63, 72
226A-C	37
251B	40
577B	38
591F	41

CURTIUS
3.13.15	36, 44, 49

DEMOSTHENES
First Olynthiac
1.1	296
1.16	14
1.19	97, 284

Second Olynthiac
2.11	284
2.29	5, 15, 20

Third Olynthiac
3.5	64

First Philippic
4.1	296
4.13ff	41, 284, 295,
4.16ff	295
4.19ff	295
4.23ff	295
4.28f	295
4.29	284bis, 295,
4.30	41, 284
4.33	41, 284
4.37	295

On the Peace
5	285
5.19	277

Second Philippic
6.19ff	42
6.28	285, 295

On the Halonnese
7	286
7.1	14
7.23ff	47
7.42f	50bis
7.43	47
7.46	47

On the Chersonnese
8.28	44
8.32f	14
8.34	15
8.68	14, 97, 285
8.73	97, 285
8.74f	60

Third Philippic
9.3f	14
9.38	6
9.46	295
9.70	285
9.71	285
9.72	43, 47, 52, 54, 58
9.73	285
9.76	285

Fourth Philippic
10.33	285
10.46	14
10.70	14
10.70ff	64

Philip's Letter
12.5	49
12.14	7
12.16	277
12.19	18, 20

On Financial Organization
13.4	207
13.13f	97, 283
13.20	5, 14
13.35	14

On the Symmories
14.1f	296
14.14	283
14.16ff	283
14.20f	167

On the Liberty of the Rhodians
15.1f	296
15.6	283
15.9	60
15.28	284
15.33	14

For the Megapolitans
16.	283
16.1ff	296

On the Treaty with Alexander
17.	286
17.20	55
17.23	14

On the Crown
18.5	42
18.9	71, 273
18.13	53
18.13ff	273
18.21	52, 62
18.25ff	42
18.28	42
18.37	50, 103
18.53	71, 273
18.56	273
18.59	273
18.66	14bis
18.70	38, 44, 46, 103bis
18.75	38, 46, 47, 52, 62, 103
18.79	41 quater.
18.80	41
18.83	37, 102, 273
18.91	161
18.94	5, 14ter, 15
18.102ff	41, 42bis
18.114	54, 64
18.118f	71, 273
18.130	15
18.133	36
18.134	34, 60
18.136	34, 115
18.140	4, 115, 277
18.153	277
18.168ff	188
18.169	129, 133, 134, 135, 141
18.170	5, 7, 98
18.173	5, 14
18.177ff	42
18.179	31, 43
18.189	14
18.205	5
18.212	5, 14, 15, 18
18.219	7, 15, 16ter, 21, 30
18.222	41, 44
18.222f	102
18.223	60, 104
18.244	43 bis
18.246	15, 18
18.248	42 ter, 275
18.249	41, 42, 44, 55, 59, 62
18.278	14
18.282	35
18.285	34, 40, 58, 115, 116
18.285ff	275
18.301	14
18.308	15bis
18.318	15
18.319	15
18.320	207

On the False Embassy
19	10
19.2	34
19.10	34, 115
19.12	14, 52, 56, 116bis,
19.13	34, 185
19.15	277

19.17	14, 35, 42bis	20.90	257
19.23	7, 15, 164	20.91	14
19.31	140, 158	20.93ff	257
19.35	34, 115	20.94	169
19.45f	164	20.95	53, 118
19.47f	62	20.100	63
19.61	277	20.128	53, 118
19.63f	277	20.132	14, 97
19.70	205, 250	20.144	39bis, 53bis
19.86	44, 50, 103bis, 163	20.146	28, 38, 40, 51, 53 quater.
19.99	11	20.149	37
19.103	34	20.150	51
19.113	34, 115	20.159	63
19.116	60	20.167	14
19.121	35, 37, 42, 49, 52, 53, 56, 62, 63, 275	*Against Midias*	
19.122	42, 205	21.2	216
19.122f	205	21.8ff	27
19.123	180, 192	21.10	46
19.124	39	21.47	221
19.126	35	21.64	62, 63
19.144	277	21.103	64
19.153ff	53	21.111	71, 187
19.154	42, 171, 181, 191	21.116	55, 71
19.162	46	21.139	64
19.163ff	37, 52, 56	21.153	55
19.175	40	21.161	71
19.180	43 bis, 45bis	21.164	63
19.185	99, 62, 63	21.171	275
19.191	30, 34, 52, 53, 59	21.173	54, 118
19.197	63	21.174	43
19.197f	49	21.179	275
19.209	34, 115	21.180	253
19.211	34	21.182	29, 58quater., 104bis, 107
19.222f	41	21.189	15
19.234	41	21.190	8
19.237	39, 62	21.194	253
19.273	10	21.197	54
19.277ff	45	21.202	55
19.280	58, 64	21.215	64
19.285	14	21.218	27, 38, 46
19.286f	59, 72, 104	21.223	253
19.290	46, 47, 64		
19.291	64	*Against Androtion*	
19.304	34, 46, 103, 115	22	35, 70
19.310	34, 115	22.1	43, 46
19.315	56, 116	22.3	46
19.331	47	22.5	35, 271
		22.5ff	279
Against Leptines		22.8ff	35
20.51	63	22.9f	271
20.74	8	22.10	54

22.20	275	24.11	38, 275, 278
22.26	6, 256	24.11ff	46bis, 103, 275, 278
22.30	13	24.12	35, 55
22.35ff	279	24.12f	39
22.36	13, 14, 75, 117, 120	24.13	35, 39bis, 115, 116, 276
22.37	7, 13, 15	24.13f	35, 55,
22.38	35, 61bis, 70, 72	24.14	39, 271, 275, 276, 277, 278
22.40	38, 70	24.15	170
22.48	35	24.17	60
22.52	14	24.19	275
22.59	35	24.20	7
22.62	275	24.20ff	169, 171
22.70	7, 15bis, 35, 277	24.21	98, 168, 170, 172, 174, 251
22.77	14	24.23	53
		24.24ff	167, 171
Against Aristocrates		24.25	98, 168, 172, 174
23.1	37, 102	24.26ff	275
23.4	13, 14	24.27	45, 66, 67, 103, 285
23.5	46bis	24.33	60, 169
23.7	279	24.39	66
23.13	37, 115	24.39f	60, 118, 285
23.14	37, 70, 102	24.41ff	7
23.18	37	24.42	43
23.22ff	279	24.45	148
23.28	221, 223, 237, 260ter	24.48	253
23.62	14	24.50	224, 151
23.90	277	24.59	148
23.92	277	24.63	60, 118, 222, 223, 253
23.92f	273	24.64	43
23.97	222	24.66	13, 97, 118
23.100ff	279	24.71	60, 66, 118, 285
23.101	279	24.99	256
23.104	39, 45	24.101	276, 277
23.110	37, 115	24.105	221, 223, 224, 237, 240, 260ter
23.141	69	24.105f	7
23.146f	97	24.112	14
23.149	49bis, 60	24.114	7, 223, 224
23.163	51	24.117	277
23.165ff	46	24.123	224, 252
23.167	51	24.123f	7
23.171	63	24.124	16
23.172	39	24.127	10, 55bis
23.173	64	24.134	48bis, 61
23.177	39	24.135	6, 14, 38
23.184	6	24.138	46bis, 61bis
23.201	7, 97	24.142	7, 96
23.209	14	24.147	7
		24.148	257
Against Timocrates		24.148ff	251
24.9	46bis, 253, 278	24.150	251
24.9ff	277	24.155	14
24.10	46	24.157	14

24.158f	35	*Against Boiotus I*	
24.160	35	39.3	14
24.164	14	39.19	275
24.178	35		
24.192ff	14	*Against Boiotus II*	
24.201ff	97, 118	40.20	10, 57
24.212ff	257	40.22	10, 57

Against Aristogiton I
Against Phaenippus

25.1	54	42.21	16
25.4	29		
25.6	36	*Against Macartatus*	
25.9	178	43.50f	7
25.14	54	43.57	251
25.16	277	43.71	250
25.20	256	43.75	221, 223
25.27	216		
25.28	253	*Against Leochares*	
25.37	36	44.35	132
25.38	15	44.38	277
25.40f	97	44.68	251
25.42	275		
25.43	216	*Against Stephanus II*	
25.44	62	46.14	251
25.47	34, 36, 41, 47	46.26	10, 222bis, 241, 242
25.55	46		
25.62	15, 277	*Against Euergus and Mnesibolus*	
25.87	36, 102	47.12	225, 226, 250, 251
25.90	161	47.20	63
25.94	36	47.21	57
25.98	216	47.34	9
25.99	96	47.41ff	48
		47.50	35
Against Aristogiton II		47.78	35
26.1	36		
26.1ff	14	*Against Olympiodorus*	
26.4	15	48.36	8
26.8	253		
26.11	60, 104	*Against Timotheus*	
26.17	36	49.6	60
26.18	14	49.9	49, 60
		49.9f	36, 49, 50bis, 60
Against Aphobus I		49.22	49, 60, 80
27.26	277		
		Against Polycles	
Against Zenothemis		50.4	39
32.31	15	50.4ff	37
32.32	123	50.12	55
		50.14	60
For Phormio			
36.53	36, 39, 50, 55, 60		

On the Trierarchic Crown
51.1   51
51.2   7
51.8f   38
51.22   277

Against Callippus
52.28   14, 64

Against Nicostratus
53.2   14
53.5   275

Against Conon
54.39   145

Against Eubulides
57.8   80
57.31ff 37
57.56   256

Against Theocrines
58   29
58.1   48
58.23   14, 42, 48bis
58.30   45
58.30ff 45, 48, 103
58.35   36, 48, 103
58.36   48
58.36ff 41, 42, 48ter, 103
58.37f   64
58.38   64
58.42ff 42, 48
58.43   41
58.53   55, 103
58.56   55, 103
58.62   7, 14bis
58.62ff 16
58.70   48

Against Neaera
59.3f   36, 276.
59.4   70, 102
59.5   59
59.8   36
59.26f   56
59.27   50
59.43   7bis, 16, 59, 97, 158, 160, 164
59.52   254
59.89f   129, 130, 131, 133, 135, 140, 148, 158, 280
59.91   271
59.105   7, 15

Letters
1.8   6
2.9   14
2.10   7, 15
3.15   14
3.16   55, 57, 59, 116bis
3.27   14
3.29   58
3.31   62, 64
3.33   14
3.45   14

Prooemia
1.1   296
3   296
6   296
7   296
12.2   14
13   14
26   296
53.1   7

Fragments
ii   295
iv   295
vi   295
vii   295
ix   295
x   295
xii   295
xiii   296

Demades
1.9   40bis
1.14   40

DEMETRIUS
On Style
289   41

DINARCHUS
Against Demosthenes
1   42
1.1   59
1.4   253
1.10   15
1.14ff   60

1.31	14, 15, 214	vi	58
1.33	64	viii	10, 54
1.38ff	14bis	xii	291
1.38	16, 49, 64	xiii	44
1.39	51	xiv	49
1.42	42, 169	xv	57
1.43	42 sex.	xvi	34
1.45	52	xviii	59bis, 104
1.48ff	57bis	xix	50
1.51	28	xxiv	61, 64
1.52	253	xxvi	34
1.53	14	xxvii	37
1.58f	57	xxx	10
1.62	42	xli	42, 44, 116, 288, 290, 291
1.63	36, 38, 41, 42, 58	xlii	10
1.69	80	xliiS	50
1.71	6, 15	xlv	292
1.76	6, 14, 18	xlvi	292
1.78ff	42	xlvii	42bis
1.80	43		
1.82f	42 bis	**DIODORUS SICULUS**	
1.84	216, 217	14.81.4	49
1.86	15	14.92.2	49, 63
1.89	40, 42	15.26.2	43
1.90	6	15.29.7	51, 60, 63
1.94	42bis, 50	15.30.5	63,
1.96	14	15.34.5	51
1.99	15	15.46.3	52
1.100	7, 16, 57	15.47.4	52
1.100f	15bis	15.71.3	39
1.107	253	15.75.3	64
1.112	6, 8	15.79.1	53
		15.84.2	47
Against Aristogiton		15.95.2	53
2	37	15.95.3	64
2.12	36, 102.	16.2.6	54
2.13	29, 36, 54, 70, 161	16.21.1	60
2.15	14	16.22.1f	64
2.16	205	16.37.3	56
2.26	6	16.74.1	63
		16.85.2ff	64
Against Philocles		16.87.1	19
3	62	16.87.3	40
3.1	62	16.88.1	54
3.2	62, 104	16.92.1f	40
3.5	62, 104	17.8.6	42
3.12	62	17.15.3	40, 287
3.17	38	17.15.4f	40
3.19	6, 214	17.111.3	53, 117bis
		18.13.6	36
Fragments		18.15.9	46
ii	29, 57, 72	18.17.6	36

18.18.2	40bis, 63	*Orestes*	
18.18.4f	78	730	209
		917ff	12

DIOGENES LAERTIUS
1.66   156
2.38   64
2.59   46
9.114   254

Fragments
Fr.626   209

EUSTATHIUS
1430 36ff   254
1669 59f   254
Od.1924   3131

DIONYSIUS HALICARN.
Ad Amm.
10   295
12   273, 296

HARPOCRATIO
Alkimachos   35, 40, 102
Ardettos   251
Ekkl.   34
Epikrates   45
heliaia   250, 251, 252, 253
Hegesippos   295
metroon   96
synkl.ekkl. 180, 192
xenikon   52

Demosthenes
44   295
57   287, 295

Dinarchus
11   287bis, 288
658   291
660   55
668   55bis

HELLENICA OXYRHYNCHIA
6.2   34, 36, 49
7.1   34, 59
7.2   45
20   207

Lysias
480   49bis, 60
483   290
525ff   290
526   63

HERODOTUS
1.125.2   255
5.29.2   255
5.72.2   257
5.79.2   255
5.97.2   216, 253
6.57   161
7.8.1   205
7.61.1   131
7.74.2   205
7.134.2   255
7.208   206
8.24.2   205
8.83.1   205

EPHORUS
Fragments
85   47

ETYMOLOGICUM MAGNUM
427.35   253
heliaia 227, 252bis, 255

EURIPIDES
Helena
878   209

Heraclidae
335   208

HESYCHIUS
gerra   131
Metichou tem   254
agora
Kerkopon   254

Iphigenia Aulidensis
514   205
515   208
825   208
1545   205, 208

HYPERIDES
Against Demosthenes
1	42, 60
1.8f	42
1.12	15bis
1.16	14
1.18	205bis
1.20	42 bis
1.21	15
1.22	15bis
1.24	6
1.25	14
1.28	14
1.29	214
1.40	34

For Lycophron
2.1	38
2.2	38
2.3	54
2.8	38
2.13	275
2.20	48, 54

For Euxenippus
3.	47
3.1	7, 15, 16, 38, 48bis
3.1f	51, 53, 60, 62bis
3.3	16, 34, 43
3.4	7, 15
3.6	253
3.7f	4, 8, 10, 30, 214
3.8	15
3.8f	7
3.9	16
3.11	16
3.12	54, 57
3.13	14
3.13ff	104
3.14	47, 116
3.15ff	57bis
3.20	57
3.24	216
3.27	6
3.27ff	16
3.28	15, 38, 60
3.29	7, 15, 16, 44, 60
3.29f	62
3.40	251
3.41	57, 60

Against Philippides
4	60, 61
4.2f	41
4.4ff	61, 104
4.11	61bis

Against Athenogenes
5.22	257

Fragments
vi	60
x	60
xii	60
xiii	60
xviii	60
xxii	60
xxiii	60
xxv	60
xxviii	60
xxxiii	60
xlviii	60
lix	60, 63
32ff	36, 60, 104
41	36
44	37
49	291
80	40
80ff	40
97	15
139	54
150	55bis, 103
172	60
182ff	18, 57, 291
190	60, 291
194	60, 291
195f	60, 291
225	291

HYPOTHESES
Aeschin.1	59, 122
Dem.7	295
Dem.19	56, 63
Dem.20	63, 42
Dem.22	43
Dem.23	46bis
Dem.24	43, 46,
Dem.25	36bis, 42, 61, 102

INSCRIPTIONS
Agora XV
1.	73, 77
7.7	39, 70

13.10ff	78		8 (1939) 172-73 n.3	107
22.11	72		8 (1939) 176-80	68
36.21	70		8 (1939) 180	55, 80, 81
38.78ff	132, 139		9 (1940) 62-3 n.8	52, 59
38.79	147		9 (1940) 341f	186
42.42	70		9 (1940) 342	108
42.145	70		9 (1940) 325-27 n.35	40, 111
42.206	63, 72		9 (1940) 327-28 n.36	74, 110
42.232ff	78		9 (1940) 332-33 n.39	110
42.244	72		9 (1940) 339-40	111
42.263	68		10 (1941) 287 l.78	38
42.303	68		10 (1941) 67 n.31	250
43.82	78		13 (1944) 231-3 n.5	41, 102, 111
43.88	78		19 (1950) 261 n.19	44
43.214f	70		21 (1952) 355-95	46, 117
44.56	71		26 (1957) 3 n.S2.13	44
49.12	71		26 (1957) 207 n.53	40, 70, 76
49.13	70		28 (1959) 239-47	37
49.14	71		29 (1960) 1-2 n.2	106
49.24	70		29 (1960) 2-4 n.3	56
49.41	50, 71, 117		33 (1964) 55-58 n.16	59
61.177	71		40 (1971) 149-50 n.3	66
62.220	59, 72		40 (1971) 280-301 n.7	48, 71, 272
			43 (1974) 157-88	56, 244, 256, 266
AGORA XVII			43 (1974) 322-24 n.3	54, 111
71	91		47 (1978) 90-91lin.54	35, 70
968	81		48 (1979) 180-93	59
			49 (1980) 263lin.28ff	256
Arch. Eph.			49 (1980) 263-64	222ter, 223
1923.36ff	57, 69, 71		52 (1983) 106 1.ii.e	40
1971.137ff	76, 115		52 (1983) 106 d10	39, 68
			54 (1985) 309-12 n.1	46
ASCSA			Suppl.8 274	61
1987.8	34		Suppl.17 2-4	182, 222, 251
Ath.Mitt.			*I. Délos*	
72.156-64	37, 102, 111		88.5	62, 72
			88.15	45
EM			88.30	35
13067	102, 111		1507.37ff	184, 191, 194
Hesperia			*IG I 2*	
3 (1934) 2-3 n.3	39		374	268
3 (1934) 3-4 n.5	74, 110		883	135, 138, 139, 155
3 (1934) 18-21	191		884	135, 136, 138, 139, 156ter, 161
4 (1935) 35-37 n.5	99			
4 (1935) 169-70 n.32	111		*IG I 3*	
5 (1936) 393-413 n.10	62ter,		21.33f	250
7 (1938) 291-92 n.18	59, 72, 104, 111		34.18f	172
8 (1939) 3-5 n.2	48		34.37ff	250
8 (1939) 5-12 n.3	51, 71, 76, 115		40.70ff	200
8 (1939) 26-27 n.6	74, 99, 110		41.37	170, 205

46.24	9	21.2	63
48bis	65	21.9ff	186
49.10	170, 205	26	65
61.1	208	26.6f	34
61.54	172	28.3	57
68.11	172	29.6	51
68.30	172	31	106
71.13f	221, 250	34.35f	51
71.16	252	34.36f	34, 74
71.33ff	186	34.37	41
71.49	250	36	66
85.11	172	36.4	56
93.15	172	36.5	61
93.17	172	36.6	49
104.11ff	255	36.7	45
104.19f	251	36.8	34
105	258	40.4	59
105.33f	259	40.7	48
105.36	259	41.17	56
105.38f	259	41.18	45
105.40	250, 259	41.19	56
105.53	172	41.20	58
105.54f	259	41.21	35
123.5f	172	42	76
182.21	172	42.3	39, 70
227.1ff	153	42.19f	34
227.5ff	153	43.7	37
237.13	172	43.76	37, 48, 58
328	65	43.91	37
1040	73, 77	44.7	58, 72, 115
1454	65	47	65
		47.23	34
IG II		60.4	47, 71
701	51	61.6f	70
		65	68, 153
IG II 2		72	106
1	76	72.3	36
1.41f	70	74.7ff	184
1.42	51, 71	77	56, 58, 72
1.51	51, 71	84.9f	50
2.8f	61	96	106, 108
5.11	48	96.4f	52, 71
6.7	56, 71	96.24	277
7.3f	56	97.14f	277
8	68	103	68, 69, 76
10.1	38, 48	103.6	57, 115
16	76	103.10f	277
16.6	39, 70	104.2	63
16.19	14	104.3	58
18.5	52, 71	105	68, 69
19.4f	59	105.6	57, 115
20	59	106	76, 106

312

106.6	44, 70	136	76, 95
107	76	136.10f	62, 72, 104
107.8	44	137	95
107.30	39, 115	137.4f	107
107.32	39, 60	138	107
107.33	37	138.4	46, 103
107.36	50, 71	139.6	60, 104
108.10	60	140.7	74
109a.7	52, 71	140.9	63
109b.8	52, 71	140.33	63
110	106	141.29	55
110.6	58, 60	141.30	51, 115
110.20	58	145	76
111.4	37	145.3f	47
111.8f	55	145.13	55, 71, 115
111.18	63	150	55
112	106	152.7f	43, 70
112.5f	57, 72	152.13	168
112.13	277	157	126
114	44	157.5	74, 76
114.4	65	172.3f	52, 103, 105
116.8	45, 115	175.2f	45
116.45	47	175.3	34
118.4	37	175.4	74
118.7	69bis	182.5	62
121	76	182.6	62
121.9	37, 70	188.13	45
123	76	189.7	39, 102
123.7	47, 71, 115	204.54f	62, 102
123.11f	277	204.82	14
124.20	49, 63, 64	204.83	46
124.21	55, 62	204.84	74
124.22	45	205	76, 107
124.23	43	205.8f	107
125.1	47	205.9	74
125.7ff	47	206	76
127.7	50, 71	206.5ff	49, 71, 103
127.15	57	206.26f	103
127.17	64	207a.	67
127.31	57	207	69bis, 126
127.36	36, 54	207d.1	64bis
127.37	49	207a.	258, 104, 105
128	76	207c.12	64bis
128.8	57, 72	207c.12ff	63
130	76	207d.23	58
130.8	38, 70	207.27	74
131.5	106	207b-d.	67
132.2	106	208	76
132.22	106	208.4	68
133.8f	107	208.4f	103
134	95	208.5f	38, 70, 102
134.6	52, 103	209.5	49, 103, 105

212	106, 171	243.6f	44, 70, 103
212.8	35, 102	244.1	74bis, 117
212.53ff	184	244.2	21, 51, 118
212.57ff	181	248	95, 106
212.65f	57, 104	249.6	68
212.66	108	253.1f	108
213.5	59, 104	253.2	74
213.8	61	263.5	74
214	95, 106	265	95, 106
215	76, 106	276.2f	108
215.5f	50, 71, 103	276.3	74
216	95, 106	276.23f	52, 111
216b. 6	35	289	102
216a.13	35	289.6	108
217	67	328	65, 76
217.13	35	328.8f	53, 71
218	67, 76	330	76
218.6f	45, 70, 103, 111	330.5	48, 103, 105
218.22	44	330.25	34
218.22f	103, 111	330.26	49, 71, 103
219.8f	107	330.32	34, 70, 117
220.4f	74	330.50	49, 71, 103
220.6f	107	333.14	54
220.7f	38, 102, 111	335	40
220.28f	38, 102, 111	336	99
223A.4	9, 40, 70, 117	336b.	100
223A.6	61	336a.5f	108
223B.1	61, 72	336.6	74
223B.7ff	52	336b.13f	108
223B.10	74, 76	337.5ff	117
223C.6	51	337.7	36
223C.10	39, 70	337.7f	70
223C.10ff	46, 71, 117	337.20ff	256
224.6f	38	337.31f	54
227	67	338.6f	63, 104
228.7ff	49, 103	339	40
228.11	64	339b.1f	108
229	76	343.2f	109
229.6f	107	343.3	74
229.7	74	344.11f	57, 104, 105
231.6	42	345	99
232.18f	62, 104	345.9f	54
233.5	50, 103	346	99
235.4f	108	346.12f	40
237.5f	47, 105	347	99
240	123	347.9ff	37, 67, 102
240.7	40	348.6	61, 104
241	123	349	76
241.5f	40	349.9f	56, 71, 104
242	123	351.10f	54
242.6f	44, 70, 103	353.9f	40
243	76, 123	354.8f	58, 104

354.32	46, 117	547	110
355.4	35	597	189
358.8	74	682.96ff	251
359	188	800	74
360.5	41, 103	838	184, 190
360.28	50, 104	897	188, 189, 190
360.45	48	911	184, 190
360.46	59, 104	945	184, 190
360.51	51, 71, 117	954	188
360.66	63, 72, 117	1009 II 76	68
361.7	74, 76	1028	67
363.7f	57, 104	1128.39	35
365.6f	45	1128.39f	47
365.6	103	1128.40	74
366	95, 106	1156.36	47, 71, 117
366.9f	109	1175	80
367.9	74	1191.5f	68
367.9f	109	1264	208
368.8	57, 104	1270	208
399	40	1272	208
403	76	1281	208
403.4f	109	1299	208
403.5	74	1302	208
405.4f	40	1303	207, 208
408.5	39, 102	1304	208
408.5f	111	1424a.350	44
408.7f	44	1443.13	56
410	76	1443.112f	51
410.1f	74, 109	1469.121f	115
412.4f	250	1492.126f	115
414a	53	1493ff	40
415	76	1544.30	44, 68, 103
415.11	49, 71, 103	1613.270	48
420.5f	109	1617.40f	115
421.3f	43, 103	1623.10ff	70
436.2ff	109	1623.35ff	51
448	99	1623.200f	44bis
448.6	47, 103	1623.210ff	44
448.31	56, 104	1623.240	61
452.11	54, 111	1623.240ff	110
454.8f	109	1623.277f	44
457	41	1623.280ff	37, 102
493	189	1623.281f	53
494	189	1623.313	56, 104
495	189	1623.329f	56
496	189	1627.247	40
497	189	1627.374ff	51, 71
498	189	1627.380	117
500	186, 207	1628.38f	57, 104
501	186	1628.40f	48
505.18	46	1628.300	47, 117
518	189	1628.351	40

1628.370	40	5433	81
1628.396f	44	5450	81
1628.437	63	5497	81
1628.438	51	5498	81
1629.13ff	34, 102	5584	105
1629.170	52, 103	5765	81
1629.273	35, 70	5787a	91
1629.520	40	5830	68
1629.643f	126	6043	68, 81
1629.869	40	6444	81
1629.871	40	6551	105
1629.890	40	6569	91
1629.958	63	7045	91
1629.959	51	7062	81
1631.215	43	7268	81
1631.350f	57, 72, 117	7374	91
1631.380	43	7642	105
1631.511	44	11370	91
1631.655ff	43, 103		
1632.19	44	*IG* VII	
1672.210	68	4252	111
1672.271f	62	4252.9f	61, 104
1672.302	54, 71	4253	111
1672.303	54	4254	111
1673.9	64, 104		
1673.65	54	*IG* XII	
1749.75ff	132, 205	5.647	207
1749.76	147		
1751.62	109	*M&L*	
1927.129	68	23.20ff	7
1965.9	67	32	205
2457.7	68	455ff	221
2811	45		
2840.5	67	*Michel*	
2841.5	67	439	205
2845.1	68	466	149
2968	61, 208		
2968.5	61	*Peek.Ker.III*	
2969	48, 208	1.4f	126
2970.5	52		
2970.6	59	*Reinmuth*	
2973	208	4	59
2976.9	52	15b.4ff	43, 53, 61
2977	208		
2978	208	*SEG*	
3207	41, 44, 48bis, 52, 70bis, 71bis, 103, 117ter	3.122	208
		10.14	250
3207.4	74, 76	10.31	250
5221.2f	48	10.370	135, 136, 137, 156
5221.3	68	12.89	57, 104
5228	35, 81	14.36	48
5432	81	14.44	43

14.47	95	298.9f	41, 103
14.51	74, 107	333.21ff	184
14.64	207	438.21	255
15.113	208	526.15	205
16.52	76	675.12	193
16.54	108		
16.193	81	**ISAEUS**	
21.109	135, 136, 137, 156	*On the Estate of Cleonymus*	
21.241	52	1.1	11
21.267	40, 102	1.7	8
21.272	35, 111		
21.274	40	*On the Estate of Hagnias*	
21.275	40	11.8	34
21.276	44, 53		
21.278	100, 108	**ISOCRATES**	
21.284	54, 111	*Panegyricus*	
21.289	74	4.157	205
21.292	110		
21.293	109	*Philippus*	
21.300	108	5.81	6
21.305	70		
21.440	188, 190	*Archidamus*	
21.525	208	6.106	205
21.552	40		
22.89	106	*Areopagiticus*	
22.93	109	7	293, 367
22.94	74	7.48	205
22.148	52	7.55	14
23.60	108	7.82	202, 207
23.78	68		
24.84	95	*On the Peace*	
24.86	106bis	8	267, 293
24.88	95	8.54f	18
24.103	109	8.76	3
24.134	184, 190	8.129	7
24.151	68		
28.103	68	*Panathenaicus*	
28.190	48	12.9	205
32.32	69		
32.279	126	*Plataicus*	
34.122	64	14	267, 293
		14.4	7
Sylloge 2			
587.180	62	*On the Exchange*	
		15	267
Sylloge 3		15.30	6
278	205	15.8	12
282	205	15.93	21
287	76, 111	15.112f	60
287.9	41, 102, 118	15.129	38, 55, 60
287.10	61	15.132	14
298	111	15.136	18, 205

15.136ff	20	**LUCIANUS**	
15.138	7	*Demosthenis Encomium*	
15.147	205	31	118
15.231	14bis		
15.313	257	**LYCURGUS**	
		Against Leocrates.	
Against Callimachus		1.1	53, 54
18.2	38	1.5	54
18.11	64	1.16	163
18.22	29, 62bis	1.19	63, 116
18.54	252	1.24	55
		1.31	7, 16
Against Lochites		1.36f	60
20.2	257	1.41	60
		1.43	8bis
ISTRUS		1.53	39, 68
Fragments		1.66	96
16	145		
		Fragments.	
JUSTINUS		iii	54
13.5.10	60	v	45
		ix	54
LEXICON PATMENSE		x-xi	54
159f	51bis, 103	xii	54bis
Dem.23.28	251, 252, 253, 255	xiv	54, 55
hekatompedon 11		xviii	8, 15
LEX. RHET. CANT.		**LYSIAS**	
rhetorike	8	*For Callias*	
hypomosia	28	5.3	14
LEXICA SEGUERIANA		*Against Andocides*	
33.25	131	6.33	29, 35
90.28	295	6.43	277
189.20f	225, 252, 253		
208.17ff	207	*For the Soldier*	
262.10ff	251, 252ter, 253bis,	9.6	52
277.10	207ter		
310.28	251	*Against Theomnestus*	
310.28ff	253	10.1	27, 48bis, 54
310.29	252bis	10.4	255
310.29f	252	10.15ff	251, 255
310.31f	256	10.16	221, 237, 240, 260
310.32ff	227, 255		
327.23	205	*Against Eratosthenes*	
335.27	295	12	10
		12.71	205
LIBANIUS		12.72	7
Declamationes.		12.75	216
32.18	180	12.76	275

Against Agoratus
13.7 17, 26
13.32 253
13.35 253
13.72 7, 15

Against Alcibiades I
14.5 208
14.7 208
14.15 208

Against Alcibiades II
15.1ff 208

For Mantitheus
16.15 49
16.18 3
16.20 54

On the Property of Aristophanes
19.19 37, 46
19.23 37
19.55 11, 254

For Polystratus
20 10

Against the Corndealers
22.2 7

For the Invalid
24.20 163

On Subverting the Democracy
25.9 15
25.27 14

On the Scrutiny of Euandrus
26.20 26
26.21ff 48bis

Against Epicrates
27.1 10, 45
27.10 14

Against Ergocles
28 286
28.2 45
28.12 45
28.29 45

Against Nicomachus
30 56
30.22 7

Against Philon
31.8 163

Olympicus
33.2 205

On the Ancestral Constitution
34 267, 286, 290

Fragments.
vi 48
xviii 49
lxv 49bis
36 38
43 38
66 251
86ff 8, 43
123 49
143 52
143 61bis
191ff 290
228 49
246 251

NEPOS
Chabr.2.2 63
Epam.6 51
Phoc.1.3 63
Timoth.3.2 55

ONOSANDER
25.2 134

PAPYRI
P.Hibeh
1.14 48
P.Oxy.
858.25ff 141
1607 48
2686 60, 63
3360 60ter, 297
P.Ryl.
1.57 134

PAUSANIAS
1.25.5 53
1.28.8 254
1.36.4 55

3.5.4	49
9.15.2	207

PHILINUS
Fragments
3	61

PHILOCHORUS
Fragments
56A	42
49	64
50	64
51	64
55	41
140	165
147	34
149	30
149A	35, 45bis, 50bis, 52bis
155	47, 62, 102, 111
156	64
158	44
159	51
160	63
199	230, 253

PHOTIUS
Biblioteca
491a	295
491b.29	295
495a.12	296

Lexicon
peristiarchos	145
lexiarch. Gram	81
heliaia	251, 252, 253

PLATO
Apologia
17D	11bis
23E	64
32A	11

Axiochus
369A	216, 253

Euthydemus
290Cf	6, 20

Gorgias
452E	199, 200, 205
455B	205
456B	205
502C	267

Hippias Major
304D	205

Ion
541C	36, 153bis
541D	47

Laches
187A	205
187E	199

Leges
659A	205
700Cff	205
755E	200, 205
758B	83
764A	205bis
765A	205
871A	205bis
881B	161
908A	205
909A	205
935B	205bis
943B	200, 205
943Af	208
946B	161
951Df	205
961Af	205
962C	205
968A	205

Meno
90B	18, 36

Phaedrus
257f	296
261A	205bis
261Aff	267bis

Respublica
492B	199, 205, 206

Symposium
175E	253
194A	254

Theaetetus
173Cf	254
176Cf	11

PLATO COMICUS
Fragments
14	57
119	45, 63
122	45

PLUTARCHUS
Demosthenes
13.3	55, 116
20.2	19
23.6	40
24.2	273
27.6	43, 103
27.4f	43

Nicias
6	10

Pericles
32.4	253

Phocion
7.5f	18, 63, 116
8.2	63
9.10	54
14.2	55
14.3f	64
15.1	63
16.1	63
16.4	63, 64
16.5	40
17.1	63
17.6	63bis
18.8	80
22.4	64
23	53
25.1	63
26.3	40
28.7	78

Solon
18.3	257
18.6	257
19.1	257
19.4	251

Themistocles
19.6	151, 160

Moralia
350B	291
486D	18
726A	292
726B	58
803D	41, 115, 292
804B	58, 116
812F	18
814B	145
835Ff	38, 271
839C	39, 115, 293
841E	52, 54, 58
841F	292
841Ff	54
842D	54
842F	50
843F	54
844A	53
845F	10, 19
846C	49, 55, 58bis
846Cf	58
846D	43, 103
847D	43, 115
847E	296
847F	47
848D	37, 44, 64, 102
848E	60, 64, 291
849A	272
851B	43

POLLUX
1.176	207
8.53	253, 295
8.87	253
8.104	132, 205
8.123	252, 253
10.159	291

POLYAENUS
1.21.2	207bis
3.9.20	49
3.9.29	38
4.2.2	59
4.2.8	58, 64
4.2.22	64
5.21	63
5.29	43

POLYBIUS
10.24.	207
21.1.3	193
29.24.6	193

POLYEUCTUS
Fragments
1   40
1f   57

PYTHEAS
Fragments
3   58
4   15

SCHOLIA
in Aeschin.
1.23   145
1.39   56
1.64   38 bis, 60
1.77   43, 103
1.163   38
2.31   35, 49, 60bis
3.24   44

in Ar. Ach.
19   194
21f   133
44   145

in Ar. Av.
109   226, 252

in Ar. Eccl.
71   45
128   145
825   47

in Ar. Eq.
898   252
255   227, 252

in Ar. Nub.
862   227

in Ar. Pax
353   207

in Ar. Plut
174   10
174f   57

in Ar. Vesp.
88   227, 252
772   227, 252

in Arist. Rhet.
1384b 15   47

in Aristid.
172.3-4   44, 63
179   64

in Dem.
1.1   46
7.15   64
17.5f   295
18.73   180, 193, 194
19.86   50, 103
19.123   193
19.162   46
19.280   58
19.290   47
21.64   63
21.218   27, 38, 46
24.9   252, 253
24.20   180, 194
24.21   227, 251bis, 252, 255

Didymus in Dem.
18.14   35

in Dion. Thr.
183.18   38

in Luc. Tim.
51   227

STRABO
10.1.6   61
7.2.3   131

SUDA
Demades   40
heliaia   251, 252, 253
heliastes   226, 251
lex. Gram.   181
lykeion   207bis
peristiarchos 145
*Thrasy-
machos*   293
Timarchos   59, 122

THEODECTES
Fragments
1   292

322

THEOPOMPUS
Fragments

30	36, 64
166	38
249	64

THRASYMACHUS
Fragments

1	267, 293

THUCYDIDES

1.44.1	186
1.67.3	196
2.12.1	196
2.19.1	198
2.21.3	199
2.22.1	172, 195-211
2.23.3	198
2.40.2	11
2.57.2	198
2.59f.	198, 199, 209, 210
2.59.3	196, 198, 209
2.60.1	198, 209
2.65	267
2.65.8f	268
2.65.10	268
3.27.3	196ter, 204, 205, 206, 210
3.36.4ff	186
4.74.3	208bis
4.114.3	196, 197
4.120.3	196, 197
5.30.5	196
5.59f	207
5.60.1	207
5.60.5	207
5.60.6	207
5.63	207
5.64.5	206
5.65	206
5.66.1	206
6.41.5	196
6.45	208
6.58.1f	208
6.75.4	196
7.33.6	207, 208
7.35.1	207, 208
8.81.1ff	207
8.93	207, 208
8.93.1	207
8.93.3	208
8.94.1	208

TIMAEUS SOPH.

exetasmos	207

TIMOCLES
Fragments

16	51
17	116

XENOPHON
Anabasis

1.3.2	206, 207
1.4.8	206
1.4.11	206bis, 207
1.4.13	207
1.7.1	206
1.7.10	207, 208
2.1.2	206
2.2.3	206
3.1.15	206
3.1.30	208
3.1.39	207
3.2.1ff	206
3.2.9	207
3.2.31ff	207
3.3.3	206
3.5.7	206
4.4.21	206
4.8.9ff	206
5.1.2	206
5.1.4ff	207
5.3.3	207
5.4.19	206
5.6.1ff	206
5.6.14	206
5.6.22	205, 207
5.6.37ff	206
5.6.37	207
5.7.2	205
5.7.35	207
6.1.3	206
6.1.18ff	206bis
6.1.25	206
6.2.4	206
6.2.9ff	207
6.4.10f	206L 6.5.12 206
6.6.8	277
6.6.11	206
6.6.27	277
7.1.7	207
7.1.21ff	208
7.3.14	207
7.6.7	206

Ath. Resp.
1.18   256

Cyropaedia
2.1.21   131
2.2.18ff 206
2.3.22   207
2.4.1   207
6.2.11   205

De Equitum Magistro
1.8   26
3.1   207ter
3.1ff   208
3.6   207
3.14   207bis
7.10   206

Hellenica
1.1.27ff 207
1.1.33   207
1.6.4f   207
1.7.7   255
1.7.8   255
1.7.9   140, 157, 161, 255
1.7.11   255
1.7.12ff 271
1.7.23   252
1.7.31   255
1.7.35   27
2.3.20   207bis, 208
2.4.8   208
2.4.10   207
2.4.11   207
2.4.23   207
2.4.24   207
2.4.27   207bis
2.4.30   206, 207
2.4.32   207
3.4.17   163
3.5.16   48
4.1.39   205
4.5.13   49, 50
4.6.3   163
4.8.13   44, 45, 50bis, 52
4.8.24   62
4.8.25ff 49 4.8.31 34
4.8.34   49
5.1.7   44
5.1.2   10, 57
5.1.5   46

5.1.7ff   46
5.1.7   49
5.1.10   40, 63
5.1.25   44, 49
5.1.26   40, 43, 48, 53, 61, 66
5.1.27   66
5.1.28   66
5.2.37   277
5.4.14   63
5.4.37   277
5.4.61   63
5.4.63   60
5.4.66   60
6.2.2   277
6.2.10   52
6.2.11   60
6.2.13ff 49
6.2.39   15, 51, 63
6.3.2   37, 39, 43, 50, 51, 53, 55
6.3.3   15, 49, 51bis
6.3.4   50
6.3.7   21, 30
6.3.7   30
6.5.2   277
6.5.5   277
6.5.33   277
6.5.49   49, 207
7.1.12ff 51, 115
7.1.25   63
7.1.33   53, 59
7.1.38   53, 59
7.1.41   60
7.2.18   64
7.3.1   277
7.3.11   277
7.4.4   43
7.5.4   64
7.5.8   206

Memorabilia
2.6.15   6, 15
3.4.1   36

Oeconomicus
4.6   205, 207
9.15   207, 208

De Vectigalibus
3.3   161
3.7   54

324